SCOTTISH LEAGUE PLAYERS' RECORDS

SCOTTISH FOOTBALL LEAGUE PREMIER DIVISION 1975/76 to 1997/98

SCOTTISH PREMIER LEAGUE 1998/99 to 1999/2000

Steve Emms

A SoccerData Publication from Tony Brown

Published in Great Britain by Tony Brown,
4 Adrian Close, Beeston, Nottingham NG9 6FL.
Telephone 0115 973 6086. E-mail soccer@innotts.co.uk
First published 2002

ISBN 1 899468 64 1

INTRODUCTION

This volume of the Scottish League Players' Records provides details of the career of every player who made an appearance in the Premier Division during the 23 years of its history or during the first two seasons of the Scottish Premier League. Wherever possible, we have included details of players appearances elsewhere, such as in the lower divisions of the Scottish League or "abroad" in England and the rest of Europe, together with details of any other clubs played for.

The statistical information has been collected over a period of time by Derek Gray, using sources such as the "Scottish League Review" and "Rothmans Football Yearbook", with any areas of doubt confirmed from local newspapers. In addition, the various club histories and 'who's whos' that have been published on Scottish clubs (though sadly limited in number) have proved an invaluable source of information.

Thanks must therefore go to all of the authors of these books, who have made their research available to the public, and to Richard Beale, whose research into players' records before 1975 has meant that we can include details of the earlier part of players' careers. Thanks also to Tony Brown for his advice and assistance in the publication of the work.

It is intended that this book will form the first of three volumes, the remaining parts providing a complete player list for the Scottish Football League Division One from 1890 to the reorganisation in 1975. Although a great deal of work has already been done on the remaining volumes, there are still large areas of research required, especially relating to the pre-war period. We would be pleased to hear from any club historian who feels that he or she can assist us in this project. Similarly, we would like to hear of any errors or omissions in the current book. Of course, all assistance will be credited, and will help to ensure that the information is as accurate as possible. Please write to the publisher or directly to the editorial team at 28 Briar Close, Evesham, Worcestershire WR11 4JQ.

Steve Emms, October 2002

KEY TO THE STATISTICS

The "Macs" will be found in their own section, following the other surnames that begin with the letter M. Under each player's name, the first line gives their place and date of birth (and sadly, in a few cases, death). Beneath this the information in broken down into six columns.

The first column lists the clubs played for, followed by a column showing the seasons at each club. The letters "L" or "T" against the season mean that the player was either on loan, or on trial at the club. This is followed by three columns giving the number of times the player appeared in the starting line-up, the number of appearances as substitute, and the number of league goals scored during the season.

The final column shows which division or league the statistics relate to. "P" indicates the Premier Division of the Scottish Football League or the Scottish Premier League, "D1", "D2", and "D3" refer to the other Scottish League divisions, while "FL" indicates that the player appeared in the English Football League or Premiership. During the 1970s and 1980s, many players spent their summers in the North American Soccer League and appearances in this league are indicated by "NA". No entry in this column indicates that the club was non-league, a foreign team, or that the player made no first team appearances that season.

In some cases an asterisk appears against a club's name. This indicates that although a player of the same name (or at least with the same initials) made the appearances listed, we have not been able to confirm that it is in fact the same player. Again, any correspondence will be appreciated.

ABBOTT Gordon Thomas K
b. Edinburgh 24.2.1979

Club		Season	App	Sub	Gls	Div
Falkirk		95/96	0	1		P

ABEL Gregor
b. Falkirk 9.4.1949

Club		Season	App	Sub	Gls	Div
Falkirk						
Bo'ness U	L					
Falkirk		69/70	23			D2
		70/71	29			D1
		71/72	18			D1
		72/73	29			D1
Clydebank		73/74	29	3		D2
		74/75	38			D2
		75/76	24			D2
		76/77	39			D1
		77/78	25	1		P
		78/79	37			D1
		79/80	9			D1
Alloa A		79/80	18			D2
		80/81	6	1		D2

ABERCROMBY Mark Henry
b. Glasgow 14.7.1974

Club		Season	App	Sub	Gls	Div
Eastercraigs						
Airdrieonians		91/92	1	3		P
		92/93				
		93/94	1	6		P
Kitchee (HK)						
East Stirlingshire		94/95	9	7		D3
		95/96	17	5	2	D3
		96/97	15	4	1	D3
		97/98	5			D3
East Fife		97/98	13	3	1	D2
		98/99	7	3		D2

ABERCROMBY William
b. Glasgow 14.9.1958

Club		Season	App	Sub	Gls	Div
St Mirren		76/77	1	2		D1
		77/78	25	5	3	P
		78/79	30	1	2	P
		79/80	14	1		P
		80/81	28	1	1	P
		81/82	30			P
		82/83	24		1	P
		83/84	33	1	4	P
		84/85	31		2	P
		85/86	19	4	2	P
		86/87	28			P
		87/88	9			P
Partick T		88/89	9	1		D1
Dunfermline A		89/90	5	4		P
Cowdenbeath		90/91	3	1		D2
East Stirlingshire		90/91	5			D2

ABOU Samassi
b. Gagnoa 4.8.1973

Club		Season	App	Sub	Gls	Div
Martigues						
Lyon						
AS Cannes						
West Ham U		97/98	12	7	5	FL
		98/99	2	1		FL
Ipswich T	L	98/99	5	1		FL
West Ham U		99/00				
Walsall	L	99/00	7	1		FL
Kilmarnock		99/00	5	5		P

ADAM Charles
b. Dundee 5.4.1962

Club		Season	App	Sub	Gls	Div
Montrose		82/83	8			D2
Downfield Jnrs		83/84				
		84/85				
St Johnstone		85/86	21	2	8	D2
		86/87	5			D2
Brechin C		86/87	32	1	12	D1
		87/88	34	1	8	D2
		88/89	29		15	D2
Dundee U		88/89	4	2		P
Partick T		89/90	6	2	2	D1
Forfar A		89/90	9		2	D1
		90/91	17	1	2	D1
		91/92	9		3	D1
Arbroath		92/93	21		3	D2
		93/94	28	1	4	D2
		94/95	31		3	D3

ADAM Stephane Lucien
b. Lille 15.5.1969

Club		Season	App	Sub	Gls	Div
Metz		95/96				
		96/97				
Heart of Midlothian		97/98	28	2	8	P
		98/99	28	1	10	P
		99/00	18	7	4	P

ADAMCZUK Dariusz
b. Sczecin 20.10.1969

Club		Season	App	Sub	Gls	Div
Eintracht Frankfurt						
Dundee		93/94	7	4	1	P
Pogon Szczecin		94/95				
Dundee		95/96	8	5		D1
		96/97	30		1	D1
		97/98	33		1	D1
		98/99	24	2	6	P
Rangers		99/00	5	5		P

ADAMS Charles Stuart Scarlett
b. Irvine 21.3.1976

Club		Season	App	Sub	Gls	Div
Kilwinning R						
Partick T		95/96	1	4		P
		96/97	26	4	8	D1
		97/98	8	7	4	D1
Clydebank		97/98	6	5	1	D2
Queen of the South		98/99	18	9	4	D2
		99/00	18	12	4	D2

ADAMS Craig
b. 17.12.1964

Club		Season	App	Sub	Gls	Div
Morton		84/85	5			P

ADAMS Derek Watt
b. Aberdeen 25.6.1975

Club		Season	App	Sub	Gls	Div
Aberdeen						
Burnley		94/95				
		95/96	0	2		FL
Ross Co		96/97	31	3	22	D3
		97/98	31	3	16	D3
		98/99	4		3	D3
Motherwell		98/99	11	15	3	P
		99/00	15	2	1	P
Ayr U	L	99/00	4			D1

ADDISON Derek
b. Dundee 8.7.1955

Club		Season	App	Sub	Gls	Div
Lochee U						
Dundee U		73/74	4			D1
		74/75	6	1	1	D1
		75/76	3		1	P
		76/77	6	7		P
		77/78	18	2	3	P
		78/79	24	4	3	P
		79/80	13	4		P
		80/81	11	3	1	P
Heart of Midlothian		81/82	32		4	D1
St Johnstone		82/83	36		2	D1
		83/84	18	1		P
		84/85	13			D1
		85/86	30		1	D2
Brechin C *		86/87	1			D1

AIRD Kenneth
b. 13.4.1947

Club		Season	App	Sub	Gls	Div
Celtic						
St Mirren		65/66	17		1	D1
		66/67	19		2	D1
St Johnstone		67/68	30	1	7	D1
		68/69	32		8	D1
		69/70	32		5	D1
		70/71	24		2	D1
		71/72	30		6	D1
		72/73	12		4	D1
Heart of Midlothian		72/73	10			D1
		73/74	17		2	D1
		74/75	12	5		D1
		75/76	26	2	7	P
		76/77	13	3		P
Toronto Metros-Croatia		77	7			NA
Arbroath *		77/78	1			D1

AITKEN Robert Sime
b. Irvine 24.11.1958

Club		Season	App	Sub	Gls	Div
St Andrews Academy						
Ayr U BC						
Celtic BC						
Celtic		75/76	12			P
		76/77	33		5	P
		77/78	33		2	P
		78/79	36		5	P
		79/80	35		3	P
		80/81	33		4	P
		81/82	33		3	P
		82/83	33		6	P
		83/84	31		5	P
		84/85	33		3	P
		85/86	36			P
		86/87	42		1	P
		87/88	43		1	P
		88/89	32			P
		89/90	18		2	P
Newcastle U		89/90	22		1	FL
		90/91	32			FL
St Mirren		91/92	34		1	P
Aberdeen		92/93	18	8	2	P
		93/94	0	1		P
		94/95	0	2		P

ALBERTZ Jorg
b. Moenchengladbach 29.1.1971

Club		Season	App	Sub	Gls	Div
Fortuna Dusseldorf		90/91				
		91/92				
		92/93				
SV Hamburg		93/94				
		94/95				
		95/96				
Rangers		96/97	31	1	10	P
		97/98	27	4	10	P
		98/99	33	1	11	P
		99/00	30	5	17	P

ALBISTON Arthur Richard
b. Edinburgh 14.7.1957

Club		Season	App	Sub	Gls	Div
Manchester U		74/75	2			FL
		75/76	2	1		FL
		76/77	14	3		FL
		77/78	27	1		FL
		78/79	32	1		FL
		79/80	25			FL
		80/81	42		1	FL
		81/82	42		1	FL
		82/83	38		1	FL
		83/84	40		2	FL
		84/85	39			FL
		85/86	37		1	FL
		86/87	19	3		FL
		87/88	5	6		FL
WBA		88/89	43		2	FL
Dundee		89/90	9	1		P
Chesterfield	L	90/91	3			FL
Chester C		91/92	44			FL
Molde BK		92/93				
Chester C		92/93	23	1		FL
Witton A		93/94				
Ayr U		93/94	1			D1
Sittingbourne						
Witton A						
Droylsden						

ALEXANDER Ian
b. Glasgow 26.12.1963

Club		Season	App	Sub	Gls	Div
Leicester Juveniles						
Rotherham U		81/82	5	6		FL
		82/83				
Motherwell		83/84	14	2	1	P
		84/85	5	3	1	D1
Morton		84/85	6	1	1	P
Pezoporikos		85/86				
Bristol R		86/87	20	2		FL
		87/88	45			FL
		88/89	42			FL
		89/90	43		1	FL
		90/91	37	2	1	FL
		91/92	41		1	FL
		92/93	41			FL
		93/94	15	3		FL

ALEXANDER Rowan Samuel
b. Ayr 28.1.1961

Club		Season	App	Sub	Gls	Div
Queen of the South		78/79	2			D1
		79/80	37		21	D2
		80/81	35	1	14	D2
		81/82	21	2	11	D1
		82/83	38		23	D2
St Mirren		83/84	10	7	3	P
		84/85	0	1		P
Brentford		84/85	17	2	2	FL
		85/86	24	4	4	FL
Morton		86/87	41	1	23	D1
		87/88	36		7	P
		88/89	31		11	D1
		89/90	38		11	D1
		90/91	34		6	D1
		91/92	30		10	D1
		92/93	30	1	10	D1
		93/94	35	1	11	D1
		94/95	26	6	9	D2
Queen of the South		95/96	0	1		D2
		96/97	5	6	2	D2
		97/98	1	5		D2

ALLAN Thomson Sandlands
b. Longridge 5.10.1946
Holy Cross Academy
Edina Hearts

Hibernian		63/64				
		64/65				
		65/66	12			D1
		66/67	30			D1
		67/68	14			D1
		68/69	13			D1
		69/70	1			D1
Dundee		72/73	29			D1
		73/74	33			D1
		74/75	34			D1
		75/76	36			P
		76/77	10			D1
		77/78	17			D1
Meadowbank T	L	78/79	2			D2
Heart of Midlothian		78/79	16			P
		79/80	8			D1
Falkirk		80/81	12			D1

ALSFORD Julian
b. Poole 24.12.1972

Watford		91/92				
Kingsbury T	L	91/92				
Staines T	L	91/92				
Watford		92/93	2	3		FL
		93/94	7	1	1	FL
Slough T	L	93/94				
Chester C		94/95	32	3		FL
		95/96	22	2		FL
		96/97	43		2	FL
		97/98	39		4	FL
Dundee U		97/98	3			P
		98/99				
Barnet	L	98/99	9		1	FL

AMATO Gabriel Omar
b. Mar Del Plata 22.10.1970
Real Mallorca

Rangers		98/99	13	7	6	P
		99/00	4	4	3	P

AMORUSO Lorenzo
b. Bari 28.6.1971

Bari		88/89				
		89/90				
		90/91				
		91/92				
		92/93				
		93/94				
		94/95				
Fiorentina		95/96				
		96/97				
Rangers		97/98	4			P
		98/99	33		1	P
		99/00	30		2	P

ANDERSEN Erik Bo
b. Randers 14.11.1970
Aalborg BK

Rangers		95/96	6		6	P
		96/97	6	11	9	P

ANDERSEN Soren Kege
b. 13.2.1966

Raith R		96/97	7		3	P

ANDERSEN Vetle Gregle
b. Kristiansand 20.4.1964

Dunfermline A		87/88	13	1		P
Lyngby		88/89				
WBA		89/90	0	1		FL
?		90/91				
		91/92				
		92/93				
		93/94				
		94/95				
		95/96				
Raith R		96/97	18	1		P
Inverness CT		97/98	30	2		D2

ANDERSON Andrew
b. 7.8.1953
Sighthill Amateurs

Partick T		71/72	2			D1
		72/73				
		73/74	14			D1
		74/75	31	1		D1
		75/76	20	2		D1
		76/77	10	2		P
		77/78	26	1	1	P
		78/79	18	2	1	P
		79/80	26			P
		80/81	21			P
		81/82	21			P

ANDERSON Arthur Alan Duncan
b. Edinburgh 21.12.1939

Falkirk		59/60	1			D2
Millwall		59/60				
		60/61	31			FL
		61/62	43			FL
Scunthorpe U		62/63	6			FL
Heart of Midlothian		63/64	8			D1
		64/65	33			D1
		65/66	34		1	D1
		66/67	29		3	D1
		67/68	22	2	4	D1
		68/69	19	2	3	D1
		69/70	34		2	D1
		70/71	34		3	D1
		71/72	28		2	D1
		72/73	30		2	D1
		73/74	27			D1
		74/75	28			D1
		75/76	22		1	P

ANDERSON Derek Christopher
b. Paisley 15.5.1972
Kilwinning R

Kilmarnock		94/95	20			P
		95/96	28			P
		96/97	16	1		P
		97/98	0	1		P
Ayr U		97/98	12		1	D1
Hibernian		98/99	6			P
Morton		98/99	16		1	D1
		99/00	28		1	D1

ANDERSON George
b. Port Glasgow 25.12.1953

Morton		69/70	2	3		D1
		70/71	23	1	1	D1
		71/72	33		1	D1
		72/73	30		2	D1
		73/74	26	1		D1
		74/75	25	1		D1
		75/76	9		1	D1
		76/77	35		2	D1
		77/78	37		9	D1
		78/79	12		1	P
		79/80	20	2	1	P
		80/81	4		1	P
Airdrieonians		80/81	19	1	1	P
		81/82	18			P
		82/83	28	1	2	D1
		83/84	27	3	1	D1
		84/85	13	3		D1
		85/86	16	2	1	D1
		86/87	1			D1

ANDERSON Iain
b. Glasgow 23.7.1977

Dundee		93/94	0	1	1	P
		94/95	4	6	1	D1
		95/96	9	8		D1
		96/97	28	7	5	D1
		97/98	32	4	6	D1
		98/99	17	11	3	P

ANDERSON Ian
b. 11.9.1954

Dundee		72/73	5	1	1	D1
		73/74	4		1	D1
		74/75	13	2	3	D1
		75/76	2			P
St Johnstone		75/76	20		1	P
		76/77	30		8	D1
Tampa Bay Rowdies		77	11		2	NA
St Johnstone		77/78	10	1		D1
Houston Hurricane		78	25		3	NA
		79	30		5	NA
		80	30		9	NA
Tampa Bay Rowdies		81	27		2	NA

ANDERSON Norman
b. Salsburgh 4.8.1957

Airdrieonians		74/75	3	6		D1
		75/76	9			D1
		76/77	8	1		D1
		77/78	10	5		D1
		78/79	26	2		D1
		79/80	36			D1
		80/81	30			P
		81/82	29		1	P
		82/83	22			D1
		83/84	19		2	D1
Ayr U		84/85	29		2	D1
		85/86	6			D1
Brechin C		85/86	13		1	D1
Queen of the South		86/87	31			D1
		87/88	2	2		D1
Stirling A		87/88	10			D2
Clyde		87/88	6			D1
		88/89	9			D1

ANDERSON Russell
b. Aberdeen 25.10.1978
Dyce Jnrs

Aberdeen		96/97	14			P
		97/98	20	6		P
		98/99	13	3		P
		99/00	34		1	P

ANDERSSON Mikael
b. 21.3.1971
Orebro

Dundee U		97/98	1	2		P

ANDERSSON Thomas
b. 20.1.1968

St Johnstone		97/98	0	3		P

ANDREWS Gary A
b. Glasgow 21.8.1969
Rangers BC
Rangers

Hamilton A		88/89	0	1		P
Queen of the South		89/90	14	10	6	D2
		90/91	2	5		D2
		91/92				
Albion R *		92/93	1			D2

ANDREWS Ian Edmund
b. Nottingham 1.12.1964
Nottingham F

Mansfield T		80/81				
Leicester C		81/82				
		82/83				
		83/84	2			FL
Middlesbrough	L	83/84				
Swindon T	L	83/84	1			FL
Leicester C		84/85	31			FL
		85/86	39			FL
		86/87	42			FL
		87/88	12			FL
Celtic		88/89	5			P
Leeds U	L	88/89	1			FL
Southampton		89/90	3			FL
		90/91	1			FL
		91/92	1			FL
		92/93				
		93/94	5			FL
		94/95				
Bournemouth		94/95	38			FL
		95/96	26			FL

ANGUS Ian Allan
b. Glasgow 19.11.1961
Eastercraigs BC

Aberdeen		80/81	15	4	1	P
		81/82	1		1	P
		82/83	3	2	3	P
		83/84	9	3		P
		84/85	21	7	2	P
		85/86	12	5	2	P
		86/87	2		1	P
Dundee		86/87	28	1	4	P
		87/88	39	1	6	P
		88/89	12	3		P
		89/90	4			P
Motherwell		90/91	14	6	2	P
		91/92	23	2	3	P
		92/93	25	6	3	P
		93/94	8	3		P
Clyde		94/95	24		5	D2
		95/96	33		2	D2
Albion R		96/97	8			D3

ANNAND Edward
b. Glasgow 24.3.1973

Partick T		91/92	0	1		D1
		92/93				
Sligo R		93/94				
		94/95				
Clyde		95/96	35		21	D2
		96/97	29		21	D2
Dundee		96/97	5		2	D1
		97/98	27	7	12	D1
		98/99	19	10	9	P
		99/00	18	9	4	P

ANNONI Enrico
b. Gloussand 10.7.1966
AS Roma

Celtic		96/97	3			P
		97/98	14	6		P
		98/99	9	5		P

ANTHONY Marc
b. Edinburgh 28.3.1978

Celtic		96/97	0	2		P
		97/98				
Clydebank		98/99	9	4	1	D1
Berwick R		99/00	32	2	9	D3

ARCHDEACON Owen Duncan
b. Greenock 4.3.1966
St Columbas High School
Celtic BC
Gourock U

Celtic		83/84	0	1	1	P
		84/85	1	2	1	P
		85/86	19	4	3	P
		86/87	12	18	2	P
		87/88	2	8		P
		88/89				
Barnsley		89/90	17	4	3	FL
		90/91	45		2	FL
		91/92	40		6	FL
		92/93	37	1	6	FL
		93/94	41	1	2	FL
		94/95	6	3	1	FL
		95/96	36	2	3	FL
Carlisle U		96/97	46		6	FL
		97/98	18		4	FL
Morton		97/98	23		1	D1
		98/99	33			D1
		99/00	4		1	D1

ARCHER Scott
b. Bellshill 2.4.1970
Hamilton Colts
Mill U
Burnbank Thistle
Fairholm
Leicester BC

Hamilton A		88/89	7	1	1	P
		89/90	19	2	1	D1
Queen of the South	L	89/90	5			D2
Hamilton A		90/91	1	1		D1
Albion R		91/92	15			D2
		92/93	9	2	1	D2
Glenafton A						
New Cumnock						
Arthurlie Jnrs						

ARCHIBALD Steven
b. Glasgow 27.9.1956
Crofoot U
Fernhill A

Clyde		74/75	2	2		D1
		75/76	14	2	2	D1
		76/77	30	1	3	D2
		77/78	14		2	D2
Aberdeen		77/78	10		4	P
		78/79	30	2	13	P
		79/80	34		12	P
Tottenham H		80/81	40	1	20	FL
		81/82	26	1	6	FL
		82/83	31		11	FL
		83/84	31	1	21	FL
Barcelona		84/85				
		85/86				
		86/87				
		87/88				
Blackburn R		87/88	20		6	FL
Hibernian		88/89	31		13	P
		89/90	8	5	2	P
St Mirren		90/91	16		2	P
Reading		91/92	1			FL
Ayr U		91/92	1			D1
Clyde		91/92	4		2	D2
Fulham		92/93	2			FL
		93/94				
East Fife		94/95	12	1	1	D2
		95/96	29	2	6	D2
		96/97	5			D1

ARKINS Vincent Thomas
b. Dublin 18.9.1970
Shamrock R
Dundee U
Shamrock R

St Johnstone		91/92	14	7	5	P
		92/93	24	2	6	P
		93/94	0	1		P
Shelbourne		94/95				
Notts Co		95/96	17	6	7	FL
		96/97	13	2	1	FL
Portadown						

ARMOUR David
b. Glasgow 11.4.1953

Rangers		76/77	0	1		P
		77/78				
		78/79	0	2		P
Ayr U		79/80	31		1	D1
		80/81	11	5	1	D1
		81/82	11	2		D1
		82/83	14	5		D1
		83/84	9		1	D1
Cowdenbeath		84/85	38	1	2	D2
		85/86	25	3		D2
		86/87	1			D2

ARMSTRONG Kenneth Charles
b. Bridgnorth 31.1.1959
Beith

Kilmarnock		78/79	4			D1
		79/80	3			P
		80/81	21	1	1	P
		81/82	39		2	D1
		82/83	19			P
Southampton		83/84	26			FL
Notts Co	L	83/84	10			FL
Birmingham C		84/85	36		1	FL
		85/86	22		1	FL
Walsall		85/86				

ARMSTRONG Lachlan J
b. Melbourne 22.3.1973
Hamilton Thistle

Dundee		92/93	1			P
		93/94	0	1		P

ARNOTT Douglas
b. Lanark 5.8.1961
Lesmagahow Jnrs
Pollok Jnrs

Motherwell		86/87	0	1		P
		87/88	0	2		P
		88/89	8	6	1	P
		89/90	23	7	4	P
		90/91	26	3	14	P
		91/92	26		8	P
		92/93	28	5	6	P
		93/94	25	4	8	P
		94/95	26	1	10	P
		95/96	23	4	3	P
		96/97	11	4	3	P
		97/98	3	4	1	P

ARTERO Javier
b. Madrid 16.4.1975
San Lorenzo

Dundee		99/00	6	3	1	P

ARTHUR Gordon George
b. Kirkcaldy 30.5.1958
Dundonald Bluebell

Stirling A		77/78	1			D1
		78/79	2			D1
		79/80	39			D1
		80/81	39			D1
		81/82	34			D2
		82/83	35			D2
		83/84	34			D2
Partick T	L	83/84	2			D1
Dumbarton		84/85	35			P
		85/86	38			D1
		86/87	31			D1
		87/88	40			D1
Raith R		88/89	39			D1
		89/90	39			D1
		90/91	34			D1
		91/92	44			D1
		92/93	17			D1
		93/94	1			P
Forfar A		93/94	24			D2
		94/95	35			D3
		95/96	33			D2
		96/97	6			D3
Arbroath		96/97	9			D3
Montrose		97/98	0	1		D3

ARTHUR James
b. Paisley 30.3.1968
Ferguslie U

Morton		86/87	0	8		D1
		87/88	5	8		P
Stranraer		88/89	7	5	3	D2

ASHWOOD W Kenneth
b. Baillieston 16.1.1958

East Stirlingshire		76/77	2		1	D2
		77/78	33	1	8	D2
		78/79	29	3	7	D2
		79/80	28	2	6	D2
		80/81	23	4	2	D1
		81/82	15	2	1	D1
		82/83	24		3	D2
Falkirk		82/83	5	1		D1
		83/84	0	2		D1
Dumbarton		83/84	31			D1
		84/85	19	6	1	P
		85/86	2		1	D1
Ayr U		85/86	15	2	4	D1
Airdrieonians		85/86	7	1	2	D1
Falkirk		86/87	9	8	2	P
Queen of the South		87/88	3			D1

AULD Robert Stewart
b. Glasgow 22.2.1958
Pollok Jnrs

Clydebank		85/86	27		1	P
		86/87	33			P
		87/88	41	1	1	D1
		88/89	33		4	D1
		89/90	25		1	D1
Airdrieonians		89/90	7	1	1	D1
		90/91				
Ayr U		91/92	21	1	1	D1

AYTON Stuart
b. Glasgow 19.10.1975
Rangers

Partick T		94/95	0	1		P
		95/96	1	4		P
		96/97	3			D1

BACQUE Herve
b. Bordeaux 13.7.1976
Lorient
AS Monaco

Luton T		98/99	2	5		FL
Motherwell		98/99	0	1		P

BAGAN David
b. Irvine 26.4.1977
Troon Jnrs

Kilmarnock		96/97	16	1		P
		97/98	4	3		P
		98/99	1	4		P
		99/00	2	1		P

BAILEY Lee
b. Edinburgh 10.71972

Hibernian		91/92	1			P
Meadowbank T		92/93	29	1	7	D1
		93/94	29	8	11	D2
		94/95	24	10	6	D2
Livingston		95/96	20	7	6	D3
		96/97	13	10	8	D2
		97/98	9	10	4	D2
Queen of the South		98/99	16	10	1	D2
		99/00	4	3	1	D2
Brechin C		99/00	20	1	2	D3

BAILLIE William Alexander
b. Hamilton 6.7.1966
Burnbank BC

Celtic		82/83				
		83/84				
		84/85				
		85/86				
		86/87				
		87/88	11	2		P
		88/89	8	1		P
		89/90				
Toronto Blizzard	L					
Celtic		90/91	8	1	1	P
St Mirren		91/92	17	1		P
		92/93	38		4	D1
Dunfermline A		93/94	14	1		D1

BAIN Alan
b. Glasgow 5.6.1962
Campsie Black Watch

Clydebank		84/85	14	7	4	D1
		85/86	6	6	1	P
		86/87	4	3		P
		87/88	6			P
Queen of the South		87/88	14	6	2	D1
		88/89	15		1	D1
		89/90	1	1		D2

BAIN Kevin
b. Kirkcaldy 19.9.1972

Dundee		89/90	0	1		P
		90/91	7			D1
		91/92				
		92/93	24			P
		93/94	4	3		P
		94/95	20		1	D1
		95/96	7	3	1	D1
		96/97	12			D1
Rotherham U	L	96/97	10	2		FL
Stirling A		97/98	11	5		D1
Brechin C		98/99	31		5	D3
		99/00	29		1	D3

BAINES Roy
b. Derby 7.2.1950

Woodpecker Bar						
Roe Farm						
Derby Co						
Hibernian		68/69				
		69/70				
		70/71	23			D1
		71/72				
Morton		72/73	24			D1
		73/74	34			D1
		74/75	33			D1
		75/76	25			D1
		76/77	1			D1
Celtic		76/77	5			P
		77/78				
		78/79	7			P
Morton		78/79	14			P
		79/80	36			P
		80/81	36			P
		81/82	36			P
		82/83	33			P
St Johnstone		83/84	26			P
		84/85	13			D1

BAIRD Ian James
b. Rotherham 1.4.1964

Southampton		82/83	9	2	2	FL
		83/84	6		1	FL
Cardiff C	L	83/84	12		6	FL
Southampton		84/85	5		2	FL
Newcastle U	L	84/85	4	1	1	FL
Leeds U		84/85	10		6	FL
		85/86	34	1	12	FL
		86/87	40		15	FL
Portsmouth		87/88	20		1	FL
Leeds U		87/88	10		3	FL
		88/89	43		10	FL
		89/90	23	1	4	FL
Middlesbrough		89/90	19		5	FL
		90/91	41	3	14	FL
Heart of Midlothian		91/92	30		6	P
		92/93	34		9	P
Bristol C		93/94	16	3	5	FL
		94/95	28	9	6	FL
		95/96	1			FL
Plymouth A		95/96	24	3	5	FL
Brighton		96/97	34	1	13	FL
		97/98	9		1	FL

BAKER David Paul
b. Newcastle 5.1.1963

Bishop Auckland						
Southampton		84/85	6	3		FL
Carlisle U		85/86	33	2	2	FL
		86/87	33	3	9	FL
Hartlepool U		87/88	38	1	19	FL
		88/89	39	1	7	FL
		89/90	43		16	FL
		90/91	43	3	12	FL
		91/92	29		13	FL
Motherwell		92/93	5	4	1	P
Gillingham		92/93	21		6	FL
		93/94	30	3	8	FL
		94/95	7	1	2	FL
York C		94/95	25	5	13	FL
		95/96	11	7	5	FL
Torquay U		95/96	20		4	FL
		96/97	10		4	FL
Scunthorpe U		96/97	21		9	FL
Hartlepool U		96/97	6		2	FL
		97/98	16		5	FL
		98/99	3	10	2	FL

BAKER Martin
b. Govan 8.6.1974

St Mirren		91/92	1			P
		92/93	29			D1
		93/94	37	1	1	D1
		94/95	23	3	2	D1
		95/96	26			D1
		96/97	31			D1
Kilmarnock		97/98	12	1		P
		98/99	23			P
		99/00	11			P

BALAVAGE John
b. Bellshill 15.10.1960

Albion R		78/79	27			D2
		79/80	33			D2
		80/81	33			D2
		81/82	31			D2
		82/83	21			D2
		83/84	20			D2
St Johnstone		84/85	5			D1
		85/86	38			D2
		86/87	26			D2
		87/88	37			D2
		88/89	38			D1
		89/90	38			D1
		90/91	2			P

BALFOUR Evan William
b. Edinburgh 9.9.1965

Whitburn Jnrs						
Airdrieonians		89/90	34	2	5	D1
		90/91	32	1	6	D1
		91/92	40	1	2	P
		92/93	26	1	1	P
		93/94	18	7		D1
		94/95				
Ayr U		95/96	12	2	1	D2

BALLANTYNE John Ian
b. Achnamara 2.11.1958

Queens Park		77/78	14	8	6	D2
		78/79	35		13	D2
Dundee U		79/80	1	1		P
Raith R		79/80	20		13	D1
		80/81	29	4	12	D1
		81/82	32	2	12	D1
		82/83	7	12	3	D1
East Stirlingshire		82/83	11		4	D2

BALTACHA Sergei Pavlovich
b. Kiev 17.2.1958

Metallist Karkhov						
Dynamo Kiev						
Ipswich T		88/89	19	1	1	FL
		89/90	3	5		FL
St Johnstone		90/91	34			P
		91/92	30	1	1	P
		92/93	25			P
		93/94				
Inverness CT		94/95	9			D3

BANGER Nicholas Lee
b. Southampton 25.2.1971

Southampton		90/91	0	6		FL
		91/92	0	4		FL
		92/93	10	17	6	FL
		93/94	4	10		FL
		94/95	4		2	FL
Oldham A		94/95	20	8	3	FL
		95/96	8	5	2	FL
		96/97	16	7	5	FL
Oxford U		97/98	18	10	3	FL
		98/99	22	10	5	FL
Dundee		99/00	2	4		P

BANNERMAN Scott John
b. Edinburgh 21.3.1979

Hutchison Vale						
Hibernian		97/98	0	1		P
		98/99	2	10		D1
		99/00	1	1		P
Alloa A		99/00	0	1		D2

BANNON Eammon John Peter
b. Edinburgh 18.4.1958

Links BC						
Heart of Midlothian		76/77	12	1	1	P
		77/78	39		12	D1
		78/79	19		5	P
Chelsea		78/79	19		1	FL
		79/80	6			FL
Dundee U		79/80	24		4	P
		80/81	34		8	P
		81/82	33	3	12	P
		82/83	31	1	9	P
		83/84	32	1	7	P
		84/85	35		10	P
		85/86	30	1	11	P
		86/87	37	2	9	P
		87/88	25	1	1	P
Heart of Midlothian		88/89	23	7	2	P
		89/90	31	2	2	P
		90/91	15	4	2	P
		91/92	10	3	2	P
		92/93	8	11	1	P
Hibernian		93/94	1			P
		94/95				
Stenhousemuir		95/96	29		1	D2

BAPTIE Crawford Bowie
b. Glasgow 24.2.1959

Cambuslang R						
Larkhall Thistle						
Baillieston Jnrs						
Falkirk		84/85	26		4	D1
		85/86	19		2	D1
Motherwell		85/86	14	2	3	P
		86/87	6	11		P
Falkirk		86/87	8			P
		87/88	35		9	P
		88/89	24	4	2	D1
		89/90	32	2	8	D1
		90/91	25	1	3	D1
		91/92	34	4	7	P
		92/93	8	1	2	P
Hamilton A		93/94	33	3	2	D1
		94/95	24	6		D1
		95/96	31		1	D1
		96/97	11	4		D2
Clyde		97/98	30			D2
Stenhousemuir		98/99	25	2	1	D3

BARNES David Oswald
b. Kingston 17.12.1962

West Ham U		80/81	1	5	1	FL
		81/82	1	2		FL
		82/83				
		83/84	11	2	2	FL
		84/85	18	2	2	FL
		85/86	0	1		FL
Scunthorpe U	L	85/86	6			FL
Aldershot		85/86	14		8	FL
		86/87	25		11	FL
		87/88	10		7	FL
Swindon T		87/88	26	2	10	FL
		88/89	17		3	FL
Bournemouth		88/89	10			FL
		89/90	1	3		FL
Northampton T		89/90	37		18	FL
		90/91	42	1	13	FL
		91/92	18		6	FL
Peterborough U		91/92	15		5	FL
		92/93	22	4	3	FL
		93/94	5	3	1	FL
Partick T		93/94	3	4		P
Hong Kong						
Torquay U		95/96	0	1		FL

BARNETT David Kwame
b. Birmingham 16.4.1967

Windsor & Eton						
Colchester U		88/89	19		1	FL
Edmonton						
WBA		89/90				
Walsall		90/91	4	1		FL
Kidderminster H						
Barnet		91/92	3			FL
		92/93	36		2	FL
		93/94	19		1	FL
Birmingham C		93/94	8	1		FL
		94/95	31			FL
		95/96				
		96/97	6			FL
Dunfermline A		97/98	21		1	P
Port Vale		97/98	8	1	1	FL
		98/99	26	1		FL
Lincoln C		99/00	20	2	3	FL
Forest Green R						

BARR Leslie
b. Dundee 18.11.1952

Montrose		71/72	21	5	6	D2
		72/73	18	1	4	D2
		73/74	30	1	9	D2
		74/75	35		7	D2
		75/76	26			D1
		76/77	31	3	2	D1
		77/78	30	2	5	D1
Dundee		78/79	21		1	D1
		79/80	26	3		P
		80/81	29			D1
		81/82	23	3		P
Montrose		82/83	24		4	D2
		83/84	31	2	3	D2
		84/85	39		2	D2
		85/86	34		5	D1
		86/87	37	1	2	D1
		87/88	25	1	2	D2
		88/89	10	8		D2

BARR Robert
b. Lennoxtown 16.5.1962
Campsie Black Watch

Queens Park		83/84	4			D2
Alloa A		83/84	2			D1
		84/85	27	2	2	D2
		85/86	31		3	D1
Hamilton A		86/87	19	4		P
		87/88				
		88/89				
Stranraer		89/90	2	1		D2
Arthurlie						
Annbank U						
Stenhousemuir		91/92	20			D2
		92/93	4	5		D2
Camelon Jnrs						

BARRON Douglas
b. Edinburgh 25.10.1961
Bainsford FANG

St Johnstone		79/80				
		80/81	1			D1
		81/82	14	3		D1
		82/83	1	4		D1
		83/84	17	3	2	P
		84/85	34	3	1	D1
		85/86	37		2	D2
		86/87	35			D2
		87/88	38		1	D2
		88/89	38			D1
		89/90	16	1		D1
		90/91	3	8		P
		91/92	1	3		P
Clydebank		92/93	23	4		D1
East Fife		92/93	5			D2
		93/94	20	2		D2
		94/95	3			D2

BARRY Roy Alexander
b. Edinburgh 19.9.1942
Musselburgh A

Heart ot Midlothian		60/61				
		61/62	3			D1
		62/63	28		1	D1
		63/64	28			D1
		64/65	16		7	D1
		65/66	17			D1
		66/67	2			D1
Dunfermline A		66/67	28		5	D1
		67/68	32			D1
		68/69	31			D1
		69/70	3			D1
Coventry C		69/70	14	1		FL
		70/71	1			FL
		71/72	27		1	FL
		72/73	40		1	FL
Crystal Palace		73/74	31		1	FL
		74/75	10	1		FL
Hibernian		75/76	25			P
East Fife		76/77	11			D1

BARTRAM Jan
b. 6.3.1962

Rangers		87/88	11		3	P

BATEMAN Alan D
b. Falkirk 4.8.1966

Stenhousemuir		84/85	15	4	1	D2
		85/86	35	1	10	D2
		86/87	34	2	5	D2
Morton		87/88	5	2		P
Alloa A		88/89	12	10	2	D2
Clyde						
East Stirlingshire		89/90	26	3	2	D2

BAVIDGE Mitchell

Dundee		75/76	0	3		P
		76/77				
		77/78				
		78/79				
		79/80				
		80/81				
		81/82				
		82/83				
		83/84				
Raith R		84/85	4	4	1	D2

BAYNE Graham
b. Kirkcaldy 22.8.1979
Newburgh

Dundee		96/97	0	2		D1
		97/98	0	2		D1
		98/99	0	2		P
		99/00	3	10	1	P

BEATTIE James
b. Glasgow 16.2.1973
Celtic

St Mirren		91/92	24			P
		92/93	2			D1
Ayr U		93/94	3			D1
Albion R		93/94	14	1		D2
		94/95	10	1		D3

BEATTIE Stuart Richard
b. Stevenston 10.7.1967
Ardeer Recreation

Rangers		85/86	5			P
Doncaster R		86/87	7			FL
		87/88	2			FL
		88/89	17		1	FL

BEAUMONT David Alan
b. Edinburgh 10.12.1963

Dundee U		83/84	1	1		P
		84/85	13	5	1	P
		85/86	10	3		P
		86/87	21	7		P
		87/88	7	3	1	P
		88/89	12	6	1	P
Luton T		88/89	15			FL
		89/90	16	3		FL
		90/91	29	4		FL
		91/92	6	3		FL
Hibernian		91/92	17	4		P
		92/93	16			P
		93/94	24	2	2	P
		94/95	7			P

BECKETT Alexander
b. 19.2.1954

St Mirren		74/75	23	1		D2
		75/76	20			D1
		76/77	32		2	D1
		77/78	30	1		P
		78/79	12			P
		79/80	19	2		P
		80/81	27	1	1	P
		81/82	27			P
Queen of the South		82/83	2			D2
		83/84				
		84/85	6	1		D2

BECKFORD Darren Richard Lorenzo
b. Manchester 12.5.1967

Manchester C		84/85	1	3		FL
		85/86	2	1		FL
Bury	L	85/86	12		5	FL
Manchester C		86/87	4			FL
Port Vale		86/87	9	2	4	FL
		87/88	36	4	9	FL
		88/89	41	1	20	FL
		89/90	40	2	17	FL
		90/91	43		22	FL
Norwich C		91/92	25	5	7	FL
		92/93	7	1	1	FL
Oldham A		92/93	6	1	3	FL
		93/94	13	9	6	FL
		94/95	0	3		FL
		95/96	12	8	2	FL
Heart of Midlothian		96/97	6	2		P
Preston NE		96/97	0	2		FL
Fulham		96/97				
Walsall		96/97	3		5	FL

BEEDIE Stuart
b. Aberdeen 16.8.1960
Lewis U

Montrose		78/79	9	1		D1
		79/80	27	7	4	D2
		80/81	35	1	9	D2
St Johnstone		81/82	25	1	5	D1
		82/83	33	1	2	D1
		83/84	34		2	P
Dundee U		84/85	18	8	3	P
		85/86	14	4	3	P
Hibernian		86/87	9		2	P
Dunfermline A		86/87	6			D1
		87/88	35	1	2	P
		88/89	22	1	2	D1
Dundee		89/90	19	2	6	P
		90/91	8	1		D1
		91/92	40		4	D1
		92/93	8	6		P
East Fife		93/94	25			D2
Montrose		93/94	12			D2
		94/95	7		2	D3

BEESLEY Darren
b. Rotherham 16.3.1981
Rotherham U

Kilmarnock		99/00	1	1		P

BELABED Rachid
b. Brussels 30.10.1980
RWD Molenbeek

Aberdeen		99/00	6	15	1	P

BELL Brian

Kello R						
Ayr U		73/74	6	12	2	D1
		74/75	2	3		D1
		75/76	0	2		P

BELL David S
b. Falkirk 22.10.1961
Camelon Mariners

Dundee		81/82	15	1	1	P
		82/83	21	7	3	P
Falkirk		83/84	11	7	1	D1
		84/85	10	1	1	D1

BELL Douglas
b. Paisley 5.9.1959
Cumbernauld

St Mirren		77/78	0	2	1	P
		78/79				
Aberdeen		79/80	4	5		P
		80/81	13	4	1	P
		81/82	11	2	1	P
		82/83	20	3	1	P
		83/84	21	3	3	P
		84/85	18	4		P
Rangers		85/86	20	3		P
		86/87	7	5	1	P
St Mirren		86/87	4			P
Hibernian		86/87	16		2	P
		87/88	8	8	1	P
Shrewsbury T		87/88	13	2	2	FL
		88/89	25	1	1	FL
Hull C	L	88/89	4			FL
Shrewsbury T		89/90	9		3	FL
Birmingham C		89/90	14	1		FL
		90/91	1			FL
Partick T		91/92	8	4		D1
		92/93				
Clyde		93/94	13	5		D1
Alloa A		94/95	5			D3
Albion R		95/96	17	4		D3

BENNEKER Armand
b. Tongeren 25.6.1969
Austria Lustenau
Schwarz-Weiss Bregenz
MVV Maastricht

Dundee U		96/97	6	1		P

BERGERSEN Kent
b. Oslo 8.2.1967
Drobak

Lyn Oslo		91				
		92				
Rosenborg Trondheim		93				
		94				
Valerengen		95				
		96				
Raith R		96/97	6		1	P
Panionos		97/98				
		98/99				
Stromgodset		99				
Stockport Co		99/00	17			FL

BERKOVIC Eyal
b. Haifa 2.4.1972
Maccabi Haifa

Southampton		96/97	26	2	4	FL
West Ham U		97/98	34	1	7	FL
		98/99	28	2	3	FL
Celtic		99/00	27	1	9	P

BERNARD Paul Robert James
b. Edinburgh 30.12.1972

Oldham A		90/91	2		1	FL
		91/92	16	5	5	FL
		92/93	32	1	4	FL
		93/94	32		5	FL
		94/95	16	1	2	FL
		95/96	7		1	FL
Aberdeen		95/96	27	4	1	P
		96/97	13	1		P
		97/98	15	2		P
		98/99	8	1	1	P
		99/00	24	1	4	P

BERRY Neil
b. Edinburgh 6.4.1963

Bolton W	81/82	2	1		FL
	82/83	8	1		FL
	83/84	9	5		FL
	84/85	6			FL
Heart of Midlothian	84/85	2	1		P
	85/86	32		2	P
	86/87	30		3	P
	87/88	31	4		P
	88/89	32		1	P
	89/90	10		1	P
	90/91	18	1	1	P
	91/92				
	92/93	16	1	1	P
	93/94	30			P
	94/95	29			P
	95/96	16	3		P
Falkirk	96/97	9			D1
	97/98	10			D1
Hamilton A	98/99	14	1	1	D1
Cowdenbeath	99/00	3			D3

BERTHE Mohammed
b. Conakry 12.9.1972

Gaz Ajaccio					
West Ham U	97/98				
Bournemouth	98/99	12	3	2	FL
Heart of Midlothian	98/99	1			P
Raith R	99/00	1			D1

BEST George
b. Belfast 22.5.1946

Manchester U	63/64	17		4	FL
	64/65	41		10	FL
	65/66	31		9	FL
	66/67	42		10	FL
	67/68	41		28	FL
	68/69	41		19	FL
	69/70	37		15	FL
	70/71	40		18	FL
	71/72	40		18	FL
	72/73	19		4	FL
	73/74	12		2	FL
Dunstable T	74/75				
Stockport Co	75/76	3		2	FL
Cork Celtic	75/76				
Los Angeles Aztecs	76	23		15	NA
Fulham	76/77	32		6	FL
Los Angeles Aztecs	77	20		11	NA
Fulham	77/78	10		2	FL
Los Angeles Aztecs	78	12		1	NA
Fort Lauderdale Strikers	78	9		4	NA
	79	19		2	NA
Hibernian	79/80	13		3	P
San Jose Earthquakes	80	26		8	NA
Hibernian	80/81	4			D1
San Jose Earthquakes	81	30		13	NA
	81/82				
Bournemouth	82/83	5			FL
Brisbane Lions					

BETT Baldur
b. Reykjavik 12.4.1980

FH Hafnarfjordur					
Hermes					
Aberdeen	96/97				
	97/98				
	98/99	1			P
	99/00	0	1		P

BETT James
b. Hamilton 25.11.1959

Dundee					
Airdrieonians	76/77	1			D1
	77/78	7			D1
Valur Reykjavik					
SK Lokeren					
Rangers	80/81	34		4	P
	81/82	35		11	P
	82/83	35		6	P
SK Lokeren	83/84				
	84/85				
Aberdeen	85/86	22	2	23	P
	86/87	38		4	P
	87/88	38		10	P
	88/89	31		5	P
	89/90	30		3	P
	90/91	36		7	P
	91/92	38		1	P
	92/93	17			P
	93/94	6			P
Heart of Midlothian	94/95	26		2	P
Dundee U	95/96	23		2	D1

BIGGINS Wayne
b. Sheffield 20.11.1961

Lincoln C	80/81	2	1	1	FL
Matlock T					
Kings Lynn					
Matlock T					
Burnley	83/84	20		8	FL
	84/85	46		18	FL
	85/86	12		3	FL
Norwich C	85/86	28		7	FL
	86/87	23	8	4	FL
	87/88	15	5	5	FL
Manchester C	88/89	29	3	9	FL
Stoke C	89/90	35		10	FL
	90/91	36	2	12	FL
	91/92	41		22	FL
	92/93	8		2	FL
Barnsley	92/93	32	2	14	FL
	93/94	12	1	2	FL
Celtic	93/94	4	5		P
Stoke C	93/94	10		4	FL
	94/95	8	9	2	FL
Luton T	94/95	6	1		FL
Oxford U	95/96	8	2	1	FL
Wigan A	95/96	15	3	2	FL
	96/97	20	13	3	FL

BILLIO Patrizio
b. Treviso 19.4.1974

Monza					
Crystal Palace	97/98	1	2		FL
Ancona	98/99				
Dundee	99/00	16	1	1	P

BINGHAM David Thomas
b. Dunfermline 3.9.1970

Oakley U					
St Johnstone	89/90	1			D1
	90/91	4	3	2	P
	91/92	7	2	1	P
Forfar A	92/93	20		6	D2
	93/94	38		13	D2
	94/95	36		22	D3
	95/96	5		3	D2
Dunfermline A	95/96	12	3	3	D1
	96/97	5	12	1	P
	97/98	18	12	5	P
Livingston	98/99	29		11	D2
	99/00	32		15	D1

BJORKLUND Joachim
b. Vaxjo 15.3.1971

Brann Bergen	90				
	91				
	92				
	93				
IFK Gothenburg	93				
	94				
	95				
Lanerossi Vicenza	95/96				
IFK Gothenburg	96				
Rangers	96/97	28			P
	97/98	31			P
Valencia	98/99				
	99/00				

BLACK Eric
b. Bellshill 1.10.1963

Aberdeen	81/82	10	3	3	P
	82/83	23	9	13	P
	83/84	14	4	6	P
	84/85	27		17	P
	85/86	23	3	8	P

BLACK Ian George
b. 4.2.1960

Heart of Midlothian	78/79	10	4		P
	79/80	17	1		D1
Hibernian	80/81	2			D1
East Fife	80/81	3			D2
Berwick R	80/81	13		2	D1
	81/82	16	2		D2

BLACK Kenneth George
b. Stenhousemuir 29.11.1963

Rangers	81/82	7	1		P
	82/83	11	4	1	P
Motherwell	83/84	17			P
Heart of Midlothian	84/85	32		7	P
	85/86	23	6	2	P
	86/87	41	1	1	P
	87/88	41	1	4	P
	88/89	33		1	P
Portsmouth	89/90	36	5	2	FL
	90/91	14	7	1	FL
Airdrieonians	91/92	33		2	P
	92/93	33		1	P
	93/94	40		1	D1
	94/95	31		2	D1
	95/96	33		2	D1
	96/97	26	2	4	D1
	97/98	24	3	1	D1
	98/99	30	1	7	D1
Raith R	99/00	23	2	3	D1

BLACK Paul Alexander
b. Aberdeen 30.10.1977

Dundee U	96/97	0	1		P

BLACK Russell Palmer
b. Dumfries 29.7.1960

Gretna					
Sheffield U	84/85	9	3		FL
	85/86	1	1		FL
Dundee	85/86	1		1	P
Halifax T	86/87	44	1	9	FL
	87/88	19	8	5	FL

BLACK Steven Scott
b. Kilmarnock 23.11.1958

Whitletts V					
Kilmarnock	78/79				
	79/80				
	80/81	0	1		P
Stranraer	81/82	28		2	D2
Whitletts V					
Cumnock Jnrs					

BLACK Thomas
b. Lanark 11.10.1962

Airdrieonians	82/83	4			D1
	83/84	32		4	D1
	84/85	37		1	D1
	85/86	10	2		D1
	86/87	24		1	D1
	87/88	27	2	1	D1
	88/89	37		4	D1
St Mirren	89/90	31		1	P
	90/91	33	1	2	P
	91/92	9		1	P
Kilmarnock	91/92	23		3	D1
	92/93	10		1	D1
	93/94	44		4	P
	94/95	31	1	5	P
	95/96	30		4	P
Stranraer	96/97	26		1	D2
	97/98	36		5	D2
	98/99	26		2	D1
	99/00	16	1		D2

BLACKLEY John Henderson
b. Polmont 12.5.1948

Gairdoch U					
Hibernian	67/68	3	1		D1
	68/69	13			D1
	69/70	31			D1
	70/71	29		2	D1
	71/72	33		2	D1
	72/73	29			D1
	73/74	31		1	D1
	74/75	21	1		D1
	75/76	34		1	P
	76/77	31			P
	77/78	7			P
Newcastle U	77/78	18			FL
	78/79	28			FL
Preston NE	79/80	27			FL
	80/81	21	2		FL
	81/82	3			FL
Hamilton A	81/82	19			D1
	82/83	19			D1
Hibernian	83/84	16			P

BLAIR Allan
b. Kirkcaldy 24.12.1954

East Fife	76/77	21			D1
	77/78	39			D1
	78/79	34			D2
	79/80	21	1		D2
Dundee	80/81	15			D1
	81/82	8	1		P
	82/83				
	83/84	2			P
Raith R	84/85	27			D2

BLAIR Raymond
b. Falkirk 12.11.1958

Dumbarton		76/77	11	2		D1
		77/78	9	10	2	D1
		78/79	26			D1
		79/80	30	3	8	D1
		80/81	21	8	8	D1
		81/82	36	3	9	D1
		82/83	28		10	D1
St Johnstone		82/83	9	1	1	D1
		83/84	34	2	4	P
		84/85	4	2		D1
Motherwell		84/85	21	10	6	D1
		85/86	17	4	2	P
East Fife		86/87	43		7	D1
		87/88	37	1	10	D1

BLAKE Noel Lloyd George
b. Kingston, Jamaica 12.1.1962
Sutton Coldfield T

Aston Villa		79/80	3			FL
		80/81				
		81/82	1			FL
Shrewsbury T	L	81/82	6			FL
Birmingham C		82/83	37		3	FL
		83/84	39		2	FL
Portsmouth		84/85	42		3	FL
		85/86	42		4	FL
		86/87	41		3	FL
		87/88	19			FL
Leeds U		88/89	44		4	FL
		89/90	7			FL
Stoke C		89/90	18			FL
		90/91	44		3	FL
		91/92	12	1		FL
Bradford C	L	91/92	6			FL
		92/93	31	1	3	FL
		93/94	7			FL
Dundee		93/94	23		2	P
		94/95	29	2		D1
Exeter C		95/96	44		2	FL
		96/97	46		6	FL
		97/98	36	2	1	FL
		98/99	4	3		FL
		99/00	2	5	1	FL

BLINKER Reginald Waldie
b. Surinam 4.6.1969

Feyenoord		86/87				
		87/88				
		88/89				
Den Bosch		88/89				
Feyenoord		89/90				
		90/91				
		91/92				
		92/93				
		93/94				
		94/95				
		95/96				
Sheffield W		95/96	9		2	FL
		96/97	33		1	FL
Celtic		97/98	13	3	1	P
		98/99	13	2	4	P
		99/00	10	7	4	P

BOAG James
b. Greenock 22.9.1949

St Mirren		81/82	2			P
Port Glasgow R		82/83				
		83/84				
		84/85				
Morton		85/86	28	1		D1
		86/87	7	16	3	D1
		87/88	27	3	8	P
		88/89	1	6		D1
		89/90	6	7	1	D1

BOAG John
b. Port Glasgow 14.2.1965

Morton		84/85	17			P
		85/86				
		86/87	13	1		D1
		87/88	15			P
		88/89	27			D1
		89/90	29	3		D1
		90/91	20		2	D1
		91/92	19			D1
		92/93	5			D1
Dumbarton *		92/93	6	1		D1

BOCO Jean Marc Adjovi
b. Benin 22.12.1963
RC Lens

Hibernian		97/98	29			P

BOLI Basile
b. Adjame 2.1.1967
Olympique Marseille

Rangers		94/95	28		2	P

BOLI Roger Zokou
b. Adjame 29.6.1965
Auxerre
Le Havre
Lens

Walsall		97/98	41		12	FL
Dundee U		98/99	3			P
Bournemouth		98/99	5	1		FL
		99/00				

BOLLAN Gary
b. Dundee 24.3.1973
Fairfield BC

Dundee U		90/91	1	1		P
		91/92	8	2	1	P
		92/93	12	3	3	P
		93/94	10	2		P
		94/95	5	2		P
Rangers		94/95	5	1		P
		95/96	4			P
		96/97				
		97/98	0	1		P
St Johnstone		98/99	32	1	4	P
		99/00	34		2	P

BONAR Paul
b. Robroyston 28.12.1976

Airdrieonians		95/96	9	3		D1
Raith R		95/96	4	1		P
		96/97	9	7	1	P
Ayr U		97/98	6	4		D1

BONE James
b. Bridge of Allan 22.9.1949
Bannockburn
Airth Castle R

Partick T		68/69	30	1	13	D1
		69/70	30	1	14	D1
		70/71				
		71/72	22		10	D1
Norwich C		71/72	13		4	FL
		72/73	26		5	FL
Sheffield U		72/73	12		6	FL
		73/74	18	1	3	FL
Celtic		73/74	3	1		D1
		74/75	2	1	1	D1
Arbroath		74/75	14		5	D1
		75/76	26		13	D1
		76/77	39		15	D1
		77/78	18		8	D1
St Mirren		77/78	13		3	P
		78/79	33		7	P
Toronto Blizzard		79	25		3	NA
St Mirren		79/80	32		6	P
Toronto Blizzard		80	25		4	NA
St Mirren		80/81	26	1	7	P
		81/82	20	6	4	P
Hong Kong R		82/83				
Heart of Midlothian		83/84	34		7	P
		84/85	16	6	4	P
Arbroath		84/85	8	1	1	D2
		85/86	15		1	D2
		86/87	5	1		D2

BONETTI Peter Philip
b. Putney 27.9.1941

Chelsea		59/60	6			FL
		60/61	36			FL
		61/62	33			FL
		62/63	39			FL
		63/64	35			FL
		64/65	41			FL
		65/66	38			FL
		66/67	38			FL
		67/68	40			FL
		68/69	41			FL
		69/70	36			FL
		70/71	28			FL
		71/72	33			FL
		72/73	23			FL
		73/74	20			FL
		74/75	8			FL
		75/76	27			FL
		76/77	31			FL
		77/78	31			FL
		78/79	16			FL
Dundee U		79/80	5			P

BONNER Patrick Joseph
b. Clochglas 24.5.1960
Rosses R
Keadue R

Leicester C	T	75/76				
Celtic		78/79	2			P
		79/80				
		80/81	36			P
		81/82	36			P
		82/83	36			P
		83/84	33			P
		84/85	34			P
		85/86	30			P
		86/87	43			P
		87/88	32			P
		88/89	26			P
		89/90	36			P
		90/91	36			P
		91/92	19			P
		92/93	33			P
		93/94	31			P
		94/95	20			P

BONNYMAN Philip
b. Glasgow 6.2.1954
Anniesland W
Rangers

Hamilton A		73/74	7	6		D2
		74/75	35		5	D2
		75/76	23		2	D1
Carlisle U		75/76	9			FL
		76/77	35	2	1	FL
		77/78	32	1	8	FL
		78/79	45		7	FL
		79/80	28		10	FL
Chesterfield		79/80	11		3	FL
		80/81	41	1	8	FL
		81/82	46		14	FL
Grimsby T		82/83	40		1	FL
		83/84	27	2	3	FL
		84/85	37		8	FL
		85/86	29		3	FL
Stoke C	L	85/86				
Grimsby T		86/87	13	3		FL
Darlington		87/88	38		3	FL
		88/89	11	1	2	FL
Dunfermline A		89/90	1			P

BOOTH Scott
b. Aberdeen 16.12.1971

Aberdeen		89/90	1	1		P
		90/91	8	11	6	P
		91/92	21	12	5	P
		92/93	21	8	13	P
		93/94	14	11	4	P
		94/95	11	1	6	P
		95/96	20	4	9	P
		96/97	8	11		P

BOOTHROYD Adrian Neil
b. Bradford 8.2.1971

Huddersfield T		89/90	9	1		FL
Bristol R		90/91	2	1		FL
		91/92	8	5		FL
Heart of Midlothian		92/93	0	4		P
Mansfield T		93/94	22	1	1	FL
		94/95	35	1		FL
		95/96	42	1	2	FL
Peterborough U		96/97	24	2	1	FL

BORTHWICK Walter Ross
b. Edinburgh 4.12.1948

Morton		65/66	2			D1
Brighton		66/67	1			FL
Dundee U	T	67/68				
East Fife		67/68				
		68/69				
		69/70				
		70/71				
		71/72	17		4	D1
		72/73	29	1	4	D1
		73/74	23		1	D1
St Mirren		74/75	35		7	D2
		75/76	10	7	3	D1
		76/77	4	6	1	D1
St Johnstone		76/77	21	1	2	D1
St Mirren		77/78	0	1		P
Dunfermline A		77/78	26	1	4	D2
		78/79	25	4	2	D2
		79/80	24			D1
		80/81	2	1		D1

BOURKE John Francis
b. Glasgow 31.12.1953

Club	Season	Apps	Sub	Goals	Div
Dumbarton U					
Dumbarton	73/74	12	4	7	D1
	74/75	29	2	5	D1
	75/76	25		17	D1
	76/77	35		19	D1
	77/78	3		3	D1
Dundee U	77/78	25	1	5	P
Kilmarnock	78/79	27		21	D1
	79/80	20	3	1	P
	80/81	26	1	5	P
	81/82	33	1	14	D1
	82/83	10	9	2	P
Dumbarton	82/83	7	1		D1
	83/84	34		13	D1
	84/85	24	2	4	P
	85/86	25	2	8	D1
	86/87	8	3	1	D1
Brechin C	86/87	13	1	5	D1
	87/88	6	8	2	D2
Kilmarnock	87/88	9		2	D1
	88/89	2			D1

BOVE Raphael
b. Australia (?)

Club	Season	Apps	Sub	Goals	Div
Heerenveen					
Dundee U	99/00	0	1		P

BOWES Mark John
b. Bangour 17.2.1973

Club	Season	Apps	Sub	Goals	Div
Gairdoch U					
Dunfermline A	91/92	12	2		P
	92/93	4			D1
	93/94	4	2		D1
	94/95	7			D1
Forfar A	95/96	27	2	2	D2
	96/97	30	2	1	D3
	97/98				
	98/99	0	1		D2

BOWMAN David
b. Tonbridge 10.3.1964

Club	Season	Apps	Sub	Goals	Div
Heart of Midlothian	80/81	16	1	1	P
	81/82	16		1	D1
	82/83	39		5	D1
	83/84	32	1		P
	84/85	9	2	1	P
Coventry C	84/85	9	1		FL
	85/86	29	1	2	FL
Dundee U	86/87	19	10		P
	87/88	34	5	1	P
	88/89	21	8	1	P
	89/90	20	4	1	P
	90/91	17	3	1	P
	91/92	37	4	3	P
	92/93	18	6		P
	93/94	35		2	P
	94/95	31			P
	95/96	16	1		D1
	96/97	26	2		P
	97/98	15	4		P
Raith R	98/99	23			D1

BOWMAN Gary
b. Glasgow 12.8.1974

Club	Season	Apps	Sub	Goals	Div
Knightswood Juveniles					
Clydebank	92/93	1			D1
	93/94	0	1		D1
	94/95	30	2	1	D1
	95/96	33		2	D1
	96/97	22			D1
St Johnstone	96/97	4			D1
	97/98	1			P
Ayr U	97/98	15			D1
	98/99	0	4		D1
	99/00	5	1		D1
St Mirren	99/00	10	9	1	D1

BOYACK Steven
b. Edinburgh 12.8.1974

Club	Season	Apps	Sub	Goals	Div
Rangers	96/97	0	1		P
	97/98				
Hull C L	97/98	12		3	FL
Dundee	98/99	8		2	P
	99/00	32	4	1	P

BOYD Crawford
b. 19.3.1952

Club	Season	Apps	Sub	Goals	Div
Queen of the South	72/73	27	2		D2
	73/74	35	1		D2
	74/75	38		1	D2
	75/76	23		2	D1
	76/77	20	1		D1
	77/78	33		1	D1
	78/79	34	1	2	D1
	79/80				
Heart of Midlothian	80/81	5			P
Queen of the South	80/81	8			D2
	81/82	30			D1

BOYD Gordon
b. Glasgow 27.3.1958

Club	Season	Apps	Sub	Goals	Div
Rangers	75/76	1			P
	76/77				
	77/78				
Fulham	78/79	1	2		FL
Rangers	79/80				
Barnsley	80/81	1	1		FL
Scunthorpe U	81/82	10	1		FL

BOYD James
b. 14.8.1956

Club	Season	Apps	Sub	Goals	Div
Clyde	74/75	4	1		D1
	75/76	11	2		D1
	76/77	34		1	D2
	77/78	38		2	D2
Motherwell	78/79	9	2		P
Clyde	79/80	19	2		D1
	80/81	7			D2

BOYD Thomas
b. Glasgow 24.11.1965

Club	Season	Apps	Sub	Goals	Div
Celtic BC					
Motherwell	83/84	13			P
	84/85	35	1		D1
	85/86	31			P
	86/87	31			P
	87/88	42		2	P
	88/89	31	5	1	P
	89/90	33		1	P
	90/91	30		2	P
Chelsea	91/92	22	1		FL
Celtic	91/92	12	1	1	P
	92/93	42			P
	93/94	38			P
	94/95	35		1	P
	95/96	34			P
	96/97	31			P
	97/98	33			P
	98/99	31			P
	99/00	10			P

BOYLE James
b. Glasgow 19.2.1967

Club	Season	Apps	Sub	Goals	Div
Queens Park	85/86	30		1	D2
	86/87	39		3	D2
	87/88	39		8	D2
	88/89	39		4	D2
Airdrieonians	89/90	30	1	1	D1
	90/91	6	5		D1
	91/92	36	1	3	P
	92/93	36	4	4	P
	93/94	17	10	1	D1
	94/95	33	1	4	D1
	95/96	36		2	D1
	96/97	19	7		D1
Partick T	97/98	36		2	D1
Livingston	98/99	34		1	D2
Alloa A	99/00	14	2	1	D2

BOYLE Steven Robert
b. 6.2.1981

Club	Season	Apps	Sub	Goals	Div
Dunfermline A	98/99	1		1	P
Brechin C	98/99	8			D3
	99/00	4			D3
Ross Co	99/00	0	3		D2

BRADBURY Andrew

Club	Season	Apps	Sub	Goals	Div
Clydebank	77/78	0	4		P

BRADLEY Mark
b. Glasgow 10.8.1976

Club	Season	Apps	Sub	Goals	Div
Heart of Midlothian	97/98	0	1		P
Stirling A	98/99	4	3		D2
Cowdenbeath	98/99	19		2	D3
	99/00	31	4	6	D3

BRANNAN Gerard Daniel
b. Prescot 15.1.1972

Club	Season	Apps	Sub	Goals	Div
Tranmere R	90/91	14	4	1	FL
	91/92	18		1	FL
	92/93	38		1	FL
	93/94	45		9	FL
	94/95	37	4	2	FL
	95/96	44			FL
	96/97	31	3	6	FL
Manchester C	96/97	11		1	FL
	97/98	27	5	3	FL
Motherwell	98/99	25		5	P
	99/00	33		5	P

BRANNIGAN Andrew
b. Glasgow 10.12.1959

Club	Season	Apps	Sub	Goals	Div
St Johnstone	78/79	14	9	5	D1
	79/80	20	7	4	D1
	80/81	13	6	1	D1
	81/82	35	3	11	D1
	82/83	39		9	D1
	83/84	9	5	1	P
	84/85	1			D1
Arbroath	84/85	34		5	D2
	85/86	37		7	D2
	86/87	28		8	D2
	87/88	33		6	D2
Jeanfield Swifts					

BRATBAKK Harold Martin
b. Norway 1.2.1971

Club	Season	Apps	Sub	Goals	Div
Rosenborg Trondheim	90				
	91				
Bodo Glimt	92				
	93				
Rosenborg Trondheim	94				
	95				
	96				
	97				
Celtic	97/98	11	7	7	P
	98/99	16	8	5	P
	99/00	0	2		P

BRAZIL Alistair
b. Currie 10.12.1958

Club	Season	Apps	Sub	Goals	Div
Currie Hearts					
Hibernian	76/77	4			P
	77/78	22	3	2	P
	78/79	17	1		P
	79/80	31	1		P
	80/81	5	2	1	D1
	81/82	23	1		P
	82/83	10	1		P
	83/84	28	1	1	P
	84/85	27	4	1	P
	85/86	21	3	2	P
Hamilton A	86/87	23	1		P
Forfar A	87/88	36			D1
	88/89	15	2		D1
	89/90	29	1	1	D1
	90/91	26	2	2	D1
	91/92	22	3		D1
Armadale Thistle					

BRCIC David
b. USA 21.1.1957

Club	Season	Apps	Sub	Goals	Div
New York Cosmos	78	1			NA
Morton	78/79	6			P
New York Cosmos	79	7			NA

BREBNER Grant Iain
b. Edinburgh 6.12.1977

Club	Season	Apps	Sub	Goals	Div
Hutchinson Vale BC					
Manchester U	95/96				
	96/97				
	97/98				
Cambridge U L	97/98	6		1	FL
Hibernian L	97/98	9		1	P
Reading	98/99	36	3	9	FL
Hibernian	99/00	27	1		P

BREMNER Desmond George
b. Aberchirder 7.9.1952

Club	Season	Apps	Sub	Goals	Div
Banks o'Dee					
Deverondale					
Hibernian	72/73	11			D1
	73/74	21		2	D1
	74/75	30		2	D1
	75/76	32		3	P
	76/77	36		4	P
	77/78	33		2	P
	78/79	31		5	P
	79/80	5			P
Aston Villa	79/80	36		3	FL
	80/81	42		2	FL
	81/82	38		3	FL
	82/83	36	1		FL
	83/84	14	3		FL
	84/85	4		1	FL
Birmingham C	84/85	30			FL
	85/86	32			FL
	86/87	40		4	FL
	87/88	37			FL
	88/89	28	1	1	FL
Fulham	89/90				
Walsall	89/90	2	4		FL

BREWSTER Craig James
b. Dundee 13.12.1966

Club	Season				
Forfar A	85/86	14	2	2	D1
	86/87	27	5	3	D1
	87/88	35	4	2	D1
	88/89	35	2	9	D1
	89/90	32	6	8	D1
	90/91	28	1	11	D1
Raith R	91/92	40	2	12	D1
	92/93	44		22	D1
Dundee U	93/94	30	3	16	P
	94/95	25	2	7	P
	95/96	23	7	17	D1
Ionikos					

BRITTON Gerard Joseph
b. Glasgow 20.10.1970
Celtic BC

Club	Season				
Celtic	90/91	0	2		P
	91/92				
Reading L	91/92	0	2		FL
Partick T	92/93	39	1	12	P
	93/94	20	2	3	P
Dundee	93/94	15	2	1	P
	94/95	23	3	12	D1
	95/96	15	10	2	D1
Dunfermline A	96/97	27	6	13	P
	97/98	12	4	3	P
	98/99	13	8	2	P
Raith R	98/99	5		1	D1
Livingston	99/00	13	5	5	D1

BRITTON Ian
b. Dundee 19.5.1954

Club	Season				
Chelsea	72/73	11	3		FL
	73/74	17		2	FL
	74/75	14	1	1	FL
	75/76	40		8	FL
	76/77	37		10	FL
	77/78	40		1	FL
	78/79	9	4		FL
	79/80	41		10	FL
	80/81	27	1	1	FL
	81/82	17	1		FL
Dundee U	82/83	7	3	1	P
Arbroath	83/84	2			D2
Blackpool	83/84	29	1	9	FL
	84/85	46		5	FL
	85/86	25	5	1	FL
Burnley	86/87	37	2	3	FL
	87/88	29	3	4	FL
	88/89	36	1	3	FL

BRODDLE Julian Raymond
b. Sheffield 1.1.1964
Plymouth A

Club	Season				
St Mirren	90/91	7	3		P
	91/92	35		2	P
	92/93	13	1		D1
Partick T	92/93	6			P
Raith R	93/94	16	2		P
	94/95	26	2	1	D1
	95/96	23	4		P
East Fife	95/96	5			D2
Ross Co	96/97	27	2		D3

BRODIE Colin
b. Glasgow 13.8.1964

Club	Season				
Clydebank	82/83	4			D1
	83/84				
	84/85	2			D1
	85/86	1			P
Partick T *	86/87	2			D1
Clydebank	86/87	6			P
	87/88	10			D1
	88/89	6			D1

BROGAN James Andrew
b. Glasgow 5.6.1944
Dumfries St Josephs
St Rochs

Club	Season				
Celtic	62/63				
	63/64	3			D1
	64/65	13		1	D1
	65/66	2			D1
	66/67	0	1		D1
	67/68	18	1	1	D1
	68/69	29		2	D1
	69/70	27	1	1	D1
	70/71	26			D1
	71/72	20	1	1	D1
	72/73	20			D1
	73/74	30			D1
	74/75	19	1		D1
Coventry C	75/76	28			FL
	76/77				
Ayr U	76/77	10			P
	77/78	3			P

BROGAN John
b. Hamilton 9.3.1954
Toll Star
Blantyre Celtic

Club	Season				
Albion R	72/73	14		3	D2
	73/74	32	2	5	D2
	74/75	31	3	7	D2
	75/76	20	1	7	D2
	76/77	21		10	D2
St Johnstone	76/77	15		6	D1
	77/78	24	1	14	D1
	78/79	36	2	14	D1
	79/80	39		22	D1
	80/81	13	2	8	D1
	81/82	32	1	16	D1
	82/83	39		26	D1
	83/84	26	2	9	P
Ayr U	84/85	5			D1
Hibernian	84/85	2	3	1	P
Hamilton A	84/85	19		6	D1
	85/86	39		23	D1
	86/87	30	7	6	P
Stirling A	87/88	39		24	D2
	88/89	30	5	15	D2
	89/90				
	90/91				
	91/92	0	1		D1
	92/93	0	1		D1

BROUGH John
b. Edinburgh 31.3.1960

Club	Season				
Heart of Midlothian	77/78	5			D1
	78/79	2			P
	79/80	31			D1
	80/81	34			P
	81/82	6			D1
	82/83				
Partick T	83/84	18			D1
	84/85	33			D1
	85/86	22			D1
	86/87	34			D1
	87/88	8			D1
	88/89	16			D1

BROWN Charles

Club	Season				
Morton	72/73	7	1	2	D1
	73/74	2	6	1	D1
	74/75	4	6	1	D1
	75/76	15	4	1	D1
	76/77	35	1	9	D1
	77/78	28	1	3	D1
Ayr U	78/79	1	1		D1
Morton	79/80	9	2	1	P
Clyde	80/81	2	1		D2

BROWN James
b. 11.8.1950

Club	Season				
Heart of Midlothian	68/69	1	1		D1
	69/70	20	1	3	D1
	70/71	33		4	D1
	71/72	34		4	D1
	72/73	31	1	2	D1
	73/74	25	3	2	D1
	74/75	18	2		D1
	75/76	33	1	3	P
	76/77	34		3	P
	77/78	15			D1
	78/79	22	4		P
Hibernian	79/80	11	2		P
	80/81	29	2	1	D1
Dunfermline A	81/82	13			D1

BROWN James
b. Irvine 3.4.1960
Beith

Club	Season				
Kilmarnock	78/79				
	79/80				
	80/81	9			P
Ayr U	81/82	10			D1
	82/83	1			D1
	83/84	27			D1
Irvine Meadow					

BROWN John
b. Stirling 26.1.1962
Blantyre Welfare

Club	Season				
Hamilton A	77/78				
	78/79				
	79/80	19			D1
	80/81	37	1	6	D1
	81/82	28		5	D1
	82/83	8			D1
	83/84	39			D1
Dundee	84/85	33	1	7	P
	85/86	28	1	11	P
	86/87	31		10	P
	87/88	19	1	3	P
Rangers	87/88	9		2	P
	88/89	29		1	P
	89/90	24	3	1	P
	90/91	25	2	1	P
	91/92	18	7	4	P
	92/93	39		4	P
	93/94	24			P
	94/95	10	3	1	P
	95/96	8	6		P

BROWN Mark
b. Motherwell 28.2.1981

Club	Season				
Rangers	99/00	1			P

BROWN Steven
b. 10.12.1958

Club	Season				
Hibernian	78/79	10	2		P
	79/80	3	2		P
	80/81	1			D1

BROWN Thomas Heron
b. Glasgow 1.4.1968
Glenafton A

Club	Season				
Clydebank	92/93	1			D1
Kilmarnock	93/94	26	5	5	P
	94/95	18	9	4	P
	95/96	19	6	6	P
	96/97	7	17	1	P
St Mirren	97/98	20	5	3	D1
	98/99	23	3	4	D1
	99/00	19	7	3	D1

BROWNE Paul
b. Glasgow 17.2.1975

Club	Season				
Aston Villa	93/94				
	94/95				
	95/96	2			FL
Raith R	96/97	4			P
	97/98	30	1		D1
	98/99	31	1		D1
	99/00	34		4	D1

BROWNLIE John Jack
b. Caldercruix 11.3.1952
Pumpherston Jnrs

Club	Season				
Hibernian	69/70	1			D1
	70/71	22	1		D1
	71/72	33		3	D1
	72/73	19			D1
	73/74	11			D1
	74/75	28		3	D1
	75/76	33		5	P
	76/77	36		3	P
	77/78	29			P
Newcastle U	78/79	34			FL
	79/80	38			FL
	80/81	14			FL
	81/82	38		2	FL
Middlesbrough	82/83	12			FL
	83/84				
Hartlepool U	84/85	19		1	FL
Vasalunds					
Berwick R	85/86	15			D2
Blyth Spartans					

BRUCE Andrew
b. Edinburgh 9.8.1964

Club	Season				
Rangers	82/83	1			P
Partick T	83/84	2			D1
Rangers	84/85	1			P
	85/86				
Heart of Midlothian	86/87	1			P
Morton	86/87	1			D1

BRUNO Pasquale
b. Lecce 19.6.1962
Fiorentina

Club	Season				
Heart of Midlothian	95/96	22		1	P
	96/97	11	2		P
	97/98				
Wigan A	97/98	1			FL
Cowdenbeath	98/99	1			D3

BRYCE Steven

b. Shotts 30.6.1969

Club	Season				
Motherwell BC					
Motherwell	88/89	3	6		P
	89/90	0	3		P
	90/91	1	3	1	P
	91/92	2	3		P
	92/93	1			P
Ayr U	92/93	14		5	D1
	93/94	12	5	2	D1

BRYCE Thomas

b. 14.1.1951

Club	Season				
Queen of the South	74/75	14	1	9	D2
	75/76	10	2	4	D1
	76/77	9	6	3	D1
	77/78	21	2	8	D1
	78/79	30	6	12	D1
	79/80	14	4	4	D2
Stenhousemuir *	80/81	2	4	1	D2
Morton	80/81	0	2		P

BRYCE Thomas

b. Johnstone 27.1.1960

Club	Season				
Ferguslie U					
Irvine Meadow					
Kilmarnock	79/80				
	80/81	3	3		P
	81/82	2	2		D1
Stranraer	82/83	28	3	2	D2
	83/84	22	9	3	D2
	84/85	39		9	D2
Queen of the South	85/86	38		15	D2
	86/87	44		20	D1
Clydebank	87/88	27	8	10	D1
	88/89	38		16	D1
	89/90	1			D1
Ayr U	89/90	34	1	10	D1
	90/91	34		11	D1
	91/92	39	2	9	D1
Clydebank	92/93	16	8	1	D1
Queen of the South	93/94	34	3	7	D2
	94/95	32	1	9	D2
	95/96	35	1	10	D2
	96/97	34	1	12	D2
	97/98	35		11	D2
Partick T	98/99	18	1	3	D2
Queen of the South	98/99	1	5		D2
Arbroath	99/00	32	2	6	D2

BRYSON James Ian Cook

b. Kilmarnock 26.11.1962

Club	Season				
Hurlford U					
Kilmarnock	81/82	7	7	3	D1
	82/83	18	9	1	P
	83/84	23	2	4	D1
	84/85	36		3	D1
	85/86	37	1	14	D1
	86/87	32		10	D1
	87/88	40	2	5	D1
Sheffield U	88/89	36	1	8	FL
	89/90	39		9	FL
	90/91	25	4	7	FL
	91/92	29	5	9	FL
	92/93	9	7		FL
Barnsley	93/94	16		3	FL
Preston NE	93/94	24	1	2	FL
	94/95	41		5	FL
	95/96	44		9	FL
	96/97	32	9	3	FL
Rochdale	97/98	12	3	1	FL
	98/99	31	8		FL

BUCHAN Martin James

b. Manchester 3.4.1977

Club	Season				
Aberdeen	95/96	1	3	1	P
	96/97	9	5		P
	97/98	9	1		P
	98/99	19	4	2	P
	99/00	5	3		P

BUDDEN John Edward

b. Croydon 17.7.1971

Club	Season				
Crystal Palace					
St Johnstone	93/94	1	1		P

BUGLIONE Martin

b. London 19.6.1968

Club	Season				
Margate					
St Johnstone	92/93	6	1	2	P
	93/94	3	6		P

BUIST Mark

b. Kirkcaldy 13.9.1975

Club	Season				
Glenrothes Strollers					
Raith R	95/96	2			P

BURCHILL Mark James

b. Broxburn 18.8.1980

Club	Season				
Celtic	98/99	5	16	9	P
	99/00	12	16	11	P

BURGESS Stuart Robert

b. Broxburn 22.10.1962

Club	Season				
Bathgate Thistle					
Albion R	80/81	11	1	1	D2
	81/82	35	2	5	D2
	82/83	36	1	4	D2
	83/84	28	2	2	D2
	84/85	9			D2
East Fife	84/85	22	3	3	D1
	85/86	34	2	9	D1
	86/87	38		12	D1
Falkirk	87/88	42		6	P
	88/89	37		10	D1
	89/90	28		2	D1
Kilmarnock	90/91	10	6		D1
	91/92	1			D1
East Fife	92/93	21			D2

BURKE Alexander

b. Glasgow 11.11.1977

Club	Season				
Kilmarnock	96/97	14	4	3	P
	97/98	16	3	3	P
	98/99	2	17		P
	99/00	3	6		P

BURLEY Craig William

b. Irvine 24.9.1971

Club	Season				
Chelsea	90/91	0	1		FL
	91/92	6	2		FL
	92/93	1	2		FL
	93/94	20	3	3	FL
	94/95	16	9	2	FL
	95/96	16	6		FL
	96/97	26	5	2	FL
Celtic	97/98	35		10	P
	98/99	20	1	9	P
	99/00	6	2	1	P
Derby Co	99/00	18		5	FL

BURLEY George Elder

b. Cumnock 3.6.1956

Club	Season				
Ipswich T	73/74	20			FL
	74/75	31			FL
	75/76	42			FL
	76/77	40		2	FL
	77/78	31		1	FL
	78/79	38		1	FL
	79/80	38			FL
	80/81	23			FL
	81/82	29			FL
	82/83	31		1	FL
	83/84	28		1	FL
	84/85	37			FL
	85/86	6			FL
Sunderland	85/86	27			FL
	86/87	27			FL
	87/88				
Gillingham	88/89	46		2	FL
Motherwell	89/90	34			P
	90/91	20			P
Ayr U	90/91	12			D1
	91/92	9			D1
	92/93	33			D1
	93/94	12	1		D1
Falkirk	93/94	1			D1
Motherwell	93/94	3	2		P
Colchester U	94/95	5	2		FL

BURNETT Albert

b. Glasgow 10.10.1955

Club	Season				
Airdrieonians	80/81	1			P
	81/82				
Dumbarton	82/83	28	2		D1
	83/84	8	4		D1
Falkirk	84/85	9		1	D1

BURNS Alexander

b. Bellshill 4.8.1973

Club	Season				
Shotts Bon Accord					
Motherwell	93/94	2	2	1	P
	94/95	7	7	3	P
	95/96	14	14	3	P
	96/97	16	14	1	P
Den Bosch	97/98				
Southend U	98/99				
Raith R	99/00	34		6	D1

BURNS Hugh

b. Lanark 13.12.1965

Club	Season				
Larkhall Academy					
Cambuslang R					
Rangers	83/84	0	5		P
	84/85	11	4		P
	85/86	26	2	3	P
	86/87	4			P
Hamilton A	86/87	5		1	P
Heart of Midlothian	87/88	23	1		P
Dunfermline A	88/89	13	2		D1
Fulham L	89/90	6			FL
Hamilton A	90/91	22	2	6	D1
	91/92	7	2		D1
Kilmarnock	91/92	28	3	4	D1
	92/93	9	1		D1
Ayr U	93/94	35		2	D1
	94/95	23		3	D1
Dumbarton	95/96	10	1	1	D1
Larkhall Thistle					

BURNS James

b. Motherwell 5.2.1965

Club	Season				
Motherwell BC					
Motherwell	82/83	2	1		P
	83/84	2	4	1	P

BURNS John Paul

b. Kirkcaldy 11.3.1978

Club	Season				
Heart of Midlothian	96/97	0	2		P
Cowdenbeath	97/98	10		3	D3
	98/99	23	4		D3
	99/00	23	3	6	D3

BURNS Thomas

b. Glasgow 16.12.1956

Club	Season				
St Mungos Academy					
St Marys BG					
Eastercraigs Amateurs					
Celtic BC					
Celtic					
Maryhill Jnrs L					
Celtic	73/74				
	74/75	0	1		D1
Harare CSC L					
Celtic	75/76	5			P
	76/77	13	9	1	P
	77/78	22	1	3	P
	78/79	28	1	3	P
	79/80	12	3		P
	80/81	32	1	4	P
	81/82	33		9	P
	82/83	17		7	P
Blackpool L	82/83				
Celtic	83/84	31	2	9	P
	84/85	25	2	7	P
	85/86	34		5	P
	86/87	14	3		P
	87/88	21	6	2	P
	88/89	30	2	2	P
	89/90	7	1		P
Kilmarnock	89/90	22		3	D2
	90/91	37		8	D1
	91/92	41		3	D1
	92/93	39		2	D1
	93/94	12			P

BURRELL Alexander

b. Edinburgh 25.5.1955

Club	Season				
Heart of Midlothian	74/75	2			D1
	75/76	6			P
	76/77	6	1		P
Falkirk	77/78	30			D2
	78/79	22			D2
	79/80	35	1	1	D2
	80/81	20			D1
	81/82	12			D1
Meadowbank T	81/82	10			D2
	82/83	15	3		D2

BURRIDGE John
b. Workington 3.12.1951

Workington		68/69	1			FL
		69/70				
		70/71	26			FL
Blackpool		70/71	3			FL
		71/72	34			FL
		72/73	22			FL
		73/74	30			FL
		74/75	38			FL
		75/76	7			FL
Aston Villa		75/76	30			FL
		76/77	35			FL
		77/78				
Southend U	L	77/78	6			FL
Crystal Palace		77/78	10			FL
		78/79	42			FL
		79/80	36			FL
QPR		80/81	19			FL
		81/82	20			FL
Wolverhampton W		82/83	42			FL
		83/84	32			FL
Derby Co	L	84/85	6			FL
Sheffield U		84/85	30			FL
		85/86	42			FL
		86/87	37			FL
Southampton		87/88	31			FL
		88/89	31			FL
Newcastle U		89/90	28			FL
		90/91	39			FL
Hibernian		91/92	35			P
		92/93	30			P
Newcastle U		93/94				
Scarborough		93/94	3			FL
Lincoln C		93/94	4			FL
Aberdeen		93/94	3			P
		94/95	3			P
Falkirk		94/95				
Dumbarton		94/95	3			D2
Manchester C		94/95	3	1		FL
Queen of the South		95/96	5			D2
Witton A		95/96				
Darlington		95/96	3			FL

BUSBY Andrew
b. Glasgow 8.12.1947

Partick T		67/68	1			D1
		68/69				
		69/70				
Airdrieonians		70/71	30		21	D1
		71/72	30	1	10	P
		72/73	32		12	P
Heart of Midlothian		73/74	27	1	12	D1
		74/75	30		11	P
		75/76	32		8	P
		76/77	25		3	P
		77/78	36		16	D1
		78/79	25		6	P
Toronto Blizzard		79	23		2	NA
		80	28		6	NA
Morton		80/81	26		5	P
		81/82	20	5		P
Queen of the South		82/83	24	4	7	D2
		83/84	9	8	4	D2

BUTCHER Terence Ian
b. Singapore 28.12.1958

Ipswich T		76/77				
		77/78	3			FL
		78/79	21		2	FL
		79/80	36		2	FL
		80/81	40		4	FL
		81/82	27		1	FL
		82/83	42			FL
		83/84	34		1	FL
		84/85	41		2	FL
		85/86	27		4	FL
Rangers		86/87	43		3	P
		87/88	11		1	P
		88/89	34		2	P
		89/90	34		3	P
		90/91	5			P
Coventry C		90/91	6			FL
		91/92				
Sunderland		92/93	37	1		FL
		93/94				
Clydebank		94/95	3			D1

BUTLER John H
b. Bellshill 25.1.1969

St Mirren		86/87	0	3		P
Stirling A	L	86/87	15		5	D2
St Mirren		87/88	1	7		P
Airdrieonians		88/89	6	10		D1
		89/90	17	2	2	D1
		90/91	9	1	3	D1
		91/92	1			P
Stranraer *		92/93	2			D2

BUTLER Lee Simon
b. Sheffield 30.5.1966

Harworth CI						
Lincoln C		86/87	30			FL
		87/88				
Aston Villa		88/89	4			FL
		89/90				
		90/91	4			FL
Hull C	L	90/91	4			FL
Barnsley		91/92	43			FL
		92/93	28			FL
		93/94	37			FL
		94/95	9			FL
		95/96	1	2		FL
Scunthorpe U	L	95/96	2			FL
Wigan A		96/97	46			FL
		97/98	17			FL
Dunfermline A		98/99	35			P
Halifax T		99/00	38			FL

BYRNE David
b. Dublin 14.11.1979

Shelbourne						
Dundee U		99/00	0	1		P

BYRNE David Stuart
b. Hammersmith 5.3.1961

Southall						
Hounslow						
Chiswick A						
Harrow B						
Hounslow						
Kingstonian						
Gillingham		85/86	18	5	3	FL
Millwall		86/87	35	5	4	FL
		87/88	17	6	2	FL
Cambridge U	L	88/89	4			FL
Blackburn R	L	88/89	4			FL
Plymouth A		88/89	13		1	FL
		89/90	28	4	1	FL
Bristol R	L	89/90	0	2		FL
Plymouth A		90/91	11	3		FL
Watford		90/91	16	1	2	FL
		91/92				
Reading	L	91/92	7		2	FL
Fulham	L	91/92	5			FL
Shamrock R		92/93				
St Johnstone		92/93	12			P
Partick T		93/94	21	2		P
Walsall	L	93/94	5			FL
Partick T		94/95	11	1		P
St Mirren		94/95	6			D1
Ayr U		95/96	8	2		D2
Albion R		95/96	17		1	D3
		96/97	29			D3

BYRNE Gordon
b. 20.12.1963

Hibernian		80/81	0	1		D1
		81/82				
		82/83	0	1		P

BYRNE Paul Peter
b. Dublin 13.6.1972

Bluebell U						
Oxford U		89/90	2	1		FL
Arsenal		90/91				
Bangor		91/92				
Celtic		92/93				
		93/94	18	4	2	P
		94/95	6		2	P
Brighton	L	94/95	8		1	FL
Southend U		95/96	38	3	5	FL
		96/97	23	9	1	FL
		97/98	9	1		FL
		98/99				
		99/00				

CADETE Jorge Paulo Santos
b. Mozambique 27.8.1968

Sporting Lisbon						
Celtic		95/96	2	4	5	P
		96/97	30	1	25	P
Celta Vigo		97/98				
		98/99				
		99/00				
Bradford C		99/00	2	5		FL

CADETTE Richard Raymond
b. Hammersmith 21.3.1965

Wembley						
Orient		84/85	19	2	4	FL
Southend U		85/86	44		25	FL
		86/87	46		24	FL
Sheffield U		87/88	26	2	7	FL
Brentford		88/89	31	1	12	FL
		89/90	7	9	1	FL
Bournemouth	L	89/90	4	4	1	FL
Brentford		90/91	19	9	6	FL
		91/92	10	1	1	FL
Falkirk		91/92	11	3	3	P
		92/93	24	7	8	P
		93/94	39		17	D1
		94/95	8		3	P
Millwall		94/95	12	4	4	FL
		95/96	0	1		FL
		96/97	7		1	FL
Clydebank		97/98	4		1	D2

CAESAR Gus Cassius
b. Tottenham 5.3.1966

Arsenal		85/86	2			FL
		86/87	6	9		FL
		87/88	17	5		FL
		88/89	2			FL
		89/90	0	3		FL
		90/91				
QPR	L	90/91	5			FL
Cambridge U		91/92				
Bristol C		91/92	9	2		FL
Airdrieonians		91/92	12			P
		92/93	29			P
		93/94	16		1	D1
Colchester U		94/95	39		1	FL
		95/96	23		2	FL
		96/97				
Partick T		97/98	0.98			D1

CAIRNEY Henry
b. Holytown 1.9.1961

Airdrieonians		80/81	14	2		P
		81/82	12			P
		82/83	19	1		D1
Stenhousemuir		83/84	31	1		D2
		84/85	39		2	D2
		85/86	29		3	D2
		86/87	35		3	D2
		87/88	39		1	D2
		88/89	36		1	D2
		89/90	39		2	D2
		90/91	39		2	D2
		91/92	18		1	D2
Brechin C		91/92	13			D2
		92/93	38			D2
		93/94	28			D1
		94/95	32			D2
		95/96	33		2	D3
		96/97	31			D2
		97/98	22			D2
		98/99	34			D3
		99/00	31			D3

CAIRNEY Joseph Thomas
b. 8.11.1956

Wishaw Jnrs						
Airdrieonians		76/77	18	6	8	D1
		77/78	29	2	22	D1
Kilmarnock		78/79	25	6	9	D1
		79/80	9	8	2	P
		80/81	5			P
Kilsyth R						

CAIRNS Mark Henry
b. Edinburgh 25.9.1969

Heart of Midlothian						
Berwick R	L	88/89	4			D2
East Stirlingshire	L	89/90	6			D2
Gala Fairydean		90/91				
		91/92				
		92/93				
		93/94				
Partick T		94/95	1			P
		95/96	3			P
		96/97	10			D1
Alloa A		97/98	29			D3
		98/99	36			D2
		99/00	20			D2

CALDWELL Alexander
b. Edinburgh 23.10.1954

Dundee		73/74	9	1		D1
		74/75	19	1		D1
		75/76	18	3	2	P
		76/77	31	3	1	D1
		77/78	18	3		D1
		78/79				
		79/80	2			P
St Johnstone		80/81	39		1	D1
		81/82	21		2	D1
		82/83	36		2	D1
		83/84	24			P
		84/85	17		3	D1
Forfar A		84/85	4	1		D1

CALDWELL Neil
b. Glasgow 25.9.1975

Rangers		94/95	1			P
Dundee U		95/96	2			D1

CALLACHAN Ralph
b. Edinburgh 29.4.1955

Heart of Midlothian		73/74	1			D1
		74/75	27	1	5	D1
		75/76	34	1	2	P
		76/77	13		2	P
Newcastle U		77/78	9			FL
Hibernian		78/79	33		9	P
		79/80	26	4	2	P
		80/81	38		4	D1
		81/82	29		4	P
		82/83	27	1	1	P
		83/84	29	4	4	P
		84/85	22	1	1	P
		85/86	3	2	1	P
Morton *		86/87	0	1		D1
Meadowbank T		86/87	26		2	D2
		87/88	26	5	1	D1
Berwick R		88/89	31		4	D2
		89/90	30	1	1	D2
		90/91	18	4		D2
		91/92	12	7		D2

CALLAGHAN Stuart
b. Calderbank 20.7.1976

Heart of Midlothian		92/93				
		93/94				
		94/95				
		95/96	0	1		P
		96/97	4			P
		97/98	1			P
		98/99	2			P
Clydebank		98/99	5			D1

CALLAGHAN Thomas
b. Cowdenbeath 6.12.1945
Lochore Welfare

Dunfermline A		62/63	5			D1
		63/64	24		6	D1
		64/65	30		1	D1
		65/66	22		4	D1
		66/67	9		2	D1
		67/68	33		8	D1
		68/69	2	3		D1
Celtic		68/69	12	3	3	D1
		69/70	12	2	2	D1
		70/71	19		2	D1
		71/72	28	2	1	D1
		72/73	27		2	D1
		73/74	16	6	2	D1
		74/75	19	3	2	D1
		75/76	22			P
San Antonio Thunder	L					
Celtic		76/77	0	1		P
Clydebank		76/77	22		2	D1
		77/78	5	3		P

CALLAGHAN William Thomas
b. Dunfermline 23.3.1967

Dunfermline A		84/85	3			D2
		85/86				
		86/87				
		87/88	8		2	P
		88/89	0	4		D1
Walsall	L	88/89	2		1	FL
Dunfermline A		89/90				
		90/91				
Montrose		91/92	11			D1
		92/93	4		1	D2
Cowdenbeath		92/93	29	1	9	D1
		93/94	33		11	D2
		94/95	18	2	5	D3
Meadowbank T		94/95	5	2	1	D2
Livingston		95/96	6	17		D3
		96/97	7	14	1	D2
		97/98	16	2	6	D2
Partick T		98/99	7	6		D2

CAMERON Colin
b. Kirkcaldy 23.10.1972

Raith R		91/92				
Sligo R		92/93				
Raith R		92/93	13	3	1	D1
		93/94	31	11	6	P
		94/95	32	2	7	D1
		95/96	30		9	P
Heart of Midlothian		95/96	4		2	P
		96/97	36		8	P
		97/98	30	1	8	P
		98/99	10	1	6	P
		99/00	31	1	8	P

CAMERON Daniel
b. Dundee 9.11.1953

Sheffield W		73/74	17		1	FL
		74/75	6			FL
Colchester U	L	74/75	5			FL
Sheffield W		75/76	8			FL
Preston NE		75/76	0	1		FL
		76/77	14	1		FL
		77/78	40			FL
		78/79	36			FL
		79/80	17			FL
		80/81	13			FL
Dundee		81/82	25		1	P

CAMERON Hugh D

Pollok Jnrs						
Kilmarnock		72/73	7	1	1	D1
		73/74	1	2		D1
		74/75	6		1	D1
Ayr U		75/76	4	9		P
Stranraer		76/77	33	3	1	D2
		77/78	16	1	2	D2
Craigmark Bruntonians						

CAMERON Ian
b. Glasgow 24.8.1966

St Mirren		83/84	5	3		P
		84/85	3	6	1	P
		85/86	3	9		P
		86/87	22	9	6	P
		87/88	36	5	8	P
		88/89	23	3	2	P
Aberdeen		89/90	6	5		P
		90/91	3	7	1	P
		91/92	4	2		P
Partick T		92/93	38	3	5	P
		93/94	37	4	1	P
		94/95	27	7	3	P
		95/96	32	3	1	P
Hibernian		96/97	9	8		P
Raith R		97/98	7	1		D1
Clyde		97/98	12		1	D2
Raith R		98/99	26	2	5	D1
Clydebank		99/00	28	4	5	D1

CAMPBELL Alan Christopher
b. Dublin 10.8.1960
Shamrock R
RC Santander
Berchem

Dundee		89/90	8	7	2	P
Forfar A		90/91	7	1	1	D1
		91/92	7	5	3	D1

CAMPBELL Calum
b. Erskine 7.11.1965
Kilbirnie Ladeside

Airdrieonians		87/88	40	2	15	D1
		88/89	32	4	14	D1
Partick T		89/90	34		18	D1
		90/91	15	11	4	D1
Kilmarnock		91/92	35	3	10	D1
		92/93	13	11	4	D1
		93/94	0	1		P
Dumbarton		93/94	12	2		D1
		94/95	4	10	1	D2

CAMPBELL Colin
b. Benbecula 1.12.1956

Hibernian		78/79	16	1	3	P
		79/80	16	5	2	P
Dundee U		80/81	2	2		P
Airdrieonians		81/82	20	5	1	P
		82/83	1	5		D1
Meadowbank T		83/84	2			D1
		84/85	5	3	1	D1
		85/86	6	7	1	D1

CAMPBELL Duncan Matthew
b. Paisley 11.9.1970
Jerviston BC

Dundee		88/89	6	2	1	P
		89/90	6	9	1	P
		90/91	10	6		D1
		91/92	11	3	2	P
		92/93	2	2		P
Hong Kong						
Malta						
Hamilton A		93/94	21	1	6	D1
		94/95	0	3		D1
Glentoran		94/95				
Queen of the South		94/95	19		9	D2
		95/96	11	6	3	D2

CAMPBELL George

Aberdeen		74/75	0	1		D1
		75/76	2			P
		76/77	4	1		P
		77/78	0	1		P

CAMPBELL John
b. 27.2.1946

Partick T		63/64	6			D1
		64/65	16			D1
		65/66	26			D1
		66/67	11	1		D1
		67/68	34			D1
		68/69	24			D1
		69/70	5			D1
		70/71				
		71/72	21			D1
		72/73	11			D1
		73/74	30			D1
		74/75	29			D1
		75/76	19	1		D1
		76/77	33	1		P
		77/78	24	7		P
		78/79	30	2		P
		79/80	33	2	1	P
		80/81	34		3	P
		81/82	2			P

CAMPBELL Robert
b. 19.5.1961

Dumbarton		78/79	10			D1
		79/80	9	1		D1
		80/81	9	5		D1
		81/82	15	1		D1
Cowdenbeath		82/83	11	1		D2
		83/84				
Dumbarton		94/85	0	1		D2

CAMPBELL Robert Fraser
b. Glasgow 12.4.1965
Glasgow U

St Mirren		82/83	1	1		P
		83/84				
		84/85	1			P
		85/86				
		86/87				
Stranraer		87/88	20	3		D2

CAMPBELL Stephen
b. Dundee 20.11.1967

Dundee		85/86	2	3		P
		86/87	2	2		P
		87/88	6	1	1	P
		88/89	18	6		P
		89/90	0	2		P
		90/91	3	3	1	D1
		91/92	29	1	3	D1
		92/93	20			P
		93/94				
		94/95				
Livingston		95/96	19		2	D3
		96/97	30		3	D2
Brechin C		97/98	29		3	D2
		98/99	27	1	2	D3
		99/00	13	4		D3

CANERO Peter
b. Glasgow 18.1.1981

Kilmarnock		99/00	6	5		P

CANDLISH Neil
b. Inverness 2.6.1968
Wishaw Thistle

Motherwell		85/86				
		86/87	1	1		P
		87/88	7	2	1	P
Kilmarnock	L	87/88	3			D1
Glentoran						
Ballymena U						
Portadown						

CANT James
b. 24.9.1953

Heart of Midlothian		72/73	1			D1
		73/74	26			D1
		74/75	8			D1
Montrose		75/76	21	2	2	D1
		76/77	16			D1
Heart of Midlothian		76/77	1	1		P
Raith R		76/77	1	1		D1

CAPALDI John
b. Newarthill
Aston Villa

Motherwell		78/79	3	5		P
		79/80	0	3		D1

CARBERRY Robert
b. 22.11.1957

Alloa A		77/78	21	2		D1
		78/79	26	2	3	D2
Motherwell		78/79	9			P
		79/80	19	2	1	D1
		80/81	5			D1

CARR Peter
b. Bishop Middleham 25.8.1951

Darlington		67/68	1			FL
		68/69	3	2		FL
		69/70	26			FL
		70/71	38	2		FL
		71/72	44		1	FL
		72/73	19			FL
Carlisle U		72/73	23			FL
		73/74	37			FL
		74/75	39		1	FL
		75/76	36	1		FL
		76/77	32			FL
		77/78	35	1		FL
Motherwell		78/79	6	1		P
New England Teamen		79	29			NA
Hartlepool U		79/80	22			FL

CARROLL Patrick
b. Bridge of Allan 23.10.1957

Hibernian		74/75	4			D1
		75/76	1			P
		76/77	5	2		P
		77/78	2	4		P
		78/79	1			P
Raith R		79/80	25	2	4	D1
		80/81	12	9	1	D1
		81/82	7	6		D1
Falkirk		82/83	12			D1

CARSON Joseph
b. Helensburgh 24.11.1953

Arbroath		73/74	9	1	1	D1
		74/75	28	1	1	D1
		75/76	22		3	D1
		76/77	31			D1
		77/78	30	5	3	D1
		78/79	32	2	2	D1
		79/80	18			D1
Motherwell		79/80	16		1	D1
		80/81	36		3	D1
		81/82	34		3	D1
		82/83	20		1	P
		83/84	20			P
Dumbarton		83/84	5			D1
Partick T		84/85	34		5	D1
		85/86	32			D1
		86/87	35		4	D1
Stranraer		87/88	20			D2
Dumbarton		87/88	2	1		D1

CARSON Thomas
b. Dumbarton 26.3.1959

Dumbarton		79/80	3			D1
		80/81	33			D1
		81/82	39			D1
		82/83	37			D1
		83/84	37			D1
Dundee		84/85	20			P
		85/86				
Hibernian		86/87	2			P
Dunfermline A		87/88	5			P
Dundee		87/88	6			P
Ipswich T	L	87/88	1			FL
Partick T *		87/88	6			D1
Queen of the South		87/88	7			D1
Dundee		88/89	2			P
		89/90	16			P
		90/91	33			D1
Dumbarton		91/92	6			D2
Raith R		92/93	27			D1
		93/94	8			P

CASCARINO Anthony Guy
b. Orpington 1.9.1962
Crockenhill

Gillingham		81/82	19	5	5	FL
		82/83	37	1	14	FL
		83/84	33	4	12	FL
		84/85	43		15	FL
		85/86	34		14	FL
		86/87	43		16	FL
Millwall		87/88	39		20	FL
		88/89	38		13	FL
		89/90	28		9	FL
Aston Villa		89/90	10		2	FL
		90/91	33	3	9	FL
Celtic		91/92	13	11	4	P
Chelsea		91/92	11		2	FL
		92/93	8	1	2	FL
		93/94	16	4	4	FL
Olympique Marseille						

CASEY James
b. Ruchazie 2.8.1957
St Gregorys
Celtic Amateurs

Maryhill Jnrs	L					
Celtic		75/76	1			P
		76/77				
		77/78	2	2		P
		78/79	1	4		P
		79/80	2	2		P
Phoenix Inferno						
Arbroath		80/81	11			D2
		81/82	11		1	D2
		82/83	9	1		D2

CAUGHEY Mark
b. Belfast 27.8.1960
Linfield

Hibernian		86/87	5	9		P
Burnley	L	86/87	8			FL
Hamilton A		86/87	4	1	3	P
		87/88	16		10	D1
Motherwell		87/88	9	6		P
Bangor						

CHALMERS Paul
b. Glasgow 31.10.1963
Eastercraigs Amateurs

Celtic		84/85	0	1	1	P
		85/86	0	3		P
Bradford C	L	85/86	2			FL
Nottingham F	T	86/87				
St Mirren		86/87	16	7	2	P
		87/88	26	10	10	P
		88/89	32		11	P
		89/90	2	7		P
Swansea C		89/90	13	3	4	FL
		90/91	12	9	2	FL
		91/92	14	7	7	FL
Dunfermline A		92/93	23	9	9	D1
Hamilton A		93/94	14	6	5	D1
		94/95	18	5	2	D1
		95/96	1			D1
Ayr U		95/96	5		1	D2
East Fife		95/96	6	2	4	D2

CHARBONNIER Lionel
b. Poitiers 25.10.1966

Auxerre		88/89				
		89/90				
		90/91				
		91/92				
		92/93				
		93/94				
		94/95				
		95/96				
		96/97				
		97/98				
Rangers		98/99	11			P
		99/00	7			P

CHARNLEY James Callaghan
b. Glasgow 11.6.1963
Rutherglen Glencairn

St Mirren		82/83	1			P
Ayr U		83/84	10	7	3	D1
		84/85				
		85/86				
		86/87				
Clydebank		87/88	27	1	10	D1
		88/89	3		1	D1
Hamilton A		88/89	8	6		P
Partick T		88/89	14		4	D1
		89/90	29		11	D1
		90/91	29	1	7	D1
St Mirren		91/92	23	3	4	P
Bolton W	L	91/92	3			FL
St Mirren		92/93	14		1	D1
Partick T		93/94	25	1	1	P
		94/95	19	1	1	P
Dumbarton		95/96	16	2	1	D1
Dundee		95/96	12		3	D1
		96/97	15		3	D1
Hibernian		96/97	9		1	P
		97/98	17	3	3	P
Clydebank		97/98	1			D2
Partick T		97/98	5			D1

CHERRY Paul Robert
b. Derby 14.10.1964

Heart of Midlothian		84/85	0	3		P
		85/86	3	2		P
Cowdenbeath		86/87	35		5	D2
		87/88	33	2	8	D2
St Johnstone		88/89	36	3	2	D1
		89/90	38	1	4	D1
		90/91	18	2		P
		91/92	24		1	P
		92/93	12	4	1	P
		93/94	31	2		P
		94/95	27		5	D1
		95/96	13	2		D1
Inverness CT		96/97	31		1	D3
		97/98	30	1	8	D2
		98/99	24	3	3	D2

CHISHOLM Gordon William
b. Glasgow 8.4.1960

Sunderland		78/79	27		1	FL
		79/80	12	1		FL
		80/81	33	1	3	FL
		81/82	20	2		FL
		82/83	32		1	FL
		83/84	36		4	FL
		84/85	31	1	1	FL
		85/86	1			FL
Hibernian		85/86	29		2	P
		86/87	21	2	2	P
		87/88	7			P
Dundee		87/88	15			P
		88/89	33	1	4	P
		89/90	34		3	P
		90/91	34		3	D1
		91/92	37	2	5	D1
Partick T		92/93	8	1		P

CHRISTENSEN Lars
b. 8.7.1964

Morton		87/88	8			P

CHRISTIE Gerard
b. Port Glasgow 13.12.1957
Irvine Meadow

Ayr U		76/77	4	2		P
		77/78	9	6	1	P
		78/79	33	4	6	D1
		79/80	25	10	9	D1
		80/81	34	4	7	D1
		81/82	27	5	5	D1
		82/83	16	4	1	D1
		83/84	19	12	1	D1
Airdrieonians		84/85	36	1	5	D1
		85/86	15	4	1	D1
		86/87	10	7	4	D1
Clydebank *		86/87	3			D1
Airdrieonians		87/88	18	10	4	D1

CHRISTIE Kevin
b. Aberdeen 1.4.1976
Lewis U

Aberdeen		94/95				
		95/96	0	2		P
		96/97				
East Fife		96/97	9		1	D1
Motherwell		96/97	3	1		P
		97/98	20	1		P
		98/99	4	1		P
Falkirk		99/00	14		2	D1

CHRISTIE Martin Peter
b. Edinburgh 7.11.1971

Meadowbank T	89/90	13			D1
	90/91				
	91/92	34		1	D1
Dundee	91/92	1			D1
	92/93	1	2		P
	93/94	1			P
Stenhousemuir	93/94	13	5		D2
	94/95	28		3	D2
	95/96	18	1		D2
	96/97	7	1		D2
	97/98	19	1	1	D2
	98/99	3		1	D3
Alloa A	99/00	20	4	1	D2

CLARK Alexander
b. Lanark 28.10.1956

Airdrieonians	74/75	1	2		D1
	75/76	18	2	7	D1
	76/77	27	5	8	D1
	77/78	37	1	7	D1
	78/79	38		23	D1
	79/80	37		22	D1
	80/81	36		10	P
	81/82	30		15	P
West Ham U	82/83	26		7	FL
Rangers	82/83	10		4	P
	83/84	27	3	9	P
	84/85	1			P
Heart of Midlothian	84/85	25		8	P
	85/86	33		12	P
	86/87	41		8	P
	87/88	11	24	6	P
	88/89	1	1	1	P
Dunfermline A	89/90	3	1		P
Partick T	89/90	1	2		D1

CLARK Christopher
b. Aberdeen 15.9.1980

Aberdeen	99/00	0	2		P

CLARK Gary
b. Glasgow 13.9.1964
Pollok Jnrs

Stenhousemuir *	84/85	1			D2
Falkirk	85/86	0	2	1	D1
	86/87	0	1		P
East Stirlingshire *	86/87	1			D2
	87/88				
Albion R	89/90	25		8	D1
Clyde	90/91	36	1	5	D1
Hamilton A	91/92	24	8	14	D1
	92/93	34	3	8	D1
	93/94	29	3	9	D1
	94/95	12	5	4	D1
	95/96	14	3	3	D1
	96/97	15	17	2	D2
	97/98	23	3	6	D1
	98/99	9	5	2	D1
Alloa A	99/00	18	14	4	D2

CLARK George
b. Renton 15.7.1958

Partick T	78/79	0	3		P
	79/80				
	80/81	20	5		P
	81/82	15	9	4	P
	82/83	3			D1
	83/84				
Stenhousemuir *	84/85	1			D2
Falkirk	85/86	5	2	3	D1
East Stirlingshire	86/87	1			D2

CLARK James Morrison
b. Kilmarnock 14.8.1952
Kilmarnock U
Glenafton A

Stirling A	72/73	11	1	1	D2
	73/74	28	4	5	D2
	74/75	31	1	2	D2
	75/76	26		2	D2
	76/77	39		5	D2
	77/78	34	1	7	D1
Kilmarnock	78/79	32		3	D1
	79/80	34		1	P
	80/81	24	3		P
	81/82	27	1	2	D1
	82/83	36		4	P
	83/84	16	1	1	P
	84/85				
Motherwell	85/86	5			P
Meadowbank T	85/86	8	1	1	D2
Kilmarnock	86/87	20	1		D1
Australia					

CLARK John
b. Edinburgh 22.9.1964
Musselburgh Windsor BC

Dundee U	82/83	1			P
	83/84	4	5	1	P
	84/85	7	3	3	P
	85/86	5	6	1	P
	86/87	28	3	3	P
	87/88	19	9	3	P
	88/89	17	3	2	P
	89/90	18	11	1	P
	90/91	17	1	2	P
	91/92	31	4	1	P
	92/93	35	2	2	P
	93/94	13	1		P
Stoke C	94/95	5			FL
Falkirk	94/95	31		8	P
	95/96	14	3	2	P
Dunfermline A	95/96	11		1	D1
	96/97	8		1	P
Ross Co	96/97	1			D3
FC Mulhouse	96/97				
Berwick R	96/97	24		2	D2
	97/98	2			D2

CLARK Martin John
b. Motherwell 13.10.1968
Hamilton A

Clyde	87/88	25	1		D1
	88/89	25		2	D1
Nottingham F	88/89				
	89/90				
Mansfield T	89/90	14		1	FL
	90/91	24			FL
	91/92	7	2		FL
Partick T	92/93	8			P
	93/94	10	1		P
Clyde	93/94	12			D1
	94/95	18			D2
Albion R	95/96	11			D3
	96/97	14	3	2	D3

CLARK Robert Brown
b. Glasgow 26.9.1945
Glasgow YMCA

Queens Park	62/63	18			D2
	63/64	30			D2
	64/65	35			D2
Aberdeen	65/66	33			D1
	66/67	34			D1
	67/68	33			D1
	68/69	14			D1
	69/70	13	1		D1
	70/71	34			D1
	71/72	22			D1
	72/73	33			D1
	73/74	34			D1
	74/75	33			D1
	75/76	20			P
San Antonio Thunder	76	19			NA
Aberdeen	76/77	27			P
	77/78	36			P
	78/79	23			P
	79/80	35			P
	80/81				
	81/82				
Clyde	82/83	4			D1

CLARK Robert Rodger
b. Hamilton 4.11.1962
Blantyre V

Rangers	80/81	0	1		P
	81/82				
Kilmarnock	82/83	23	2	3	P
	83/84	36	1	11	D1
	84/85	6			D1
Motherwell	84/85	8	2	1	D1
	85/86	1	1		P
Kilmarnock	86/87	34		2	D1
	87/88	10			D1
Albion R	87/88	7			D2
	88/89	37			D2
	89/90	31	1		D1
	90/91	37		8	D2
	91/92	36		5	D2
Stirling A	92/93	7			D1

CLARKE Paul
b. Ardrossan 11.10.1956
Kilmarnock Star
Ardrossan Winton R

Kilmarnock	74/75				
	75/76	18	2	1	D1
	76/77	33		1	P
	77/78	34	1	7	D1
	78/79	37		1	D1
	79/80	35		3	P
	80/81	23			P
	81/82	35		4	D1
	82/83	34			P
	83/84	30		1	D1
	84/85	36	3	3	D1
	85/86	38		6	D1

CLARKE Stephen
b. Saltcoats 29.8.1963
Beith

St Mirren	82/83	31			P
	83/84	33		2	P
	84/85	33			P
	85/86	31		3	P
	86/87	20	5	2	P
Chelsea	86/87	15	1		FL
	87/88	38		1	FL
	88/89	36			FL
	89/90	24		3	FL
	90/91	17	1	1	FL
	91/92	31		1	FL
	92/93	18	2		FL
	93/94	39			FL
	94/95	29			FL
	95/96	21	1		FL
	96/97	31			FL
	97/98	22	4	1	FL

CLARKE Stephen
b. Coatbridge 13.1.1963
Bellshill YM
Bellshill A

Hamilton A	84/85	34		2	D1
	85/86	23	3	5	D1
	86/87	20	5	2	P
	87/88	14	3	2	D1
Forfar A	87/88	19		3	D1
	88/89	16	2	2	D1
Clyde	89/90	28		7	D1
	90/91	24		1	D1
	91/92	28		7	D2
	92/93	26	3	10	D2
	93/94	16		2	D1
Blantyre V					
Bellshill YM					

CLELAND Alexander
b. Glasgow 10.12.1970

Dundee U	87/88	1			P
	88/89	7	2		P
	89/90	12	3		P
	90/91	16	4	2	P
	91/92	24	7	4	P
	92/93	21	3		P
	93/94	32	1	1	P
	94/95	18		1	P
Rangers	94/95	10			P
	95/96	21	4	1	P
	96/97	32			P
	97/98	27	2	3	P
Everton	98/99	16	2		FL
	99/00	3	6		FL

CLELAND Bruce
b. Paisley 26.9.1958
Glasgow U
Maryhill

Albion R	77/78	10	2	1	D2
	78/79	31		24	D2
Motherwell	79/80	15	1	1	D1
	80/81	8	7	8	D1
	81/82	25	6	15	D1
	82/83	2	3	1	P
Ayr U	82/83	3		1	D1
Berwick R	82/83	4	4		D2
	83/84				
Queen of the South	84/85	1			D2
Albion R	84/85	24	4	1	D2
	85/86	31	2	3	D2
Stranraer	86/87	31	1	13	D2
	87/88	19	4	8	D2

CLINGING Ian

b. Motherwell 12.6.1958						
Carluke R						
Motherwell		77/78	9	2	3	P
		78/79	29	5	5	P
		79/80	31	1	9	D1
		80/81	17		2	D1
		81/82	17	5	2	D1
		82/83	2	6		P
Kilmarnock		82/83	3			P
South China						
Morton		83/84	19	6	7	D1
		84/85	25	2	1	P
		85/86	11	14	4	D1
		86/87	43		7	D1
		87/88	24		2	P
		88/89	34	3	7	D1
Forfar A		89/90	20	4	6	D1
		90/91	4	9	1	D1
Berwick R		91/92	2			D2

CLINTON Andrew

b. Irvine 4.2.1967						
Morton		83/84	1			D1
		84/85	0	1		P

CLOUGHERTY Mark

b. Glasgow 20.9.1951						
East Fife		74/75	34		2	D2
		75/76	6	4		D1
Falkirk		76/77	34	1	2	D1
		77/78	15	2	1	D2
Clyde		77/78	21			D2
		78/79	37			D1
		79/80	29		1	D1
Dumbarton		80/81	32		1	D1
		81/82	21	1		D1
		82/83	36			D1
		83/84	38			D1
		84/85	28			P
		85/86	37			D1
		86/87	26			D1
		87/88	4			D1

CLUNIE David

Heart of Midlothian		66/67	0	3		D1
		67/68				
		68/69	15			D1
		69/70	34		3	D1
		70/71	29		1	D1
		71/72	5			D1
		72/73	25		1	D1
		73/74	31			D1
		74/75	27			D1
		75/76	26			P
		76/77	29	1		P
Berwick R *		77/78	1			D2
St Johnstone		77/78	34			D1

COBIAN Juan

b. Buenos Aires 11.9.1975						
Boca Juniors						
Sheffield W		98/99	9			FL
Charlton A		99/00				
Aberdeen		99/00	2	1		P

COCARD Christophe

b. Bernay 23.11.1967						
Olympique Lyon						
Kilmarnock		99/00	24	1	8	P

COCHRANE John

b. Bellshill 27.4.1959						
Preston NE		76/77	1		1	FL
		77/78				
		78/79	2	2	1	FL
Dundee U		79/80	0	1		P
Morton		80/81	20	3	2	P
		81/82	14	6	2	P
		82/83	27	5	1	P
Hamilton A		83/84	11	8		D1
Queen of the South		83/84	5	1	2	D2
Partick T		84/85	10		2	D1
Cowdenbeath		84/85	27			D2
		85/86	19	1	3	D2

COCKBURN James Hammond

b. Kilwinning 11.9.1958						
Kilwinning Abbey R						
Ardrossan Winton R						
Kilmarnock		77/78				
		78/79				
		79/80	1			P
		80/81	24	2		P
		81/82	20	1		D1
		82/83	20	1		P
		83/84	29	3		D1
		84/85	24	6		D1
		85/86	23	5	1	D1
		86/87	21			D1
		87/88	3			D1
Auchinleck Talbot						
Kilwinning R						

CODY Stephen

b. Calderbank 1.6.1969						
Kilmarnock		89/90	12	8		D2
Falkirk		90/91	12	5	1	P
		91/92	2	3	1	P
Stranraer		92/93	20	9	1	D2
		93/94	29		3	D2
		94/95	16			D1
Queen of the South		94/95	5	1		D2
		95/96	13	3	1	D2
Albion R		96/97	8	1	1	D3
		97/98	7			D3

COHEN Abraham

b. Cairo 14.11.1956						
Maccabi Tel Aviv						
Liverpool		79/80	3	1	1	FL
		80/81	13	1		FL
Maccabi Tel Aviv		81/82				
		82/83				
		83/84				
		84/85				
		85/86				
		86/87				
Rangers		87/88	4	3		P

COLE Anthony Richard

b. Gateshead 18.9.1972						
Middlesbrough						
St Johnstone		92/93	7			P
		93/94	1			P
Berwick R		94/95	22			D2
		95/96	8		1	D2

COLGAN Gerry

b. Glasgow 20.6.1951						
Queens Park		72/73	20	1		D2
		73/74	18	1	4	D2
		74/75	26	4	1	D2
		75/76	19	4	4	D2
		76/77	33		11	D2
Clydebank		77/78	22	1	2	P
		78/79	37		2	D1
		79/80	27	2	1	D1
		80/81	8	2		D1
Hamilton A		80/81	8	1		D1
		81/82	10	5		D1
		82/83	3			D1
Stranraer		83/84				

COLGAN Nicholas Vincent

b. Drogheda 19.9.1973						
Drogheda U						
Chelsea		92/93				
		93/94				
Crewe A	L	93/94				
Chelsea		94/95				
		95/96				
		96/97	1			FL
		97/98				
Brentford	L	97/98	5			FL
Reading	L	97/98	5			FL
Chelsea		98/99				
Hibernian		99/00	24			P

COLLINS Derek J

b. Glasgow 15.4.1969						
Renfrew Waverley						
Morton		87/88	28		1	P
		88/89	36		1	D1
		89/90	36	2		D1
		90/91	36	1	2	D1
		91/92	44		1	D1
		92/93	41			D1
		93/94	35	2	1	D1
		94/95	33		1	D2
		95/96	36	1	1	D1
		96/97	35			D1
		97/98	34		3	D1
		98/99	18			D1
Hibernian		98/99	16			D1
		99/00	23	1		P

COLLINS Gerard

b. Glasgow 12.3.1955						
Maryhill						
St Rochs						
Stranraer	L	79/80	2			D2
St Rochs		80/81				
Albion R		81/82	32		1	D2
		82/83	34	1		D2
		83/84	1			D2
Ayr U		83/84	32		5	D1
		84/85	34		8	D1
		85/86	8		1	D1
Hamilton A		85/86	10	3	1	D1
		86/87	36	1	2	P
		87/88	32	1	2	D1
		88/89	10	1		P
Partick T		88/89	22		1	D1
		89/90	8			D1

COLLINS John Angus Paul

b. Galashiels 31.1.1968						
Gala Academy						
St Margarets BC						
Celtic BC						
Hutchison Vale BC						
Hibernian		85/86	16	3	1	P
		86/87	26	4	1	P
		87/88	43	1	6	P
		88/89	35		2	P
		89/90	35		6	P
Celtic		90/91	35		1	P
		91/92	36	2	11	P
		92/93	43		8	P
		93/94	38		8	P
		94/95	33	1	8	P
		95/96	26	3	11	P
Monaco		96/97				
		97/98				
Everton		98/99	19	1	1	FL
		99/00	33	2	2	FL

COLQUHOUN John Mark

b. Stirling 14.7.1963						
Grangemouth Int. BC						
Stirling A		80/81	8	5		D1
		81/82	36	1	13	D2
		82/83	39		21	D2
		83/84	15		11	D2
Celtic		83/84	11	1	2	P
		84/85	14	5	2	P
Heart of Midlothian		85/86	36		8	P
		86/87	42	1	13	P
		87/88	43	1	15	P
		88/89	34	2	5	P
		89/90	36		6	P
		90/91	36		7	P
Millwall		91/92	27		3	FL
Sunderland		92/93	12	8		FL
Heart of Midlothian		93/94	38	3	6	P
		94/95	23	8	2	P
		95/96	20	11	4	P
		96/97	4	7		P
St Johnstone		96/97	6		1	D1

COMBE Alan

b. Edinburgh 3.4.1974						
Kelty Hearts						
Cowdenbeath		92/93	18			D1
St Mirren		93/94	16			D1
		94/95	20	1		D1
		95/96	21			D1
		96/97	36			D1
		97/98	30			D1
Dundee U		98/99	10			P
		99/00	35			P

CONN Alfred James
b. Edinburgh 5.4.1952

Tynecastle A						
Leeds U						
Rangers		67/68				
Musselburgh Windsor	L					
Rangers		68/69	1	1		D1
		69/70	8	4		D1
		70/71	23	2	4	D1
		71/72	21	2	3	D1
		72/73	18	2	12	D1
		73/74	7	4	4	D1
Tottenham H		74/75				
		75/76	7	1		FL
		76/77	12	1		FL
Celtic		76/77	13	1	2	P
		77/78	9	1		P
		78/79	12	1	6	P
Derby Co		78/79				
Hercules Alicante	T	79/80				
Pittsburgh Spirit						
San Jose Earthquakes		80	2			NA
Hartford Hellions						
Heart of Midlothian		80/81	13	4	3	P
Blackpool		80/81	3			FL
Motherwell		81/82	17	5	2	D1
		82/83	4	1	1	P

CONN Samuel Craig
b. Lanark 26.10.1961

Falkirk	80/81	15	2	1	D1
	81/82	5	4	2	D1
Albion R	82/83	32	3	8	D2
	83/84	29	1	5	D2
	84/85	28	3	2	D2
	85/86	31	2	6	D2
	86/87	17		4	D2
Clydebank	86/87	19		1	P
Falkirk	87/88	34	2	2	P
Airdrieonians	88/89	31		8	D1
	89/90	29	2	2	D1
	90/91	18	3	1	D1
	91/92	26	1	5	P
	92/93	4	10		P
	93/94	0	2		D1
Albion R	93/94	31		1	D2
	94/95	7		2	D3
Cowdenbeath	94/95	19		2	D3
	95/96	16	2	3	D3
	96/97	28		2	D3

CONNAGHAN Denis
b. Glasgow 9.1.1945

Celtic						
Yoker A						
Queen of the South	T					
Renfrew Jnrs						
St Mirren		66/67	23			D1
Baltimore Bays		67	7			NA
St Mirren		67/68				
		68'69	21			P
		69/70	15			P
		70/71	33			P
Celtic		71/72	14			
		72/73	4			P
		73/74	8			P
		74/75	6			P
		75/76				
		76/77				
Clydebank		76/77				
Ayr U		77/78				
Morton		77/78	25			P
		78/79	16			P
Clyde		79/80	17			D1
Arthurlie						

CONNELLY George
b. Fife 1.3.1949

Tulliallan Thistle						
Celtic		64/65				
		65/66				
		66/67				
		67/68				
		68/69	6	1	1	D1
		69/70	7			D1
		70/71	22	2	3	D1
		71/72	32			D1
		72/73	32			D1
		73/74	14		1	D1
		74/75	15			D1
		75/76	1	2		P
Falkirk	L	76/77	8		2	D1
Tulliallan Thistle						
Sauchie						

CONNOLLY John
b. Barrhead 13.6.1950

Glasgow U					
St Johnstone	67/68	1		1	D1
	68/69	13		6	D1
	69/70	21		6	D1
	70/71	34		17	D1
	71/72	27		11	D1
Everton	71/72	2			FL
	72/73	41		7	FL
	73/74	26		5	FL
	74/75	22	2	3	FL
	75/76	14	1	1	FL
Birmingham C	76/77	37		5	FL
	77/78	12	8	4	FL
Newcastle U	78/79	34		8	FL
	79/80	8	7	2	FL
Hibernian	80/81	29	3	8	D1
	81/82	1	1		P
Gateshead	81/82				
	82/83				
Blyth Spartans	82/83				
Gateshead	83/84				

CONNOLLY Patrick Martin
b. Dunfermline 25.6.1970

Dundee U	88/89	2			P
	89/90	12	3	5	P
	90/91	7	3	2	P
	91/92	1	4		P
	92/93	32	10	16	P
	93/94	21	7	5	P
	94/95	4	2		P
	95/96	3	3	1	D1
Airdrieonians	95/96	6		3	D1
	96/97	24	11	8	D1
	97/98	22	1	8	D1
St Johnstone	97/98	2	2		P
	98/99	6	3	1	P
	99/00	9	2	1	P
Morton	99/00	5		5	D1

CONNOR Robert
b. Kilmarnock 4.8.1960

Ayr U BC					
Ayr U	77/78	9			P
	78/79	27	2		D1
	79/80	36	2	9	D1
	80/81	38	1	8	D1
	81/82	29	1		D1
	82/83	39		4	D1
	83/84	39		7	D1
Dundee	84/85	34		7	P
	85/86	35		2	P
	86/87	2			P
Aberdeen	86/87	30	2	4	P
	87/88	32	2	1	P
	88/89	36		4	P
	89/90	33		1	P
	90/91	29		6	P
	91/92	11			P
	92/93	5	1		P
	93/94	21	4	1	P
Kilmarnock	94/95	27	1		P
	95/96	22	1		P
Ayr U	96/97	18		1	D2
Partick T	97/98	2			D1
Queen of the South	97/98	24		1	D2

CONROY Michael George
b. Johnstone 31.7.1957

Port Glasgow Jnrs					
Celtic	77/78	5		1	P
	78/79	20	1	4	P
	79/80	13	5	2	P
	80/81	14	1		P
	81/82	6	2	1	P
Hibernian	82/83	22		1	P
	83/84	9	1	1	P
Blackpool	84/85	41		2	FL
	85/86	25			FL
Wrexham	86/87	23	2	2	FL
Leyton Orient	87/88	2	1		FL
Cork C					

CONROY Michael Kevin
b. Glasgow 31.12.1965

Coventry C						
Clydebank		83/84	2			D1
		84/85	16	10	11	D1
		85/86	23	5	7	P
		86/87	31	5	9	P
		87/88	20	2	11	D1
St Mirren		87/88	9	1	1	P
Reading		88/89	9	4	4	FL
		89/90	27	7	2	FL
		90/91	29	4	1	FL
Burnley		91/92	38		24	FL
		92/93	38	1	6	FL
Preston NE		93/94	28	4	12	FL
		94/95	22	3	10	FL
Fulham		95/96	38	2	9	FL
		96/97	40	3	21	FL
		97/98	10	1	2	FL
Blackpool		97/98	5	1		FL
		98/99	7	1		FL
Chester C	L	98/99	11	4	3	FL
Blackpool		99/00				

CONSIDINE Douglas
b. Edinburgh 15.5.1957

Aberdeen	78/79	3	3		P
	79/80	14			P
	80/81	8	4		P
Dunfermline A	81/82	30	4	3	D1
	82/83	18		1	D1

CONVERY John
b. Newtonards 1.4.1980

Glenavon					
Celtic	99/00	0	1		P

CONWAY Christopher Thomas
b. Glasgow 17.7.1983

St Johnstone	99/00	0	1		P

COOPER David
b. Hamilton 25.2.1956

Hamilton Avondale					
Clydebank	74/75	25	1	4	D2
	75/76	26		13	D2
	76/77	28		11	D1
Rangers	77/78	34	1	6	P
	78/79	26	4	6	P
	79/80	25	5	2	P
	80/81	17	8	3	P
	81/82	29	1	3	P
	82/83	26	5	5	P
	83/84	32	2	6	P
	84/85	32		5	P
	85/86	28	4	4	P
	86/87	42		8	P
	87/88	21	12	1	P
	88/89	9	14	1	P
Motherwell	89/90	31		6	P
	90/91	34		6	P
	91/92	38	1	3	P
	92/93	42	1	2	P
	93/94	2	8		P
Clydebank	93/94	14	4		D1
	94/95	19	2	1	D1

COOPER Neale James
b. Darjeeling 24.11.1963

Aberdeen	80/81	4	1		P
	81/82	22	5	3	P
	82/83	29	2	2	P
	83/84	25	1		P
	84/85	17	3	1	P
	85/86	20	3		P
Aston Villa	86/87	13			FL
	87/88	6	1		FL
Rangers	88/89	11	3	1	P
	89/90	2	1		P
	90/91				
Reading	91/92	6	1		FL
Dunfermline A	91/92	21			P
	92/93	33		2	D1
	93/94	30		2	D1
	94/95	14	1		D1
	95/96	2	2		D1
Ross Co	96/97	4			D3
	97/98	0	1		D3

COOPER Neil
b. Aberdeen 12.8.1959

Aberdeen		74/75	0	1		D1
		75/76	1	1		P
		76/77				
		77/78	1			P
		78/79	3	4	1	P
		79/80	1			P
Barnsley		79/80	20		3	FL
		80/81	27	3	2	FL
		81/82	10		1	FL
Grimsby T		81/82	16		1	FL
		82/83	24		1	FL
		83/84	7			FL
St Mirren		83/84	23	2		P
		84/85	10			P
		85/86	28	2		P
		86/87	38		1	P
		87/88	27		1	P
		88/89	30			P
Hibernian		89/90	27			P
		90/91	11			P

COPLAND John
b. Paisley 21.3.1947

Stranraer						
Dundee U		70/71	10	2	2	D1
		71/72	24	2	9	D1
		72/73	33		1	D1
		73/74	27		1	D1
		74/75	33		3	D1
		75/76	13		2	P
St Mirren		76/77	12		1	D1
		77/78	31		1	P
		78/79	36		1	P
		79/80	35			P
		80/81	33		2	P
		81/82	36			P
		82/83	18			P

CORMACK Michael
b. Inverurie 13.3.1965

Deveronvale						
Montrose						
Motherwell		82/83	0	4		P
		83/84	5	5		P
		84/85	1	2	1	D1
Kilmarnock		84/85	13	5	1	D1
		85/86				
Falkirk		86/87	2	2		P
Cove R						

CORMACK Peter Barr
b. Granton 17.7.1946

Tynecastle BC						
Heart of Midlothian						
Hibernian		62/63	1		1	D1
		63/64	6		1	D1
		64/65	32		9	D1
		65/66	32		15	D1
		66/67	30		13	D1
		67/68	29	1	11	D1
		68/69	29		15	D1
		69/70	23		11	D1
Nottingham F		69/70	1			FL
		70/71	41		9	FL
		71/72	32		7	FL
Liverpool		72/73	30		8	FL
		73/74	40	2	9	FL
		74/75	33	3	3	FL
		75/76	16	1	1	FL
		76/77				
Bristol C		76/77	19	1	6	FL
		77/78	25	1	6	FL
		78/79	14	3	3	FL
		79/80	1	3		FL
Hibernian		79/80	10	4		P
		80/81	3	3	1	D1
		81/82				
		82/83				
Partick T		83/84	0	1		D1

CORR Barry John
b. Glasgow 13.1.1981

Celtic		98/99	0	1		P

CORRIGAN Dennis
b. 31.10.1960

Svenborg						
Dundee		79/80	2	5	1	P
		80/81	1	2		D1
East Fife		81/82	5			D2

CORRIGAN Martyn Alexander
b. Glasgow 14.8.1977

Gairdoch U						
Falkirk		96/97	8	9		D1
		97/98	24	4		D1
		98/99	21	3	3	D1
Motherwell		99/00	18	1	1	P

COUSAR Robert
b. Kilmarnock 9.10.1961

Hurlford						
St Mirren		83/84	1	1		P
Stranraer		84/85	20	3		D2
		85/86	21	4		D2

COWAN Steven J
b. Paisley 17.2.1963

Aberdeen		80/81	3	2	1	P
		81/82	3	10	3	P
		82/83	0	2	2	P
		83/84	5			P
		84/85	6	10	5	P
Hibernian		85/86	36		19	P
		86/87	23	6	4	P
		87/88	5			P
Motherwell		87/88	32		9	P
		88/89	12	7	2	P
Albion R		89/90	6		2	D1
Portadown						

COWAN Thomas
b. Bellshill 28.8.1969

Clyde		88/89	16		2	D1
Rangers		88/89	3	1		P
		89/90	1	2		P
		90/91	4	1		P
Sheffield U		91/92	20			FL
		92/93	21			FL
		93/94	4			FL
Stoke C	L	93/94	14			FL
Huddersfield T		93/94	10			FL
		94/95	37		2	FL
		95/96	43		2	FL
		96/97	42		4	FL

COWELL James
b. Bellshill 28.7.1961

Shettleston Jnrs						
Heart of Midlothian		84/85	0	1		P
East Stirlingshire	L	85/86	1			D2
Ayr U		85/86	20	3	2	D1
		86/87	17	11	4	D2
		87/88	39		6	D2
		88/89	21	9	2	D1
		89/90	3	2		D1
Clyde		89/90	4	6		D1
Falkirk		89/90	3	6		P
		90/91	0	3		D1
East Fife		90/91	14	4		D2
		91/92	4			D2
Dumbarton		91/92	1	7		D2
		92/93	0	7		D2

COWIE George Alexander
b. Buckie 6.5.1961

Buckie Thistle						
West Ham U		81/82	5	1		FL
		82/83	1	1		FL
Heart of Midlothian		83/84	35		1	P
		84/85	14	1		P
		85/86	8			P
		86/87	9	1	1	P
Morton *		86/87	3			D1
Dunfermline A		87/88	10	4		P
		88/89				
Morton		89/90	5			D1
		90/91	10	9		D1

COYLE John
b. Helensburgh 23.10.1964

Campsie Black Watch						
Clydebank		86/87	7	4		P

COYLE Joseph
b. Glasgow 24.6.1957

Dumbarton		77/78	2	1		D1
		78/79	25	5	2	D1
		79/80	36		4	D1
		80/81	25		3	D1
		81/82	32	3	6	D1
Airdrieonians		82/83	8	3	1	D1
Dumbarton		83/84	39		15	D1
		84/85	28	6	7	P
		85/86	2			D1
Morton		85/86	5	10		D1
		86/87	1	2		D1

COYLE Owen Columba
b. Glasgow 14.7.1966

Renfrew YM						
Dumbarton		85/86	11	5	5	D1
		86/87	33	10	17	D1
		87/88	38	3	14	D1
		88/89	3			D2
Clydebank		88/89	36		16	D1
		89/90	27		17	D1
Airdrionians		89/90	10		10	D1
		90/91	24	4	20	D1
		91/92	40	3	11	P
		92/93	42		9	P
Bolton W		93/94	25	5	7	FL
		94/95	8	11	5	FL
		95/96	2	3		FL
Dundee U		95/96	20	8	5	D1
		96/97	6	4		P
Motherwell		96/97	15		7	P
		97/98	34	2	10	P
		98/99	26		7	P
Dunfermline A		98/99	11		1	P
		99/00	23	7	9	D1

COYLE Ronald Paul
b. Glasgow 19.8.1961

Celtic BC						
Celtic		78/79				
		79/80				
		80/81				
		81/82				
		82/83				
		83/84				
		84/85	0	1		P
		85/86	1			P
Clyde	L	86/87	8			D1
Middlesbrough		86/87	1	2		FL
Rochdale		87/88	23	1	1	FL
Raith R		87/88	16		3	D1
		88/89	36		1	D1
		89/90	28		2	D1
		90/91	34	1	1	D1
		91/92	27	2		D1
		92/93	35		1	D1
		93/94	41		1	P
		94/95	9			D1
		95/96	22	2		P
Ayr U		95/96	4			D2
		96/97	29	1		D2
Albion R		97/98	16	3		D3
East Fife		98/99	25	1		D2

COYLE Thomas
b. Glasgow 9.1.1959

Shettleston Jnrs						
Dumbarton		78/79	8	3		D1
		79/80	8	13		D1
		80/81	31			D1
		81/82	38			D1
		82/83	38		1	D1
		83/84	38	1	7	D1
		84/85	34	2	3	P
		85/86	24	5	6	D1
		86/87	43		5	D1
		87/88	0	1		P
St Johnstone		87/88	38		13	D2
		88/89	24	6	2	D1
Clydebank		89/90	26	1	7	D1
		90/91	12	3	4	D1

COYNE Brian
b. Glasgow 13.2.1959

St Roch						
Celtic		77/78				
		78/79				
Shrewsbury T		79/80	1			FL
Motherwell		80/81	2	1		D1
		81/82	19	1	2	D1
		82/83	6	6		P
Falkirk		83/84	0	1		D1
Worcester C						
Newtown						

COYNE Thomas
b. Glasgow 14.11.1962
Hillwood BC

Clydebank		81/82	29	2	9	D1
		82/83	38		19	D1
		83/84	11		10	D1
Dundee U		83/84	13	5	3	P
		84/85	17	4	3	P
		85/86	9	4	2	P
		86/87	4	6	1	P
Dundee		86/87	20		9	P
		87/88	43		33	P
		88/89	26		9	P
Celtic		88/89	4	3		P
		89/90	17	6	7	P
		90/91	24	2	18	P
		91/92	32	7	15	P
		92/93	5	5	3	P
Tranmere R		92/93	9	3	1	FL
Motherwell		93/94	26		12	P
		94/95	30	1	16	P
		95/96	9	5	4	P
		96/97	24	3	11	P
		97/98	33	1	15	P
Dundee		98/99	8	8		P
		99/00	0	2		P
Falkirk	L	99/00	6	2	1	D1

CRABBE Scott
b. Edinburgh 8.2.1970

Heart of Midlothian		86/87	3	2		P
		87/88	2	3		P
		88/89	1			P
		89/90	27	8	12	P
		90/91	13	8	3	P
		91/92	37	4	15	P
		92/93	4	4	1	P
Dundee U		92/93	22	5	4	P
		93/94	10	11	2	P
		94/95	5	4		P
		95/96	1	1		D1
Falkirk		96/97	10	2		D1
		97/98	27	4	5	D1
		98/99	36		10	D1
		99/00	35		14	D1

CRAIB Mark
b. St Andrews 8.2.1970

Dundee		88/89	2	2		P
		89/90	20	2	1	P
		90/91	17	2		D1
		91/92	20			D1
Montrose		92/93	38		2	D2
		93/94	23		3	D2
		94/95	22		2	D3
		95/96	26	1		D2
		96/97	26		1	D3
		97/98	36			D3
		98/99	31			D3
		99/00	33		2	D3

CRAIG Albert Hughes
b. Glasgow 3.1.1962
Yoker A

Dumbarton		81/82	9	4	2	D1
		82/83	23	8	7	D1
		83/84	21	5	4	D1
		84/85	35		4	P
		85/86	29	3	6	D1
Hamilton A		86/87	12	4	5	P
Newcastle U		86/87	5	1		FL
		87/88	1	2		FL
Hamilton A	L	87/88	6		1	D1
Newcastle U		88/89	0	1		FL
Northampton T	L	88/89	2		1	FL
Dundee		88/89	6		2	P
		89/90	12	8	2	P
		90/91	3	9	3	D1
		91/92	24	2	7	D1
Partick T		92/93	26	3	1	P
		93/94	37	1	14	P
		94/95	30		2	P
		95/96	9		2	P
Falkirk		95/96	14		3	P
		96/97	10	3	2	D1
		97/98	16	10	5	D1
Stenhousemuir		98/99	32		7	D3
Partick T		99/00	28	1	4	D2

CRAIG David William
b. Glasgow 11.6.1969
Milngavie W

Partick T		89/90	6	3	1	D1
		90/91	0	3		D1
East Stirlingshire		91/92	34			D2
		92/93	16		2	D2
		93/94	38		4	D2
Dundee U		94/95	3	3		P
Hamilton A		95/96	17		1	D1
Raith R		96/97	28		2	P
		97/98	3			D1
Hamilton A		97/98	32		2	D1
Ayr U		98/99	22	9	2	D1
		99/00	23		3	D1

CRAIG John
b. 10.4.1953

Aberdeen		73/74	4	4		D1
		74/75	8			D1
Partick T		74/75	4	2		D1
		75/76	26		3	D1
		76/77	31			P
		77/78	30		2	P
		78/79	1			P
Heart of Midlothian		78/79	14	4		P
		79/80	6			P
		80/81	0	1		P

CRAIG Joseph
b. Bridge of Allan 14.5.1954
Lornshill Academy
Sauchie

Partick T		72/73	18	4	8	D1
		73/74	32	1	7	D1
		74/75	31		15	D1
		75/76	22	2	14	D1
		76/77	2			P
Celtic		76/77	34		16	P
		77/78	19	1	5	P
		78/79	0	1		P
Blackburn R		78/79	28	2	5	FL
		79/80	16	1	3	FL
		80/81	0	1		FL
Hamilton A		80/81	7		3	D1
		81/82	32	1	9	D1
		82/83	11	3	2	D1

CRAIG Michael John
b. Glasgow 20.9.1977

Aberdeen		95/96	0	1		P
		96/97	2	3	1	P
		97/98				
Montrose		98/99	15		5	D3
		99/00	15	4	1	D3

CRAIG Thomas Brooks
b. Glasgow 21.11.1950
Drumchapel Amateurs

Aberdeen		66/67				
		67/68	13	1	1	D1
		68/69	30	1	7	D1
Sheffield W		68/69	1			FL
		69/70	40		5	FL
		70/71	35	4	5	FL
		71/72	36		10	FL
		72/73	39		10	FL
		73/74	37		4	FL
		74/75	22		4	FL
Newcastle U		74/75	19	1	2	FL
		75/76	39	1	9	FL
		76/77	40		9	FL
		77/78	24		3	FL
Aston Villa		77/78	4			FL
		78/79	23		2	FL
Swansea C		79/80	33		6	FL
		80/81	14	5	3	FL
		81/82				
Carlisle U		81/82	18		3	FL
		82/83	30	6	4	FL
		83/84	34		2	FL
		84/85	10		1	FL
Hibernian		84/85	10	1		P

CRAIGAN Stephen James
b. Comber 29.10.1976
Bangor
Blantyre V

Motherwell		97/98	9	5		P
		98/99	6	4		P
		99/00	3	2		P

CRAINEY Stephen Danial
b. Glasgow 22.6.1981

Celtic		99/00	5	4		P

CRAINIE Daniel
b. Kilsyth 24.5.1962
Celtic BC

Celtic		81/82	14	2	7	P
		82/83	3	4		P
		83/84	0	2		P
Wolverhampton W		83/84	27	1	3	FL
		84/85	13			FL
Blackpool	L	84/85	6			FL
Wolverhampton W		85/86	23		1	FL
Celtic		85/86	0	3		P
Melbourne Hellas						
Dundee	T	85/86				
South Melbourne						
Woolongong City						
Airdrieonians		90/91	19	9	1	D1
		91/92	0	3		P
Kilmarnock		92/93	3	6	1	D1
		93/94	6	8	1	P
Ballymena U	L	94/95				
Ross Co		95/96	5			D3

CRAMB Colin
b. Lanark 23.6.1974

Hamilton A		90/91	2	1	2	D1
		91/92	2	10	1	P
		92/93	25	8	7	P
Southampton		93/94	0	1		FL
Falkirk		94/95	6	2	1	P
Heart of Midlothian		94/95	3	3	1	P
Doncaster R		95/96	20	1	7	FL
		96/97	40	1	18	FL
Bristol C		97/98	34	6	9	FL
		98/99	4	9		FL
Walsall	L	98/99	4		4	FL
Crewe A		99/00	33	4	6	FL

CRAMOND Gordon Alexander
b. Aberdeen 13.9.1949 d. Ayr 11.1.1989
Banks o'Dee

Dundee		67/68				
		68/69				
Montrose		69/70				
		70/71				
		71/72	33		3	D2
		72/73	34	1	13	D2
		73/74	8		2	D2
St Johnstone		73/74	27		3	D1
		74/75	33		2	P
		75/76	25		2	P
Ayr U		75/76	9			P
		76/77	23	4	5	P
		77/78	33	1	4	P
		78/79	39		4	D1
		79/80	18	2	1	D1
Kilmarnock		79/80	15		1	P
		80/81	16	2	2	P
		81/82				
Brechin C		82/83	1			D2

CRAWFORD Stephen
b. Dunfermline 9.1.1974

Raith R		92/93	10	10	3	D1
		93/94	24	12	5	P
		94/95	28	4	11	D1
		95/96	21	7	3	P
Millwall		96/97	40	2	11	FL
Hibernian		97/98	35		9	P
		98/99	28	7	14	D1
		99/00	1	2		P
Dunfermline A		99/00	25		16	D1

CRAWLEY Gerard
b. Glasgow 3.7.1962

Queens Park		80/81	23	3	3	D2
		81/82	35		10	D1
		82/83	32		4	D1
Dumbarton		83/84	19	6	1	D1
		84/85	16	5	1	P
		85/86	20			D1
Brechin C		86/87	5	1		D1
St Johnstone		86/87	3	1		D2

CREANEY Gerard Thomas
b. Coatbridge 13.4.1970

Nottingham F BC						
Celtic BC						
Celtic		89/90	2	4	1	P
		90/91	22	9	7	P
		91/92	21	11	4	P
		92/93	23	3	9	P
		93/94	17	1	5	P
Portsmouth		93/94	18		11	FL
		94/95	39		18	FL
		95/96	3		3	FL
Manchester C		95/96	6	9	3	FL
Oldham A	L	95/96	8	1	2	FL
Manchester C		96/97	1	4	1	FL
Ipswich T	L	96/97	6		1	FL
Manchester C		97/98				
Burnley	L	97/98	9	1	8	FL
Chesterfield	L	97/98	3	1		FL
St Mirren		98/99	11	1	3	D1

CRUIKSHANK James Fergus
b. Glasgow 13.4.1941

Drumchapel Amateurs						
Queens Park		59/60	30			D2
Heart of Midlothian		60/61	4			D1
		61/62	5			D1
		62/63	6			D1
		63/64	34			D1
Queens Park	L	63/64	1			D2
Heart of Midlothian		64/65	34			D1
		65/66	34			D1
		66/67	34			D1
		67/68	20			D1
		68/69	31			D1
		69/70	29			D1
		70/71	32			D1
		71/72	20			D1
		72/73	11			D1
		73/74	11			D1
		74/75	27			D1
		75/76	35			P
		76/77	27			P
Dumbarton *		77/78	3			D1

CUNNINGTON Edward
b. Kilbride 12.11.1969

Chelsea						
Dunfermline A		90/91	6	1		P
		91/92	35	1		P
		92/93	26	8		D1
		93/94	7	2		D1
Dumbarton		93/94	13		3	D1
Glentoran		94/95				
Coleraine		95/96				
Hamilton A		96/97	8			D2
		97/98	25	3	2	D1
		98/99	33		1	D1
		99/00	31	1	4	D2

CURCIC Sasa
b. Belgrade 14.2.1972

OFK Belgrade						
Partizan Belgrade						
Bolton W		95/96	28		4	FL
Aston Villa		96/97	17	5		FL
		97/98	3	4		FL
Crystal Palace		97/98	6	2	1	FL
		98/99	4	11	4	FL
Motherwell		99/00	3	3		P

CURRAN Henry
b. Glasgow 9.10.1966

Eastercraigs BC						
Dumbarton		84/85	0	2		P
		85/86	5	1		D1
		86/87	8			D1
Dundee U		86/87	3			P
		87/88	1	4		P
		88/89	3	3		P
St Johnstone		89/90	26	5	3	D1
		90/91	35		9	P
		91/92	36	3	8	P
		92/93	32	2	8	P
		93/94	39		3	P
		94/95	22	4	4	D1
Partick T		95/96	3	5		P
Dunfermline A		96/97	18	2	2	P
		97/98	15	2	1	P
Morton		97/98	9		1	D1
		98/99	33		5	D1
		99/00	28		9	D1

CURRAN Jeffrey Francis
b. Glasgow 15.4.1961

St Mirren		79/80	0	2		P
		80/81	3	2		P
		81/82	5			P
Airdrieonians		82/83				
Stirling A		82/83	0	1		D2
Pollok Jnrs		83/84				
		84/85				
Arbroath		85/86	37	1	5	D2
		86/87	3			D2

CUTHBERTSON William Scott
b. Hamilton 24.10.1965

Eddlewood BC						
Kilmarnock		82/83	1	1		P
		83/84	7	5	1	D1
		84/85	18	5	6	D1
		85/86	22	6	6	D1
		86/87	11	7	3	D1
		87/88	20	9	4	D1
		88/89	0	1	1	D1
Stirling A		88/89	9	4	3	D2
		89/90	6	2		D2

CZACHOWSKI Piotr
b. Warsaw 7.11.1966

Legia Warsaw						
Dundee		93/94	18		1	P

DAILLY Christian Eduard
b. Dundee 23.10.1973

Dundee U		90/91	16	2	5	P
		91/92	5	3		P
		92/93	8	6	4	P
		93/94	29	9	3	P
		94/95	30	3	4	P
		95/96	20	10	1	D1
Derby Co		95/96				
		96/97	31	5	3	FL
		97/98	30		1	FL
		98/99	1			FL
Blackburn R		98/99	14	3		FL
		99/00	43		4	FL

DAIR Jason
b. Dunfermline 15.6.1974

Raith R		91/92	0	4		D1
		92/93	10	5	1	D1
		93/94	35	3	6	P
		94/95	12	6	1	D1
		95/96	19	1	3	P
Millwall		96/97	21	3	1	FL
Raith R		97/98	15	10		D1
		98/99	27		3	D1
Dunfermline A		98/99	9	1		P
		99/00	22	2	1	D1

DALGLISH Kenneth Mathieson
b. Dalmarnock 4.3.1951

Glasgow U						
Possilpark YMCA						
Drumchapel Amateurs						
Celtic						
Cumbernauld U	L					
Celtic		68/69				
		69/70	2			D1
		70/71	1	2		D1
		71/72	31		17	D1
		72/73	32		22	D1
		73/74	31	2	18	D1
		74/75	33		16	D1
		75/76	35		24	P
		76/77	35		14	P
Liverpool		77/78	42		20	FL
		78/79	42		21	FL
		79/80	42		16	FL
		80/81	34		8	FL
		81/82	42		13	FL
		82/83	42		18	FL
		83/84	33		7	FL
		84/85	36		6	FL
		85/86	17	4	3	FL
		86/87	12	6	6	FL
		87/88	0	2		FL
		88/89				
		89/90	0	1		FL

DALZIEL Gordon
b. Motherwell 16.3.1962

Queens Park *		78/79	3			D2
		79/80	0	1		D2
Rangers		79/80	1			P
		80/81				
		81/82	14	3	6	P
		82/83	7	7	3	P
Manchester C		83/84	4	1		FL
Partick T		84/85	19	6	6	D1
		85/86	13	5		D1
East Stirlingshire		86/87	10		2	D2
Raith R		86/87	11		7	D2
		87/88	41	1	25	D1
		88/89	34	2	11	D1
		89/90	39		20	D1
		90/91	39		25	D1
		91/92	38	1	26	D1
		92/93	44		33	D1
		93/94	20	7	8	P
		94/95	25	6	15	D1
Ayr U		95/96	16	7	4	D2
		96/97	0	1		D2

DARGO Craig Peter
b. Edinburgh 3.1.1978

Links U						
Raith R		95/96	0	1		P
		96/97	1	4		P
		97/98	21	6	8	D1
		98/99	21	1	8	D1
		99/00	25		12	D1

DASOVIC Nick Robert
b. Vancouver 5.12.1968

Trelleborg						
St Johnstone		96/97	14			D1
		97/98	18	1		P
		98/99	31		1	P
		99/00	13			P

DAVID Lionel
b. Nantes 28.9.1966

La Roche Sur Yon						
Dundee		92/93	8			P
		93/94	1			P

DAVIDSON Alan
b. Airdrie 17.4.1960

Airdrieonians		80/81	1			P
		81/82	9			P
Queen of the South		82/83	39			D2
		83/84	39			D2
		84/85	27			D2
		85/86	39			D2
		86/87	38			D1
		87/88	29			D1
		88/89				
		89/90	24			D2
		90/91	32			D2
		91/92	23			D2
		92/93	8			D2
		93/94	14			D2
Albion R		94/95	21			D3
		95/96				
		96/97	1			D3

DAVIDSON Callum Iain
b. Stirling 25.6.1976

St Johnstone		94/95	4	3	1	D1
		95/96	2			D1
		96/97	18	2	2	D1
		97/98	15		1	P
Blackburn R		97/98	1			FL
		98/99	34		1	FL
		99/00	28		2	FL

DAVIDSON Duncan
b. Elgin 5.7.1954

Aberdeen		73/74	0	5		D1
		74/75	2	14	2	D1
		75/76				
		76/77	8	5	3	P
		77/78	17	7	8	P
		78/79	7	2	2	P
		79/80	2	5	1	P
		80/81	0	4		P
Tulsa Roughnecks		81	9		2	NA
Toronto Blizzard		81	12		2	NA
See Bee		81/82				
Toronto Blizzard		82	9		2	NA
See Bee		82/83				
Manchester C		83/84	2	4	1	FL

DAVIDSON Gerard						
b. Aberdeen 28.2.1961						
Sunnybank Jnrs						
Dundee		78/79	3	3		D1
		79/80				
		80/81	0	1		D1
		81/82	1	3		P
		82/83	6	1		P
DAVIDSON Hugh Norman						
b. Dundee 3.8.1980						
Dundee U		99/00	17	7		P
DAVIDSON Lee						
b. 18.11.1967						
Dundee		86/87	0	1		P
DAVIDSON Stuart William						
b. Glasgow 3.8.1979						
Kilmarnock		99/00	0	2		P
Queen of the South	L	99/00	1	1		D2
DAVIDSON Victor Salvatore Ferla						
b. Glasgow 8.11.1950						
Glasgow U						
Celtic		67/68				
Giffnock North	L					
Ashfield	L					
Celtic		68/69				
		69/70	1		1	D1
		70/71	6	1	5	D1
		71/72	5		5	D1
		72/73	1	1		D1
		73/74	3			D1
		74/75				
Motherwell		75/76	29	6	5	P
		76/77	30	1	6	P
		77/78	29		8	P
Blackpool		77/78	23	2	3	FL
Celtic		78/79	12		1	P
		79/80	5		2	P
		80/81				
Phoenix Inferno						
DAVIES John						
b. Glasgow 25.9.1966						
Clydebank		85/86	3			P
		86/87	10	4		P
Jonkoping						
Clydebank		87/88	18	4	3	D1
		88/89	38		3	D1
		89/90	31		5	D1
		90/91	14		1	D1
St Johnstone		90/91	13	8	1	P
		91/92	37	3		P
		92/93	33	5	4	P
		93/94	30	2	9	P
		94/95	1	2		D1
Airdrieonians		94/95	25		3	D1
		95/96	33	2	3	D1
		96/97	31		6	D1
		97/98	11	8	1	D1
Ayr U		97/98	8			D1
		98/99	27	2	3	D1
		99/00	7			D1
Motherwell		99/00	7	1		P
DAVIES William McIntosh						
b. Glasgow 31.5.1964						
Pollok U						
Rangers		81/82	1	3		P
		82/83	2	2		P
		83/84	0	3	1	P
Jonkoping		84/85				
		85/86				
Elfsborg		86/87				
St Mirren		87/88	18			P
		88/89	26	1	4	P
		89/90	22	7	1	P
Leicester C		90/91	5	1		FL
Dunfermline A		90/91	26			P
		91/92	22	11		P
		92/93	39	2	10	D1
		93/94	3	1		D1
Motherwell		93/94	6	4		P
		94/95	31		4	P
		95/96	26	7	2	P
		96/97	20	5	1	P
		97/98	12	5	2	P
DAWSON Alistair John						
b. Govan 25.2.1958						
Rangers		75/76	3			P
		76/77	1			P
		77/78	1	1		P
		78/79	23		1	P
		79/80	32			P
		80/81	22		2	P
		81/82	25		1	P
		82/83	24	1		P
		83/84	28			P
		84/85	25	1	1	P
		85/86	23	1	1	P
		86/87	6	1		P
Blackburn R		87/88	20	2		FL
		88/89	3	3		FL
		89/90	9	3		FL
Airdrieonians		90/91	9	1	1	D1
DAWSON Robert McQuillan						
b. Stirling 1.8.1963						
Fallin Violet						
Stirling A		81/82	18			D2
		82/83	34	2		D2
		83/84	31	2	2	D2
		84/85	33	1		D2
		85/86	39			D2
		86/87	39			D2
St Mirren		87/88	16	8		P
		88/89	9			P
		89/90	1			P
		90/91	13	1		P
		91/92	5	2		P
		92/93	34			D1
		93/94	38		3	D1
		94/95	29		2	D1
		95/96	8			D1
Clyde		95/96	8			D2
DAY Raymond						
b. Glasgow 29.10.1963						
Bishopbriggs BC						
St Johnstone		81/82				
		82/83	0	1		D1
		83/84	3	1		P
Hamilton A		84/85	19	2	1	D1
		85/86	2	2		D1
Stranraer		86/87	34			D2
		87/88	24	1	3	D2
		88/89	0	1		D2
Cumnock Jnrs						
DE CLERK Mark						
Aberdeen		80/81	1			P
DE VOS Jason Richard						
b. Ontario 2.1.1974						
Darlington		96/97	8			FL
		97/98	24		3	FL
		98/99	12		2	FL
Dundee U		98/99	23	2		P
		99/00	35		2	P
DEANS John Kelty						
b. Johnstone 30.7.1946						
Neilston V						
Motherwell		66/67	2		11	D1
		67/68	21		11	D1
		68/69	33		30	D2
		69/70	29		16	D1
		70/71	31		9	D1
		71/72	6		2	D1
Celtic		71/72	21		19	D1
		72/73	30	1	21	D1
		73/74	24	2	24	D1
		74/75	18	1	9	D1
		75/76	29		15	P
Luton T		76/77	13	1	6	FL
Carlisle U	L	76/77	4		2	FL
Partick T	L	76/77	4	2	2	P
Adelaide Juventus						
Shelbourne		77/78				
Adelaide Juventus						
Partick T	T	80/81				
DEAS Paul Andrew						
b. Perth 22.2.1972						
St Johnstone						
Kinnoull Jnrs	L					
St Johnstone		90/91	0	1		P
		91/92	17	1		P
		92/93	25		1	P
		93/94	35	1		P
		94/95	7		1	D1
Stirling A		94/95	9	1		D2
		95/96	9	1		D2
		96/97	32		1	D1
		97/98	33			D1
Livingston		98/99	35		5	D2
		99/00	33		2	D1
DELAUNAY Jean Pierre						
b. Harfleur 17.1.1966						
Le Havre						
Dundee U		99/00	1			P
DEMPSEY James						
b. Bellshill 28.7.1959						
Lanark U						
Motherwell		78/79	10			P
		79/80	10			D1
Clyde		80/81	18	3	2	D2
		81/82	38		1	D2
		82/83	29		2	D1
		83/84	25	2		D1
Falkirk		84/85	37		7	D1
		85/86	36		1	D1
		86/87	35			P
		87/88	25	2	1	P
Partick T		88/89	30	4	1	D1
		89/90	1			D1
Dumbarton		89/90	29			D2
		90/91	35	1	1	D2
		91/92	28	2		D2
		92/93	3			D2
Stirling A		92/93	4			D1
Alloa A *		93/94	3			D2
DEMPSEY Samuel George						
b. Bellshill 15.10.1974						
Airdrieonians		92/93	0	1		P
		93/94				
East Stirlingshire		94/95	0	1		D2
DEMPSIE Mark William						
b. Bellshill 19.10.1980						
Hibernian		98/99	5	3		D1
		99/00	7	1		P
DEMPSTER John						
Queen of the South		71/72	26		5	D2
		72/73	32	1	3	D2
		73/74	33	2	16	D2
		74/75	38		21	D2
		75/76	24		6	D1
		76/77	36	1	6	D1
		77/78	29	3	2	D1
		78/79	30	2	6	D1
St Mirren		79/80	2	1		P
Clyde		80/81	15		5	D2
DEN BIEMEN Ivo Johannes						
b. Wamel 4.2.1967						
SV Leones						
Montrose		90/91	32	4	5	D2
		91/92	37	5	6	D1
Dundee		92/93	23	1	3	P
Dunfermline A		93/94	33	8	3	D1
		94/95	19	12	5	D1
		95/96	16	10	1	D1
		96/97	21	7	1	P
		97/98	11	14		P
		98/99	0	2		P
Ross Co		98/99	2			D3
Falkirk		98/99	24			D1
		99/00	15		1	D1
DENHAM Greig Paterson						
b. Glasgow 5.10.1976						
Cumbernauld U						
Motherwell		95/96	11	2		P
		96/97	5	4		P
		97/98	18			P
		98/99	0	1		P
		99/00	6			P
DENNIS Shaun						
b. Kirkcaldy 20.12.1969						
Lochgelly Albert						
Raith R		88/89	9	1		D1
		89/90	18			D1
		90/91	35		1	D1
		91/92	42			D1
		92/93	31		1	D1
		93/94	43		3	P
		94/95	26		1	D1
		95/96	25			P
		96/97	16			P
Hibernian		96/97	4		1	P
		97/98	5			P
		98/99	29	2	3	D1
		99/00	23	1		P

DENNY James
b. 13.3.1950

Rangers		71/72	7	2		D1
		72/73	6			D1
		73/74	0	1		D1
		74/75	6	1		D1
		75/76	6	3		P
		76/77	5			P
		77/78				
		78/79				
Heart of Midlothian		79/80	34			D1
		80/81	19			P
Stirling A		81/82	20			D2
Irvine V						

DE ORNELAS Fernando
b. 29.7.1976

Celtic		99/00	0	2		P

DI CANIO Paolo
b. Rome 9.7.1968

Lazio						
Ternana						
Lazio						
Juventus						
Napoli						
Juventus						
AC Milan						
Celtic		96/97	25	1	12	P
Sheffield W		97/98	34	1	12	FL
		98/99	5	1	3	FL
West Ham U		98/99	12	1	4	FL
		99/00	29	1	16	FL

DIBBLE Andrew Gerard
b. Cwmbran 8.5.1965

Cardiff C		81/82	1			FL
		82/83	20			FL
		83/84	41			FL
Luton T		84/85	13			FL
		85/86	7			FL
Sunderland	L	85/86	12			FL
Luton T		86/87	1			FL
Huddersfield T	L	86/87	5			FL
Luton T		87/88	9			FL
Manchester C		88/89	38			FL
		89/90	31			FL
		90/91	3			FL
Aberdeen	L	90/91	5			P
Middlesbrough	L	90/91	19			FL
Manchester C		91/92	2			FL
Bolton W	L	91/92	13			FL
WBA	L	91/92	9			FL
Manchester C		92/93	1	1		FL
		93/94	11			FL
		94/95	14	1		FL
		95/96				
Rangers		96/97	7			P
Sheffield U		97/98				
Luton T		97/98	1			FL
Middlesbrough		97/98	2			FL

DICK James
b. Bellshill 21.6.1972

Airdrieonians		90/91	0	3		D1
		91/92				
		92/93	0	1		P
St Mirren		93/94	31	4	4	D1
		94/95	24	1	2	D1
		95/96	24	2	2	D1
		96/97	24	1	3	D1
		97/98	13	2	2	D1
Ayr U		97/98	4			D1
		98/99	1	3		D1
Airdrieonians		99/00	19	3		D1

DICKSON John
b. c1949 d. Kirkcaldy 12.1.1998

Leeds U						
Lochore Welfare						
Cowdenbeath		68/69				
		69/70				
		70/71	26	3	8	D1
		71/72	33		12	D2
		72/73	7		5	D2
St Mirren		72/73	29		15	D1
		73/74	29	1	7	D1
Ayr U		74/75	13	4	4	D1
		75/76	8	2		P
		76/77				
Elgin C						
Dunfermline A *		77/78	8		3	D2
East Fife *		78/79	35		9	D2
		79/80	4	3		D2

DICKSON Joseph Ronald
b. Glasgow 24.3.1965

Clydebank		82/83	1	5		D1
		83/84	29	2		D1
		84/85	35			D1
		85/86	27	1	1	P
		86/87	32	3		P
		87/88	20	6	1	D1
		88/89	29	2		D1
		89/90	30		1	D1
		90/91	20	1		D1
		91/92	12	1		D1
Queen of the South		92/93	27	2		D2

DIJKSTRA Sieb
b. Kerkrade 20.10.1966

Roda JC Kerkrade						
AZ67 Alkmaar						
Hasselt KSC						
Motherwell		91/92	1			P
		92/93	35			P
		93/94	44			P
QPR		94/95	11			FL
		95/96				
Bristol C	L	95/96	8			FL
Wycombe W	L	95/96	13			FL
Dundee U		96/97	22			P
		97/98	36			P
		98/99	26	1		P

DINDELEUX Frederic
b. Lille 16.1.1974

Lille Olympique						
Kilmarnock		99/00	28		1	P

DINNIE Alan
b. Glasgow 14.5.1963

Partick T		87/88	38			D1
		88/89	31		1	D1
		89/90	14		2	D1
Dundee		89/90	21	1		P
		90/91	25		3	D1
		91/92	24	6		D1
		92/93	26		1	P
		93/94	7			P
		94/95	1			D1
Partick T		94/95	23	2	2	P
		95/96	31			P
		96/97	13	1	1	P
Albion R *		97/98	2			D3

DOAK Martin
b. Greenock 11.5.1964

Morton		82/83	4	5		P
		83/84	24	5	2	D1
Falkirk		84/85	7		2	D1
Morton		84/85	13	6	3	P
		85/86	24		7	D1
		86/87	37	1	6	D1
		87/88	27	6		P
Adelaide Hellas		88/89				
		89/90				
Morton		90/91	33		1	D1
		91/92	43		9	D1
		92/93	27	4	1	D1
		93/94	15		4	D1

DOBBIN James
b. Dunfermline 17.9.1963

Whitburn BC						
Celtic		80/81				
		81/82				
		82/83				
		83/84	1	2	2	P
Motherwell	L	83/84	1			P
Doncaster R		83/84	11		2	FL
		84/85	15	2	1	FL
		85/86	25	6	6	FL
		86/87	5		4	FL
Barnsley		86/87	30		4	FL
		87/88	14	2	2	FL
		88/89	36	5	5	FL
		89/90	28			FL
		90/91	8	6		FL
Grimsby T						

DOCHERTY Brian
b. Johnstone 24.4.1960

St Mirren		77/78	14	2	1	P
		78/79	1	1		P
		79/80	7	4		P
Arbroath		80/81	37	1	2	D2
		81/82	27	1	4	D2
		82/83	10	7	3	D2

DOCHERTY Daniel
b. Cambuslang 12.4.1961

Morton		80/81	1			P
		81/82	31	4	3	P
		82/83	20	5	1	P
Clyde		83/84	2	4	2	D1
Morton		83/84	23	3	4	D1
		84/85	32	4	1	P
		85/86	9			D1
Dumbarton		85/86	15	3	2	D1
		86/87	18	4		D1
Queen of the South		87/88	39		2	D1

DOCHERTY Gerald
b. Broxburn 17.2.1965

Armadale Thistle						
Partick T		81/82	0	1		P
		82/83	4	3		P

DOCHERTY James
b. Broxburn 8.11.1956

East Stirlingshire		77/78	25		14	D2
		78/79	21	1	14	D2
Chelsea		78/79	2	1		FL
Dundee U		79/80	1	1		P
Heart of Midlothian		79/80	1	3		D1
		80/81	0	1		P
St Johnstone		80/81	26	4	11	D1
		81/82	16	3	2	P
Partick T		82/83	1	3		D1
		83/84	0	3		P
Meadowbank T		83/84	3			D2
Dunfermline A		83/84	3	1		D1

DOCHERTY John

Aberdeen		75/76	1			P

DOCHERTY Peter
b. Edinburgh 3.10.1962

Hibernian		79/80	2	1		P
		80/81				
		81/82	2			P
Berwick R		82/83	9	2		D2

DOCHERTY Robert John
b. Glasgow 11.9.1965

St Mirren BC						
St Mirren		77/78				
		78/79				
		79/80				
		80/81				
		81/82				
		82/83				
Hamilton A	L	83/84	7			D1
East Stirlingshire	L	84/85	0	1		D2
Dundee		84/85	0	1		P
Hibernians Valletta		85/86				
Partick T		86/87	2	1		D1
Kilmarnock		86/87	12	3	1	D1
Hamilton A	T	87/88	0	1		D1
Dumbarton		87/88	19	2	5	D1
		88/89	31		7	D2
Stirling A		89/90	9	1	5	D2
		90/91	27	3	4	D2
		91/92	23	5		D1
		92/93	3	4		D1
Dumbarton		92/93	26	6	1	D1
		93/94	0	1		D1
		94/95				
East Stirlingshire		95/96	4	2		D3
Stranraer		96/97	25	6	3	D2
		97/98	20	6	3	D2
Albion R		97/98	11		1	D3
		98/99	6			D3

DOCHERTY Stephen
b. Glasgow 18.2.1976

Pollok Jnrs						
Partick T		92/93	0	1		P
		93/94				
		94/95	0	1		P
		95/96	19	5	3	P
		96/97	8	14	1	D1
Clydebank		97/98	30		2	D2
		98/99	17	11	2	D1
Partick T		99/00	17	1	1	D2

DODDS David
b. Dundee 23.9.1958

Club		Season				
Dundee U		77/78	2	8	1	P
Arbroath	L	77/78	6			D1
Dundee U		78/79	19	8	10	P
		79/80	14	7	6	P
		80/81	23	1	14	P
		81/82	35		14	P
		82/83	34	2	22	P
		83/84	31	2	15	P
		84/85	24	2	8	P
		85/86	30		12	P
Neuchatel Xamax						
Aberdeen		86/87	25	1	4	P
		87/88	22	1	9	P
		88/89	17	6	4	P
		89/90	0	1		P
Rangers		89/90	4	10	4	P
		90/91	3			P

DODDS William
b. New Cumnock 5.2.1969

Club		Season				
Chelsea		86/87	0	1		FL
		87/88				
Partick T	L	87/88	19	11	7	D1
Chelsea		88/89				
Dundee		89/90	29	1	13	P
		90/91	37		15	D1
		91/92	41		19	D1
		92/93	41		16	P
		93/94	23	1	5	P
St Johnstone		93/94	20		6	P
Aberdeen		94/95	35		15	P
		95/96	28	3	17	P
		96/97	31		15	P
		97/98	29	5	10	P
		98/99	6			P
Dundee U		98/99	29	1	17	P
		99/00	15		9	P
Rangers		99/00	16	2	10	P

DODS Darren
b. Edinburgh 7.6.1975

Club	Season				
Hibernian	94/95	1			P
	95/96	14	1		P
	96/97	17	3		P
	97/98	29		1	P
St Johnstone	98/99	34		2	P
	99/00	22		2	P

DOESBURG Michel Johannes
b. Beverwyk 10.8.1968

Club	Season				
Haarlem	86/87				
	87/88				
	88/89				
	89/90				
Wageningen	90/91				
	91/92				
Heerenveen	92/93				
	93/94				
	94/95				
	95/96				
AZ67 Alkmaar	95/96				
	96/97				
	97/98				
Motherwell	98/99	29	1		P
	99/00	17	2		P
Dunfermline A	99/00	5	1		D1

DOHERTY James Hugh
b. Kilmarnock 13.9.1958
Fenwick BC

Club	Season				
Kilmarnock	76/77	4	4		P
	77/78	7	8	4	D1
	78/79	8	6	2	D1
	79/80	2	8	1	P
	80/81	8	4	2	P
Clyde	81/82	35	3	7	D2
	82/83	20	4	5	D1
	83/84	21	4	4	D1
	84/85	37		1	D1
	85/86	22	5	2	D1
	86/87	20	3		D1
Queen of the South	87/88	30	5	10	D1
	88/89	12	6	2	D1
Stranraer	88/89	7		2	D2
	89/90	0	1		D2

DOIG Kevin
b. Glasgow 6.11.1975

Club	Season				
Kilmarnock	97/98	1			P
Queen of the South	98/99	9			D2

DOLAN James
b. Salsburgh 22.2.1969
Motherwell BC

Club	Season				
Motherwell	88/89	3	2		P
	89/90	5	7		P
	90/91	4	4	1	P
	91/92	28	4	2	P
	92/93	15	10	2	P
	93/94	32	4		P
	94/95	31			P
	95/96	24	3		P
	96/97	18			P
Dundee U	96/97	11	2		P
	97/98	21	5		P
	98/99	4	1		P
Dunfermline A	98/99	10			P
	99/00	19			D1

DONALD Graeme Still
b. Stirling 14.4.1974
Gairdoch U

Club	Season				
Hibernian	91/92	3	2	3	P
	92/93	1	3		P
	93/94	2	4		P
	94/95				
	95/96	2	11	1	P
	96/97	8	3	1	P
	97/98	1	3		P
Stirling A	98/99	18	4	3	D2
	99/00	36		1	D2

DONALDSON Alistair
b. 27.11.1943

Club	Season				
Dundee	63/64				
	64/65	30			D1
	65/66	29			D1
	66/67	6			D1
	67/68	24			D1
	68/69	33			D1
	69/70	34			D1
	70/71	29			D1
	71/72	3			D1
Falkirk	71/72	13			D1
	72/73				
	73/74	34			D1
	74/75	38			D2
	75/76	20			D1
Dundee	76/77	29			D1
	77/78	22			D1
	78/79	39			D1
	79/80	36			P
	80/81				
Raith R	81/82	18			D1

DONALDSON George
b. 24.11.1954

Club	Season				
Rangers	72/73	3	2		D1
	73/74				
Heart of Midlothian	74/75	10	4	1	D1
	75/76	2			P
Dunfermline A	76/77	13	2	1	D2
	77/78				
Meadowbank T	78/79	1			D2

DONNELLY John
b. Glasgow 8.3.1961
Notts Co

Club	Season				
Motherwell	78/79	14	2	2	P
	79/80	7	2		D1
Dumbarton	80/81	14	2	4	D1
	81/82	31	3	5	D1
	82/83	28		8	D1
Leeds U	82/83	13	1	1	FL
	83/84	23	2	3	FL
	84/85	0	1		FL
Partick T	84/85	10		7	D1
	85/86	27	2	10	D1
	86/87	6			D1
Dunfermline A	86/87	30		7	D1
	87/88	2	2		P
East Fife	87/88	4			D1
Stranraer	88/89	16	1	1	D2

DONNELLY Simon Thomas
b. Glasgow 1.12.1974
Clyde BC
Queens Park BC
Celtic BC

Club	Season				
Celtic	92/93				
	93/94	10	2	5	P
	94/95	7	10		P
	95/96	35		6	P
	96/97	20	9	4	P
	97/98	21	9	10	P
	98/99	20	3	5	P
Sheffield W					

DORNAN Andrew
b. Aberdeen 19.8.1961

Club	Season				
Aberdeen	80/81	2			P
	81/82				
Motherwell	82/83	19			P
	83/84	26		2	P
	84/85	18	3	1	D1
	85/86	25	1		P
	86/87	0	1		P
Walsall	86/87	43			FL
	87/88	30	1		FL
	88/89	26			FL
	89/90	18		1	FL
Montrose	90/91	17			D2
	91/92	24			D1

DORNER Mario
b. Baden 21.3.1970
Linzer ASK
Krems
Admira Wacker
VfB Modling

Club	Season				
Motherwell	97/98	1	1		P
Darlington	97/98	25	2	10	FL
	98/99	9	13	3	FL

DOUGLAS Robert James
b. Lanark 24.4.1972
Forth W

Club	Season				
Meadowbank T	93/94	4			D2
Livingston	94/95	8			D3
	95/96	24			D2
	96/97	36			D2
Dundee	97/98	36			D1
	98/99	35			P
	99/00	35			P

DOW Andrew James
b. Dundee 7.2.1973
Sporting Club 85

Club		Season				
Dundee		91/92	0	5		D1
		92/93	8	6	1	P
Chelsea		93/94	13	1		FL
		94/95				
Bradford C	L	94/95	5			FL
Chelsea		95/96	1			FL
Hibernian		95/96	8		1	P
		96/97	17	5	2	P
		97/98	23	9		P
Aberdeen		98/99	22	3		P
		99/00	35		5	P

DOWIE John
b. Hamilton 12.12.1955
Calder Blantyre

Club	Season				
Rangers	71/72				
Fulham	72/73				
	73/74	1			FL
	74/75	14	1	2	FL
	75/76	14	4		FL
	76/77	3			FL
Celtic	77/78	12	2		P
Houston Hurricane	78	21		1	NA
Celtic	78/79				
Doncaster R	79/80	9			FL
	80/81	12			FL
Clyde	81/82	4	5		D1
Doveton					
Brunswick Juventus					

DOYLE James
b. Glasgow 1.10.1961

Club	Season				
Partick T	78/79	4	3		P
	79/80	32	1	1	P
	80/81	22	1		P
	81/82	33		2	P
	82/83	29		3	D1
	83/84	26		4	D1
Motherwell	84/85	15			D1
	85/86	16		1	P
	86/87	4	2		P
Partick T *	87/88	1	1		D1
Dumbarton	88/89	11	3	1	D2
	89/90	18	3	1	D2

DOYLE John
b. Caldercruix 11.5.1951 d. Kilmarnock 19.10.1981
Viewpark Boys Guild

Club	Season				
Ayr U	70/71	10	2	1	D1
	71/72	34		3	D1
	72/73	34		6	D1
	73/74	23		1	D1
	74/75	28		7	D1
	75/76	23		6	P
Celtic	75/76	5			P
	76/77	33		4	P
	77/78	20	5	2	P
	78/79	23	2	2	P
	79/80	22	2	7	P
	80/81	1	4		P

DRINKELL Kevin Smith
b. Grimsby 18.6.1960

Grimsby T		76/77	3	1	2	FL
		77/78	20	6	5	FL
		78/79	20	8	7	FL
		79/80	31	2	16	FL
		80/81	41		7	FL
		81/82	23	5	6	FL
		82/83	39		17	FL
		83/84	35	1	15	FL
		84/85	30	5	14	FL
Norwich C		85/86	41		22	FL
		86/87	42		16	FL
		87/88	38		12	FL
Rangers		88/89	32		12	P
		89/90	2	2		P
Coventry C		89/90	21	1	5	FL
		90/91	11	4		FL
		91/92	2	2		FL
Birmingham C	L	91/92	5		2	FL
Falkirk		92/93	33	2	7	P
		93/94	18	2	5	D1
Stirling A		93/94	10	1	1	D1
		94/95	8	2	2	D2

DRIZIC Milos
b. Nis 21.12.1960
Red Star Belgrade

Dunfermline A		90/91	5		1	P
		91/92	1			P

DUARTE Sergio
b. 20.1.1968

Dunfermline A		97/98	9	7		P

DUFFIELD Peter
b. Middlesbrough 4.2.1969

Middlesbrough		86/87				
Sheffield U		87/88	7	4		FL
Halifax T	L	87/88	12		6	FL
Sheffield U		88/89	25	13	11	FL
		89/90	2	3	2	FL
		90/91	0	2		FL
Rotherham U	L	90/91	17		4	FL
Sheffield U		91/92	0	2		FL
		92/93				
Blackpool	L	92/93	3	2	1	FL
Crewe A	L	92/93	0	2		FL
Stockport Co	L	92/93	6	1	4	FL
Hamilton A		93/94	33	3	19	D1
		94/95	36		20	D1
Airdrieonians		95/96	19	5	6	D1
Raith R		95/96	9		5	P
		96/97	23	10	5	P
		97/98	5	4	1	D1
Morton		97/98	25		9	D1
		98/99	2	1		D1
Falkirk		98/99	10	7	3	D1
Darlington	L	98/99	10	4	2	FL
		99/00	21	12	12	FL

DUFFY Bernard John
b. Kilmarnock 28.7.1961

Stranraer *		83/84	1			D2
Annbank U		84/85				
		85/86				
St Mirren		86/87	1			P
Annbank U		87/88				
Stranraer		88/89	39			D2
		89/90	39			D2
		90/91	30			D2
		91/92	36			D2
		92/93	15			D2
		93/94	30	2		D2
		94/95	8	1		D1
		95/96	9			D2
		96/97	27			D2
		97/98	1			D2
Albion R *		97/98	2			D3

DUFFY Cornelius
b. Glasgow 5.6.1967
Dundee U
South Africa
Dundee U

Falkirk		90/91	20	5	2	P
		91/92	39		2	P
		92/93	33	1	5	P
		93/94	23		10	D1
Dundee		93/94	12		2	P
		94/95	23	1	3	D1
		95/96	31		3	D1
Dundee U		96/97	6	7	1	P
		97/98	1	6		P
		98/99	12	3		P
Ayr U		99/00	28			D1

DUFFY James
b. Glasgow 27.4.1959

Morton		81/82	20			P
		82/83	27			P
		83/84	38		2	D1
		84/85	34		1	P
Dundee		85/86	36			P
		86/87	42		2	P
		87/88	5			P
		88/89				
		89/90	8			P
Partick T		90/91	34		2	D1
		91/92	37	1	2	D1
Dundee		92/93	39			P
		93/94	32			P
		94/95	16			D1
		95/96	19			D1
		96/97	2			D1
Stranraer *		96/97	0	1		D2

DUNCAN Arthur
b. Falkirk 5.12.1947
Gairdoch U

Partick T		65/66	15		9	D1
		66/67	27		6	D1
		67/68	25		5	D1
		68/69	33		9	D1
		69/70	17		4	D1
Hibernian		69/70	17		3	D1
		70/71	24	1	4	D1
		71/72	27	2	11	D1
		72/73	33		10	D1
		73/74	33		6	D1
		74/75	30	1	12	D1
		75/76	35	1	13	P
		76/77	30		2	P
		77/78	28	3	5	P
		78/79	35		1	P
		79/80	26	2		P
		80/81	39		1	D1
		81/82	32		1	P
		82/83	31	4	2	P
		83/84	25	2	2	P
Meadowbank T		84/85	27	6		D1
		85/86				
		86/87	0	1		D2

DUNCAN Cameron
b. Shotts 4.8.1965

Sunderland		85/86	1			FL
		86/87				
Motherwell		87/88	43			P
		88/89	17			P
Partick T		89/90	25			D1
		90/91	20			D1
Ayr U		90/91	11			D1
		91/92	15			D1
		92/93	41			D1
		93/94	31			D1
		94/95	29			D1
		95/96	21			D2
Albion R		96/97	10			D3

DUNLOP Andrew
b. Ayr 29.12.1957

St Mirren		76/77	0	2		D1
		77/78	6	2		P
		78/79	36			P
		79/80	8			P
		80/81	2			P
Partick T		81/82	34			P
		82/83	13	2		D1
		83/84	38		4	D1
Morton		84/85	9		1	P

DUNLOP Raymond
b. 20.6.1952

Stenhousemuir		72/73	2			D2
		73/74	36			D2
		74/75	38			D2
		75/76	25			D2
		76/77	38			D2
Heart of Midlothian		77/78	34			D1
		78/79	18			P
Queen of the South		79/80	18			D2
		80/81	19			D2

DUNLOP William
b. 12.2.1966
Bo'ness U

Hamilton A		86/87	1			P

Hastings U
Pumpherston

DUNNE Liam
b. Dublin 1.9.1971
Bohemians

St Johnstone		91/92	9	8		P
		92/93	4	4	2	P

DURIE Gordon
b. Paisley 6.12.1965
Hill o'Beath

East Fife		81/82	8	5	1	D2
		82/83	17	8	2	D2
		83/84	32	2	16	D2
		84/85	9		7	D1
Hibernian		84/85	22		8	P
		85/86	23	2	6	P
Chelsea		85/86	1			FL
		86/87	18	7	5	FL
		87/88	26		12	FL
		88/89	32		17	FL
		89/90	14	1	5	FL
		90/91	24		12	FL
Tottenham H		91/92	31		7	FL
		92/93	17		3	FL
		93/94	10		1	FL
Rangers		93/94	23	1	12	P
		94/95	16	4	6	P
		95/96	21	6	17	P
		96/97	14	2	5	P
		97/98	14	12	4	P
		98/99	1	4		P
		99/00	1	6		P

DURRANT Ian
b. Glasgow 29.10.1966

Rangers		84/85	5			P
		85/86	30		2	P
		86/87	39		4	P
		87/88	39	1	10	P
		88/89	8		2	P
		89/90				
		90/91	3	1	1	P
		91/92	9	4		P
		92/93	19	11	3	P
		93/94	14	9		P
		94/95	16	10	4	P
Everton	L	94/95	4	1		FL
Rangers		95/96	6	9		P
		96/97	4	4		P
		97/98	1	7		P
Kilmarnock		98/99	36		4	P
		99/00	32		4	P

DZIEKANOWSKI Dariusz Pavel
b. Warsaw 30.9.1962
FSO Cars
Widzew Lodz
Legia Warsaw

Celtic		89/90	31	2	8	P
		90/91	11	3	2	P
		91/92	0	1		P
Bristol C		91/92	16	1	4	FL
		92/93	24	2	3	FL

Legia Warsaw
FC Yverdon Sports
1FC Cologne

EADIE Kenneth William
b. Paisley 26.2.1961
Johnstone Thistle

Kilmarnock		80/81	4	1	1	P
		81/82	9	5	3	D1
		82/83	6	1		P
Brechin C		83/84	19	2	5	D1
		84/85	30	4	17	D1
		85/86	34		22	D1
Falkirk		86/87	35	2	6	P
		87/88	12	3	3	P
Clydebank		87/88	14		5	D1
		88/89	34		21	D1
		89/90	37		21	D1
		90/91	38		29	D1
		91/92	39		22	D1
		92/93	36		20	D1
		93/94	19	2	11	D1
		94/95	26	3	9	D1
		95/96	26	2	10	D1
Airdrieonians		96/97	9	6	7	D1
Queen of the South		97/98	19	4	8	D2
		98/99	15	5	5	D2
		99/00	5	4	4	D2

EASTON Craig
b. Bellshill 26.2.1979

Dundee U		96/97	1	1		P
		97/98	20	9	1	P
		98/99	28	2	1	P
		99/00	22	10	1	P

EDINHO Amaral Neto Edon Do
b. Brazil 21.2.1967
Chaves
Vitoria Guimares

Bradford C		96/97	15		5	FL
		97/98	34	7	10	FL
		98/99	1	2		FL
Dunfermline A		98/99	5	4	1	P

EDVALDSSON Johannes
b. Reykjavik 3.9.1950

Valur Reykjavik						
Capetown C						
Valur Reykjavik						
Metz						
Holbaek						
Dundee U	T	74/75				
Celtic		75/76	35		7	P
		76/77	13	4	5	P
		77/78	33	3	10	P
		78/79	34		1	P
		79/80	5	3	2	P
		80/81				
Tulsa Roughnecks		81	32		5	NA
Hannover 96						
Motherwell		82/83	33		2	P
		83/84	20		4	P

EDWARDS Alexander
b. 14.3.1946

Dunfermline A		61/62	2			D1
		62/63	16		3	D1
		63/64	30		3	D1
		64/65	24		4	D1
		65/66	29		7	D1
		66/67	29		8	D1
		67/68	28		5	D1
		68/69	32		7	D1
		69/70	25	1	4	D1
		70/71	21	1	1	D1
		71/72	3	1		D1
Hibernian		71/72	16		3	D1
		72/73	26			D1
		73/74	31			D1
		74/75	12	1	1	D1
		75/76	25		1	P
		76/77	22	3		P
		77/78	5	1		P
Arbroath		78/79	6			D1
		79/80	1	2		D1

EDWARDS Keith
b. Middlesbrough 16.7.1957

Sheffield U		75/76	2	1		FL
		76/77	30	1	18	FL
		77/78	32	4	11	FL
Hull C		78/79	46		24	FL
		79/80	41		19	FL
		80/81	38	2	13	FL
		81/82	5		1	FL
Sheffield U		81/82	41		35	FL
		82/83	37	5	13	FL
		83/84	44		33	FL
		84/85	29		13	FL
		85/86	32	3	20	FL
Leeds U		86/87	24	6	6	FL
		87/88	4	4		FL
Aberdeen		87/88	6	3	2	P
Hull C		87/88	9		3	FL
		88/89	44		26	FL
		89/90	2			FL
Stockport Co		89/90	26	1	10	FL
Huddersfield T		89/90	6	4	4	FL
		90/91	10	8	4	FL
Plymouth A	L	90/91	3		1	FL

ELI Roger
b. Bradford 11.9.1965

Leeds U		84/85	0	1		FL
		85/86	1			FL
Wolverhampton W		85/86	14			FL
		86/87	2	2		FL
Cambridge U		86/87				
Crewe A		87/88	20	7	1	FL
Pontefract Colliery						
York C		88/89	3	1	1	FL
Bury		88/89	0	2		FL
Burnley		89/90	24	5		FL
		90/91	15	11	10	FL
		91/92	29	4	10	FL
		92/93	2	9		FL
Hong Kong						
Scunthorpe U		94/95	0	2		FL
Partick T		94/95	0	2		P

ELLIOT Barry Robert
b. Carlisle 24.10.1978

Celtic		96/97	0	1		P
		97/98				
Clydebank		98/99	4		2	D1

ELLIOT David
b. Glasgow 13.11.1969

Celtic BC						
Celtic		88/89	2	2		P
		89/90	0	1		P
Partick T		90/91	37		13	D1
St Mirren		91/92	21	7	1	P
		92/93	38	2	5	D1
		93/94	24	2	8	D1
		94/95	26	2	3	D1
Falkirk		95/96	31	1		P
		96/97	8	9	1	D1
Hibernian		96/97	5	2		P
		97/98	4			P
		98/99	8			D1
Partick T		99/00	10	1	2	D2

ELLIOTT John
b. Edinburgh 4.7.1980

Whitehill Welfare						
Dundee		96/97	1	3		D1
		97/98	1	16	2	D1
		98/99	8	3		P
		99/00	0	1		P

ELLIOTT Paul Marcellus
b. Lewisham 18.3.1964

Charlton A		81/82	36	2	1	FL
		82/83	25			FL
Luton T		82/83	13		1	FL
		83/84	38		2	FL
		84/85	9		1	FL
		85/86	3	3		FL
Aston Villa		85/86	23		2	FL
		86/87	33	1	5	FL
Pisa		87/88				
		88/89				
Celtic		89/90	25	1		P
		90/91	27		2	P
Chelsea		91/92	35		3	FL
		92/93	7			FL

ENGLISH Isaac
b. Paisley 12.11.1971

Partick T		89/90	3	3	2	D1
		90/91	7	6	2	D1
		91/92	12	14	5	D1
		92/93	3	10		P
		93/94	25	11	4	P
		94/95	6	5	2	P
St Johnstone		94/95	4	5		D1
		95/96	0	1		D1
Ayr U		95/96	8		5	D2
		96/97	17		7	D2
		97/98	0	1		D1
Stranraer		97/98	9	11	2	D2
		98/99				
Partick T		99/00	7	7	1	D2

ERWIN Henry
b. Bellshill 5.12.1961

Airdrieonians		78/79	1			D1
		79/80	12	4		D1
		80/81	19	2	2	P
		81/82	10	1		P
Stenhousemuir		82/83	33			D2
		83/84	35		1	D2
		84/85	33			D2
		85/86	39		8	D2
		86/87	31	1	4	D2
		87/88	36	1	7	D2
		88/89	36		5	D2
Alloa A		89/90	26	4		D1
East Stirlingshire		90/91	25	3		D2

ESKILSSON Hans
b. 23.1.1966

Heart of Midlothian		95/96	9	2	2	P

ESSANDOH Roy
b. Belfast 17.2.1976

Glentoran						
Motherwell		95/96	0	4		P
		96/97	0	1		P
Cumbernauld U						
East Fife		97/98	5			D2
Austria						
VPS Vaasa		00/01				
Wycombe W						

ESSON Ryan
b. Aberdeen 19.3.1980

Parkvale						
Aberdeen		99/00	1			P

EUSTACE John
b. Solihull 3.11.1979

Coventry C						
Dundee U		98/99	8	3	1	P
Coventry C		99/00	12	4	1	FL

EVANS Barry D
b. Glasgow 8.10.1957

Morton		75/76	21	1		D1
		76/77	23	2	2	D1
		77/78	3	3		D1
		78/79	15	2		P
		79/80				
Clydebank		80/81	31	1	2	D1
Stenhousemuir		81/82	17	1		D2
		82/83	4			D2
Queen of the South		82/83	11			D1

EVANS Gareth John
b. Coventry 14.1.1967

Coventry C		85/86	5	1		FL
		86/87	0	1		FL
Rotherham U		86/87	34		9	FL
		87/88	28	1	4	FL
Hibernian		87/88	10	2	3	P
		88/89	32	3	5	P
		89/90	23	4	3	P
		90/91	11	4	2	P
Stoke C	L	90/91	5		1	FL
Northampton T	L	90/91	2			FL
Hibernian		91/92	26	15	6	P
		92/93	23	17	6	P
		93/94	23	17	4	P
		94/95	16	8		P
		95/96	12	11	2	P
Partick T		96/97	29		9	D1
		97/98	17	3	5	D1
Airdrieonians		98/99	21	5	6	D1
		99/00	25		4	D1

FAIRLIE James
b. Baillieston 1.5.1957

Calderbank YC						
Hamilton A		74/75				
		75/76	13	2		D1
		76/77	39		5	D1
		77/78	38	1	6	D1
		78/79	36	1	13	D1
		79/80	38	1	11	D1
		80/81	33		13	D1
		81/82	33	1	10	D1
		82/83	38		15	D1
		83/84	10			D1
Airdrieonians		83/84	17	1		D1
		84/85	38		8	D1
		85/86	34	1	2	D1
		86/87	14		3	D1
Clydebank		86/87	27		1	P
Motherwell		87/88	8	4	1	P
Hamilton A		87/88	21		4	D1
		88/89	20		3	P
Clyde		88/89	7		1	D1
		89/90	19	6	2	D1

FALCO Mark Peter
b. Hackney 22.10.1960

Tottenham H		78/79	1			FL
		79/80	7	2	2	FL
		80/81	3		1	FL
		81/82	21		5	FL
		82/83	11	5	5	FL
Chelsea	L	82/83	3			FL
Tottenham H		83/84	32	4	13	FL
		84/85	42		22	FL
		85/86	40		18	FL
		86/87	5	1		FL
Watford		86/87	33		14	FL
Rangers		87/88	9	5	5	P
QPR		87/88	15	4	5	FL
		88/89	22	5	12	FL
		89/90	11	10	5	FL
		90/91	17	3	5	FL
		91/92	19	2	4	FL
Millwall						
Enfield						
Worthing						
Enfield						
Cornard						
Worthing						
Hitchin T						

FALCONER William Henry
b. Aberdeen 5.4.1966

Club		Season				
Lewis U						
Aberdeen		82/83	0	1		P
		83/84	4	4	1	P
		84/85	10	6	4	P
		85/86	2	6		P
		86/87	1	7		P
		87/88	32	4	8	P
Watford		88/89	30	3	5	FL
		89/90	23	7	3	FL
		90/91	32	3	4	FL
Middlesbrough		91/92	25		5	FL
		92/93	22	6	5	FL
Sheffield U		93/94	21	2	3	FL
Celtic		93/94	14		1	P
		94/95	19	7	4	P
		95/96	0	2		P
Motherwell		95/96	15		5	P
		96/97	21		2	P
		97/98	21	1	3	P
Dundee		98/99	31	2	4	P
		99/00	31		13	P

FALLIS Ian B
d. 1977

Club		Season				
Queens Park		72/73	18	5	7	D2
		73/74	35		12	D2
Kilmarnock		74/75	10	6	4	D1
		75/76	26		10	D1
		76/77	32	1	10	P
		77/78	4	2		D1

FALLON James
b. Cambuslang 24.3.1950

Club		Season				
Clydebank		71/72	36		6	D2
		72/73	34			D2
		73/74	34	1	5	D2
		74/75	38		1	D2
		75/76	25			D2
		76/77	39			D1
		77/78	3			P
		78/79	38		1	D1
		79/80	39		1	D1
		80/81	32	2	1	D1
		81/82	38		3	D1
		82/83	39			D1
		83/84	39			D1
		84/85	31			D1
		85/86	20			P

FANNING James

Club		Season				
Clydebank		76/77	25			D1
		77/78	3			P
		78/79	26	2	1	D1

FARMER Francis

Club		Season				
Hibernian		78/79	0	1		P
		79/80	2			P
Stirling A		80/81	2	2		D1

FARNINGHAM Raymond Paul
b. Dundee 10.4.1961

Club		Season				
Dundee Celtic BC						
Forfar A		78/79	1			D2
		79/80	36	2	5	D2
		80/81	34		4	D2
		81/82	39		5	D2
		82/83	21		3	D2
		83/84	37		6	D2
		84/85	31		4	D1
		85/86	37		2	D1
		86/87	1	1		D1
Motherwell		86/87	27	2	3	P
		87/88	25	4	6	P
		88/89	17	1	3	P
Dunfermline A		88/89	13			D1
		89/90	11	7		P
		90/91	6	4		P
		91/92	4		1	P
Partick T		91/92	33		7	D1
		92/93	35	2	8	P
		93/94	2			P
Dundee		93/94	20	4	4	P
		94/95	25	2	3	D1
		95/96	13	5	3	D1
		96/97	3	5		D1
		97/98	0	1		D1
Forfar A		97/98	9		1	D2

FARQUHAR Gary Robert
b. Wick 23.2.1971

Club		Season				
Brora R						
St Johnstone		94/95	11	6	2	D1
		95/96	10	5	1	D1
		96/97	3	2		D1
		97/98	3	1	1	P
Inverness Clachnacuddin						
Inverness CT		98/99	9	3		D2

FARRELL David
b. Glasgow 29.10.1969

Club		Season				
Hibernian		90/91	1	1		P
		91/92	3	3		P
		92/93	10	3		P
		93/94	26	9	2	P
		94/95	15	4		P
		95/96	7	1		P
Partick T		96/97	31		2	D1
		97/98	11			D1
Airdrieonians		97/98	9	4	1	D1
		98/99	20	4	1	D1
		99/00	14	2		D1

FARRELL Isaac

Club		Season				
Rangers						
Motherwell		75/76				
		76/77	1			P

FARRELL Peter John
b. Liverpool 10.1.1957

Club		Season				
Ormskirk						
Bury		75/76	1	1		FL
		76/77	31	1	4	FL
		77/78	9		4	FL
		78/79	8	3	1	FL
Port Vale		78/79	27		4	FL
		79/80	31	1	5	FL
		80/81	24	1	1	FL
		81/82	2	2		FL
Rochdale		82/83	43		9	FL
		83/84	24	1	8	FL
		84/85	4	1		FL
Crewe A		84/85	7	1	1	FL
Iceland						
Crewe A		85/86	19	1	1	FL
Sweden						
Hamilton A		86/87	3			P

FASHANU Justinus Soni
b. Hackney 19.2.1961 d. 1998

Club		Season				
Norwich C		78/79	13	3	5	FL
		79/80	31	3	11	FL
		80/81	40		19	FL
Nottingham F		81/82	31	1	3	FL
Southampton	L	82/83	9		3	FL
Notts Co		82/83	15		7	FL
		83/84	17		5	FL
		84/85	31	1	8	FL
Brighton		85/86	16		2	FL
Retired						
Manchester C		89/90	0	2		FL
West Ham U		89/90	2			FL
Leyton Orient		89/90	3	2		FL
Leatherhead		90/91				
Torquay U		91/92	21		10	FL
		92/93	20		5	FL
Airdrieonians		92/93	16		5	P
Heart of Midlothian		93/94	10	1	1	P

FAULCONBRIDGE Craig
b. Nuneaton 20.4.1978

Club		Season				
Coventry C						
Dunfermline A		97/98	0	7	1	P
		98/99	1	5		P
Wrexham		99/00	23	12	8	FL

FEENEY Lee
b. Newry 21.3.1978

Club		Season				
Linfield						
Rangers		98/99	0	1		P

FELLENGER David
b. Edinburgh 6.6.1969

Club		Season				
Hibernian		88/89	0	2		P
		89/90	8	4	1	P
		90/91	8	4	1	P
		91/92	4	2		P
		92/93	1	4	2	P
		93/94				
Cowdenbeath		94/95	23	1		D3

FERGUSON Allan Thomas
b. Lanark 21.3.1969

Club		Season				
Netherdale Community						
Armadale Thistle						
Hamilton A		87/88	6			D1
		88/89	31			P
		89/90	34			D1
		90/91	37			D1
		91/92	16			D1
		92/93	36			D1
		93/94	40			D1
		94/95	24			D1
		95/96	26			D1
		96/97	27			D2
		97/98	25			D1
St Johnstone		98/99	2	1		P
		99/00	3			P

FERGUSON Barry
b. Glasgow 2.2.1978

Club		Season				
Rangers		96/97	1			P
		97/98	6	1		P
		98/99	23		1	P
		99/00	31		4	P

FERGUSON Derek
b. Glasgow 31.7.1967

Club		Season				
Rangers		83/84	1			P
		84/85	7	1		P
		85/86	12	7		P
		86/87	26	4		P
		87/88	31	1	4	P
		88/89	12	4	2	P
		89/90	3	2		P
Dundee		89/90	4			P
Heart of Midlothian		90/91	25	3	2	P
		91/92	37	1	1	P
		92/93	37		1	P
Sunderland		93/94	41			FL
		94/95	23			FL
Falkirk		95/96	26			P
		96/97	13	1	3	D1
		97/98	0	4		D1
Dunfermline A		98/99	18	3		P
Partick T		99/00	7			D2
Ross Co		99/00	10			D2

FERGUSON Duncan
b. Stirling 27.12.1971

Club		Season				
Dundee U		90/91	8	1	1	P
		91/92	37	1	14	P
		92/93	30		12	P
Rangers		93/94	7	3	1	P
		94/95	1	3	1	P
Everton		94/95	22	1	7	FL
		95/96	16	2	5	FL
		96/97	31	2	10	FL
		97/98	28	1	11	FL
		98/99	13		4	FL
Newcastle U		98/99	7		2	FL
		99/00	17	6	6	FL

FERGUSON Eric
b. Fife 12.2.1965

Club		Season				
Clydebank		83/84	15	1	7	D1
Rangers		83/84	2	2		P
		84/85	8	1	1	P
		85/86	0	1		P
Dunfermline A		86/87	23	10	6	D1
		87/88	9	5	4	P
Clydebank *		87/88	4			D1
Raith R		88/89	6	2		D1
Cowdenbeath		88/89	10		5	D2

FERGUSON Graeme William
b. Stirling 3.3.1971

Club		Season				
Gairdoch U						
Aberdeen		91/92	0	4		P
		92/93	0	1		P
Clydebank		93/94	14	2	2	D1
		94/95	9	3		D1
Clyde		95/96	26	1		D2
		96/97	20	1		D2
Forfar A		97/98	27	1		D2
		98/99	19			D2
		99/00	3			D3

FERGUSON Iain John H
b. Newarthill 4.8.1962

Club		Season				
Fir Park BC						
Dundee		79/80	9	4	5	P
		80/81	7	4	1	D1
		81/82	34		12	P
		82/83	25	3	9	P
		83/84	33		12	P
Rangers		84/85	24	4	6	P
		85/86	1	3		P
Dundee		86/87	2	1	2	P
Dundee U		86/87	35	1	16	P
		87/88	33	6	11	P
Heart of Midlothian		88/89	23	6	5	P
		89/90	1	10	1	P
Charlton A	L	89/90	1			FL
Bristol C	L	89/90	8	3	2	FL
Heart of Midlothian		90/91	7	5	2	P
Motherwell		90/91	13	2	8	P
		91/92	9	11		P
		92/93	11	4	2	P
		93/94	1			P
Airdrieonians		93/94	26	2	9	D1
		94/95	0	3		D1
Portadown						
Dundee		96/97	5	8	1	D1

FERGUSON Ian
b. Glasgow 15.3.1967

Clyde		84/85	1	1		D1
		85/86	18	1	4	D1
		86/87	5			D1
St Mirren		86/87	35		4	P
		87/88	22		6	P
Rangers		87/88	8		1	P
		88/89	30		6	P
		89/90	21	3		P
		90/91	10	1	1	P
		91/92	12	4	1	P
		92/93	29	1	4	P
		93/94	35		5	P
		94/95	13	3	1	P
		95/96	16	2	2	P
		96/97	17	6	1	P
		97/98	9	2		P
		98/99	4	9		P
		99/00	0	2		P
Dunfermline A		99/00	12		2	D1

FERGUSON Ian
b. Dunfermline 5.8.1968

Lochgelly Albert						
Raith R		87/88	6	3	4	D1
		88/89	19	9	4	D1
		89/90	12	20	6	D1
		90/91	27	6	8	D1
		91/92	7	2	1	D1
Heart of Midlothian		91/92	12	18	4	P
		92/93	9	15	4	P
		93/94	3	3	1	P
St Johnstone		93/94	22		3	P
		94/95				
		95/96	3	7	1	D1
		96/97	3	5	2	D1
		97/98	1	1		P
Ayr U		97/98	32	1	8	D1
		98/99	9	13	8	D1
Livingston		98/99	3	1		D2
Morton		99/00	3	4		D1
Hamilton A		99/00	8	2	4	D2

FERGUSON Paul
b. Dechmont 12.3.1975

Stoneyburn U						
Motherwell		95/96	1			P
East Fife		95/96	5	1		D2

FERGUSON Riccardo R
b. Kilmarnock 8.8.1956

Bellfield YC						
Hamilton A		74/75	36			D2
		75/76	26			D1
		76/77	37			D1
		77/78	36			D1
		78/79	39			D1
		79/80	35			D1
		80/81	38			D1
		81/82	36			D1
		82/83	36			D1
		83/84	27			D1
		84/85	39			D1
		85/86	37			D1
Morton	L	86/87	1			D1
Hamilton A		86/87	8			P
		87/88	22			D1
Partick T	L	87/88	1			D1
Queen of the South		88/89	28			D1

FERRAZ Joaquim Miguel Leitao de Freitas
b. Parades 16.5.1974

Belenenses						
Dundee U		99/00	15	13	6	P

FERRERA Juan Francisco
b. Uruguay 13.7.1970

Defensor						
Dundee U		94/95	0	1		P

FERREYRA Victor
b. Cordoba 24.2.1965

San Lorenzo						
Dundee U		91/92	20	3	5	P
		92/93	3	4		P
Mitsubishi						

FILIPPI Joseph
b. Ayrshire 3.11.1953

Prestwick Star						
Coventry C		69/70				
Ayr U		70/71	3			D1
		71/72	33		3	D1
		72/73	27			D1
		73/74	31	1	2	D1
		74/75	29	1	2	D1
		75/76	18	1		P
		76/77	34		3	P
		77/78	6	3		P
Celtic		77/78	11	1		P
		78/79	19	1		P
		79/80				
Clyde		80/81	35	1		D2
Glenafton A						

FINDLAY William McCall
b. Kilmarnock 29.8.1970

Hibernian		88/89	2	1	1	P
		89/90	5	4		P
		90/91	21	5	2	P
		91/92	8	1		P
		92/93	3	4		P
		93/94	15	5	3	P
		94/95	12	6	1	P
Kilmarnock		94/95	5	4		P
		95/96	2	1		P
		96/97	15	4	1	P
		97/98	2	3		P
Ayr U		97/98	6		1	D1
		98/99	15	7	2	D1
Queen of the South		99/00	3	4	1	D2

FINNIGAN Anthony
b. Wimbledon 17.10.1962

Fulham						
Corinthian Casuals						
Crystal Palace		84/85	10	1	1	FL
		85/86	34	2	3	FL
		86/87	36	5	6	FL
		87/88	14	3		FL
Blackburn R		88/89	13	4		FL
		89/90	8	11		FL
Hull C		90/91	15	3	1	FL
Swindon T		90/91	2	1		FL
Hong Kong						
Brentford		91/92	3			FL
Hong Kong						
Barnet		92/93				
Dulwich Hamlet						
Fulham		94/95	7	4		FL
		95/96	1	1		FL
Falkirk		95/96	8	1	1	P

FITZGERALD Darren
b. Belfast 13.10.1978

Rangers		94/95				
		95/96				
		96/97	0	1		P
		97/98				

FITZPATRICK Anthony Charles
b. Glasgow 3.3.1956

St Mirren		73/74	4	5		D2
		74/75	20		2	D2
		75/76	22	2		D1
		76/77	36	1	2	P
		77/78	34		2	P
		78/79	36		3	P
Bristol C		79/80	41			FL
		80/81	34		1	FL
St Mirren		81/82	24		1	P
		82/83	26		2	P
		83/84	28			P
		84/85	30		1	P
		85/86	29		3	P
		86/87	23	4		P
		87/88	24	2	1	P
		88/89	0	1		P

FLAVELL Robert William
b. Berwick 7.3.1956

Burnley		73/74				
		74/75				
		75/76				
Halifax T		75/76	14			FL
		76/77	33		3	FL
		77/78	44		4	FL
Chesterfield		78/79	27	2	2	FL
Barnsley		79/80	25			FL
Halifax T		80/81	1			FL
Vaster Haminge						
Hibernian		81/82	27	5	1	P
		82/83	3	1		P
Motherwell		82/83	25	1	6	P
		83/84	2	3		P
Dundee U		83/84	0	1		P
Berwick R		83/84	18	1	1	D2
		84/85	16			D2

FLECK Robert William
b. Glasgow 11.8.1965

Rangers		83/84	1			P
Partick T	L	83/84	1	1	1	D1
Rangers		84/85	1	7		P
		85/86	9	6	3	P
		86/87	35	5	19	P
		87/88	15	6	7	P
Norwich C		87/88	18		7	FL
		88/89	29	4	10	FL
		89/90	25	2	7	FL
		90/91	23	6	5	FL
		91/92	35	1	11	FL
Chelsea		92/93	28	3	2	FL
		93/94	7	2	1	FL
Bolton W	L	93/94	6	1	1	FL
Chelsea		94/95				
Bristol C	L	94/95	10		1	FL
Norwich C		95/96	37	4	10	FL
		96/97	33	3	4	FL
		97/98	23	4	2	FL
Reading		97/98	3	2		FL
		98/99	2	2	1	FL

FLEETING James Taylor
b. Glasgow 8.4.1955

Kilbirnie Ladeside						
Norwich C		76/77	0	1		FL
		77/78				
Tampa Bay Rowdies		78	28		2	NA
Ayr U		78/79	16			D1
		79/80	35	1	2	D1
		80/81	39		3	D1
		81/82	31	4		D1
		82/83	20			D1
Clyde		83/84	1	1		D1
Morton		84/85	5		1	P
Clyde		85/86	15	4	1	D1

FLEMING Christopher G
b. Maybole ?.?.1957

Maybole Jnrs						
Kilmarnock		74/75				
		75/76	1			D1
		76/77	1			P
Stranraer *		77/78	15	6	1	D2
Jnr football		78/79				
		79/80				
		80/81				
		81/82				
		82/83				
Brechin C		83/84	5	7		D1

FLEMING Derek Adam
b. Falkirk 5.12.1973

Broxburn A						
Meadowbank T		92/93	3	1		D1
		93/94	38		2	D2
		94/95	7		1	D2
Dunfermline A		94/95	29		1	D1
		95/96	25	8	3	D1
		96/97	23	3	2	P
		97/98	1	1		P
Dundee		97/98	15	2		D1
Livingston		97/98	9		2	D2
Dundee		98/99	1			P
Livingston		98/99	14	1	3	D2
		99/00	17	8	1	D1

FLEMING George
b. Edinburgh 22.9.1948

Salvesens BC						
Heart of Midlothian		64/65				
		65/66				
		66/67	16		1	D1
		67/68	19	9	5	D1
		68/69	30	1	5	D1
		69/70	19	5	3	D1
		70/71	26	4	7	D1
		71/72	2	1		D1
Dundee U		71/72	12		1	D1
		72/73	31		3	D1
		73/74	31	1	4	D1
		74/75	25		5	D1
		75/76	30	2	3	P
		76/77	28	3	1	P
		77/78	36		9	P
		78/79	33		3	P
		79/80	23	2	2	P
St Johnstone		80/81	39		1	D1
		81/82	36	1		D1
		82/83	15	4		D1

FLEMING Ian John Hosea
b. Maybole 15.1.1953
Craigmark Bruntonians

Kilmarnock	70/71	1			D1
	71/72	4	1	1	D1
	72/73	12	1	1	D1
	73/74	32	1	33	D2
	74/75	27	2	11	D1
	75/76	9	4	5	D1
Aberdeen	75/76	11	1	2	P
	76/77	13	4	4	P
	77/78	20	5	5	P
	78/79	4	8	1	P
Sheffield W	78/79	6		1	FL
	79/80	7			FL
Dundee	79/80	16		3	P
	80/81	7	1	1	D1
	81/82	13	3	1	P
	82/83	8			P
Brechin C	82/83	24		4	D1
	83/84	33	5	10	D1
	84/85	15	4		D1
	85/86	35		1	D1
	86/87	15	1		D1

FLEMING Richard

Rangers					
Kilwinning R					
Ayr U	68/69				
	69/70	34			D1
	70/71	34			D1
	71/72	12			D1
	72/73	33		7	D1
	73/74	34		1	D1
	74/75	34		2	D1
	75/76	31		1	P
	76/77	32			P
	77/78	34	1		P
Hibernian	78/79	11	1		P
Berwick R	79/80	12			D1

FLETCHER John Ernest
b. Hertfordshire 11.4.1953

Arbroath	71/72	19		9	D2
	72/73	3	8		P
	73/74	32		8	P
	74/75	32	2	4	P
	75/76	17	2	4	D1
	76/77	33	1	9	D1
	77/78	36		9	D1
	78/79	30	2	5	D1
Dundee	79/80	12	4	1	P
	80/81	6	1	1	D1
Montrose	81/82	15	3	4	D2
	82/83	22	4	4	D2

FLIES Brian
b. Netherlands

Dundee U T	93/94	1			P

FLOGEL Thomas
b. Vienna 7.6.1971

Austria Vienna	89/90				
	90/91				
	91/92				
	92/93				
	93/94				
	94/95				
	95/96				
	96/97				
Heart of Midlothian	97/98	13	16	5	P
	98/99	18	2	2	P
	99/00	28	1	1	P

FLOOD John Gerard
b. Glasgow 25.12.1960

Sheffield U	78/79	5	2		FL
	79/80	10	1	1	FL
	80/81	1			FL
Airdrieonians	80/81	13		3	P
	81/82	25	3	2	P
	82/83	24	1	9	D1
	83/84	33	3	11	D1
	84/85	37		17	D1
	85/86	26	4	11	D1
	86/87	41	2	8	D1
	87/88	35	3	7	D1
Partick T	88/89	33	2	8	D1
	89/90	26	7	9	D1
	90/91	7		1	D1
	91/92	4	2		D1

FORBES Graeme Scott Alexander
b. Forfar 29.7.1958
Lochee U

Motherwell	80/81	26	2	4	D1
	81/82	31		6	D1
	82/83	17	8	1	P
	83/84	28	4	1	P
	84/85	34	2	4	D1
	85/86	27			P
	86/87	5			P
Walsall	86/87	40		3	FL
	87/88	44		3	FL
	88/89	45		1	FL
	89/90	44		2	FL
	90/91				
Dundee	91/92	3			D1
Montrose	91/92	9			D1
	92/93	12			D2

FORD Donald
b. Linlithgow 25.10.1944
Vale of Avon
Bo'ness U

Heart of Midlothian	64/65	7		2	D1
	65/66	9			D1
	66/67	5			D1
	67/68	29		11	D1
	68/69	23	4	6	D1
	69/70	24	5	8	D1
	70/71	32		11	D1
	71/72	30		15	D1
	72/73	32		9	D1
	73/74	29		18	D1
	74/75	21	1	13	D1
	75/76	2			P
Falkirk	76/77	19	2	5	D1

FORD Robert Alan Cameron
b. Edinburgh 14.12.1949

Falkirk	68/69	2			D1
	69/70	19		1	D2
	70/71	6	5	1	D1
	71/72	0	3		D1
Dundee	71/72	19	1		D1
	72/73	19	4	2	D1
	73/74	31		1	D1
	74/75	28		1	D1
	75/76	29	1	2	P
	76/77	34	3	4	D1
	77/78	13	5		D1
Montrose	78/79	25		1	D1
Raith R	78/79	12		1	D1
	79/80	37		7	D1
	80/81	36	1	1	D1
	81/82	25	8	3	D1
Dunfermline A	82/83	8	2		D1
Meadowbank T	82/83	10	3		D2

FORREST Gordon Ian
b. Dunfermline 14.1.1977

Raith R	95/96	0	1		P
Livingston	96/97	5		1	D2
	97/98	26	1	4	D2
	98/99	2	3		D2
East Fife	99/00	23	3	1	D3

FORREST Robert
b. Hamilton 9.8.1960
Penicuik A

Dunfermline A	81/82	8	3	1	D1
	82/83	34	1	8	D1
	83/84	26	6	3	D2
	84/85	37		1	D2
	85/86	36		2	D2
	86/87	40	1	1	D1
	87/88	3			P
Arbroath	87/88	22		12	D2
	88/89	23	6	7	D2
Meadowbank T	88/89	7		2	D1
	89/90	19	8	6	D2
	90/91	18	8	6	D1

FORSYTH Alan
b. Glasgow 23.4.1955

Dundee U	75/76	14			P
	76/77	5	1		P
	77/78	1			P
Raith R	78/79	31			D1
	79/80	34		3	D1
	80/81	33		5	D1
	81/82	31		1	D1
	82/83	17			D1
	83/84	9		1	D1
Dunfermline A	83/84	20		1	D2
	84/85	17	1		D2

FORSYTH Alexander
b. Swinton 5.2.1952

Partick T	68/69	0	1		D1
	69/70				
	70/71				
	71/72	33		4	P
	72/73	17		1	P
Manchester U	72/73	8			FL
	73/74	18	1	1	FL
	74/75	39		1	FL
	75/76	28		2	FL
	76/77	3	1		FL
	77/78	3			FL
Rangers	78/79	16		4	P
	79/80	8		1	P
	80/81	1			P
	81/82				
Motherwell	82/83	18	1		P
Hamilton A	83/84	34		3	D1
	84/85	28	1	6	D1
Queen of the South	85/86	1	1		D2

FORSYTH Stewart
b. Inch 26.10.1961

Arbroath	79/80	9	3		D1
	80/81	27	1	1	D2
	81/82	27		1	D2
	82/83	33			D2
	83/84	35		1	D2
	84/85	4			D2
Dundee	84/85	10	3		P
	85/86	7	2	1	P
	86/87	25	3		P
	87/88	41		1	P
	88/89	33			P
	89/90	33	1	1	P
	90/91	18	3		D1
	91/92	11	4		D1
Montrose	92/93	14		1	D2

FORSYTH Thomas
b. Glasgow 23.1.1949
Stonehouse Thistle

Motherwell	67/68	12	2		D1
	68/69	33		13	D2
	69/70	34			P
	70/71	33		3	P
	71/72	32			P
	72/73	5		1	P
Rangers	72/73	21			D1
	73/74	18			P
	74/75	30		1	P
	75/76	28		1	P
	76/77	25			P
	77/78	31			P
	78/79	17			P
	79/80	16			P
	80/81	15	7		P
	81/82	12			P

FOSTER Wayne Paul
b. Leigh 11.9.1963

Bolton W	81/82	20	3	2	FL
	82/83	21	3	4	FL
	83/84	27	3	3	FL
	84/85	24	4	4	FL
Preston NE	85/86	25	6	3	FL
Heart of Midlothian	86/87	23	8	4	P
	87/88	23	6	4	P
	88/89	8	1	1	P
	89/90	14	3	1	P
	90/91	21	7	1	P
	91/92	1	6		P
	92/93	7	4		P
	93/94	8	10	1	P
	94/95				
Hartlepool U L	94/95	4		1	FL
Partick T	94/95	16		7	P
	95/96	19		1	P
Falkirk	96/97	10	4	1	D1
St Mirren	96/97	8		2	D1
Livingston	97/98	5	9	3	D2

FOTHERINGHAM Mark
b. Dundee 22.10.1983

Celtic	99/00	1	1		P

FOURNA David
b. Dumbarton 28.10.1963
Pollok Jnrs

Clydebank	86/87	5	1		P
	87/88	6	4	1	D1

FOWLER James
b. Stirling 26.10.1980

Kilmarnock	99/00	1	4		P

FRAIL Stephen Charles
b. Glasgow 10.8.1969

Dundee		87/88	2	2		P
		88/89	21	2	1	P
		89/90	6			P
		90/91	25	1		D1
		91/92	2	1		D1
		92/93	7			P
		93/94	28	4		P
Heart of Midlothian		93/94	9		2	P
		94/95	25		2	P
		95/96				
		96/97	4	5		P
		97/98	6	5		P
Tranmere R		97/98	4	2		FL
		98/99	5			FL
St Johnstone		99/00	9			P

FRAME Alexander

Partick T		75/76	2	2		D1
		76/77	3	1	1	P
		77/78	6		2	P

FRANCIS Trevor John
b. Plymouth 19.4.1954

Birmingham C		70/71	21	1	15	FL
		71/72	39		12	FL
		72/73	31		6	FL
		73/74	37		6	FL
		74/75	23		13	FL
		75/76	35		17	FL
		76/77	42		21	FL
		77/78	42		25	FL
		78/79	8	1	3	FL
Nottingham F		78/79	19	1	6	FL
		79/80	30		14	FL
		80/81	18		6	FL
		81/82	2			FL
Manchester C		81/82	26		12	FL
Sampdoria		82/83				
		83/84				
		84/85				
		85/86				
		86/87				
Rangers		87/88	8	10		P
QPR		87/88	8	1		FL
		88/89	19		7	FL
		89/90	3	1	5	FL
Sheffield W		89/90	10	2		FL
		90/91	18	20	4	FL
		91/92	0	20	1	FL
		92/93	1	4		FL
		93/94	0	1		FL

FRASER Alexander W
b. Glasgow 31.8.1967

Hamilton Thistle						
Celtic						
Hamilton A		87/88	2			D1
		88/89	2	6		P
Portadown						

FRASER Campbell Grant
b. Dundee 22.7.1957

Heart of Midlothian		75/76	5	10		P
		76/77	20	2		P
		77/78	39		2	D1
		78/79	36		3	P
		79/80	36		12	D1
		80/81	0	1	1	P
Dundee		80/81	30		5	D1
		81/82	31		6	P
		82/83	34		5	P
		83/84	29		3	P
Rangers		84/85	27	1	3	P
		85/86	7	1	2	P
		86/87	16		1	P
Raith R		87/88	24		1	D1
		88/89	23		3	D1
		89/90	23		2	D1
		90/91	13			D1
Dundee		90/91	7			D1
		91/92	12			D1
Montrose		91/92	8			D1
		92/93	18		5	D2

FRASER Gary
b. Glasgow 1.11.1965

Gartcosh						
Queens Park		83/84	11	4	3	D2
		84/85	22	6	5	D2
		85/86	31	5	11	D2
Motherwell		86/87	2	6		P
		87/88	8	6		P
Queen of the South		88/89	31		7	D1
		89/90	17		5	D2
		90/91	22	6	3	D2
		91/92	3	7		D2
		92/93	6	4		D2

FRASER John
b. Dunfermline 17.1.1978

Oakley U						
Dunfermline A		96/97	2			P
		97/98	3	4		P
		98/99	2	4		P
Ross Co		99/00	16	10	1	D2

FRASER Scott
b. Edinburgh 28.4.1963

Rangers		83/84	7			P
		84/85	0	2		P
East Fife		85/86	4			D1
Berwick R *		85/86	13	2	1	D2
Fawkner Azzuri						
Berwick R		89/90	37		3	D2
		90/91	22	6		D2
Cowdenbeath		91/92	19	10	2	D2

FRENCH Hamish Mackie
b. Aberdeen 7.2.1964

Keith						
Dundee U		87/88	20	1	2	P
		88/89	12	6	3	P
		89/90	7	5	2	P
		90/91	16	3	3	P
		91/92	5	1	1	P
Dunfermline A		91/92	31		2	P
		92/93	36	2	12	D1
		93/94	31	5	15	D1
		94/95	24	1	12	D1
		95/96	21	2	4	D1
		96/97	34	1	3	P
		97/98	33	1	2	P
		98/99	15	6	2	P
		99/00	13	8	3	D1

FRIAR John Paul
b. Glasgow 6.6.1963

Leicester C		80/81	15			FL
		81/82	23			FL
		82/83	18	2		FL
Rotherham U		82/83	15			FL
		83/84	5			FL
Motherwell	L	83/84	1	1		P
Charlton A		84/85	32			FL
		85/86	4			FL
Northampton T	L	85/86	14			FL
Aldershot		86/87	29		1	FL
Dover A		87/88				
		88/89				
		89/90				
		90/91				
Partick T		91/92	1			D1
East Stirlingshire		91/92	11		2	D2
		92/93	0	1		D2
Albion R		93/94	0	1		D2
		94/95				
		95/96	5			D3

FRIDGE Leslie Francis
b. Inverness 27.8.1968

Chelsea		85/86	1			FL
St Mirren		86/87	1			P
		87/88	3			P
Stirling A	L	87/88	3			D2
Arbroath		87/88	1			D2
St Mirren		88/89	15			P
		89/90	8			P
		90/91	10			P
		91/92	17			P
		92/93	18			D1
Clyde		93/94	42			D1
		94/95	25	1		D2
Raith R		95/96	1			P
Irish football		96/97				
Inverness CT		97/98	15			D2
		98/99	14			D2
		99/00	27			D1

FRITH James J
b. Motherwell 28.12.1969

Rangers						
Hamilton A		87/88	1	3	1	D1
		88/89	0	2		P
Brechin C	L	88/89	4		1	D2
Cowdenbeath		89/90	2	5		D2
Larkhall Thistle						

FRYE James F
b. Irvine 2.2.1956

Queen of the South		75/76	2	2		D1
Stranraer		76/77	39		24	D2
		77/78	39		27	D2
Dundee U		78/79	5	4	1	P
Ayr U		79/80	37		16	D1
		80/81	25	5	10	D1
		81/82	28	7	13	D1
		82/83	22	7	7	D1
		83/84	2			D1
Clyde		83/84	30		17	D1
		84/85	37		19	D1
		85/86	27	3	12	D1
Airdrieonians		86/87	13	8	2	D1
Queen of the South		87/88	14	15	7	D1
		88/89				
		89/90				
		90/91				
		91/92				
		92/93	0	1		D2

FULLARTON James
b. Glasgow 20.7.1974

St Mirren		91/92	0	1		P
		92/93	24	1		D1
		93/94	37			D1
		94/95	13	4	1	D1
		95/96	19	3	2	D1
Bastia		96/97				
Crystal Palace		97/98	19	6	1	FL
		98/99	7			FL
Bolton W	L	98/99	1			FL

FULTON David
b. Glasgow 2.9.1966

Clydebank		86/87	2	3	1	P
		87/88	2	6		D1
Dumbarton		88/89	7			D2

FULTON Mark A J
b. Johnstone 16.9.1959

Johnstone Burgh						
St Mirren		79/80	28			P
		80/81	25			P
		81/82	28	1		P
		82/83	30		3	P
		83/84	28	2	1	P
		84/85	18		1	P
Hibernian		85/86	29	1		P
		86/87	9			P
Hamilton A		86/87	15			P
		87/88	4			D1

FULTON Stephen
b. Greenock 10.8.1970

Celtic BC						
Celtic		88/89	1	2		P
		89/90	13	3		P
		90/91	19	2		P
		91/92	18	12	2	P
		92/93	3	3		P
Bolton W		93/94	4			FL
Peterborough U	L	93/94	3			FL
Falkirk		94/95	25	3	3	P
		95/96	4	1		P
Heart of Midlothian		95/96	26		2	P
		96/97	25	4	1	P
		97/98	36		5	P
		98/99	27		2	P
		99/00	16	10	1	P

FYFE Graham
b. 18.8.1951

Rangers		69/70	4			D1
		70/71	11	3	3	P
		71/72	9	5	6	P
		72/73	3	3	2	P
		73/74	7	6	7	P
		74/75	6	4	4	P
		75/76	1	2		P
Hibernian		76/77	9	1	1	P
Dumbarton		77/78	28		4	D1
		78/79	25	6	7	D1

GAHAGAN John

b. Glasgow 24.8.1958

Clydebank		77/78	4	1		P
Shettleston		78/79				
Motherwell		79/80	14	3	3	D1
		80/81	25	9	1	D1
		81/82	37	2	7	D1
		82/83	26	2	4	P
		83/84	25	5	7	P
		84/85	17	14	5	D1
		85/86	13	8	3	P
		86/87	5	14		P
		87/88	11	12		P
		88/89	10	4	2	P
		89/90	7	19	3	P
		90/91	1			P
Morton		90/91	34	1	6	D1
		91/92	6	2	2	D1
		92/93	16	3	2	D1
		93/94	7	6		D1

GALLACHER James

b. Clydebank 29.3.1951

Arbroath						
Clydebank		72/73	18			D2
		73/74	35			D2
		74/75	35			D2
		75/76				
		76/77	36			D1
		77/78	30			P
		78/79	35			D1
		79/80	39			D1
		80/81	36			D1
		81/82	39			D1
		82/83	35			D1
		83/84	39			D1
		84/85	37			D1
		85/86	35			P
		86/87	38			P
		87/88	33			D1
		88/89	33			D1
		89/90	34			D1
		90/91	24			D1
		91/92	2			D1

GALLACHER John Anthony

b. Glasgow 26.1.1969

Falkirk		87/88	0	2		P
		88/89	9	7	5	D1
Newcastle U		89/90	21	7	6	FL
		90/91	1			FL
		91/92				
Hartlepool U		92/93	16	5	1	FL
		93/94	2		1	FL
Falkirk		93/94	2	4		D1
Berwick R		94/95	11	8	2	D2
		95/96	4			D2

GALLACHER Kevin William

b. Clydebank 23.11.1966

Duntocher BC						
Dundee U		85/86	19	1	3	P
		86/87	29	8	10	P
		87/88	24	2	4	P
		88/89	29	2	9	P
		89/90	17		1	P
Coventry C		89/90	15		3	FL
		90/91	32		11	FL
		91/92	33		8	FL
		92/93	19	1	6	FL
Blackburn R		92/93	9		5	FL
		93/94	27	3	7	FL
		94/95	1		1	FL
		95/96	14	2	2	FL
		96/97	34		10	FL
		97/98	31	2	16	FL
		98/99	13	3	5	FL
		99/00	3	2		FL
Newcastle U		99/00	15	5	2	FL

GALLACHER Paul James

b. Glasgow 16.8.1979

Lochee U						
Dundee U		99/00	1			P
Airdrieonians	L	99/00	9			D1

GALLACHER Stuart

b. Bangour 25.2.1972

Dunfermline A		90/91	1			P
		91/92				
		92/93				
Berwick R		93/94	2	2		D2

GALLAGHER Brian

b. Glasgow 8.9.1958

Radnor Park Juveniles						
Dumbarton		77/78	33	1	10	D1
		78/79	32		8	D1
		79/80	39		11	D1
		80/81	33		14	D1
Kilmarnock		81/82	34	1	10	D1
		82/83	33	1	9	P
		83/84	34	1	11	D1
St Mirren		84/85	30	2	9	P
		85/86	30	1	6	P
		86/87	18	5	1	P
		87/88	8	5		P
Partick T		88/89	11	2	1	D1
		89/90	15	7		D1
		90/91	3	2	1	D1
Albion R *		91/92	10			D2

GALLAGHER Edward Adam

b. Glasgow 21.11.1964

Harmony Row						
Campsie Black Watch						
Partick T		85/86	14	9	4	D1
		86/87	14	16	5	D1
		87/88	31	3	13	D1
		88/89	3		2	D1
Hamilton A		88/89	12	2	3	P
Dunfermline A		88/89	4	3	1	D1
		89/90	4	10	1	P
		90/91	1	2		P
		91/92	3	1		P
Dundee		91/92	14	9	11	D1
		92/93	2	2		P
St Mirren		92/93	18	1	12	D1
		93/94	11	5	5	D1

GALLAGHER John

b. 12.12.1951

Heart of Midlothian		71/72	3			D1
		72/73	5			D1
		73/74	5			D1
		74/75	4			D1
		75/76	14			P
		76/77	35		4	P
		77/78	7			D1
Dumbarton		78/79	39			D1
		79/80	38			D1
		80/81	23			D1
		81/82	31			D1

GALLOWAY Michael

b. Oswestry 30.5.1965

Holyrood Star						
Tynecastle BC						
Berwick R						
Mansfield T		83/84	12	5		FL
		84/85	23	8	3	FL
		85/86	4	2		FL
Halifax T		85/86	19			FL
		86/87	43		3	FL
		87/88	17		2	FL
Heart of Midlothian		87/88	22	3	6	P
		88/89	30	1	2	P
Celtic		89/90	29	4	2	P
		90/91	3	4	1	P
		91/92	26	8	2	P
		92/93	29	1	3	P
		93/94	16	6		P
		94/95	11			P
Leicester C	L	94/95	4	1		FL

GALLOWAY Steven George

b. Hannover 13.2.1963

Sutton U						
Crystal Palace		84/85	2	2	1	FL
		85/86	1			FL
Cambridge U	L	85/86	1			FL
?		86/87				
		87/88				
St Mirren		88/89	2	2		P

GARCIN Eric

b. Avignon 6.12.1965

Toulouse						
Motherwell		97/98	7	4	1	P
Dundee		98/99	2	1		P

GARDINER John

b. Glasgow 2.4.1958

Aberdeen		78/79	2			P
Dundee U		79/80				
		80/81				
Airdrieonians	L	80/81	10			P
Dundee U		81/82				
Forfar A	L	81/82	5			D2
Dundee U		82/83				
		83/84	2			P
Motherwell		84/85	24			D1
		85/86	32			P
		86/87	22			P
Montrose *		87/88	1			D2

GARDNER James

b. Dunfermline 27.9.1967

Queens Park		86/87	1			D2
		87/88	0	1		D2
		88/89				
Motherwell		89/90	1			P
		90/91				
		91/92	6	6		P
		92/93	1	2		P
St Mirren		93/94	14	7	1	D1
		94/95	17	3		D1
Stirling A		95/96	29		1	D1

GARDNER Patrick

b. Dunfermline ?.?.1943

Belshill A						
Queen of the South		62/63	1			D1
		63/64	19		2	D1
Raith R		64/65				
		65/66				
		66/67				
Dunfermline A		67/68	32		11	D1
		68/69	30		12	D1
		69/70	29	2	7	D1
		70/71	33		8	D1
		71/72	12	2	3	D1
Dundee U		71/72	11			D1
		72/73	33		13	D1
		73/74	21	3	4	D1
		74/75	7		1	D1
Motherwell		74/75	17	1	1	D1
		75/76	12	4	4	P
Arbroath		76/77	32	5	2	D1

GARDNER Robert Lee

b. Ayr 11.7.1970

Aberdeen		87/88	1			P
		88/89				
		89/90				
		90/91				
Oxford U	L	90/91	2	5		FL
Ayr U		91/92	16			D1
		92/93	2			D1
Meadowbank T		93/94	10	6		D2
Arbroath		94/95	22	1	6	D3
		95/96	15	2	3	D3
		96/97	10			D3
Albion R		96/97	16		5	D3
		97/98	32		10	D3
		98/99	24	11	2	D3
Clydebank		99/00	33	1	4	D1

GARNER William

b. Stirling 24.7.1955

Campsie Black Watch						
Aberdeen		75/76	7	1		P
		76/77	36			P
		77/78	35		1	P
		78/79	12			P
		79/80	20			P
		80/81	2			P
Celtic		81/82	1			P
Alloa A		82/83	35		5	D1
Rochdale	L	82/83	4			FL
Alloa A		83/84	20		2	D1
Cove R						
Rosslyn Sports						
Keith						
Berwick R		90/91	19	1	1	D2
		91/92	27			D2

GASCOIGNE Paul John
b. Gateshead 27.5.1967

Newcastle U	84/85	0	2		FL
	85/86	28	3	9	FL
	86/87	21	3	5	FL
	87/88	34	1	7	FL
Tottenham H	88/89	31	1	6	FL
	89/90	34		6	FL
	90/91	26		7	FL
Lazio	91/92				
	92/93				
	93/94				
	94/95				
Rangers	95/96	27	1	14	P
	96/97	23	3	13	P
	97/98	14	6	3	P
Middlesbrough	97/98	7			FL
	98/99	25	1	3	FL
	99/00	7	1	1	FL

GATTUSO Gennaro Ivan
b. Corigliano Calabro 9.1.1978

Perugia	95/96				
	96/97				
Rangers	97/98	22	7	3	P
	98/99	3	2		P
Salernita	98/99				
AC Milan	99/00				

GAULD Stuart R Thomas
b. Edinburgh 26.3.1964

Heart of Midlothian	81/82	2			D1
	82/83	17			D1
	83/84	2	1		P

GAVIGAN Edward
b. Glasgow 7.12.1963

Morton	81/82	1			P
	82/83	7	9	1	P

GAVIN Mark
b. Holytown 10.12.1963

Rochdale					
Heart of Midlothian	87/88	5	2		P
	88/89	0	2		P
?	89/90				
	90/91				
	91/92				
	92/93				
	93/94				
	94/95				
	95/96				
	96/97				
Morton	97/98	1			D1

GEDDES Alexander Robert
b. Inverness 12.8.1960

Ross Co					
Dundee	80/81	20			D1
	81/82	28			P
	82/83	1			P
	83/84	24			P
	84/85	16			P
	85/86	36			P
	86/87	44			P
	87/88	38			P
	88/89	34			P
	89/90	12			P
Kilmarnock	90/91	10			D1
	91/92	38			D1
	92/93	33			D1
	93/94	44			P
	94/95	12			P
	95/96	2			P
Raith R	95/96	9			P
	96/97	3			P
	97/98				
	98/99				
Brechin C	99/00	36			D3

GEDDES Andrew
b. 27.10.1959

Dundee	80/81	18		7	D1
	81/82				
	82/83				
	83/84	9	2	2	P

GEMMELL Thomas
b. Glasgow 16.10.1943

Meadow Thistle Amateurs					
Coltness U					
Celtic	61/62				
	62/63	2			D1
	63/64	31			D1
	64/65	30		3	D1
	65/66	34		4	D1
	66/67	34		9	D1
	67/68	34		4	D1
	68/69	31		8	D1
	69/70	29		9	D1
	70/71	19		1	D1
	71/72	3			D1
Nottingham F	71/72	18		5	FL
	72/73	21		1	FL
Miami Toros					
Dundee	73/74	30		1	D1
	74/75	25			D1
	75/76	16	3	3	P
	76/77	20		4	D1

GEOGHEGAN Andrew

Petershill					
Aberdeen	71/72	5			D1
	72/73	1			D1
	73/74				
	74/75	1			D1
	75/76	16			P
Ayr U	76/77	21			P
	77/78	1			P
St Johnstone	77/78	16			D1
	78/79	20			D1
	79/80	2			D1

GERVAISE Anthony
b. Paisley 10.5.1955

Eadie Star					
Clydebank	77/78	4		1	P
	78/79	1	3		D1
	79/80	30	2		D1
	80/81	31		1	D1
	81/82	26	2		D1
	82/83	33			D1
	83/84	32			D1
Hamilton A	84/85	8	1		D1
Queen of the South	85/86	28	2		D2
Stranraer *	86/87	5	1		D2

GIBSON Andrew
b. Dechmont 2.2.1969

Gairdoch U					
Stirling A	87/88	4	1		D2
	88/89	4	8	1	D2
Aberdeen	89/90				
	90/91				
	91/92	2	3		P
	92/93	1		1	P
	93/94	1	1		P
Partick T	93/94	6	5		P
	94/95	9	2	1	P
	95/96	8	14	1	P
Clyde	96/97	33	2	2	D2
	97/98	33		4	D2
Forfar A *	98/99	8	1	1	D2

GIBSON Charles
b. Dumbarton 12.6.1961

St Anthonys					
Shrewsbury T	81/82	2	4		FL
East Stirlingshire	82/83	30	7	6	D2
	83/84	36	1	13	D2
	84/85	14		6	D2
Clydebank	84/85	9	5	2	D1
	85/86	11	5	1	P
	86/87	3			P
Stenhousemuir L	86/87	5			D2
Stirling A	86/87	27		7	D2
	87/88	37		9	D2
	88/89	39		18	D2
Dumbarton	89/90	36		20	D2
	90/91	25	1	4	D2
	91/92	37		9	D2
	92/93	36	6	7	D1
	93/94	44		13	D1
	94/95	21	5	6	D2
	95/96	23	6	2	D1

GIBSON Ian
b. Hamilton 24.7.1956

Partick T	76/77	12	1	2	P
	77/78	32		4	P
	78/79	21	4		P
	79/80	23	5	2	P
	80/81	8		2	P
Dundee U	80/81	13	1	1	P
	81/82	4	3		P
Morton	82/83	6	1	1	P
Dundee U	82/83				
St Johnstone	82/83	7		1	D1
	83/84	31	3	3	P
	84/85	21	5	1	D1
	85/86	33		1	D2
	86/87	30		3	D2
Raith R	87/88	30	1	4	D1
	88/89	37		5	D1
Arbroath	89/90	23	1	1	D2
	90/91	3			D2

GIBSON Ian
b. Fenwick 3.2.1956

Nairn Co					
Aberdeen	75/76	0	2		P
	76/77	0	1	1	P
	77/78	9		3	P
Kilmarnock	78/79	24		9	D1
	79/80	31	1	3	P
	80/81	10	3		P
Canberra					
Altrincham					
South Liverpool					

GIBSON James
b. Bellshill 19.2.1980

Rangers	99/00	0	1		P

GIBSON John
b. Hull 23.12.1950

Clydebank BG					
Clydebank Star					
Partick T	67/68				
	68/69	3		1	D1
	69/70	0	1		D1
	70/71				
	71/72	13	7	5	D1
	72/73	18	2	3	D1
	73/74	20	6	3	D1
	74/75	3	3	1	D1
Ayr U	74/75	2	3		D1
	75/76				
St Mirren	76/77	0	1		D1
Celtic	76/77	1	2		P
	77/78				
East Fife	78/79	15	9	2	D2
	79/80				
Forfar A	80/81	4	4		D2
Stirling A	81/82	2	2		D2
Sauchie Jnrs					

GIBSON John
b. Blantyre 20.4.1967

St Ninians BG					
Blantyre V					
Hamilton A	86/87	1	1		P
	87/88	0	1		D1
Hastings T					
Alloa A	88/89	38		4	D2
	89/90	30	2	4	D1
	90/91	21		4	D2
	91/92	20	3	2	D2
	92/93	9	9		D2
	93/94	8	6	2	D2
Stirling A	93/94	16	5	1	D1
	94/95	32	2	4	D2
	95/96	18	11	6	D2
	96/97	28	8	1	D1
	97/98	19	6	1	D1
Stenhousemuir	98/99	17	5	3	D2

GIBSON William
b. St Andrews 3.4.1953

Heart of Midlothian	73/74	10	2	6	D1
	74/75	27	3	9	D1
	75/76	24	4	8	P
	76/77	31		15	P
	77/78	36	3	20	D1
	78/79	33	1	6	P
	79/80	39		17	D1
	80/81	30	2	4	P
Partick T	81/82	2		1	P
Raith R	81/82	24	3	9	D1
	82/83	4	2		D1
Cowdenbeath	82/83	22		13	D2

GILL Wayne
b. Chorley 28.11.1975

Blackburn R	97/98				
Dundee U	97/98	0	2		P
Blackburn R	98/99				
	99/00				
Blackpool	99/00	12			FL

GILLESPIE Gary Thomson
b. Bonnybridge 5.7.1960

Grangemouth Int. BC					
Falkirk	77/78	22			D2
Coventry C	78/79	14	1		FL
	79/80	38		1	FL
	80/81	37		1	FL
	81/82	40		2	FL
	82/83	42		2	FL
Liverpool	83/84				
	84/85	10	2	1	FL
	85/86	14		3	FL
	86/87	37			FL
	87/88	35		4	FL
	88/89	15		1	FL
	89/90	11	2	4	FL
	90/91	30		1	FL
Celtic	91/92	24		2	P
	92/93	18			P
	93/94	25	2		P
Coventry C	94/95	2	1		FL

GILLESPIE James
b. Glasgow 4.11.1957

Standard Wettern					
Motherwell	83/84	12	3		P
Morton	84/85	17	3	5	P
	85/86	8	2	3	P
Clyde	85/86	11	6	4	D1

GILLHAUS Hans
b. Helmond 5.11.1963

PSV Eindhoven					
Aberdeen	89/90	19	1	8	P
	90/91	35		14	P
	91/92	24	5	5	P

GILLIES Richard Charles
b. Glasgow 24.8.1976

St Mirren	92/93	2	6	1	D1
	93/94	10	12	2	D1
	94/95	13	11	3	D1
	95/96	28	5	3	D1
	96/97	29		6	D1
Aberdeen	97/98	5	16		P
	98/99	4	7		P
	99/00	3	7	1	P
St Mirren	99/00	2	2		D1

GILMOUR James
b. Bellshill 17.12.1961

Bargeddie					
Queens Park	81/82	21	13	7	D1
	82/83	36	1	10	D1
	83/84	36		10	D2
Partick T	84/85	10	7		D1
Falkirk	84/85	3	3		D1
	85/86	29	1	15	D1
	86/87	28	5	5	P
	87/88	10		1	P
Kilmarnock	87/88	25	3	8	D1
	88/89	14	2	3	D1
Stirling A	88/89	12	2	1	D2
	89/90	7	12	2	D2
Clyde	90/91	17	11	6	D1
Dumbarton	91/92	36	1	19	D2
	92/93	5		1	D1
	93/94	1	5		D1
Bo'ness U	94/95				
Alloa A	95/96	20	5	2	D3
	96/97	14	2	2	D3
	97/98	7	8	2	D3
	98/99	0	1		D2

GILZEAN Ian Roger
b. Enfield 10.12.1969

Tottenham H					
Dundee	92/93	17	7	5	P
Doncaster R L	92/93	3			FL
Northampton T	93/94	29	4	10	FL
Ayr U	94/95	21	2	3	D1

GINSBURG Ben Z
b. Tel Aviv 12.12.1964

Maccabi Tel Aviv					
Rangers	89/90	4			P

GIVEN Charles James
b. Port Glasgow 12.6.1956

Johnstone Burgh	77/78				
Clydebank	78/79	38		3	D1
	79/80	36	2	2	D1
	80/81	38		7	D1
	81/82	39		6	D1
	82/83	34		6	D1
	83/84	33	2	9	D1
	84/85	37		7	D1
	85/86	30			P
	86/87	14	13	2	P
	87/88				
Stirling A	88/89	33	2	2	D2
	89/90	31	1		D2

GLASS Stephen
b. Dundee 23.5.1976

Aberdeen	94/95	11	8	1	P
	95/96	32		3	P
	96/97	20	4	1	P
	97/98	30	1	2	P

GLAVIN Ronald Michael
b. Glasgow 27.3.1951

Lochend R					
Partick T	67/68				
	68/69	0	1		D1
	69/70	5	3	2	D1
	70/71				
	71/72	29		2	D1
	72/73	33		9	D1
	73/74	31		9	D1
	74/75	11		3	D1
Celtic	74/75	19	1	5	
	75/76	10			P
	76/77	34		19	P
	77/78	28		9	P
	78/79	9	1	3	P
Barnsley	79/80	42		20	FL
	80/81	36	1	18	FL
	81/82	26	1	7	FL
	82/83	33	2	17	FL
	83/84	34	1	11	FL
Belenenses	84/85				
Barnsley	85/86	5	1		FL
Stockport Co	86/87	5	5	1	FL
Cowdenbeath	86/87	2			D2
St Louis Steamers					
Farsley Celtic					

GLENNIE Robert
b. Dundee 2.10.1957

Aberdeen	77/78	3			P
Dundee	77/78	13		1	D1
	78/79	36	1	1	D1
	79/80	35			P
	80/81	39			D1
	81/82	35			P
	82/83	23	2		P
	83/84	26	1	2	P
	84/85	28	1		P
	85/86	32	1	2	P
	86/87	17	1		P
	87/88	19			P
Raith R	88/89	16			D1
	89/90	7			D1
Forfar A	89/90	19		1	D1
Arbroath	90/91	2			D2
	91/92				
	92/93				
	93/94	11			D2

GODFREY Peter James
b. Falkirk 22.10.1957

Stenhousemuir	79/80	2		1	D2
Linlithgow Rose					
Meadowbank T	80/81	2			D2
	81/82	29	1	6	D2
	82/83	38		3	D2
	83/84	37		3	D1
	84/85	19			D1
St Mirren	84/85	15		1	P
	85/86	34		3	P
	86/87	37	1	1	P
	87/88	24			P
	88/89	27		1	P
	89/90	22		2	P
	90/91	14			P
Falkirk	90/91	11			P
	91/92	15	1	2	P
Arbroath	92/93	11		2	D2
Stenhousemuir	92/93	19			D2
	93/94	29		1	D2
	94/95	17	3		D2

GOLDTHORP John

Lesmagahow Jnrs					
Motherwell	67/68	11		3	D1
	68/69	11	1	9	D2
	69/70	18		4	D1
	70/71	18	1	2	D1
	71/72	22	4	6	D1
	72/73	15	6	3	D1
	73/74	24	2	10	D1
	74/75	23	4	6	D1
	75/76	0	3		P
Morton	75/76	8		5	D1
	76/77	20	6	11	D1
	77/78	34		20	D1
Airdrieonians	78/79	31		16	D1
St Johnstone	79/80	22	6	7	D1

GOMES Sergio Henrique
b. Juiz de Fora 27.7.1969

Amora					
Dundee U	94/95	11	3	3	P
	95/96				
Kuwait SC					

GOOD Iain David
b. Glasgow 9.8.1977

Queens Park					
Aberdeen	95/96				
	96/97				
	97/98				
	98/99	0	1		P

GOODMAN Donald Ralph
b. Leeds 9.5.1966

Collingham					
Bradford C	83/84	0	2		FL
	84/85	23	2	5	FL
	85/86	19	1	4	FL
	86/87	23		5	FL
WBA	86/87	10		2	FL
	87/88	34	6	7	FL
	88/89	30	6	15	FL
	89/90	39		21	FL
	90/91	16	6	8	FL
	91/92	11		7	FL
Sunderland	91/92	20	2	11	FL
	92/93	41		16	FL
	93/94	34	1	10	FL
	94/95	17	1	3	FL
Wolverhampton W	94/95	24		3	FL
	95/96	43	1	16	FL
	96/97	19	8	6	FL
	97/98	29	1	8	FL
Motherwell	98/99	8		1	P
	99/00	25	4	7	P

GOODWIN James
b. Waterford 20.11.1981

Tramore					
Celtic	99/00	1			P

GORAM Andrew Leslie
b. Bury 13.4.1964

WBA					
Oldham A	81/82	3			FL
	82/83	38			FL
	83/84	22			FL
	84/85	41			FL
	85/86	41			FL
	86/87	42			FL
	87/88	9			FL
Hibernian	87/88	33		1	P
	88/89	36			P
	89/90	34			P
	90/91	35			P
Rangers	91/92	44			P
	92/93	34			P
	93/94	8			P
	94/95	18	1		P
	95/96	30			P
	96/97	25			P
	97/98	24			P
Motherwell	98/99	13			P
	99/00	22			P

GORDON Alan

Club		Season	Apps	Sub	Gls	Div
Heart of Midlothian		61/62	22		5	D1
		62/63	16		12	D1
		63/64	10		1	D1
		64/65	29		19	D1
		65/66	15		6	D1
		66/67	19	1	6	D1
Durban U						
Heart of Midlothian		68/69	15		6	D1
Dundee U		68/69	4			D1
		69/70	25	3	11	D1
		70/71	31		16	D1
		71/72	14	1	7	D1
Hibernian		71/72	13		4	D1
		72/73	33		27	D1
		73/74	27	1	16	D1
		74/75	10		4	D1
Dundee		74/75	13	3	5	D1
		75/76	17	3	3	P

GORDON Dale Andrew
b. Great Yarmouth 9.1.1967

Club		Season	Apps	Sub	Gls	Div
Norwich C		84/85	21	2	3	FL
		85/86	3	3	1	FL
		86/87	40	1	5	FL
		87/88	16	5	3	FL
		88/89	38		5	FL
		89/90	26		3	FL
		90/91	35	1	7	FL
		91/92	15		4	FL
Rangers		91/92	23		5	P
		92/93	18	4	1	P
West Ham U		93/94	8		1	FL
		94/95				
Peterborough U	L	94/95	6		1	FL
West Ham U		95/96	0	1		FL
Millwall	L	95/96	6			FL
Bournemouth		96/97	14	2		FL

GORDON Ian
b. Bangour 30.6.1960
Livingston

Club		Season	Apps	Sub	Gls	Div
Airdrieonians		78/79	3	3		D1
		79/80	38	1	6	D1
		80/81	24			P
		81/82	33	2	1	P
		82/83	32		3	D1
		83/84	27		4	D1
Dunfermline A		84/85	8	1	1	D2
		85/86	15			D2
Raith R		86/87	23		1	D2

GORDON Stuart Love
b. Paisley 14.7.1960
Harmony Row
Kilbirnie Ladeside
Pollok Jnrs

Club		Season	Apps	Sub	Gls	Div
Clydebank		85/86	3			P
		86/87	22	7	9	P
		87/88	3	2		D1
Hamilton A		87/88	21	7	9	D1
		88/89	21	3	5	P
		89/90	4	2	1	D1
Queen of the South		89/90	25		8	D2
		90/91	32	4	7	D2
		91/92	36		2	D2
		92/93	16	6		D2
Auchinleck Talbot						

GOSS Jeremy
b. Cyprus 11.5.1965

Club		Season	Apps	Sub	Gls	Div
Norwich C		83/84	0	1		FL
		84/85	1	4		FL
		85/86				
		86/87	1			FL
		87/88	20	2	2	FL
		88/89				
		89/90	3	4		FL
		90/91	14	5	1	FL
		91/92	29	4	1	FL
		92/93	25			FL
		93/94	34		6	FL
		94/95	19	6	2	FL
		95/96	9	7	1	FL
Heart of Midlothian		96/97	7	3		P

GOTTSKALKSSON Olafur
b. Keflavik 12.3.1968

Club		Season	Apps	Sub	Gls	Div
IA Akranes		88				
		89				
KR Reykjavik		90				
		91				
		92				
		93				
Keflavik		94				
		95				
		96				
		97				
Hibernian		97/98	16			P
		98/99	36			D1
		99/00	12			P

GOUGH Charles Richard
b. Stockholm 5.4.1962

Club		Season	Apps	Sub	Gls	Div
Dundee U		80/81	0	4		P
		81/82	26	4	1	P
		82/83	34		8	P
		83/84	33		3	P
		84/85	33		6	P
		85/86	31		5	P
		86/87	3		1	P
Tottenham H		86/87	40		2	FL
		87/88	9			FL
Rangers		87/88	31		5	P
		88/89	35		4	P
		89/90	26			P
		90/91	26			P
		91/92	33		2	P
		92/93	25		2	P
		93/94	37		3	P
		94/95	25		1	P
		95/96	29		3	P
		96/97	24		1	P
Kansas City Wizards						
Rangers		97/98	35			P

GOULD Jonathan
b. London 18.7.1968
Bradford C

Club		Season	Apps	Sub	Gls	Div
Celtic		97/98	35			P
		98/99	28			P
		99/00	28	1		P

GOURLAY Archibald Murdoch
b. Greenock 29.6.1969

Club		Season	Apps	Sub	Gls	Div
Morton		85/86	0	2		D1
		86/87				
		87/88	2			P
Newcastle U		88/89	0	1		FL
		89/90				
Morton	L	89/90	4			D1
Newcastle U		90/91	2			FL
Motherwell		91/92	0	1		P
		92/93	0	2		P
		93/94				
Hartlepool U		94/95	0	1		FL

GOURLAY Iain
b. 23.10.1957

Club		Season	Apps	Sub	Gls	Div
Clydebank		77/78	12	2		P
		78/79	4	1		D1
East Stirlingshire		79/80	34		3	D2
		80/81	33		1	D1
		81/82	21	5		D1

GOWER Mark
b. Edmonton 5.10.1978

Club		Season	Apps	Sub	Gls	Div
Tottenham H		96/97				
		97/98				
		98/99				
Motherwell	L	98/99	8	1	1	P
Tottenham H		99/00				

GRADY James
b. Paisley 14.3.1971
Arthurlie Jnrs

Club		Season	Apps	Sub	Gls	Div
Clydebank		94/95	30	6	7	D1
		95/96	35	1	10	D1
		96/97	36		8	D1
Dundee		97/98	36		15	D1
		98/99	20	6	3	P
		99/00	18	13	6	P

GRAHAM Alisdair
b. Lanark 17.8.1980
Musselburgh Jnrs

Club		Season	Apps	Sub	Gls	Div
Heart of Midlothian		99/00	0	1		P

GRAHAM Alistair Slowey
b. Glasgow 11.8.1966
Anniesland Waverley

Club		Season	Apps	Sub	Gls	Div
Clydebank		84/85	1			D1
Stenhousemuir		84/85	1			D2
Clydebank		85/86	1	1		P
		86/87				
Albion R		87/88	26	2	10	D2
		88/89	38	1	15	D2
		89/90	28	3	7	D1
Ayr U		90/91	38		8	D2
		91/92	40		14	D1
		92/93	30		9	D1
Motherwell		92/93	4		1	P
		93/94	2	3		P
Raith R		93/94	35	1	5	P
		94/95	25	2	6	D1
		95/96	18	7	5	P
Falkirk		95/96	8			P
		96/97	5	2		D1
Ayr U		97/98	5	7	2	D1
Albion R		97/98	2		1	D3
Clyde		97/98	12	3	4	D2
Partick T		97/98	2	2		D1
TPV Tampere						
Stirling A		98/99	23		5	D2
		99/00	35		17	D2

GRAHAM Andrew
b. Irvine 11.12.1956
Johnstone Burgh

Club		Season	Apps	Sub	Gls	Div
Dundee U		77/78	1			P
		78/79				
		79/80	2			P
		80/81				
		81/82	1			P
Stirling A	L	82/83	4			D2
Forfar A	L	82/83	2			D2
Stirling A		83/84	5			D2
		84/85	37			D2
		85/86	39			D2
		86/87	39			D2
		87/88	37			D2
		88/89	34			D2
		89/90	5			D2
		90/91				
Kilmarnock		91/92	11			D1

GRAHAM Arthur
b. Castlemilk 26.10.1952
Cambuslang R

Club		Season	Apps	Sub	Gls	Div
Aberdeen		69/70	4	1	2	D1
		70/71	31		5	D1
		71/72	27	2	4	D1
		72/73	19	4		D1
		73/74	31	1	3	D1
		74/75	34		11	D1
		75/76	31		4	P
		76/77	35		5	P
Leeds U		77/78	40		9	FL
		78/79	39		8	FL
		79/80	26	1	3	FL
		80/81	40		3	FL
		81/82	38		9	FL
		82/83	39		5	FL
Manchester U		83/84	33	4	5	FL
		84/85				
Bradford C		85/86	23	2	2	FL
		86/87	5	1		FL

GRAHAM David

Club		Season	Apps	Sub	Gls	Div
Heart of Midlothian		73/74	4			D1
		74/75				
		75/76	1			P
Meadowbank T		76/77	4			D2
Berwick R		76/77	3			D2

GRAHAM David
b. Edinburgh 6.10.1978

Club		Season	Apps	Sub	Gls	Div
Rangers		98/99	0	3		P
Dunfermline A		98/99	14	6	2	P
		99/00	0	15	2	D1

GRAHAM John
b. c1940
Strathclyde

Third Lanark		63/64	31		7	D1
Dundee U		64/65	16		1	D1
Falkirk		64/65	14		4	D1
		65/66	34		17	D1
		66/67	30	1	12	D1
		67/68	29		13	D1
		68/69	23	3	7	D1
Hibernian		69/70	22		10	D1
		70/71	20	2	4	D1
Ayr U		71/72	34		14	D1
		72/73	28		7	D1
		73/74	31		10	D1
		74/75	29	3	12	D1
		75/76	34	1	16	P
		76/77	5	3	3	P
Falkirk		76/77	17	7		D1
		77/78	11	3		D2
		78/79	11	4	3	D2
		79/80	1			D2

GRAHAM Robert
b. Motherwell 22.11.1944

Liverpool		64/65	14			FL
		65/66	1			FL
		66/67	3		1	FL
		67/68	2	2	1	FL
		68/69	11	1	5	FL
		69/70	42		13	FL
		70/71	13	1	5	FL
		71/72	10	1	2	FL
Coventry C		71/72	13		2	FL
		72/73	6		1	FL
Tranmere R	L	72/73	10		3	FL
Motherwell		73/74	33		13	D1
		74/75	31	1	11	D1
		75/76	34		5	P
		76/77	28	5	8	P
Hamilton A		77/78	38		10	D1
		78/79	38		18	D1
		79/80	30		11	D1
		80/81	9	3	3	D1
Queen of the South						

GRAHAM Thomas
b. Glasgow 31.3.1955
Arthurlie
Aston Villa

Barnsley		78/79	27		12	FL
		79/80	9	2	1	FL
Halifax T		80/81	32	2	9	FL
		81/82	36	1	8	FL
Doncaster R		82/83	9	2	2	FL
Motherwell		82/83	0	1		P
Scunthorpe U		82/83	12	1	3	FL
		83/84	25	2	4	FL
		84/85	38		9	FL
		85/86	27	4	5	FL
Scarborough		86/87				
		87/88	44		7	FL
		88/89	40	3	4	FL
		89/90	20	4		FL
Halifax T		89/90	21		1	FL
		90/91	23		3	FL
		91/92	12	2		FL

GRANT Alexander
b. 27.11.1957

Aberdeen		77/78	0	2		P
Meadowbank T *		77/78	2			D2
East Stirlingshire		78/79	35	1	8	D2
		79/80	32		14	D2
		80/81	29	2	5	D1
		81/82	11	5	3	D1

GRANT Alexander
b. Glasgow 27.2.1962

Queens Park		79/80	0	2		D2
		80/81	1	3	1	D2
		81/82	21	2	2	D1
		82/83	31		3	D1
		83/84	35		17	D2
Ayr U		84/85	33		7	D1
		85/86	24	5	2	D1
Clydebank		86/87	32		6	P
Falkirk		87/88	9	11		P
Partick T		88/89	8	6	1	D1
		89/90	1	2		D1
East Stirlingshire	L	89/90	5		2	D2
Stranraer		90/91	33	1	4	D2
		91/92	28	3	5	D2
		92/93	36	2	11	D2
		93/94	32		6	D2
		94/95	21	5	2	D1
		95/96	18	4	6	D2

GRANT Andrew John
b. Glasgow 9.1.1975

Dunfermline A		91/92	0	1		P

GRANT Bernard
b. Rutherglen 6.8.1962
EK Dynamo

Motherwell		83/84	5	1		P
Stirling A		84/85	20		3	D2
		85/86	27		1	D2
		86/87	20	1		D2
Kilbirnie Ladeside		87/88				
		88/89				
Dumbarton		89/90	7			D2

GRANT Brian Joseph
b. Bannockburn 19.6.1964
Fallin Violet

Stirling A		81/82	0	1		D2
		82/83	1			D2
		83/84	16	8	3	D2
Aberdeen		84/85				
		85/86				
		86/87	12	3	4	P
		87/88	4	3	1	P
		88/89	23	3	6	P
		89/90	28	3	6	P
		90/91	32		2	P
		91/92	33		6	P
		92/93	29		3	P
		93/94	26	4	2	P
		94/95	32		2	P
		95/96	22	3		P
		96/97	2			P
Hibernian		96/97	9	3		P
		97/98	1	4		P
Dundee		97/98	5	3		D1
		98/99	0	4		P
Stirling A		98/99	2	6		D2

GRANT Peter
b. Glasgow 30.8.1965
St Aloysius Chapelhall
Celtic BC

Celtic		83/84	2	1		P
		84/85	19	1	4	P
		85/86	26	4	1	P
		86/87	32	5	1	P
		87/88	36	1	2	P
		88/89	20	1		P
		89/90	24	2		P
		90/91	27	1		P
		91/92	20	2		P
		92/93	27	4	2	P
		93/94	27	1		P
		94/95	27	1	2	P
		95/96	30	1	3	P
		96/97	21	2		P
Norwich C		97/98	33	2	3	FL
		98/99	31	2		FL

GRANT Roderick John
b. Gloucester 16.9.1966
Strathbrock Jnrs

Cowdenbeath		86/87	23	1	4	D2
		87/88	29	3	11	D2
		88/89	7	1	2	D2
St Johnstone		88/89	28		5	D1
		89/90	33	4	19	D1
		90/91	29	1	7	P
		91/92	17	8	2	P
Dunfermline A		92/93	18	14	4	D1
Partick T		93/94	35	2	13	P
		94/95	14	9	5	P
St Johnstone		95/96	19	8	5	D1
		96/97	31	2	19	D1
		97/98	19	15	6	P
		98/99	14	11	4	P
		99/00	1	2		P
Ayr U		99/00	9	4	2	D1

GRAY Andrew Arthur
b. Lambeth 22.2.1964
Dulwich Hamlet

Crystal Palace		84/85	19	2		FL
		85/86	29	1	10	FL
		86/87	26	4	6	FL
		87/88	17		6	FL
Aston Villa		87/88	19		1	FL
		88/89	15	3	3	FL
QPR		88/89	11		2	FL
Crystal Palace		89/90	35		6	FL
		90/91	27	3	4	FL
		91/92	25		2	FL
Tottenham H		91/92	14		1	FL
		92/93	9	8	1	FL
Swindon T	L	92/93	3			FL
Tottenham H		93/94	0	2	1	FL
Marbella		94/95				
Falkirk		95/96	16			P
		96/97	13	5	1	D1
Bury		97/98	21		1	FL
Millwall		97/98	12		1	FL

GRAY Andrew Mullen
b. Glasgow 30.11.1955
Clydebank Strollers

Dundee U		73/74	25	1	16	D1
		74/75	33		20	D1
		75/76	3			P
Aston Villa		75/76	30		10	FL
		76/77	36		25	FL
		77/78	31	1	13	FL
		78/79	15		6	FL
Wolverhampton W		79/80	35		12	FL
		80/81	25	2	9	FL
		81/82	28	1	5	FL
		82/83	33		10	FL
		83/84	9		2	FL
Everton		83/84	23		5	FL
		84/85	21	5	9	FL
Aston Villa		85/86	35		5	FL
		86/87	18	1		FL
		87/88				
Notts Co	L	87/88	3	1		FL
WBA		87/88	30	2	10	FL
		88/89	2	1		FL
Rangers		88/89	3	10	5	P

GRAY Colin
b. Glasgow 10.1.1967
Anniesland U

Clydebank		86/87	0	1		P
		87/88	2	1		P

GRAY Donal
b. Newry 22.5.1977
Portadown

Partick T		94/95	0	1		P

GRAY John
b. Hamilton ?.?.1953
Blantyre Celtic

Dundee		70/71				
		71/72				
		72/73	3	2	1	D1
		73/74	0	3		D1
Partick T		74/75	2	5		D1
Australia						
Ayr U		76/77	0	2		P
Hamilton A		76/77	2	1		D1
East Fife		76/77	13	2	1	D1

GRAY Steven
b. Irvine 7.2.1967

Aberdeen		85/86	10	3	1	P
		86/87	9	4	1	P
		87/88	4	3		P
		88/89	4			P
Airdrieonians		89/90	30	1	8	D1
		90/91	13	2	1	D1
		91/92	0	2	1	P

GRAY Stuart
b. Harrogate 18.12.1973
Celtic BC

Celtic						
Giffnock North	L					
Celtic		92/93	1			P
		93/94				
Bournemouth	L	93/94				
Celtic		94/95	8	3		P
		95/96	3	2	1	P
		96/97	7	4		P
Morton		97/98	14		1	D1
Reading		97/98	7			FL
		98/99	25	2	2	FL
		99/00	12	3		FL

GREIG John
b. Edinburgh 11.9.1942
Edina Hearts
Whitburn

Rangers		61/62	11		7	D1
		62/63	27		5	D1
		63/64	34		4	D1
		64/65	34		4	D1
		65/66	32		7	D1
		66/67	32		2	D1
		67/68	32		11	D1
		68/69	33		6	D1
		69/70	30		7	D1
		70/71	26		8	D1
		71/72	28		8	D1
		72/73	30		7	D1
		73/74	30	2	6	D1
		74/75	21	1	1	D1
		75/76	36		2	P
		76/77	30			P
		77/78	28	1	2	P

GRIFFIN Daniel Joseph
b. Belfast 10.8.1977

Club	Season	Apps	Sub	Goals	Lge
St Johnstone	94/95	3			D1
	95/96	22	9	1	D1
	96/97	26	3	1	D1
	97/98	10	3		P
	98/99	14	5	1	P
	99/00	26	3	1	P

GRIFFIN James
b. Hamilton 1.1.1967

Club	Season	Apps	Sub	Goals	Lge
Fir Park BC					
Motherwell	85/86	1			P
	86/87				
	87/88	4	2		P
	88/89	1			P
	89/90	6	5		P
	90/91	22	1	4	P
	91/92	22		1	P
	92/93	24	1	1	P
	93/94	1	2		P

GUERIN Vincent
b. 22.11.1965

Club	Season	Apps	Sub	Goals	Lge
Heart of Midlothian	98/99	9	11	1	P

GUIVARC'H Stephane
b. 6.9.1970

Club	Season	Apps	Sub	Goals	Lge
Auxerre					
Guingamp					
Rangers	98/99	11	3	5	P

GUNN Bryan James
b. Thurso 22.12.1963

Club	Season	Apps	Sub	Goals	Lge
Invergordon BC					
Aberdeen	82/83	1			P
	83/84				
	84/85	2			P
	85/86	10			P
	86/87	2			P
Norwich C	86/87	29			FL
	87/88	38			FL
	88/89	37			FL
	89/90	37			FL
	90/91	34			FL
	91/92	25			FL
	92/93	42			FL
	93/94	41			FL
	94/95	21			FL
	95/96	43			FL
	96/97	39			FL
	97/98	4			FL
Hibernian	97/98	12			P

GUNTWEIT Cato
b. Drammen 6.8.1975

Club	Season	Apps	Sub	Goals	Lge
Brann Bergen					
Aberdeen	99/00	20		3	P

HACKETT Gary Stuart
b. Stourbridge 11.11.1962

Club	Season	Apps	Sub	Goals	Lge
Bromsgrove R					
Shrewsbury T	83/84	29	2	3	FL
	84/85	36	2	5	FL
	85/86	42		6	FL
	86/87	35	4	3	FL
Aberdeen	87/88	6	9		P
Stoke C	87/88	1			FL
	88/89	45	1	5	FL
	89/90	18	8	2	FL
WBA	89/90	9	5	2	FL
	90/91	0	5		FL
	91/92	13	2		FL
	92/93	4	6	1	FL
Peterborough U	93/94	18	4	1	FL
Chester C	94/95	30	5	5	FL

HAGEN David
b. Edinburgh 5.5.1973

Club	Season	Apps	Sub	Goals	Lge
Rangers	92/93	5	3	2	P
	93/94	4	2	1	P
	94/95	16	4	3	P
Heart of Midlothian	94/95	0	2		P
	95/96	5	2	1	P
Falkirk	95/96	21	4		P
	96/97	31	3	1	D1
	97/98	25	8	4	D1
	98/99	9	3		D1
	99/00	33	2	6	D1

HAIR Ian
b. 8.8.1954

Club	Season	Apps	Sub	Goals	Lge
Aberdeen	73/74	18		1	D1
	74/75	26	1	4	D1
	75/76	24	5		P
	76/77	1			P
Montrose	76/77	26		1	D1
	77/78	34			D1
	78/79	30	1	3	D1
	79/80	13			D2
	80/81	19		2	D2

HALL Henry Begg

Club	Season	Apps	Sub	Goals	Lge
Kirkintilloch Rob Roy					
Dundee	64/65				
Stirling A	65/66	29		14	D1
	66/67	22	1	2	D1
	67/68	29	1	3	D1
	68/69				
St Johnstone	68/69	21		19	D1
	69/70	28	1	15	D1
	70/71	31		18	D1
	71/72	26		9	D1
	72/73	34		16	D1
	73/74	28		7	D1
	74/75	17	1	1	D1
Dundee U	75/76	25	1	8	P
	76/77	1	7		P
Forfar A	77/78	37		1	D2
	78/79	25	4	2	D2

HALL Norman

Club	Season	Apps	Sub	Goals	Lge
Clydebank	71/72	29	2		D2
	72/73	32	1		D2
	73/74	31			D2
	74/75	34		2	D2
	75/76	26		1	D2
	76/77	25	3	1	D1
	77/78	27			P
	78/79	38		3	D1
	79/80	21	6		D1

HALLIDAY Stephen William
b. Sunderland 3.5.1976

Club	Season	Apps	Sub	Goals	Lge
Charlton A					
Hartlepool U	93/94	7		4	FL
	94/95	19	9	5	FL
	95/96	36	3	7	FL
	96/97	28	3	8	FL
	97/98	21	10	5	FL
Motherwell	98/99	2	2		P
	99/00	1	4		P

HALLUM Carsten
b. 9.9.1969

Club	Season	Apps	Sub	Goals	Lge
Raith R	96/97	6			P

HALPIN John William
b. Broxburn 15.11.1961

Club		Season	Apps	Sub	Goals	Lge
Celtic BC						
Armadale Thistle						
Hibernian	T					
Celtic		81/82	2	1		P
		82/83				
South China	L					
Celtic		83/84	1	3		P
		84/85				
Sunderland	L	84/85				
Carlisle U		84/85	17	2	1	FL
		85/86	33		5	FL
		86/87	7			FL
		87/88	23		3	FL
		88/89	33		7	FL
		89/90	17			FL
		90/91	18	3	1	FL
Rochdale		91/92	22	9	1	FL
Gretna						

HAMILL Alexander
b. Coatbridge 30.10.1961

Club	Season	Apps	Sub	Goals	Lge
Tottenham H					
Heart of Midlothian	80/81	20	1	1	P
	81/82	16	4	2	D1
Hamilton A	82/83	26	6	2	D1
	83/84	35			D1
	84/85	35		2	D1
	05/00	35			D1
	86/87	8	1		P
Forfar A	86/87	29			D1
	87/88	44		1	D1
	88/89	37	1	1	D1
	89/90	38			D1
	90/91	37			D1
	91/92	39			D1
	92/93	39			D2
	93/94	25	2	1	D2
Cowdenbeath	93/94	9			D3
	94/95	4	2		D3
East Fife	94/95	15	1	2	D1
	95/96	12	3		D2

HAMILTON Brian
b. Paisley 5.8.1967

Club	Season	Apps	Sub	Goals	Lge
St Mirren	85/86	8	1		P
	86/87	26	2	3	P
	87/88	26	1		P
	88/89	23		1	P
Hibernian	89/90	26	2	1	P
	90/91	25	1	2	P
	91/92	37	3	3	P
	92/93	38	2	1	P
	93/94	40	2	2	P
	94/95	17	1		P
Heart of Midlothian	94/95	13		2	P
	95/96	8	4		P
Falkirk	96/97	18	1	1	D1
	97/98	3	10		D1
	98/99	12	4	2	D1
Ayr U	98/99	2	1		D1
Stranraer	98/99	1			D1

HAMILTON Derek M
b. Kilwinning 26.8.1958

Club	Season	Apps	Sub	Goals	Lge
Beith Jnrs					
Aberdeen	78/79	9	1		P
	79/80	11	2	3	P
	80/81	5	3		P
	81/82	1			P
	82/83	0	2		P
St Mirren	83/84	23			P
	84/85	12	1		P
	85/86	21	2		P
	86/87	36			P
	87/88	19			P
	88/89	2			P
Stranraer	89/90	0	1		D2
Morton	90/91	2	2		D1

HAMILTON Gordon S
b. 17.10.1951

Club	Season	Apps	Sub	Goals	Lge
Sighthill YC					
Hamilton A	69/70				
	70/71				
	71/72	33	1	3	D2
	72/73	36		1	D2
	73/74	28	2	4	D2
	74/75	12	1	1	D2
	75/76	5			D1
Clyde	75/76	21		1	D1
	76/77	39		4	D2
Falkirk	77/78	17	1		D2
	78/79	11		1	D2
St Johnstone	78/79	15			D1
Airdrieonians	79/80	25		2	D1
	80/81	0	2		P
Berwick R	80/81	26		6	D1
Stranraer	81/82	9	2		D2

HAMILTON Graeme John
b. Stirling 22.1.1974

Club	Season	Apps	Sub	Goals	Lge
Gairdoch U					
Falkirk	91/92	2	1		P
	92/93				
	93/94	7			D1
	94/95	2	1		P
	95/96	0	1		P
East Stirlingshire	96/97	20	1		D3
	97/98	3	1		D3

HAMILTON James
b. Aberdeen 9.2.1976

Club	Season	Apps	Sub	Goals	Lge
Keith					
Dundee	93/94	0	1		P
	94/95	23	5	12	D1
	95/96	30	3	14	D1
	96/97	12		1	D1
Heart of Midlothian	96/97	12	6	5	P
	97/98	20	12	14	P
	98/99	20	5	6	P
Aberdeen	98/99	6	1	1	P
	99/00	3	4		P
Dundee U	99/00	8	5	1	P

HAMILTON John Turner
b. Glasgow 10.7.1949

Club	Season	Apps	Sub	Goals	Lge
Hibernian	69/70	20	2	4	D1
	70/71	8	1	1	D1
	71/72	21	1	6	D1
	72/73	4	4	1	D1
Rangers	73/74	4	3	1	D1
	74/75	2	1		D1
	75/76	22		1	P
	76/77	22	1	3	P
	77/78	3	1		P
Millwall	78/79	1	1		FL
St Johnstone	78/79	18	1	2	D1
	79/80	20	1	3	D1

HAMILTON Lindsay
b. 30.5.1957

Club	Season	Apps	Sub	Gls	Div
St Johnstone	75/76	9	1		P
	76/77	19	2		D1
	77/78				
Alloa A	78/79	23	6	5	D2
	79/80	28	2	3	D2
	80/81	6	3		D2

HAMILTON Lindsay
b. Bellshill 7.12.1967

Club	Season	Apps	Sub	Gls	Div
Stenhousemuir	82/83	1			D2
	83/84	38			D2
	84/85	39			D2
	85/86	29			D2
	86/87	13			D2
	87/88				
East Stirlingshire	88/89	1			D2
Clydebank	89/90	1			D1
Stirling A	89/90	5			D2
St Johnstone	90/91	34			P
	91/92	43			P
Dunfermline A	92/93	39			D1
	93/94	27			D1
	94/95				
East Fife	95/96	35			D2
	96/97	30			D1
Queens Park	97/98	24			D3
Partick T	97/98	5			D1
Stenhousemuir	98/99	34			D3
	99/00	33			D2

HAMILTON Stephen T
b. Glasgow 7.10.1960

Club	Season	Apps	Sub	Gls	Div
Heart of Midlothian	79/80	5			D1
	80/81	12			P
East Fife	81/82	32			D2
	82/83	39		1	D2
East Stirlingshire	83/84	34		1	D2
	84/85	31			D2
	85/86	11			D2

HAMILTON Steven James
b. Baillieston 19.3.1975
Troon Jnrs

Club	Season	Apps	Sub	Gls	Div
Kilmarnock	96/97	6			P
	97/98	5	1		P
	98/99	5			P
Raith R	99/00	11	4		D1

HAMMEL Steven
b. Rutherglen 18.2.1982

Club	Season	Apps	Sub	Gls	Div
Motherwell	99/00	3	1		P

HANCOCK Stephen A
b. Sheffield 10.9.1953

Club	Season	Apps	Sub	Gls	Div
Heart of Midlothian	75/76	2	2		P
Meadowbank T	76/77	36		7	D2
	77/78	32	2	5	D2
	78/79	26	5	2	D2
Stenhousemuir	79/80	39		11	D2
	80/81	37	1	20	D2
Forfar A	81/82	33	1	9	D2
	82/83	4	1	1	D2

HANNAH David
b. Coatbridge 4.8.1974
Hamilton Thistle

Club	Season	Apps	Sub	Gls	Div
Dundee U	92/93	0	5		P
	93/94	6	4	2	P
	94/95	31	1	2	P
	95/96	4	3	1	D1
	96/97	9	3	2	P
Celtic	96/97	14	4		P
	97/98	9	6		P
	98/99	5	4		P
Dundee U	98/99	13		1	P
	99/00	33		6	P

HANNAH Robert
b. c1958
Celtic BC
Bellshill A

Club	Season	Apps	Sub	Gls	Div
Celtic	75/76	0	2		P
	76/77				
Ayr U	77/78	11	6		P
	78/79	5			D1
St Johnstone	79/80	4			D1
East Stirlingshire	79/80	1	3		D2

HANSEN Allan David
b. Alloa 13.6.1955
Sauchie Jnrs

Club	Season	Apps	Sub	Gls	Div
Partick T	73/74	0	1		D1
	74/75	26	3		D1
	75/76	21		2	D1
	76/77	35		4	P
Liverpool	77/78	18			FL
	78/79	34		1	FL
	79/80	38		4	FL
	80/81	36		1	FL
	81/82	35			FL
	82/83	34			FL
	83/84	42		1	FL
	84/85	41			FL
	85/86	41			FL
	86/87	39			FL
	87/88	39		1	FL
	88/89	6			FL
	89/90	31			FL

HANSEN John Angus McDonald
b. Sauchie 3.2.1950
Sauchie BC

Club	Season	Apps	Sub	Gls	Div
Partick T	67/68	2			D1
	68/69	18			D1
	69/70	26	5		D1
	70/71				
	71/72	23			D1
	72/73	10	1		D1
	73/74	15	2		D1
	74/75	33		2	D1
	75/76	26		1	D1
	76/77	33	1	2	P
	77/78	3			P

HARE M (Billy)
Fir Park BC

Club	Season	Apps	Sub	Gls	Div
Motherwell	78/79	1			P

HARO Mark
b. Irvine 21.10.1971
Glenrothes Strollers

Club	Season	Apps	Sub	Gls	Div
Dunfermline A	90/91	2	6		P
	91/92	7	3		P
	92/93	2			D1
Montrose	93/94	8			D2
	94/95	34		5	D3
	95/96	19			D2
	96/97	30		2	D3
Ross Co	97/98	31	1	4	D3
	98/99	26		1	D3

HARPER Joseph Montgomerie
b. Greenock 11.1.1948
Larkfield BC

Club	Season	Apps	Sub	Gls	Div
Morton	64/65	3		1	D1
	65/66	12		6	D1
Huddersfield T	66/67	5		1	FL
	67/68	21	2	3	FL
Morton	68/69	34		25	D1
	69/70	6		4	D1
Aberdeen	69/70	24		6	D1
	70/71	30	1	19	D1
	71/72	34		33	D1
	72/73	13		11	D1
Everton	72/73	20		7	FL
	73/74	20	3	5	FL
Hibernian	73/74	13		9	D1
	74/75	34		12	D1
	75/76	22		5	P
Aberdeen	76/77	34		18	P
	77/78	31		17	P
	78/79	25	3	19	P
	79/80	8	3	3	P
	80/81	1			P
Peterhead					
Keith					

HARPER Kevin Patrick
b. Oldham 15.1.1976
Hutchison Vale

Club	Season	Apps	Sub	Gls	Div
Hibernian	93/94	1	1		P
	94/95	15	8	5	P
	95/96	14	2	3	P
	96/97	23	3	5	P
	97/98	20	7	1	P
	98/99	0	2	1	D1

HARRIS Colin
b. Sanquhar 22.2.1961
Exit Thistle

Club	Season	Apps	Sub	Gls	Div
Raith R	79/80	1	2		D1
	80/81	23	2	9	D1
	81/82	16	6	1	D1
	82/83	36		18	D1
	83/84	19	1	4	D1
Dundee	83/84	9	5	2	P
	84/85	13	2	1	P
Hibernian	84/85	2	5	2	P
	85/86	10	10	2	P
Raith R	86/87	26	1	22	D2
	87/88	33		14	D1
Hamilton A	87/88	8		6	D1
	88/89	27	1	5	P
	89/90	35		9	D1
	90/91	24	3	7	D1
	91/92	27	5	8	D1
	92/93	14	13	6	D1
Cowdenbeath	92/93	5			D1
	93/94	9	1	1	D2
Clydebank	93/94	16	4	1	D1
	94/95	7	1		D1
Meadowbank T	94/95	5	1	1	D2
Queen of the South	95/96	25	8	9	D2

HARRISON Thomas Edward
b. Edinburgh 22.1.1974

Club	Season	Apps	Sub	Gls	Div
Heart of Midlothian	90/91	0	3		P
	91/92	0	1		P
	92/93	3	1	1	P
	93/94	1			P
Dunfermline A	94/95	1	1		D1
Clyde	95/96	21	6	4	D2
	96/97	3	5		D2
York C	96/97	0	1		FL
Carlisle U	97/98	6	4		FL
Berwick R	97/98	12	2		D3
East Fife	98/99	17			D2
Montrose	99/00	1			D3

HARROW Andrew
b. Kirkcaldy 6.11.1956

Club	Season	Apps	Sub	Gls	Div
Cowdenbeath	73/74	23	2	5	D2
	74/75	37	1	6	D2
	75/76	24		7	D2
	76/77	7	1		D2
Raith R	76/77	28		5	D2
	77/78	37	1	10	D2
	78/79	38		10	D1
	79/80	33	2	12	D1
	80/81	8	2	5	D1
Luton T	80/81	3	1		FL
Aberdeen	80/81	9	3	1	P
	81/82	3	3	2	P
Motherwell	82/83	17		2	P
	83/84	26	3	6	P
	84/85	36	1	9	D1
	85/86	15	5	2	P
Raith R	86/87	31	5	10	D2
	87/88	18	10	2	D1
East Fife	88/89	24	8	2	D2
	89/90	8			D2

HART Michael
b. Bellshill 10.2.1980

Club	Season	Apps	Sub	Gls	Div
Aberdeen	98/99	5	9		P
	99/00	2	1		P
Livingston	99/00	3			D1
Morton	99/00	1	9		D1

HARTLEY Paul
b. Glasgow 19.10.1976
Mill U

Club	Season	Apps	Sub	Gls	Div
Hamilton A	94/95	10	6		D1
	95/96	29	2	11	D1
Millwall	96/97	35	9	4	FL
Raith R	97/98	28	2	10	D1
	98/99	18		4	D1
Hibernian	98/99	6	7	5	D1
	99/00	14	10	1	P
Morton	99/00	3		1	D1

HARVEY Gerard
b. Falkirk 18.3.1962
Bonnybridge

Club	Season	Apps	Sub	Gls	Div
St Johnstone	81/82				
	82/83				
	83/84	0	1		P
Stirling A	84/85	0	1		D2
East Stirlingshire	84/85	10	3	2	D2
	85/86	11	7		D2
	86/87	4			D2
	87/88	26	2		D2
	88/89	9	5	2	D2

HARVEY Graham
b. Musselburgh 23.4.1961

Ormiston Primrose						
Hibernian		82/83	11	2	1	P
		83/84	8	8	2	P
		84/85	2	1		P
Dundee		84/85	7		2	P
		85/86	25	5	5	P
		86/87	28	5	12	P
		87/88	10	19	4	P
		88/89	11	9	4	P
		89/90	4	2	1	P
Airdrieonians		89/90	20	7	8	D1
		90/91	24	3	11	D1
		91/92	0	2		P
Hong Kong		92/93				
		93/94				
		94/95				
Livingston		95/96	6	12	3	D3
		96/97	27	2	15	D2
		97/98	25	5	15	D2

HARVEY Paul Edward
b. Glasgow 28.8.1968

Manchester U						
Clydebank		87/88	23	6	1	D1
		88/89	19	10	1	D1
		89/90	34		3	D1
		90/91	36		2	D1
		91/92	38	3	4	D1
		92/93	37	2	5	D1
		93/94	26		3	D1
Airdrieonians		93/94	9	4	1	D1
		94/95	33		2	D1
		95/96	27	7	2	D1
Raith R		96/97	10	8		P
		97/98	1			D1
Dumbarton		98/99	7	2		D3
Livingston		98/99	1	3		D2
Queen of the South		99/00	9		2	D2
Motherwell		99/00	6	7		P

HARVIE Scott Smith
b. Glasgow 22.11.1968

Rothes						
Aberdeen		87/88	1			P
		88/89				
		89/90	1	1		P
Coleraine		90/91				
Partick T		91/92	7	2		D1
		92/93				
St Mirren		93/94	4	2	1	D1

HATELEY Mark Wayne
b. Derby 7.11.1961

Coventry C		78/79	1			FL
		79/80	2	2		FL
		80/81	17	2	3	FL
		81/82	31	3	13	FL
		82/83	35		9	FL
Portsmouth		83/84	38		22	FL
AC Milan		84/85				
		85/86				
		86/87				
AS Monaco		87/88				
		88/89				
		89/90				
Rangers		90/91	30	3	10	P
		91/92	29	1	21	P
		92/93	36	1	21	P
		93/94	40	2	22	P
		94/95	23		13	P
QPR		95/96	10	4	2	FL
		96/97	8	5	1	FL
Rangers		96/97	4		1	P
Leeds U	L	96/97	5	1		FL
Hull C		97/98	4	5		FL
		98/99	8	4	3	FL
Ross Co		99/00	2			D2

HATHER John

Aberdeen		75/76	0	1		P

HAWKE Warren Robert
b. Durham 20.9.1970

Sunderland		88/89	1	3		FL
		89/90	1	7	1	FL
		90/91	3	4		FL
		91/92	2	2		FL
Chesterfield	L	91/92	7		1	FL
Sunderland		92/93	0	2		FL
Carlisle U	L	92/93	8		2	FL
Northampton T	L	92/93	7		1	FL
Raith R		93/94	1	1		P
Scarborough		93/94	0	1		FL
Berwick R		93/94	20		12	D2
		94/95	35		16	D2
Morton		95/96	34	1	13	D1
		96/97	25	7	7	D1
		97/98	32		10	D1
		98/99	27	4	3	D1
		99/00	9	6	1	D1
Queen of the South		99/00	17		4	D2

HAY Christopher Drummond
b. Glasgow 28.8.1974

Clarkston BC						
Giffnock North						
Celtic		93/94	2			P
		94/95	2	3		P
		95/96	1	3		P
		96/97	4	10	4	P
Swindon T		97/98	30	6	14	FL
		98/99	16	11	6	FL
		99/00	27	4	10	FL

HAY Douglas

Clydebank		74/75	11	4	1	D2
		75/76	25		3	D2
		76/77	20		1	D1
		77/78	12	2	1	P

HAY Garry
b. Irvine 7.9.1977

Kilmarnock		99/00	8	2	2	P

HAYES Archibald David Mackie
b. Glasgow 10.6.1953

Morton		69/70	3	1		D1
		70/71	9			D1
		71/72	27			D1
		72/73	30		1	D1
		73/74	34			D1
		74/75	31			D1
		75/76	25			D1
		76/77	37			D1
		77/78	30		2	D1
		78/79	28			P
		79/80	21			P
		80/81	31			P
		81/82	35			P
		82/83	9	1		P
		83/84	4	1		D1
Queen of the South		84/85	6			D2
Partick T		84/85	6			D1

HAYES Martin
b. Walthamstow 21.3.1966

Arsenal		85/86	11		2	FL
		86/87	31	4	19	FL
		87/88	17	10	1	FL
		88/89	3	14	1	FL
		89/90	8	4	3	FL
Celtic		90/91	3	4		P
		91/92				
Coventry C	L	91/92				
Wimbledon	L	91/92	1	1		FL
Swansea C		92/93	8	7		FL
		93/94	22		4	FL
		94/95	14	10	4	FL

HEALY Colin
b. Cork 14.3.1980

Wilton U						
Celtic		98/99	2	1		P
		99/00	8	2	1	P

HEDDLE Ian Alexander
b. Dunfermline 21.3.1963

Dunfermline A		83/84	1			D2
		84/85	3		1	D2
		85/86	25		3	D2
		86/87	10		2	D1
St Johnstone		86/87	19		2	D2
		87/88	35	1	9	D2
		88/89	35	1	2	D1
		89/90	38	1	5	D1
		90/91	3	5		P
Australia						
Forfar A		92/93	37	1	6	D2
		93/94	39		8	D2
		94/95	25	5	1	D3
		95/96	6	2		D2
Brechin C		95/96	7	1		D3
		96/97	11	5		D2
		97/98	8	1	1	D2

HEGARTY Paul A
b. Edinburgh 25.7.1954

Tynecastle BC						
Hamilton A		72/73	36		7	D2
		73/74	31		10	D2
Dundee U		74/75	10	7	4	D1
		75/76	31	2	8	P
		76/77	36		6	P
		77/78	36		4	P
		78/79	36		5	P
		79/80	27			P
		80/81	33		3	P
		81/82	36		2	P
		82/83	36		3	P
		83/84	36		4	P
		84/85	33		2	P
		85/86	36		5	P
		86/87	21	2	4	P
		87/88	40	1	1	P
		88/89	27	2	1	P
		89/90	5			P
St Johnstone		89/90	14		1	D1
Forfar A		90/91	32			D1
		91/92	8		1	D1

HENDERSON Atholl
b. Perth 7.10.1957

St Johnstone		75/76	4	4		P
Celtic		76/77				
Forfar A		77/78	3	3	1	D2
		78/79	18	4	6	D2
		79/80	5	4	2	D2
Brechin C		79/80	21	4	6	D2
		80/81	23	8	3	D2
		81/82	13	7	4	D2
		82/83	5	2	1	D2

HENDERSON James
b. Glasgow 18.3.1966

Falkirk		86/87	1			P
East Stirlingshire		86/87	8			D2
Stenhousemuir		86/87	2			D2
Oakleigh		87/88				
		88/89				
Ayr U		89/90	1			D1
East Stirlingshire		89/90	10		1	D2
Albion R		90/91	26	9	2	D2
		91/92	4	3	3	D2

HENDERSON Nicholas Sinclair
b. Edinburgh 8.2.1969

Raith R		90/91	1			D1
		91/92				
Cowdenbeath		92/93	30	2	5	D1
		93/94	22		9	D2
Falkirk		93/94	8	2	2	D1
		94/95	14	7	5	P
		95/96	0	9		P
Partick T		95/96	12	4	1	P
		96/97	12	4	2	D1
		97/98	28	5	4	D1
Hamilton A		98/99	24	4		D1
		99/00	19	2	6	D2
Clyde		99/00	6	1		D2

HENDERSON William Martin Melville
b. Kirkcaldy 3.5.1956

Rangers		73/74				
		74/75				
		75/76	23	3	10	P
		76/77	4	3		P
		77/78				
Hibernian	L	77/78	4	2		P
Philadelphia Fury		78	17		3	NA
Airdrieonians		78/79	1	1		D1
Leicester C		78/79	31	2	4	FL
		79/80	32	4	5	FL
		80/81	16	6	3	FL
Chesterfield		81/82	44		13	FL
		82/83	40		10	FL
		83/84	3			FL
Port Vale		83/84	27		7	FL
Spalding U						
Bourne T						
Spalding U						

HENDRIE Thomas
b. Edinburgh 24.10.1955

Dundee		75/76	2			P
Arbroath		76/77	0	3		D1
Dundee		77/78				
Goole T		78/79				
		79/80				
Meadowbank T		80/81	18	4		D2
		81/82	35	4	7	D2
		82/83	35		13	D2
		83/84	39		4	D1
		84/85	37	1	4	D1
		85/86	37	1		D2
		86/87	39			D2
		87/88	32		1	D1
		88/89	19	5		D1
		89/90				
		90/91	25	4		D1
		91/92				
Berwick R		92/93	26	4		D2

HENDRY Edward Colin James
b. Keith 7.12.1965

Dundee		83/84	1	3		P
		84/85	3	1		P
		85/86	10	10		P
		86/87	3	10	2	P
Blackburn R		87/88	44		12	FL
		88/89	38		7	FL
		89/90	5	2		FL
Manchester C		89/90	25		3	FL
		90/91	32		1	FL
		91/92	0	6	1	FL
Blackburn R		91/92	26	4	4	FL
		92/93	41		1	FL
		93/94	22	1		FL
		94/95	38		4	FL
		95/96	33		1	FL
		96/97	35		1	FL
		97/98	34		1	FL
Rangers		98/99	16	3		P
		99/00	1	1		P
Coventry C		99/00	9			FL

HENDRY Ian
b. Glasgow 19.10.1959

Aston Villa		77/78				
		78/79				
Hereford U		78/79	15			FL
		79/80	6			FL
Hibernian		80/81				
		81/82	0	1		P

HENDRY John
b. Glasgow 6.1.1970

Dundee		88/89	0	2		P
Forfar A		89/90	10		6	D1
Tottenham H		90/91	2	2	2	FL
		91/92	1	4	1	FL
Charlton A	L	91/92	1	4	1	FL
Tottenham H		92/93	2	3	2	FL
		93/94	0	3		FL
		94/95				
Swansea C	L	94/95	8		2	FL
Motherwell		95/96	8	8	2	P
		96/97	5	1		P
		97/98	10	3	1	P
Stirling A		98/99	6	1	2	D2

HENRY Fabrice
b. Argenteuil 13.2.1968

Basle						
Hibernian		99/00	6	3		P

HENRY James
b. Dundee 4.2.1949

Carnoustie Jnrs						
Dundee U		67/68				
		68/69				
		69/70	24		2	D1
		70/71	29	2	1	D1
		71/72	19		1	D1
		72/73	12		3	D1
		73/74	8			D1
Aberdeen		73/74	6			D1
		74/75	11			D1
		75/76	1			P
San Antonio Thunder		76	18			NA
Forfar A		76/77				
		77/78				

HENRY John
b. Vale of Leven 31.12.1971

Clydebank		90/91	2	1	1	D1
		91/92	32	3	1	D1
		92/93	32		12	D1
		93/94	42	2	7	D1
Kilmarnock		94/95	28	2	4	P
		95/96	22	6	3	P
		96/97	18	4	2	P
		97/98	13	14	1	P
		98/99	7	4	3	P
Falkirk		98/99	11	1	5	D1
Kilmarnock		99/00	1			P
Falkirk		99/00	21		3	D1

HESSEY Sean Peter
b. Whiston 19.9.1978

Liverpool						
Leeds U		97/98				
Wigan A		97/98				
Huddersfield T		97/98	0	1		FL
		98/99	7	3		FL
Kilmarnock		99/00	7	4		P

HETHERSTON Peter
b. Bellshill 6.11.1964

Bargeddie U						
Falkirk		84/85	9	3	2	D1
		85/86	15	7	2	D1
		86/87	33	3	3	P
Watford		87/88	2	3		FL
Sheffield U		87/88	11			FL
Falkirk		88/89	26	5	3	P
		89/90	14	8	2	D1
		90/91	22	4	4	D1
Raith R		91/92	31		1	D1
		92/93	44		4	D1
		93/94	33		5	P
Aberdeen		94/95	13	9		P
		95/96	9	2		P
Airdrieonians		95/96	7	2	4	D1
		96/97	5			D1
Partick T		97/98	5		1	D1
		98/99				
Raith R		99/00	3	11	2	D1

HEWITT John
b. Aberdeen 9.2.1963

Middlefield Wasps						
Hilton Academy						
Aberdeen		79/80	2	2		P
		80/81	9	12	2	P
		81/82	22	3	11	P
		82/83	9	7	5	P
		83/84	22	10	9	P
		84/85	11	10	3	P
		85/86	18	5	6	P
		86/87	29	5	11	P
		87/88	26	11	1	P
		88/89	21	6	3	P
Celtic		89/90	8	4		P
		90/91	1	3		P
Middlesbrough	L	91/92	0	2		FL
St Mirren		91/92	14		3	P
Deveronvale		92/93				
St Mirren		92/93	25	3	5	D1
		93/94	27	4	4	D1
		94/95	9	7	2	D1
		95/96				
Ross Co		96/97	2	5	1	D3

HIGGINS Anthony
b. Glasgow 3.6.1954

Hibernian		72/73	11		3	D1
		73/74	5	3	2	D1
		74/75	5	1	3	D1
		75/76	1	3		P
		76/77	4	1	2	P
		77/78	24		7	P
		78/79	21	2	4	P
		79/80	20	2	2	P
Partick T		79/80	11	1		P
		80/81	21		7	P
		81/82	14	9	2	P
Morton		82/83	3	2		P
		83/84	1	4		D1
Stranraer		84/85	4	6	4	D2
		85/86	15	8	3	D2
		86/87	7	3	2	D2

HIGNETT Craig John
b. Prescot 12.1.1970

Liverpool						
Crewe A		88/89	1			FL
		89/90	30	5	8	FL
		90/91	31	7	13	FL
		91/92	32	1	13	FL
		92/93	14		8	FL
Middlesbrough		92/93	18	3	4	FL
		93/94	25	4	5	FL
		94/95	19	7	8	FL
		95/96	17	5	5	FL
		96/97	19	3	4	FL
		97/98	28	8	7	FL
Aberdeen		98/99	13		2	P

HILL Hugh
b. Hamilton 4.7.1957

Albion R		76/77	18	2	5	D2
		77/78	33	3	3	D2
		78/79	34	2	5	D2
		79/80	35		4	D2
		80/81	33	1	8	D2
		81/82	5		1	D2
Arbroath		81/82	14	2		D2
		82/83	31	3	4	D2
		83/84	34		3	D2
		84/85	9	2		D2
East Fife		84/85	28		1	D1
		85/86	23	1		D1
		86/87	16		2	D1
Falkirk		87/88	22	12	1	P
Brechin C		88/89	22	3		D2
		89/90	36	1	2	D2
		90/91	32	4	2	D1
		91/92	14	6		D2

HINDS Peter R
b. Barbados 8.6.1962

Jujita						
Dundee U		89/90	7	6		P
Maritimo						

HOGARTH Myles
b. Falkirk 30.3.1975

Heart of Midlothian		95/96	1			P
		96/97				
Airdrieonians		97/98	12			D1
Hamilton A		97/98	5			D1
Falkirk		98/99	5			D1
		99/00	36			D1

HOGG Graeme James
b. Aberdeen 17.6.1964

Manchester U		83/84	16		1	FL
		84/85	29			FL
		85/86	17			FL
		86/87	11			FL
		87/88	9	1		FL
WBA	L	87/88	7			FL
Portsmouth		88/89	41		1	FL
		89/90	36	3	1	FL
		90/91	20			FL
Heart of Midlothian		91/92	13	5	1	P
		92/93	20	2	2	P
		93/94	16	1		P
		94/95	0	1		P
Notts Co		94/95	17			FL
		95/96	10			FL
		96/97	35			FL
		97/98	4			FL
Brentford		97/98	17		2	FL

HOGGAN Wilson
b. Falkirk 17.7.1948
Linlithgow Rose

Falkirk		68/69	12	4		D1
		69/70	30	1	4	D2
		70/71	28	2	4	D1
		71/72	32		3	D1
		72/73	28	2	3	D1
		73/74	25		3	D1
		74/75	7		3	D2
Dundee		74/75	25		5	D1
		75/76	16	4	5	P
		76/77	23	4	2	D1
		77/78	0	1		D1
Alloa A *		77/78	10			D1
Stenhousemuir *		77/78	1			D2
Falkirk		78/79	30	2	1	D2
		79/80	17	3		D2
		80/81	36		2	D1
		81/82	39		4	D1
		82/83	27		4	D1

HOLMES Derek
b. Lanark 18.10.1978
Royal Albert

Heart of Midlothian		96/97	1			P
		97/98	0	1	1	P
Cowdenbeath	L	97/98	13		5	D3
Heart of Midlothian		98/99	1	5		P
Raith R		98/99	13	1	6	D1
Ross Co		99/00	20	5	8	D2

HOLMES James B
b. Hamilton 8.12.1954
Partick T

Morton		76/77	39			D1
		77/78	38	1		D1
		78/79	35			P
		79/80	33		2	P
		80/81	34			P
		81/82	35			P
		82/83	35			P
		83/84	37			D1
		84/85	36		1	P
		85/86	35		1	D1
		86/87	41		3	P
		87/88	38			P
Falkirk		87/88	6			P
		88/89	38			D1
		89/90	7	2		D1
Alloa A		89/90	8			D1
Arbroath		90/91	37			D2

HOLT Gary
b. Irvine 9.3.1973
Stoke C

Kilmarnock		95/96	17	9		P
		96/97	10	2	1	P
		97/98	25	2	2	P
		98/99	33		3	P
		99/00	35			P

HOLT John W
b. Dundee 21.11.1956
Invergowrie BC

Dundee U		72/73				
		73/74				
		74/75				
		75/76	13	3		P
		76/77	4	4		P
		77/78	13	2	3	P
		78/79	26	1	3	P
		79/80	16	1	4	P
		80/81	22	2		P
		81/82	26	2	1	P
		82/83	18	7	4	P
		83/84	26	6	2	P
		84/85	23	2		P
		85/86	20	7		P
		86/87	15	3		P
		87/88	5	1		P
Dunfermline A		87/88	35		1	P
		88/89	13		1	D1
Dundee		88/89	10	1		P
		89/90	2			P
		90/91	4	4		D1
Forfar A		90/91	14	1		D1
		91/92	36			D1
Deveronvale		92/93				
Montrose		93/94	0	1		D2

HONEYMAN Graham

East Fife		70/71				
		71/72	27	4	3	D1
		72/73	15	6	5	D1
		73/74	6	3		D1
		74/75	12	15	2	D2
		75/76	9	4	2	D1
West Adelaide Hellas		76/77				
		77/78				
Dundee U		78/79	2	1		P

HONOR Christian Robert
b. Bristol 5.6.1968

Bristol C		85/86	1			FL
		86/87	1	1		FL
Torquay U	L	86/87	3			FL
Bristol C		87/88	14	3		FL
		88/89	24	2		FL
		89/90	4	10	1	FL
Hereford U	L	89/90	2	1		FL
Swansea C	L	90/91	2			FL
Airdrieonians		91/92	30			P
		92/93	28	1	3	P
		93/94	32	2	2	D1
		94/95	1			D1
Cardiff C	L	94/95	10			FL
?		95/96				
		96/97				
Partick T		97/98	2			D1

HOOD Henry Anthony
b. Glasgow 3.10.1944
Campsie Black Watch
St Rochs

Queens Park		61/62				
Brunswick BC						
Clyde		62/63	15		5	D1
		63/64				
		64/65	11		4	D1
Sunderland		64/65	24		8	FL
		65/66				
		66/67	7		1	FL
Clyde		66/67	27		10	D1
		67/68	34		13	D1
		68/69	26		7	D1
Celtic		68/69	7		5	D1
		69/70	25	3	8	D1
		70/71	27	3	22	D1
		71/72	24		11	D1
		72/73	22	7	12	D1
		73/74	28	3	7	D1
		74/75	21	6	8	D1
		75/76	7	7	1	P
San Antonio Thunder		76	20		10	NA
Motherwell		76/77	6	9		P
Queen of the South		77/78	31	1	4	D1

HORN Robert David
b. Edinburgh 3.8.1977

Heart of Midlothian		96/97	1			P
		97/98				
Cowdenbeath		98/99	8			D3
Forfar A		99/00	6			D3

HOTSON John

St Johnstone		72/73	14		1	D1
		73/74	17	5	1	D1
		74/75	5	2		D1
		75/76	13	4	1	P
Morton		76/77	10	9	1	D1

HOUCHEN Keith Morton
b. Middlesbrough 25.7.1960

Chesterfield		77/78				
Hartlepool U		77/78	13		4	FL
		78/79	38	1	12	FL
		79/80	35	6	14	FL
		80/81	42	3	17	FL
		81/82	32		18	FL
Leyton Orient		81/82	14		1	FL
		82/83	32		10	FL
		83/84	28	2	9	FL
York C		83/84	1	6	1	FL
		84/85	35		13	FL
		85/86	20	5	6	FL
Scunthorpe U		85/86	9		2	FL
Coventry C		86/87	20		2	FL
		87/88	13	8	3	FL
		88/89	10	3	2	FL
Hibernian		88/89	7		2	P
		89/90	27	2	8	P
		90/91	17	4	1	P
Port Vale		91/92	18	3	4	FL
		92/93	26	2	6	FL
Hartlepool U		93/94	34		8	FL
		94/95	32		13	FL
		95/96	36	2	6	FL
		96/97	2	3		FL

HOUSTON David
b. Glasgow 4.12.1956

Clydebank		76/77	8	2	3	D1
		77/78	23	3	1	P
		78/79	38		2	D1
		79/80	36		3	D1
		80/81	33		1	D1
		81/82	5	2		D1
Alloa A		82/83	39		3	D1
		83/84	38		2	D1
		84/85	8		3	D2
Dunfermline A		85/86	7	8		D2
Clyde		86/87	2	3		D1
Albion R		87/88	26	1		D2
		88/89	3			D2

HOUSTON Douglas A
b. 13.4.1943
Giffnock North

Queens Park		60/61	29		8	D2
		61/62	27		7	D2
Dundee		62/63	17		4	D1
		63/64	8			D1
		64/65	5			D1
		65/66	15		3	D1
		66/67	11		1	D1
		67/68	25		1	D1
		68/69	32			D1
		69/70	30		2	D1
		70/71	32	1		D1
		71/72	28			D1
		72/73	33		5	D1
Rangers		73/74	9	1		D1
Dundee U		73/74	6			D1
		74/75	25	1	3	D1
		75/76	33		2	P
		76/77	20	1		P
St Johnstone		77/78	39			D1
		78/79	7	1		D1

HOUSTON Robert Joseph
b. Glasgow 23.1.1952
Rutherglen Glencairn

Partick T		72/73	9			D1
		73/74	31	2	2	D1
		74/75	33		2	D1
		75/76	22		2	D1
		76/77	18	2	1	P
		77/78	28	4	7	P
		78/79	31	2	4	P
		79/80	3	1		P
Kilmarnock		79/80	24	1	6	P
		80/81	14	1		P
Morton		80/81	3	5		P
		81/82	19	6	4	P
		82/83	35	1	1	P
		83/84	37		3	D1

HOWIE Scott
b. Glasgow 4.1.1972

Clyde		91/92	15			D2
		92/93	39			D2
		93/94	1			D1
Norwich C		93/94	1	1		FL
Motherwell		94/95	3			P
		95/96	36			P
		96/97	30			P
Reading		97/98	7			FL
		98/99	42			FL
		99/00	35	1		FL

HUGGINS David

Hibernian		79/80	3			P
East Fife		80/81	1			D2

HUGHES James
b. Glasgow 9.1.1960
Clyde Valley

Kilmarnock		78/79				
		79/80	0	2		P
		80/81	9	4	2	P
Pollok Jnrs		81/82				
East Stirlingshire		82/83	3	1	1	D2
Pollok Jnrs		83/84				
		84/85				
Falkirk		85/86	24	5	4	D1
		86/87	4	8		P
Queen of the South		87/88	36	2	17	D1
		88/89	9		1	D1
Clydebank		88/89	9	5	1	D1
		89/90	10	1	3	D1
Dumbarton		89/90	24	1	7	D2
		90/91	5	4		D2
		91/92	3	3		D2

HUGHES John
b. Edinburgh 9.9.1964

Berwick R		88/89	27		10	D2
		89/90	14		4	D2
Swansea C		89/90	16	8	4	FL
Falkirk		90/91	31	1	2	P
		91/92	38		2	P
		92/93	15			P
		93/94	28	1	3	D1
		94/95	17	3		P
Celtic		95/96	26		2	P
		96/97	5	1		P
Hibernian		96/97	4			P
		97/98	24	1	1	P
		98/99	22	1	3	D1
		99/00	20			P

HUGHES Martin
b. Glasgow 20.1.1962

Clydebank BC						
Clydebank		80/81				
		81/82	13	3	1	D1
		82/83	38		5	D1
		83/84	39		3	D1
		84/85	38		8	D1
		85/86	21	6	2	P
		86/87	8			P
Airdrieonians		86/87	19		2	D1
		87/88	9	6	1	D1
Kilmarnock		88/89	3			D1
Stirling A		88/89	16	2	2	D2
		89/90	1	4		D2

HUGHES Stephen
b. Motherwell 14.11.1982

Rangers		99/00	0	1		P

HUISTRA Peter
b. Goenga 18.1.1967

FC Twente						
Rangers		90/91	10	17	4	P
		91/92	25	7	5	P
		92/93	27	3	4	P
		93/94	10	11	6	P
		94/95	15		3	P
Sanfrecce Hiroshima						
Lierse SK						

HUMPHRIES Mark
b. Glasgow 23.12.1971

Cove R						
Aberdeen		91/92	2			P
		92/93				
Leeds U		93/94				
		94/95				
Bristol C		94/95	4			FL
Raith R		95/96	9			P
Ayr U		96/97	22			D2

HUNTER Alistair Robert
b. Glasgow 4.10.1949

Drumchapel Amateurs						
Rangers	T					
Leicester C	T					
Johnstone Burgh						
Kilmarnock		69/70				
		70/71	30			D1
		71/72	34			D1
		72/73	12			D1
Celtic		72/73	15			D1
		73/74	26			D1
		74/75	18			D1
		75/76	1			P
Motherwell		76/77	8			P
		77/78				
St Mirren		77/78	7			P
Clydebank		78/79				

HUNTER Donald
b. Dumbarton 1.4.1955

St Mirren		76/77	39			D1
		77/78	19			P
Dumbarton		78/79	15			D1
		79/80	6			D1
		80/81	6			D1
Alloa A		81/82	39			D2
		82/83	39			D1
		83/84	38			D1
		84/85	7			D2

HUNTER Gordon
b. Wallyford 3.5.1967

Musselburgh Windsor						
Hibernian		83/84	1			P
		84/85	5	1		P
		85/86	25			P
		86/87	25	4		P
		87/88	36			P
		88/89	33		1	P
		89/90	34			P
		90/91	20		1	P
		91/92	37		2	P
		92/93	22			P
		93/94	29		1	P
		94/95	29		2	P
		95/96	22			P
		96/97	16	1		P
Australia						
Dundee		98/99	3			P
Cowdenbeath		98/99	2		1	D3
Hamilton A		99/00	21	1	1	D2

HUNTER James Addison
b. Johnstone 20.12.1964

Morton		85/86	26	1		D1
		86/87	43			D1
		87/88	36	2		P
		88/89	35			P
		89/90	36			P
		90/91	38			P
		91/92	3			P
		92/93				
		93/94	21		1	P
		94/95	6	2		P
		95/96	0	1		P
		96/97	3			P

HURLOCK Terence Alan
b. Hackney 22.9.1958

Leytonstone & Ilford						
Brentford		80/81	42		4	FL
		81/82	40		2	FL
		82/83	39		3	FL
		83/84	32		4	FL
		84/85	40		3	FL
		85/86	27		2	FL
Reading		85/86	16			FL
		86/87	13			FL
Millwall		86/87	13		1	FL
		87/88	27	1	4	FL
		88/89	34		3	FL
		89/90	29			FL
Rangers		90/91	29	2		P
Southampton		91/92	27	2		FL
		92/93	30			FL
		93/94	2			FL
Millwall		93/94	13			FL
Fulham		94/95	27		1	FL

HUTCHINSON Robert
b. Glasgow 19.6.1953

Montrose		72/73	8	2	1	D2
		73/74	25	3	7	D2
Dundee		74/75	21	2	7	D1
		75/76	18	3	5	P
		76/77	35		12	D1
		77/78	8	1	1	D1
Hibernian		77/78	20		6	P
		78/79	19	3	4	P
		79/80	18	7	3	P
Wigan A		80/81	34	1	3	FL
Tranmere R		81/82	26	3	4	FL
		82/83	6		2	FL
Mansfield T		82/83	25		3	FL
		83/84	10			FL
Tranmere R		83/84	21		4	FL
Bristol C		84/85	31		4	FL
		85/86	42		4	FL
		86/87	18	1	1	FL
Walsall		86/87	8	6		FL
		87/88	0	2		FL
Blackpool	L	87/88	3	3		FL
Carlisle U	L	87/88	12	1	2	FL

HUTCHINSON Thomas A
b. Glasgow 12.5.1971

Tullibody Hearts						
St Mirren		89/90	0	1		P
		90/91	0	2		P
Stenhousemuir		91/92	2			D2

HUTCHISON Roderick
b. Lennoxtown 25.3.1955

Clyde		74/75	0	1		D1
Pollok Jnrs						
Morton		76/77	2	2	1	D1
		77/78	21	5	1	D1
		78/79	16	2	1	P
		79/80	31	4	5	P
		80/81	11	5	3	P
		81/82	35	1	5	P
		82/83	30		4	P
Hamilton A		83/84	18		2	D1
Queen of the South		83/84	2			D2
Partick T		83/84	7	1		D1
		84/85	10		2	D1
East Fife		84/85	3			D1
Petershill						
Kilsyth R						

HUXFORD Richard John
b. Scunthorpe 25.7.1969

Kettering T						
Barnet		92/93	33		1	FL
Millwall		93/94	25	6		FL
Birmingham C	L	93/94	5			FL
Millwall		94/95	0	1		FL
Bradford C		94/95	33		1	FL
		95/96	21	5	1	FL
		96/97	1	1		FL
Peterborough U	L	96/97	7			FL
Burnley		96/97	2	7		FL
		97/98	4			FL
Dunfermline A		97/98	9	1		P
		98/99	22	3		P
		99/00	2		1	D1

HYSLOP Derek
b. Girvan 6.9.1957

St Mirren		75/76	6	3		D1
		76/77	36	3	17	D1
		77/78	16	5	4	P
		78/79	3	5	2	P
Clyde		79/80	20	5		D1
		80/81	2	1		D2
Arbroath		80/81	23		5	D2
		81/82	19	3	1	D2
Cowdenbeath		81/82	9		3	D2
		82/83	17		1	D2
		83/84	5			D2
Queen of the South		83/84	1		2	D2
Brechin C		83/84	18	4	4	D1
		84/85	3	2		D1
East Fife		84/85	8		2	D1
Queen of the South		84/85	11	1	2	D2
Stenhousemuir		85/86	2	1		D2

HYSLOP John
b. 11.3.1957

Ayr U		75/76	1			P
		76/77	3	2		P
		77/78	18	3		P
		78/79	5	1		D1
		79/80	6			D1
Stranraer		80/81	28	2		D2
		81/82	17	1		D2

INGLIS John
b. Edinburgh 16.10.1966

East Fife		83/84	0	4	1	D2
		84/85	3	6		D1
		85/86	24	6		D1
		86/87	11	2		D1
Brechin C		86/87	15			D1
		87/88	25	1	3	D2
		88/89	11	1	1	D2
Meadowbank T		88/89	10	2	1	D1
		89/90	37	1	3	D1
St Johnstone		90/91	31		1	P
		91/92	39	1		P
		92/93	39			P
		93/94	25		1	P
		94/95	5			D1
Aberdeen		94/95	16	1	1	P
		95/96	24		1	P
		96/97	15			P
		97/98	25		1	P
		98/99	16	1	1	P
Bulgaria						

INGLIS Neil David
b. Glasgow 10.9.1974

Rangers						
Falkirk		95/96	1			P
Morton		96/97	4			D1
Clydebank		97/98	5			D2
		98/99	1			D1
Linfield		98/99				
Queens Park		98/99	11			D3
		99/00	36			D3

INGOLFSSON Haruldur

b. 1.8.1970

IF Elfsborg						
Raufass IL						
Aberdeen		96/97	1	5		P

INGRAM Alexander David

b. Edinburgh 2.1.1945

Queens Park						
Ayr U		66/67	23	2	4	D1
		67/68				
		68/69				
		69/70	16		7	D1
Nottingham F		69/70	16		3	FL
		70/71	12			FL
Ayr U		707/1	16		4	D1
		71/72	23	3	5	D1
		72/73	32		5	D1
		73/74	18	3	3	D1
		74/75	26	3	8	D1
		75/76	31	1	5	P
		76/77	6	6	2	P

INNES Christopher

b. Broxburn 13.7.1976

Stenhousemuir		96/97	23	1	1	D2
		97/98	30		2	D2
Kilmarnock		98/99	4		1	P
St Mirren		98/99	9			D1
Kilmarnock		99/00	5			P
Falkirk		99/00	2			D1

IORFA Dominic

b. Lagos 1.10.1968

Royal Antwerp						
QPR		89/90	0	1		FL
		90/91	1	1		FL
		91/92	0	1		FL
Galatasaray						
Peterborough U		92/93	3	23	1	FL
		93/94	24	10	8	FL
Southend U		94/95	4	4	1	FL
		95/96	1	1		FL
Falkirk		95/96	3	1	1	P

IRELAND Craig

b. Dundee 29.11.1975

Aberdeen						
Dunfermline A		95/96	10			D1
		96/97	7	2	1	P
		97/98	12		1	P
		98/99	21	2		P
		99/00	1	2		D1
Dundee		99/00	14		1	P

IRONS David J

b. Glasgow 18.7.1961

Kello R						
Ayr U		84/85	29	5	6	D1
		85/86	36	1	6	D1
		86/87	4		1	D2
Clydebank		86/87	17	6	1	P
		87/88	31		6	D1
Dunfermline A		87/88	11		1	P
		88/89	31		6	D1
		89/90	13	10	2	P
		90/91	24	10	4	P
		91/92	1	1		P
Partick T		91/92	40	1	8	D1
		92/93	43		2	P
St Johnstone		93/94	1			P
		94/95	34		2	D1
		95/96	9	8		D1
Clydebank		95/96	8		1	D1
		96/97	35			D1

IRVINE Alan James

b. Broxburn 29.11.1962

Falkirk		82/83	1			D1
		83/84	21	2	2	D1
		84/85	32	2	5	D1
		85/86	32	2	6	D1
		86/87	17	1	4	P
Liverpool		86/87	0	2		FL
Dundee U		87/88	4	3		P
Shrewsbury T		87/88	3	3	1	FL
		88/89	29	2	5	FL
		89/90				
St Mirren		90/91	8	3		P
		91/92	25	3	3	P
		92/93				
East Fife		93/94	22	8	9	D2
		94/95	1	13		D2

IRVINE Brian Alexander

b. Bellshill 24.5.1965

Falkirk		83/84	3			D1
		84/85	35			D1
Aberdeen		85/86	1			P
		86/87	19	1	3	P
		87/88	14	2	1	P
		88/89	21	6	2	P
		89/90	28	3	1	P
		90/91	29		2	P
		91/92	41		4	P
		92/93	39		5	P
		93/94	42		7	P
		94/95	17		1	P
		95/96	17	1	3	P
		96/97	24	1	1	P
Dundee		97/98	36		1	D1
		98/99	33		3	P
Ross Co		99/00	32		6	D2

IRVINE James Alan

b. Glasgow 12.7.1958

Queens Park		77/78	3	1		D2
		78/79	6	2		D2
		79/80	36	2	5	D2
		80/81	38		4	D2
Everton		81/82	25		3	FL
		82/83	7	7	1	FL
		83/84	19	2		FL
Crystal Palace		84/85	34	1	5	FL
		85/86	41		3	FL
Albion R	L	85/86	1			D2
Alloa A	L	85/86	1			D1
Crystal Palace		86/87	33		4	FL
Dundee U		87/88	11	5	2	P
		88/89	6	1	1	P
		89/90	1			P
Blackburn R		89/90	13	12	1	FL
		90/91	23	4	2	FL
		91/92	4	2		FL

IRVINE William

b. Whitburn 26.5.1956

Whitburn Jnrs						
Celtic						
Alloa A		77/78	23	1	4	D1
		78/79	29	1	13	D2
Motherwell		78/79	9		4	P
		79/80	37		13	D1
		80/81	31	3	12	D1
		81/82	39		20	D1
		82/83	2			P
Hibernian		82/83	21	3	4	P
		83/84	36		19	P
		84/85	25		3	P
		85/86	2	1		P
Falkirk		85/86	7	1		D1
Ayr U *		86/87	20		6	D2

IRVINE William

b. Stirling 28.12.1963

Dunipace Thistle						
Stirling A		82/83	10	1	2	D2
		83/84	26	2	12	D2
		84/85	35	2	21	D2
		85/86	29	1	17	D2
Hibernian		86/87	6	6	2	P
Dunfermline A		86/87	6	1	2	D1
		87/88	0	5		P
		88/89				
Airdrieonians		89/90	11	10	7	D1
Albion R		89/90	5		2	D1
Meadowbank T		90/91	31	3	8	D1
		91/92	16	12	5	D1
		92/93	6	3	4	D1
Berwick R		92/93	20	1	9	D2
		93/94	37	1	15	D2
		94/95	36		11	D2
		95/96	35		13	D2
Alloa A		96/97	33		12	D3
		97/98	33		18	D3
		98/99	33		15	D2
		99/00	36		13	D2

JACK James Ross

b. Inverness 21.3.1959

Everton		76/77				
		77/78				
		78/79	1		1	FL
		79/80				
Norwich C		79/80				
		80/81	5	6		FL
		81/82	24	11	10	FL
		82/83	2	8		FL
Lincoln C		83/84	34	2	9	FL
		84/85	18	6	7	FL
Dundee		85/86	5	1		P
		86/87	21	7	4	P
		87/88	0	4		P
Dunfermline A		87/88	21	4	4	P
		88/89	34	2	18	D1
		89/90	34	2	16	P
		90/91	27	5	8	P
Kilmarnock		91/92	27	10	8	D1
		92/93	11	7	5	D1
Montrose		92/93	6		2	D2
		93/94	0	3		D2
Ayr U		93/94	14	4		D1

JACK Matthias

b. Leipzig 15.2.1969

Chemie Leipzig						
Stahl Brandenburg						
Oldenburg						
Rot Weiss Essen						
VFL Bochum						
Fortuna Dusseldorf						
Hibernian		99/00	20	2	1	P

JACK Paul Dunn

b. Malaya 15.5.1965

Fallin MW						
Arbroath		85/86	8	6		D2
		86/87	35		1	D2
		87/88	31			D2
		88/89	23	2	5	D2
Airdrieonians		89/90	24	2	2	D1
		90/91	33	2		D1
		91/92	17	6	1	P
		92/93	32	1	3	P
		93/94	32	3	1	D1
		94/95	29			D1
		95/96	9	5		D1
		96/97	30		1	D1
		97/98	27	5	2	D1
		98/99	21	1		D1
		99/00	29	1	1	D1

JACKSON Christopher

b. Edinburgh 29.10.1973

Hibernian		92/93	0	1		P
		93/94	8	4		P
		94/95				
		95/96	19	4	2	P
		96/97	15	4		P
		97/98	11	4		P
Stirling A		98/99	21	1	1	D2
Cowdenbeath		99/00	5			D3
Clydebank		99/00	5			D1
East Fife		99/00	11			D3

JACKSON Colin MacDonald

b. Falkirk 8.10.1946

Rangers						
Sunnybank A						
Rangers		63/64				
		64/65				
		65/66	1			D1
		66/67	4	1		D1
		67/68				
		68/69	10			D1
		69/70	3			D1
		70/71	34		2	D1
		71/72	24	1	2	D1
		72/73	7			D1
		73/74	18		4	D1
		74/75	33		3	D1
		75/76	33		2	P
		76/77	30		4	P
		77/78	35		3	P
		78/79	28		1	P
		79/80	29		2	P
		80/81	29			P
		81/82	21			P
Morton		82/83	5	1		P
Partick T		82/83				

JACKSON Darren					
b. Edinburgh 25.7.1966					
Meadowbank T	85/86	36	3	17	D2
	86/87	9		5	D2
Newcastle U	86/87	16	7	3	FL
	87/88	24	7	2	FL
	88/89	13	2	2	FL
Dundee U	88/89	1			P
	89/90	24	1	7	P
	90/91	30	3	12	P
	91/92	24	4	11	P
Hibernian	92/93	35	1	13	P
	93/94	29	10	7	P
	94/95	30	1	10	P
	95/96	36		9	P
	96/97	30		11	P
Celtic	97/98	9	14	3	P
	98/99	4	2		P
Heart of Midlothian	98/99	9		1	P
	99/00	31	4	6	P

JAMES Kevin Francis					
b. Edinburgh 3.12.1975					
Musselburgh A					
Falkirk	94/95	1			P
	95/96	10	4	2	P
	96/97	17	1	3	D1
	97/98	17		4	D1
	98/99	11	2		D1
Heart of Midlothian	98/99	1	4		P
	99/00	8	2		P

JAMIESON William George					
b. Barnsley 27.4.1963					
Edina Hearts					
Tynecastle BC					
Hibernian	80/81	19	9	12	D1
	81/82	8	4	5	P
	82/83	16	3	4	P
	83/84	32	1	4	P
	84/85	12	13	2	P
Hamilton A	85/86	39		2	D1
	86/87	14	1		P
	87/88	41		4	D1
	88/89	34		1	P
	89/90	19			D1
Dundee	89/90	14			P
	90/91	38		2	D1
	91/92	38		4	D1
Partick T	92/93	26	3	3	P
	93/94	42	1	1	P
	94/95	15			P
Heart of Midlothian	94/95	13	2	3	P
	95/96	2	3		P
Ayr U	95/96	20		1	D2
	96/97	26		3	D2
	97/98	6			D1
Partick T	98/99	25		2	D2

JARDINE Ian J					
b. Irvine 17.2.1955					
Fenwick Amateurs					
Irvine V					
Kilmarnock	76/77	9	3		P
	77/78	34	2	2	D1
	78/79	27	2	2	D1
	79/80	2	2	1	P
Partick T	79/80	11	6	1	P
	80/81	23	3	1	P
	81/82	22	2	4	P
	82/83	17		4	D1
	83/84	31	1	2	D1
Anorthosis	84/85				
Heart of Midlothian	85/86	19	3	7	P
	86/87	12	3	1	P
	87/88	6	12	2	P
	88/89	2	13	1	P
Partick T	89/90	12			D1

JARDINE William Pullar					
b. Edinburgh 31.12.1948					
United Crossroads					
Edinburgh A					
Rangers	66/67	14		2	D1
	67/68	6	3		D1
	68/69	15	3	4	D1
	69/70	10	4		D1
	70/71	32		1	D1
	71/72	31		5	D1
	72/73	34		2	D1
	73/74	34		3	D1
	74/75	34		9	D1
	75/76	18	7	2	P
	76/77	36		2	P
	77/78	32		5	P
	78/79	35			P
	79/80	35		3	P
	80/81	29	2	3	P
	81/82	36		1	P
Heart of Midlothian	82/83	39		2	D1
	83/84	33			P
	84/85	34			P
	85/86	35			P
	86/87	34		1	P
	87/88	9			P

JARVIE Andrew					
b. Annathill 5.10.1948					
Kirkstyle					
Kilsyth R					
Airdrieonians	67/68	18	1	6	D1
	68/69	27		5	D1
	69/70	34		17	D1
	70/71	34		16	D1
	71/72	28		8	D1
Aberdeen	72/73	33	1	15	D1
	73/74	32		13	D1
	74/75	27	5	9	D1
	75/76	30	2	4	P
	76/77	18	2	9	P
	77/78	35		12	P
	78/79	24	2	4	P
	79/80	22	8	12	P
	80/81	16	7	5	P
	81/82	3	7	2	P
Airdrieonians	82/83	19	2	4	D1
	83/84	6		1	D1
St Mirren	83/84	10	3	2	P
	84/85	1			P
	85/86	2		1	P

JEAN Earl Jude					
b. St Lucia 9.10.1971					
Felgueires					
Ipswich T	96/97	0	1		FL
Rotherham U	96/97	7	11		FL
Plymouth A	97/98	16	20	4	FL
	98/99	21	8	3	FL
Hibernian	99/00	0	5		P

JEFFREY Michael Richard					
b. Liverpool 11.8.1971					
Bolton W	88/89	7	2		FL
	89/90	1	3		FL
	90/91				
	91/92	1	1		FL
Doncster R	91/92	11			FL
	92/93	29	1	12	FL
	93/94	8		1	FL
Newcastle U	93/94	2			FL
	94/95				
Rotherham U	95/96	22		5	FL
Fortuna Sittard	96/97				
	97/98				
	98/99				
Kilmarnock	99/00	10	8	2	P

JEFFRIES James					
b. Musselburgh 22.11.1950					
Heart of Midlothian	71/72	7			D1
	72/73	8			D1
	73/74	23	1		D1
	74/75	27	1		D1
	75/76	26	3		P
	76/77	18	2	3	P
	77/78	38		1	D1
	78/79	26	2		P
	79/80	32		1	D1
	80/81	12	1		P
Berwick R	81/82	22			D2
	82/83	38			D2

JENKINS Grant R					
b. Dundee 11.4.1958					
Jeanfield Swifts					
Dunfermline A	80/81	9	2	2	D1
	81/82	31	4	7	D1
	82/83	21	1	3	D1
	83/84	26	3	6	D2
	84/85	25	8	9	D2
	85/86	23	14	14	D2
	86/87	28	12	6	D1
	87/88	12	4		P
St Johnstone	87/88	8	7	1	D2
	88/89	24	9	9	D1
	89/90	20	8	3	D1

JENKINS Iain					
b. Prescot 24.11.1972					
Everton	90/91	1			FL
	91/92	1	2		FL
	92/93	1			FL
Bradford C	92/93	6			FL
Chester C	93/94	30	4		FL
	94/95	40			FL
	95/96	12	1		FL
	96/97	39			FL
	97/98	34		1	FL
Dunfermline A	97/98	7			P
Dundee U	98/99	5	1		P
	99/00	1			P

JENKINSON Leigh					
b. Thorne 9.7.1969					
Hull C	87/88	2	1	1	FL
	88/89	6	5		FL
	89/90	9	13		FL
	90/91	12	14		FL
Rotherham U L	90/91	5	2		FL
Hull C	91/92	41	1	8	FL
	92/93	25	1	4	FL
Coventry C	92/93	2	3		FL
	93/94	10	6		FL
Birmingham C L	93/94	2	1		FL
Coventry C	94/95	10	1	1	FL
St Johnstone	95/96	18		2	D1
	96/97	22	3	6	D1
	97/98	16	8	3	P
Wigan A	98/99	3	4		FL
Heart of Midlothian	98/99	3	2		P
Dundee U	99/00	1	3		P

JESS Eoin					
b. Aberdeen 13.12.1970					
Aberdeen	88/89	1	1		P
	89/90	7	4	3	P
	90/91	20	7	13	P
	91/92	33	6	12	P
	92/93	28	3	12	P
	93/94	38	3	6	P
	94/95	15	10	1	P
	95/96	25		3	P
Coventry C	95/96	9	3	1	FL
	96/97	19	8		FL
Aberdeen	97/98	35		9	P
	98/99	36		14	P
	99/00	25	1	5	P

JOHANSSON Jonaton					
b. Stockholm 16.8.1975					
Flora Tallinn					
TPS Turku	95				
	96				
Flora Tallinn	96/97				
Rangers	97/98	1	5		P
	98/99	13	12	8	P
	99/00	8	8	6	P

JOHNSON Gavin					
b. Stowmarket 10.10.1970					
Ipswich T	88/89	4			FL
	89/90	3	3		FL
	90/91	5	2		FL
	91/92	33	9	5	FL
	92/93	39	1	5	FL
	93/94	16		1	FL
	94/95	14	3		FL
Luton T	95/96	4	1		FL
Wigan A	95/96	27		3	FL
	96/97	37			FL
	97/98	18	2		FL
Dunfermline A	98/99	18			P

JOHNSON Ian Grant
b. Dundee 24.3.1972

Dundee U		91/92	10		1	P
		92/93	15	2	1	P
		93/94	8	2		P
		94/95	12	1	1	P
		95/96	25	3	4	D1
		96/97	2	5		P
Burnley	L	97/98				
Huddersfield T		97/98	28	1	1	FL
		98/99	36		4	FL
		99/00				

JOHNSON Thomas
b. Newcastle 15.1.1971

Notts Co		88/89	6	4	4	FL
		89/90	34	6	18	FL
		90/91	29	8	16	FL
		91/92	31		9	FL
Derby Co		91/92	12		2	FL
		92/93	34	1	8	FL
		93/94	31	6	13	FL
		94/95	14		7	FL
Aston Villa		94/95	11	3	4	FL
		95/96	17	6	5	FL
		96/97	10	10	4	FL
Celtic		96/97	3	1	1	P
		97/98	1	1		P
		98/99	3		3	P
		99/00	7	3	9	P

JOHNSTON Allan
b. Glasgow 14.12.1973

Heart of Midlothian		92/93	2		1	P
		93/94	5	23	1	P
		94/95	9	12	1	P
		95/96	30	3	9	P
Stade Rennes						
Sunderland		96/97	4	2	1	FL
		97/98	38	2	11	FL
		98/99	40		7	FL
		99/00				
Birmingham C	L	99/00	7	2		FL
Bolton W		99/00	17	2	3	FL

JOHNSTON David

Dundee		68/69	4			D1
		69/70	3		1	D1
		70/71	25	3	1	D1
		71/72	33		4	D1
		72/73	18		1	D1
		73/74	25	2		D1
		74/75	22	3		D1
		75/76	32		2	P
		76/77	21	1		D1
		77/78	22	5		D1
Montrose		78/79	21			D1
		79/80	18		2	D2
		80/81	3			D2

JOHNSTON Forbes Duthie S
b. Aberdeen 3.8.1971
Musselburgh A

Falkirk		91/92	10	2		P
		92/93	17	5	1	P
		93/94	14	1	1	D1
		94/95	3			P
		95/96	3	3		P
Airdrieonians		96/97	15	6	1	D1
		97/98	21	7	1	D1
		98/99	26	5	1	D1
		99/00	16	3		D1

JOHNSTON Harold
b. Glasgow 24.12.1949

Montrose		71/72	26	4	3	D2
		72/73	30	1	2	D2
		73/74	31	4	3	D2
		74/75	34	4	7	D2
		75/76	26		8	D1
		76/77	2	1		D1
Partick T		76/77	12	1	3	P
		77/78	1			P
Brechin C		78/79	17		2	D2
Montrose		79/80	34	3	5	D2
		80/81	28	4	2	D2
		81/82	25	1	4	D2
Stenhousemuir		82/83	28	2	1	D2
		83/84	2	1		D2

JOHNSTON Maurice John Giblin
b. Glasgow 30.4.1963
Milton Battlefield

Partick T		81/82	30	2	9	P
		82/83	39		21	D1
		83/84	14		10	D1
Watford		83/84	28	1	20	FL
		84/85	9		3	FL
Celtic		84/85	27		14	P
		85/86	31	1	15	P
		86/87	39	1	23	P
Nantes		87/88				
		88/89				
Rangers		89/90	36		15	P
		90/91	29		11	P
		91/92	10	1	5	P
Everton		91/92	21		7	FL
		92/93	7	6	3	FL
Heart of Midlothian		93/94	31		4	P
		94/95	3	1	1	P
Falkirk		94/95	10		1	P
		95/96	31		5	P
Kansas City Wiz						

JOHNSTON Samuel
b. Glasgow 13.4.1967

St Johnstone		84/85	2	1		D1
		85/86	21	6	2	D2
		86/87	38	1	6	D2
		87/88	38	1	11	D2
		88/89	21	9	3	D1
		89/90	34	3	7	D1
		90/91	0	1		P
Ayr U		90/91	24		9	D1
Partick T		90/91	8		1	D1
		91/92	19	1	2	D1
		92/93	11	4	1	P
Ballymena U		93/94				
Stranraer		93/94	2			D2
Coleraine		94/95				
		95/96				
		96/97				
		97/98				
Partick T		98/99	4	11		D2

JOHNSTON William

St Mirren		75/76	13	1		D1
		76/77	34	1		D1
		77/78	2			P
		78/79				
Falkirk		79/80	26		1	D2

JOHNSTON William McClure
b. Glasgow 19.12.1946
Lochore Welfare

Rangers		64/65	17		5	D1
		65/66	31		9	D1
		66/67	21		5	D1
		67/68	30	1	18	D1
		68/69	29		18	D1
		69/70	29		12	D1
		70/71	25		9	D1
		71/72	23	1	11	D1
		72/73	4		2	D1
WBA		72/73	22			FL
		73/74	35		2	FL
		74/75	38		7	FL
		75/76	39		6	FL
		76/77	34		1	FL
		77/78	32		2	FL
		78/79	3	4		FL
Vancouver Whitecaps		79	27		1	NA
Birmingham C		79/80	15		1	FL
Vancouver Whitecaps		80	14		2	NA
Rangers		80/81	21	6	2	P
		81/82	6	2		P
Vancouver Whitecaps		82	18			NA
Heart of Midlothian		82/83	24	3	6	D1
		83/84	2	19	2	P
		84/85	4	6	1	P
East Fife		84/85	3			D1

JOHNSTONE Derek Joseph
b. Dundee 4.11.1953
St Francis BC
St Columbas

Rangers		70/71	13	4	6	D1
		71/72	16	1	7	D1
		72/73	31		4	D1
		73/74	31		1	D1
		74/75	27		14	D1
		75/76	32	1	15	P
		76/77	27		15	P
		77/78	33		25	P
		78/79	31		9	P
		79/80	31	2	14	P
		80/81	23	3	4	P
		81/82	27	1	9	P
		82/83	18		6	P
Chelsea		83/84	0	2		FL
Dundee U	L	83/84	2	2		P
Chelsea		84/85	1	1		FL
Rangers		84/85	11		1	P
		85/86	8			P
Partick T		86/87	4			D1

JONES Alexander
b. Blackburn 27.11.1964

Oldham A		82/83	2			FL
		83/84	2			FL
		84/85	3	1		FL
Stockport Co	L	84/85	3			FL
Oldham A		85/86	18		1	FL
Preston NE		86/87	46		1	FL
		87/88	22			FL
		88/89	8	9	3	FL
		89/90	3			FL
Carlisle U		89/90	36		4	FL
		90/91	26			FL
Rochdale		91/92	12	1		FL
Motherwell		91/92	12		1	P
Rochdale		92/93	28	1	2	FL
		93/94	3	1		FL

JONES Graeme Anthony
b. Gateshead 13.3.1970
Bridlington T

Doncaster R		93/94	24	4	4	FL
		94/95	25	7	12	FL
		95/96	31	1	10	FL
Wigan A		96/97	39	1	31	FL
		97/98	28	5	9	FL
		98/99	8	12	3	FL
St Johnstone		99/00	15	4	3	P

JONES Thomas
b. Aldershot 7.10.1964
Weymouth

Aberdeen		87/88	14	14	3	P
Swindon T		88/89	40			FL
		89/90	43	1	2	FL
		90/91	42	1		FL
		91/92	37	4	4	FL
Reading		92/93	21		1	FL
		93/94	11	6		FL
		94/95	18	2	1	FL
		95/96	13	8		FL

JONSSON Gunnlaugar
b. Iceland 29.11.1974

Motherwell		97/98	2			P

JONSSON Sigurdur
b. Akranes 27.9.1966
FH Hafnarfjordur
IA Akranes

Sheffield W		84/85	2	1		FL
		85/86	9	1	2	FL
Barnsley	L	85/86	5			FL
Sheffield W		86/87	12	1		FL
		87/88	11	2	1	FL
		88/89	25	3	1	FL
Arsenal		89/90	0	5	1	FL
		90/91	2			FL
Orebro		91/92				
		92/93				
		93/94				
		94/95				
		95/96				
		96/97				
Dundee U		97/98	14	1		P
		98/99	12	2	1	P
		99/00	14			P

JORGENSEN Henrik
b. Fredericia 16.2.1966
Viborg

Dundee U		94/95	1	1		P

JOYCE Stephen

Ayr U BC

Ayr U		73/74				
		74/75	0	2		D1
		75/76				
		76/77	3			P

JUANJO (PEREZ, Juan Jose Carricondo)

b. Barcelona 4.5.1977

Barcelona

Heart of Midlothian		98/99	1	11		P
		99/00	2	13	3	P

KANCHELSKIS Andrei

b. Kirovgrad 23.1.1969

Shaktyor Donetsk

Manchester U		90/91	1			FL
		91/92	28	6	5	FL
		92/93	14	13	3	FL
		93/94	28	3	6	FL
		94/95	25	5	14	FL
Everton		95/96	32		16	FL
		96/97	20		4	FL
Fiorentina		97/98				
Rangers		98/99	30	1	7	P
		99/00	25	3	4	P

KANE Anthony

b. 12.6.1960

Lanark U

Motherwell		78/79	2			P
		79/80	8	5		D1
		80/81				

KANE Paul James

b. Edinburgh 20.6.1965

Hibernian		83/84	12	1	1	P
		84/85	30	4	8	P
		85/86	30	2	5	P
		86/87	33	4	1	P
		87/88	44		10	P
		88/89	35		5	P
		89/90	31		3	P
		90/91	21			P
Oldham A		90/91	12	5		FL
		91/92	1	3		FL
Aberdeen		91/92	22	3	2	P
		92/93	13	14	4	P
		93/94	39		3	P
		94/95	27		2	P
		95/96				
Barnsley	L	95/96	4			FL
Aberdeen		96/97				
St Johnstone		97/98	24	3	1	P
		98/99	33	1	3	P
		99/00	33	1	1	P

KAVEN Mikko

b. Lahti 19.2.1975

HJK Helsinki

Motherwell		98/99	16			P

KAY Alan

b. Glasgow 2.8.1961

Partick T		81/82	4			P
		82/83	29	1		D1
		83/84	18	5	3	D1
Dumbarton		84/85	36		3	P
		85/86	19	2		D1
		86/87	18	2		D1
		87/88	18	3	1	D1

KAY Robert

b. Edinburgh 24.10.1949

United Crossroads

Heart of Midlothian		70/71	13			D1
		71/72	18			D1
		72/73	15			D1
		73/74	14		1	D1
		74/75	28			D1
		75/76	23	1		P
		76/77	29	2		P
Celtic		77/78	5			P
York C		78/79	46			FL
		79/80	41		3	FL
		80/81	36		1	FL
		81/82	37		4	FL
Northallerton						

KELLACHAN Daniel

b. 24.1.1953

Blantyre Celtic

Hamilton A	T					
Partick T		72/73	9			D1
		73/74	32	1		D1
		74/75	26			D1
		75/76	25			D1
		76/77				
		77/78	2			P
Hamilton A		78/79	31			D1
		79/80	25	1		D1
		80/81	3			D1
Petershill						
Glenafton						
Lesmagahow						

KELLY Colin John

b. London 19.10.1961

Hibernian		80/81	2			D1
Montrose		81/82	20			D2
Dundee		82/83	35			P
		83/84	10			P

KELLY James

Partick T		76/77	1	5		P
		77/78	0	1		P

KELLY Norman

b. Belfast 10.10.1970

Oldham A		87/88	0	1		FL
		88/89	0	1		FL
		89/90				
Wigan A	L	89/90	0	4		FL
Dunfermline A		90/91	1	1		P
		91/92	8			P
		92/93	4			D1
Raith R		93/94	1	3		P

KELLY Patrick

b. Kirkcaldy 26.4.1978

Celtic		96/97	1			P
Newcastle U		97/98				
Reading	L	97/98	3			FL
Newcastle U		98/99				

KELLY William

Ayr U		75/76	1	1		P
		76/77	6	3		P
		77/78	27			P
		78/79	16	2		D1
		79/80	14			D1

KEMBLE Benito

b. Surinam 27.8.1968

Robin Hood

NEC Nijmegen

EVC Eindhoven

Tranmere R	T					
Motherwell		99/00	25		1	P

KEMP Brian

b. Falkirk 30.11.1964

Gairdoch U

Falkirk		82/83	2	2	1	D1
		83/84	14	4	2	D1
		84/85	6	5		D1
East Stirlingshire	L	84/85	14			D2
Falkirk		85/86	4	2		D1
		86/87	17	3		P
Stirling A		86/87	11		3	D2
		87/88	37	1	4	D2
		88/89	32	2	5	D2
Stenhousemuir		89/90	39		4	D2
		90/91	33			D2
		91/92	20		1	D2
		92/93	2		1	D2
East Stirlingshire		92/93	36		3	D2
		93/94	19		3	D2
Alloa A		93/94	12		1	D2
		94/95	20	4	1	D3

KENNEDY Alexander

b. Irvine 25.6.1963

Craigmark Burntonians

Motherwell		83/84	8	3		P
		84/85	14	2	2	D1
		85/86	18	2	1	P
		86/87	26		1	P
		87/88	1	1		P
		88/89	1			P
Partick T		89/90	22		1	D1
		90/91	2			D1
		91/92	9		1	D1

KENNEDY Andrew John

b. Stirling 8.10.1964

Sauchie A

Rangers		82/83	12	1	3	P
		83/84	0	2		P
Everton		84/85				
Seiko						
Birmingham C		84/85	4	3	4	FL
		85/86	27	5	6	FL
		86/87	5	4	1	FL
Sheffield U	L	86/87	8	1	1	FL
Birmingham C		87/88	15	13	7	FL
Blackburn R		88/89	23	2	10	FL
		89/90	26	8	13	FL
Watford		90/91	13	5	3	FL
		91/92	4	3	1	FL
Bolton W	L	91/92	1			FL
Brighton		92/93	26	4	8	FL
		93/94	8	4	2	FL
Gillingham		94/95	0	2		FL
Hong Kong						
Witton A						
Hastings T						
Hendon						

KENNEDY Ian

Motherwell		73/74	6	6		D1
		74/75	5			D1
		75/76	1	1		P
		76/77	24	5	2	P
		77/78	4	7		P
		78/79	5			P
Clyde *		79/80	11	1		D1

KENNEDY John

b. Falkirk 3.3.1953

Falkirk		71/72	5			D1
		72/73	14			D1
		73/74				
Partick T		74/75	1			D1
Stirling A		75/76	22		1	D2
		76/77	34	2	2	D2
		77/78	2	4	2	D1
		78/79	35	1	2	D1
		79/80	31	1	3	D1
		80/81	37		2	D1
		81/82	12			D2
St Johnstone		82/83	16			D1
		83/84	8	3		P

KENNEDY John

b. Bellshill 18.8.1983

Celtic		99/00	1	4		P

KENNEDY Stewart J

b. Stirling 31.8.1949

Camelon Juniors

Dunfermline A		67/68				
		68/69				
Linlithgow Rose						
Stenhousemuir		71/72	36			D2
		72/73	28			D2
Rangers		73/74	1			D1
		74/75	34			D1
		75/76	12			P
		76/77	31			P
		77/78	22			P
		78/79				
		79/80				
Forfar A		80/81	33			D2
		81/82	17			D2
		82/83	37			D2
		83/84	37			D2
		84/85	23			D1
		85/86	13			D1
		86/87	38			D1
		87/88	44			D1
		88/89	31			D1
		89/90	3			D1
		90/91	5			D1
St Johnstone		91/92	1			P

KENNEDY Stuart Robert

b. Grangemouth 31.5.1953

Bothkennor YM

Falkirk		71/72	1			D1
		72/73	34			D1
		73/74	12	1		D1
		74/75	34	2	1	D2
		75/76	26			D1
Aberdeen		76/77	32		1	P
		77/78	34			P
		78/79	32			P
		79/80	35		1	P
		80/81	31			P
		81/82	34		1	P
		82/83	25			P

KERIMOGLU Tugay
b. Istanbul 24.8.1970

Club	L	Season	Apps	Sub	Gls	Div
Galatasaray		87/88				
		88/89				
		89/90				
		90/91				
		91/92				
		92/93				
		93/94				
		94/95				
		95/96				
		96/97				
		97/98				
		98/99				
Rangers		99/00	9	7	1	P

KERNAGHAN Alan Nigel
b. Otley 25.4.1967

Club	L	Season	Apps	Sub	Gls	Div
Middlesbrough		84/85	8		1	FL
		85/86	2	4		FL
		86/87	10	3		FL
		87/88	24	11	6	FL
		88/89	5	18		FL
		89/90	34	3	4	FL
		90/91	23	1		FL
Charlton A	L	90/91	13			FL
Middlesbrough		91/92	38		2	FL
		92/93	22		2	FL
		93/94	6		1	FL
Manchester C		93/94	23	1		FL
		94/95	18	4	1	FL
Bolton W	L	94/95	9	2		FL
Manchester C		95/96	4	2		FL
Bradford C	L	95/96	5			FL
Manchester C		96/97	9	1		FL
		97/98	1			FL
St Johnstone		97/98	28		2	P
		98/99	26		3	P

KERR Alan
b. Irvine 7.5.1976

Club	L	Season	Apps	Sub	Gls	Div
Troon Jnrs						
Kilmarnock		96/97	2	2		P
		97/98				
Hamilton A		98/99	1	1		D1
Queen of the South		99/00	13	8	1	D2

KERR Dylan
b. Valletta 14.1.1967

Club	L	Season	Apps	Sub	Gls	Div
Sheffield W						
Arcadia Shepherds						
Leeds U		88/89	1	2		FL
		89/90	2	3		FL
		90/91				
		91/92				
Doncaster R	L	91/92	7		1	FL
Blackpool	L	91/92	12		1	FL
Leeds U		92/93	3	2		FL
Reading		93/94	45		2	FL
		94/95	35	1	1	FL
		95/96	4	4	2	FL
Carlisle U		96/97	0	1		FL
Kilmarnock		96/97	27			P
		97/98	20			P
		98/99	16			P

KERR James
b. Hamilton 17.1.1959

Club	L	Season	Apps	Sub	Gls	Div
Stonehouse Violet		78/79				
Dundee U		79/80	2			P
		80/81				
Airdrieonians		81/82	3	5		P
Raith R		82/83	28	1	5	D1
		83/84	38	1	16	D1
		84/85	3			D2
Brechin C		84/85	31		3	D1
		85/86	35		2	D1
Falkirk		86/87	34	2	2	P
		87/88	3	4		P
Hamilton A		87/88	22	2		D1
		88/89	8	1		P
Partick T		88/89	25	1	2	D1
		89/90	33	2	1	D1
Stirling A		90/91	38		1	D2
		91/92	40			D1
		92/93	26			D1
		93/94	4		1	D1
Albion R		94/95	12		1	D3
Arbroath		94/95	10			D3
		95/96	4	3		D3
		96/97	1			D3

KERR James Stewart Robert
b. Bellshill 13.11.1974

Club	L	Season	Apps	Sub	Gls	Div
Celtic		96/97	25	1		P
		97/98				
		98/99	4			P
		99/00	4			P

KERR Michael
b. Greenock 6.4.1971

Club	L	Season	Apps	Sub	Gls	Div
Dundee		89/90	0	2		P

KEY Lance William
b. Kettering 13.5.1968

Club	L	Season	Apps	Sub	Gls	Div
Histon						
Sheffield W		90/91				
		91/92				
		92/93				
		93/94				
Oldham A	L	93/94	2			FL
Portsmouth	L	93/94				
Sheffield W		94/95				
Oxford U	L	94/95	6			FL
Sheffield W		95/96				
Lincoln C	L	95/96	5			FL
Hartlepool U	L	95/96	1			FL
Rochdale		95/96	14			FL
		96/97				
Dundee U		96/97	4			P
Rochdale		97/98	19			FL
		98/99				

KHARINE Dmitri Victorvitch
b. Moscow 16.8.1968

Club	L	Season	Apps	Sub	Gls	Div
CSKA Moscow						
Chelsea		92/93	5			FL
		93/94	40			FL
		94/95	31			FL
		95/96	26			FL
		96/97	5			FL
		97/98	10			FL
		98/99	1			FL
Celtic		99/00	4			P

KIDD Albert
b. Dundee 16.10.1957

Club	L	Season	Apps	Sub	Gls	Div
Brechin C		76/77	18			D2
Arbroath		77/78	39		5	D1
		78/79	36		8	D1
		79/80	20		6	D1
Motherwell		79/80	16		5	D1
		80/81	37		13	D1
Dundee		81/82	21	9	2	P
		82/83	15	4	4	P
		83/84	18	7	1	P
		84/85	11	12	3	P
		85/86	4	9	2	P
		86/87	6	1		P
Falkirk		86/87	12	3		P

KIDD Walter Joseph
b. Edinburgh 10.3.1958

Club	L	Season	Apps	Sub	Gls	Div
Newtongrange Star						
Heart of Midlothian		77/78	21	2		D1
		78/79	29	1		P
		79/80	27	7	2	D1
		80/81	25		1	P
		81/82	29	1		D1
		82/83	37			D1
		83/84	31		1	P
		84/85	33		1	P
		85/86	28			P
		86/87	33	2		P
		87/88	16	2		P
		88/89	20			P
		89/90	12	5	1	P
		90/91	1	3		P
Airdrieonians		91/92	32			P
		92/93	30	1		P
		93/94				
Heart of Midlothian		94/95	1			P
		95/96				
Falkirk		96/97	1			D1

KILGOUR Robert
b. Edinburgh 20.10.1956

Club	L	Season	Apps	Sub	Gls	Div
Meadowbank T		75/76	13	2		D2
		76/77	8			D2
		77/78				
Hibernian		78/79	5			P
		79/80				
St Johnstone		80/81	31			D1
		81/82	36			D1
		82/83	13	1		D1
		83/84	28	1	1	P
		84/85	32	2		D1

KING Colin

Club	L	Season	Apps	Sub	Gls	Div
Clydebank		77/78	6			P

KINNAIRD Paul
b. Glasgow 11.11.1966

Club	L	Season	Apps	Sub	Gls	Div
Norwich C		84/85				
		85/86				
Dundee U		86/87	5	2		P
		87/88	7	4		P
Motherwell		87/88	10			P
		88/89	24			P
St Mirren		88/89	2	4		P
		89/90	22	3		P
		90/91	18	5	4	P
		91/92	1	2		P
Partick T		91/92	13		2	D1
		92/93	14	6	1	P
Shrewsbury T	L	92/93	4		1	FL
St Johnstone		92/93	2	6		P
Partick T		93/94	2	1		P
		94/95				
Dunfermline A		95/96	6	3		D1
Scarborough		95/96	3			FL
Ayr U		95/96	16	2	2	D2
		96/97	13	14	2	D2
Stranraer		97/98	25	7	4	D2
		98/99	21		1	D1
Ross Co		98/99	10		1	D3
		99/00	22	6	7	D2

KINNELL Andrew

Club	L	Season	Apps	Sub	Gls	Div
Cowdenbeath		69/70				
		70/71	32		4	D1
		71/72	36			D2
St Johnstone		72/73	20			D1
		73/74	15	4		D1
		74/75	29	1		D1
		75/76	25			P

KINSEY Stephen
b. Manchester 2.1.1963

Club	L	Season	Apps	Sub	Gls	Div
Manchester C		80/81	1			FL
		81/82	13	3		FL
		82/83	12	1	1	FL
Chester C	L	82/83	3		1	FL
Chesterfield	L	82/83	3			FL
Manchester C		83/84	16	7	7	FL
		84/85	33	2	7	FL
		85/86	12	1		FL
Minnesota Strikers						
Los Angeles Galaxy						
Warrington T						
Tacoma Stars						
Molde BK						
Rochdale		91/92	3	3	1	FL
St Mirren		91/92	1	5		P
Fort Lauderdale						
Molde BK						
Macclesfield T		93/94				
Radcliffe B						

KIRIAKOV Ilian
b. Pavlikeni 4.8.1967

Club	L	Season	Apps	Sub	Gls	Div
Anorthosis						
Aberdeen		96/97	26	1	1	P
		97/98	15			P
		98/99	17	5		P
		99/00	6	2		P

KIRK Andrew
b. Belfast 29.5.1979

Club	L	Season	Apps	Sub	Gls	Div
Glentoran						
Heart of Midlothian		98/99	0	5		P
		99/00	1	3		P

KIRK Stephen David
b. Kirkcaldy 3.1.1963

Club	L	Season	Apps	Sub	Gls	Div
East Fife		79/80	24	1	2	D2
Stoke C		80/81				
		81/82	12			FL
East Fife		82/83	25		8	D2
		83/84	32	1	5	D2
		84/85	38		8	D1
		85/86	39		14	D1
Motherwell		86/87	33	2	10	P
		87/88	29	9	4	P
		88/89	32	1	14	P
		89/90	32	2	8	P
		90/91	18	11	2	P
		91/92	28	10	6	P
		92/93	26	14	10	P
		93/94	25	11	7	P
		94/95	6	12	2	P
Falkirk		94/95	11		5	P
		95/96	16	4	4	P
Raith R		95/96	6	1	1	P
		96/97	19	7	1	P
		97/98	0	3		D1
East Fife		97/98	11	6	3	D2
		98/99	17	10	5	D2
		99/00	5	6	2	D3

KIRKWOOD David Stewart

b. St Andrews 27.8.1967

Leven Royals					
East Fife	83/84	5	9	2	D2
	84/85	13	14	4	D1
	85/86	29	5	2	D1
	86/87	35		4	D1
Rangers	86/87	0	1		P
	87/88	2			P
East Fife	88/89	5		2	D2
Heart of Midlothian	89/90	10	9		P
	90/91	8	1	1	P
Airdrieonians	91/92	27	9	9	P
	92/93	17	10	2	P
	93/94	28	1	10	D1
Raith R	94/95	9	10	1	D1
	95/96	25	3	2	P
	96/97	13	4	1	P
	97/98	15	1		D1
	98/99	5	1		D1
	99/00	3	1		D1

KIRKWOOD William J

b. Edinburgh 1.9.1958

Dundee U	76/77	3	1	1	P
	77/78	16	11	4	P
	78/79	32	2	9	P
	79/80	22	6	3	P
	80/81	24	5	10	P
	81/82	29	3	2	P
	82/83	26	5	4	P
	83/84	24	2	9	P
	84/85	18	5	1	P
	85/86	13	2	1	P
Hibernian	86/87	26		1	P
Dundee U	86/87	11		1	P
	87/88	0	1		P
Dunfermline A	87/88	24			P
Dundee	87/88	9			P
	88/89	10	2		P

KIWOMYA Andrew Derek

b. Huddersfield 1.10.1967

Barnsley		85/86	1			FL
		86/87				
Sheffield W		86/87				
Retired						
Dundee		92/93	11	10	1	P
Rotherham U		93/94	4	3		FL
Halifax T		94/95				
Scunthorpe U		94/95	9		3	FL
Bradford C		95/96	7	9	2	FL
		96/97	20	7	1	FL
Luton T	L	96/97	5		1	FL
Burnley	L	97/98	1	2		FL
Notts Co		97/98	0	2		FL

KLOS Stefan

b. Dortmund 16.8.1971

Eintracht Dortmund					
Borussia Dortmund	90/91				
	91/92				
	92/93				
	93/94				
	94/95				
	95/96				
	96/97				
	97/98				
	98/99				
Rangers	98/99	18			P
	99/00	24			P

KNOX Archibald

b. 1.5.1947

Errol R					
Forfar A					
St Mirren	70/71	28		7	D1
	71/72	20	1	4	D2
Dundee U	71/72	11		3	D1
	72/73	10		1	D1
	73/74	21	7	8	D1
	74/75	1	4		D1
	75/76	2			P
Montrose	76/77	13		3	D1
Forfar A	76/77	21		3	D2
	77/78	33	1	3	D2
	78/79	27	4	2	D2
	79/80	29	3		D2

KOMBAURE Antoine

b. Noumba 16.11.1963

Sion					
Aberdeen	96/97	30		3	P
	97/98	13			P

KOPEL Frank

b. Falkirk 28.3.1949

Manchester U	67/68	1	1		FL
	68/69	7	1		FL
Blackburn R	68/69	4	2		FL
	69/70	5			FL
	70/71	11			FL
	71/72	3			FL
Dundee U	71/72	8		1	D1
	72/73	32	1	1	D1
	73/74	31	1	1	D1
	74/75	30		1	D1
	75/76	29	1		P
	76/77	20	2		P
	77/78	33			P
	78/79	11	3	2	P
	79/80	31		1	P
	80/81	27	6		P
	81/82	6	1		P
Arbroath	81/82	18			D2
	82/83	35		1	D2
	83/84	9			D2
Dundee U	83/84				

KOZMA Istvan

b. Paszto 3.12.1964

Bordeaux					
Dunfermline A	89/90	32	1	6	P
	90/91	32	2	2	P
	91/92	18	5		P
Liverpool	91/92	3	2		FL
	92/93	0	1		FL

KPEDEKPO Malcolm

b. Aberdeen 27.8.1976

Hermes					
Aberdeen	94/95	0	1		P
	95/96	1	4		P
	96/97	0	5		P

KRISTENSEN Karl

b. 17.8.1968

Morton	87/88	0	1		P

KRIPOKAPIC Miodrag

b. Niksic Crna Gora 6.9.1950

Red Star Belgrade					
Dundee U	88/89	18	6	1	P
	89/90	25	1		P
	90/91	24			P
	91/92				
	92/93	8			P
Motherwell	93/94	42		1	P
	94/95	16			P
	95/96	13			P
Raith R	95/96	5			P
	96/97	6			P
Hamilton A	97/98	2			D1
	98/99	0	1		D1

KROMHEER Elroy Patrick

b. Amsterdam 15.1.1970

VVV Volendaam					
Motherwell	92/93	11	1	1	P
Reading					

KUZNETSOV Oleg

b. Kiev 2.3.1963

Dynamo Kiev					
Rangers	90/91	2			P
	91/92	16	2		P
	92/93	8	1		P
	93/94	4	2	1	P

KYLE Graham

b. Paisley 15.12.1961

Cumbernauld U					
Morton	82/83	3			P
	83/84	4			D1
Queen of the South	84/85	1			D2
Partick T	85/86	2			D1
Stenhousemuir	85/86	1			D2

LAING Derek

Dundee	74/75	1			D1
	75/76	18	1	1	P
	76/77	2	6	1	D1
	77/78	0	2		D1

LAING Derek James

b. Haddington 11.11.1973

Dunfermline A	91/92	0	3		P
	92/93	11	2	3	D1
	93/94	11	16	8	D1
	94/95	2	4		D1
Morton	94/95	9	3	2	D2
	95/96	3	23	1	D1
Queen of the South	96/97	5	4		D2

LAMBERT Paul

b. Glasgow 7.8.1969

Linwood R					
St Mirren	85/86	0	1		P
	86/87	24	12	2	P
	87/88	25	11	2	P
	88/89	8	8	2	P
	89/90	19	6	3	P
	90/91	30	1	2	P
	91/92	36	4	2	P
	92/93	38	1	1	D1
	93/94	3			D1
Motherwell	93/94	30	2	3	P
	94/95	36		1	P
	95/96	35		2	P
Borussia Dortmund	96/97				
Celtic	97/98	25	1	2	P
	98/99	33		1	P
	99/00	25		1	P

LAMBIE Duncan

Armadale Thistle					
Dundee	70/71	1			D1
	71/72	20	3	1	D1
	72/73	12	2		D1
	73/74	24	7	6	D1
	74/75	1	1	1	D1
St Johnstone	74/75	27	1	4	D1
	75/76	26		3	P
	76/77	15	1	1	D1
Germany	77/78				
Hibernian	78/79	4	2		P
	79/80	9	1		P

LAMONT William Fleming

b. Falkirk 24.7.1966

Armadale Thistle					
Cowdenbeath	89/90	35			D2
	90/91	32			D2
	91/92	26			D2
	92/93	25			D1
	93/94				
Falkirk	94/95	5	3		P
	95/96	7			P
Ayr U	95/96	4			D2
Alloa A	95/96	1			D3
	96/97	1			D3
Berwick R	96/97	3			D2
East Stirlingshire	96/97	3			D3

LANDELS Graeme John

b. Broxburn 27.3.1978

ICI Juveniles					
Raith R	95/96	0	1		P

LANGFIELD James

b. Paisley 22.12.1979

Dundee	98/99	1	1		P
	99/00	1			P

LAPSLEY John

b. Edinburgh 24.11.1951

Linlithgow Rose					
Airdrieonians	72/73				
	73/74				
	74/75	25	1	1	D1
	75/76	14	3	1	D1
	76/77	28	2	2	D1
	77/78	32	7		D1
	78/79	38		6	D1
	79/80	30		11	D1
Partick T	79/80	2	1		P
	80/81	14	9		P
	81/82	18	5		P
Ayr U	82/83	4	1		D1
Cowdenbeath	82/83	1			D2
East Stirlingshire	82/83	3			D2
Stenhousemuir	82/83	1			D2
Falkirk	82/83	2			D1
Hamilton A	82/83	2			D1
Partick T	82/83	0	1		D1
Dunfermline A	83/84	17		1	D2
Brechin C	84/85	6			D1

LARNACH Michael

b. Lybster 9.11.1952

Clydebank		72/73	35		17	D2
		73/74	18	2	3	D2
		74/75	26	4	7	D2
		75/76	25	1	7	D2
		76/77	39		25	D1
		77/78	17		4	P
Newcastle U		77/78	12	2		FL
Motherwell		78/79	26	6	4	P
		79/80	17	3	3	D1
		80/81	6			D1
Ayr U		80/81	7	6	1	D1
		81/82	6	8		D1
		82/83	22		7	D1
Stenhousemuir		83/84	12		2	D2
Clydebank		83/84	25	1	7	D1
		84/85	35	2	10	D1
		85/86	23		3	P

LARSSON Henrik

b. Helsingborg 20.9.1971

Hogaborgs		89				
		90				
		91				
Helsingborgs		92				
		93				
Feyenoord		93/94				
		94/95				
		95/96				
		96/97				
Celtic		97/98	34	1	16	P
		98/99	35		29	P
		99/00	8	1	7	P

LARUSSON Bjarnolafur

b. Iceland 11.3.1976

IBV Vestmannnayar		93				
		94				
		95				
		96				
		97				
Hibernian		97/98	3	4	1	P
Walsall		98/99	33	3	3	FL
		99/00	12	11		FL

LATAPY Russell Nigel

b. Trinidad 2.8.1968

Aston Villa						
Hibernian		98/99	23		6	D1
		99/00	28		9	P

LATCHFORD David Barry

b. Birmingham 27.9.1952

Birmingham C		68/69	4			FL
		69/70	16			FL
		70/71	8			FL
		71/72	11			FL
		72/73	32			FL
		73/74	25			FL
		74/75	39			FL
		75/76	40			FL
		76/77	30			FL
		77/78	1			FL
Motherwell		78/79	8			P
Bury		78/79	2			FL
Barnsley		79/80				
Redditch U						
Cheltenham T						
East Worle						

LATCHFORD Peter William

b. Kings Heath 27.9.1952

Monyhull Hospital						
Redditch T						
Sutton Coldfield T						
Finn Harps GAA						
WBA		69/70				
		70/71				
		71/72				
		72/73	26			FL
		73/74	42			FL
		74/75	13			FL
Celtic	L	74/75	10			D1
		75/76	35			P
		76/77	31			P
		77/78	36			P
		78/79	27			P
		79/80	36			P
		80/81				
		81/82				
		82/83				
		83/84	3			P
		84/85	2			P
		85/86	6			P
		86/87	1			P
Clyde		87/88	12			D1

LAUCHLAN James Harley

b. Glasgow 2.2.1977

Kilmarnock		93/94	0	1		P
		94/95	2			P
		95/96	5			P
		96/97	7	2	1	P
		97/98	22			P
		98/99	14			P
		99/00	29		2	P

LAUCHLAN Martin Thomas

b. Rutherglen 1.10.1980

Partick T		97/98	5	5		D1
		98/99	22	5	5	D2
St Johnstone		99/00	0	5		P

LAUDRUP Brian

b. Vienna 22.2.1969

Brondby		85/86				
		86/87				
		87/88				
		88/89				
Bayer Uerdingen		89/90				
Bayern Munich		90/91				
		91/92				
Fiorentina		92/93				
AC Milan	L	93/94				
Rangers		94/95	33		10	P
		95/96	22		2	P
		96/97	33		16	P
		97/98	26	2	5	P

LAVETY Barry

b. Paisley 21.8.1974

St Mirren		91/92	3	2	2	P
		92/93	32	10	8	D1
		93/94	35	7	10	D1
		94/95	29	2	7	D1
		95/96	27	2	11	D1
Hibernian		96/97	6	4		P
		97/98	22	4	7	P
		98/99	22	5	5	D1
St Mirren		99/00	21	8	16	D1

LAW Robert

b. Bellshill 24.12.1965

Stonehouse Violet						
Partick T		84/85	1			D1
		85/86	14	2	3	D1
		86/87	28	3	2	D1
		87/88	17	4	1	D1
		88/89	33			D1
		89/90	27	1	1	D1
		90/91	25	2		D1
		91/92	25	6	2	D1
		92/93	34			P
		93/94	25			P
		94/95	2	3		P
St Mirren		95/96	15	5		D1
Ayr U		95/96	6			D2
		96/97	10	6		D2
Stenhousemuir		97/98	21	4	1	D2

LAWRENCE Alan

b. Edinburgh 19.8.1964

Meadowbank T		84/85	25	11		D1
		85/86	38		17	D2
		86/87	29		6	D2
Dundee		86/87	3	1	1	P
		87/88	14	8	1	P
		88/89	8	2		P
Meadowbank T		88/89	3		4	D1
Airdrieonians		88/89	7		2	D1
		89/90	29	5	9	D1
		90/91	38		13	D1
		91/92	26	5	7	P
		92/93	23	12	2	P
		93/94	20	7	5	D1
		94/95	24	8	11	D1
Heart of Midlothian		95/96	17	9	5	P
Airdrieonians		96/97	10	17	3	D1
		97/98	5	4		D1
Partick T		97/98	17		3	D1
Stenhousemuir		98/99	33		8	D3
		99/00	31	3		D2

LAWRIE Andrew

b. Galashiels 24.11.1978

Falkirk		95/96	1			P
		96/97	7	5		D1
		97/98	5	1	1	D1
East Fife		98/99	13		1	D2
Falkirk		99/00	33	2	4	D1

LECLERQ Fabien Christian Rene

b. Lille 19.10.1972

OSC Lille						
Heart of Midlothian		99/00	8	2		P

LEE Iain Caird Cameron

b. Hamilton 7.7.1967

Alloa A		88/89	30		2	D2
		89/90	35	1	4	D1
St Johnstone		90/91	1	4		P
		91/92				
Cowdenbeath		92/93	18	1		D1
		93/94	24	1	1	D2
East Stirlingshire		93/94	10		3	D2
		94/95	36		10	D3
		95/96	31	2	4	D3
Forfar A		96/97	31	2	3	D3
		97/98	20	1		D2

LEHMANN Dirk

b. Aachen 16.8.1971

Energie Cottbus						
Fulham		98/99	16	10	2	FL
Hibernian		99/00	18	12	7	P

LEHTONEN Joni

b. Finland 23.8.1970

Ilves Tampere						
Motherwell		96/97	4	2		P

LEIGHTON James

b. Johnstone 24.7.1958

Aberdeen		78/79	11			P
		79/80	1			P
		80/81	35			P
		81/82	36			P
		82/83	35			P
		83/84	36			P
		84/85	34			P
		85/86	26			P
		86/87	42			P
		87/88	44			P
Manchester U		88/89	38			FL
		89/90	35			FL
		90/91				
		91/92				
Reading	L	91/92	8			FL
Dundee		91/92	13			D1
		92/93	8			P
Hibernian		93/94	44			P
		94/95	36			P
		95/96	36			P
		96/97	35			P
		97/98	34			P
		98/99	22			P
		99/00	26			P

LEITCH Donald Scott

b. Motherwell 6.10.1969

Shettleston						
Dunfermline A		90/91	9	5	3	P
		91/92	29	4	4	P
		92/93	34	8	9	D1
Heart of Midlothian		93/94	24	4	2	P
		94/95	18	3		P
		95/96	4	2		P
Swindon T		95/96	7			FL
		96/97	36			FL
		97/98	25	1	1	FL
		98/99	23	1		FL
		99/00	28	1		FL

LEKOVIC Dragoje

b. Sivac 21.11.1967

Buducnost						
Kilmarnock		94/95	20			P
		95/96	33			P
		96/97	30			P
		97/98	13			P

LEMAJIC Zoran

b. Niksic 8.11.1960

CS Maritimo						
Dunfermline A		96/97	8			P

LENNON Daniel Joseph

b. Whitburn 6.4.1970

Hibernian		87/88	0	1		P
		88/89	0	1		P
		89/90				
		90/91	6			P
		91/92	3	8	1	P
		92/93	7	6		P
		93/94	3	2	1	P
Raith R		93/94	7			P
		94/95	19	1		D1
		95/96	30	3	5	P
		96/97	35		5	P
		97/98	32		4	D1
		98/99	21	4		D1
Ayr U		99/00	3	4	1	D1
Ross Co		99/00	7			D2
Partick T		99/00	19		2	D2

LENNOX Gary
b. Kilwinning 6.12.1969

Queens Park	86/87	2	5		D2
	87/88	9	6	1	D2
	88/89	24	4	2	D2
	89/90				
Brechin C	90/91	12		2	D1
Falkirk	91/92	15	11		P
	92/93	17	3	2	P
Ayr U	93/94	23		1	D1

LENNOX Robert
b. Saltcoats 30.8.1943

Star of the Sea Amateurs					
Ardeer Recreation					
Celtic	61/62	1			D1
	62/63	4			D1
	63/64	7		1	D1
	64/65	22		9	D1
	65/66	24		15	D1
	66/67	26	1	13	D1
	67/68	28		32	D1
	68/69	27	1	12	D1
	69/70	19	1	14	D1
	70/71	22	2	10	D1
	71/72	24	2	12	D1
	72/73	15	8	11	D1
	73/74	17	2	12	D1
	74/75	9	5	5	D1
	75/76	25	5	10	P
	76/77	2	3	2	P
	77/78	1	2		P
Houston Hurricane	78	30		3	NA
Celtic	78/79	6	8	4	P
	79/80	19	9	6	P

LEONARD Peter

St Mirren	74/75	1	1		D2
	75/76	3	1	2	D1
	76/77	0	2		D1
	77/78	3	6	1	P
Motherwell	78/79	2	4		P

LEVEIN Craig
b. Dunfermline 22.10.1964

Cowdenbeath	81/82	14	1		D2
	82/83	29			D2
	83/84	15			D2
Heart of Midlothian	83/84	20	2		P
	84/85	35	1	1	P
	85/86	33		2	P
	86/87	12			P
	87/88	21			P
	88/89	8	1		P
	89/90	35			P
	90/91	33		4	P
	91/92	36		2	P
	92/93	37		3	P
	93/94	30		3	P
	94/95	24			P
	95/96	1			P

LIDDELL Francis James
b. Stirling 10.7.1953

Alloa A	75/76	0	2		D2
	76/77	31	1	3	D2
	77/78	26		2	D1
Heart of Midlothian	78/79	31			P
	79/80	37		3	D1
	80/81	24		2	P
Australia	81/82				
	82/83				
	83/84				
Dunfermline A	84/85	3		1	D2
Stenhousemuir	84/85	5	2		D2
St Johnstone	85/86	24			D2
Australia					

LIDDELL Gary
b. Bannockburn 27.8.1954

Leeds U	72/73				
	73/74				
	74/75				
	75/76				
	76/77				
Grimsby T	76/77	14		4	FL
	77/78	37	1	12	FL
	78/79	21	5	6	FL
	79/80	14	6	2	FL
	80/81	4	3		FL
Heart of Midlothian	80/81	13		2	P
	81/82	9	2	2	D1
Doncaster R	81/82	13		1	FL
	82/83	12	12	3	FL

LIDDLE James H
b. Edinburgh 9.4.1958

Bonnyrigg Rose					
Whitehill Welfare					
Cowdenbeath	78/79	25	3	5	D2
	79/80	31	4	11	D2
	80/81	37		18	D2
	81/82	32		9	D2
	82/83	18		6	D2
Forfar A	82/83	12		2	D2
	83/84	36		22	D2
	84/85	33	2	11	D1
	85/86	22	1	8	D1
Cowdenbeath *	86/87	2			D2
Hamilton A	86/87	6	3	3	P
Meadowbank T	86/87	5	3		D2
	87/88	5	2		D1

LILLEY David William
b. Bellshill 31.10.1977

Queen of the South	95/96	23			D2
	96/97	20	2	1	D2
	97/98	2			D2
	98/99	27			D2
	99/00	2			D2
Aberdeen	99/00	14	3		P

LILLEY Derek Symon
b. Paisley 9.2.1974

Morton	91/92	13	12	3	D1
	92/93	16	6	4	D1
	93/94	34	4	5	D1
	94/95	34	1	16	D2
	95/96	35		14	D1
	96/97	25		15	D1
Leeds U	96/97	4	2		FL
	97/98	0	13	1	FL
Heart of Midlothian	98/99	3	1	1	P

LINDQVIST Stefan
b. 18.3.1967

Halmstad					
Neuchatel Xamax					
Motherwell	97/98	5	1	1	P

LINDSAY James

Fir Park BC					
Motherwell	76/77	1	1		P
	77/78	3	1		P
	78/79	7	8	1	P
Ayr U	79/80	2	10	1	D1
Stirling A	80/81	1	2		D1
Petershill					

LINIGHAN David
b. Hartlepool 9.1.1965

Hartlepool U	81/82	6			FL
	82/83	6		1	FL
	83/84	19	4	1	FL
	84/85	15	2	2	FL
	85/86	38	1	1	FL
Derby Co	86/87				
Shrewsbury T	86/87	24		1	FL
	87/88	41		1	FL
Ipswich T	88/89	40	1	2	FL
	89/90	41			FL
	90/91	45		10	FL
	91/92	36		3	FL
	92/93	42		1	FL
	93/94	38		3	FL
	94/95	31	1		FL
	95/96	2			FL
Blackpool	95/96	29		4	FL
	96/97	42		1	FL
	97/98	26	3		FL
Dunfermline A	98/99	1			P

LLOYD David A
b. Glasgow 18.10.1960

Lesmagahow					
Alloa A	81/82	0	2		D2
	82/83	28	7	5	D1
	83/84	26	6	10	D1
	84/85	34	2	16	D2
	85/86	0	1		D1
Clydebank	85/86	13	5	7	P
Clyde	85/86	16		7	D1
	86/87	6	6	1	D1
St Johnstone	86/87	22	2	5	D2
	87/88	0	3	1	D2
Raith R	87/88	10	19	6	D1
Stranraer	88/89	31	4	11	D2
Stirling A	89/90	31	3	15	D2
	90/91	34	1	14	D2
	91/92	9	1	2	D1

LOCKE Gary
b. Edinburgh 11.6.1975

Whitehill Welfare					
Heart of Midlothian	92/93	0	1		P
	93/94	29	4		P
	94/95	3	6		P
	95/96	29		4	P
	96/97	11			P
	97/98	16	5		P
	98/99	22	3	1	P
	99/00	9	4		P

LOGAN Alan
b. Glasgow 22.7.1961

St Mirren	79/80	14	1	5	P
	80/81	8	9	5	P
	81/82	5	15	1	P
	82/83	7	6	3	P
	83/84	2	6	1	P
Partick T	84/85	33		12	D1
	85/86	23	6	3	D1
	86/87	8	1	2	D1
Queen of the South	86/87	5		1	D1
Partick T	87/88	15	9	3	D1
Arbroath	88/89	1			D2
Raith R	88/89	16	9	6	D1
	89/90	16	10	6	D1
	90/91	17	12	4	D1
	91/92				
Montrose	92/93	17	4	4	D2

LORIMER David James
b. Bellshill 26.1.1974

Albion R BC					
Hamilton A BC					
Hamilton A	92/93	1	5	1	D1
	93/94	9	9		D1
	94/95	15	12	2	D1
	95/96	5	10		D1
	96/97	0	3		D2
Raith R	96/97	1	2		P
Clydebank	97/98	1	2		D2
Stirling A	97/98	0	5	1	D1
Albion R	98/99	31	5	10	D3
Stenhousemuir	99/00	9	7	1	D2

LOVE Alistair James
b. Edinburgh 9.5.1955

Melbourne Thistle					
WBA	73/74				
Southend U	74/75	6	5		FL
Newport Co	75/76	41	1	2	FL
Partick T	76/77	12	4		P
	77/78	16	9	2	P
	78/79	13	3		P
	79/80	2	4		P
Ayr U	79/80	11	1	1	D1
	80/81	22	6	3	D1
	81/82	19			D1
Falkirk	82/83	19			D1
	83/84	4	1		P

LOVE Graeme
b. Bathgate 7.12.1973

Hibernian	91/92	1			P
	92/93	1			P
	93/94	3	1		P
	94/95	11	1		P
	95/96	11	3		P
	96/97	6	1		P
Ayr U	97/98	12			D1
Queen of the South	97/98	12			D2
Clydebank	98/99	7		1	D1

LOVELL Stuart
b. Sydney 9.1.1972

Reading	90/91	22	8	2	FL
	91/92	16	8		FL
	92/93	18	4	8	FL
	93/94	43	2	20	FL
	94/95	25	5	11	FL
	95/96	28	7	7	FL
	96/97	17	9	5	FL
	97/98	8	7	1	FL
Hibernian	98/99	26	5	11	D1
	99/00	19	7	1	P

LOVERING Paul James
b. Glasgow 25.11.1975

Neilston Jnrs					
Clydebank	94/95	3			D1
	95/96	11	10	1	D1
	96/97	25	1		D1
	97/98	32		4	D2
	98/99	12			D1
Hibernian	98/99	17		1	D1
	99/00	9	1		P

LOWNDES Nathan Peter
b. Salford 2.6.1977

Leeds U	95/96				
Watford	96/97	0	3		FL
	97/98	1	3		FL
St Johnstone	98/99	12	17	2	P
	99/00	16	9	10	P

LUMSDEN James

Clydebank	75/76	23	1	1	D2
	76/77	27	1	1	D1
	77/78	20	4	1	P

LUNA Francisco

Dundee	99/00	5	4	3	P

LYALL Kenneth
b. Edinburgh 23.3.1963

Rangers	81/82	3			P
	82/83	2	2		P
	83/84	1			P
Motherwell	83/84	16	1	2	P
	84/85	2			D1
St Johnstone	84/85	29		3	D1
Brechin C	85/86	14	2		D1
	86/87	21	6	1	D1
	87/88	4	1		D2

LYNCH Andrew
b. 3.3.1951
Glasgow U
Renfrew Jnrs

Queens Park	68/69				
Kirkintilloch Rob Roy					
Heart of Midlothian	69/70	13		2	D1
	70/71	20		4	D1
	71/72	16	1	2	D1
	72/73	7	3	3	D1
Celtic	72/73	0	1		D1
	73/74	1	2		D1
	74/75	5	2	2	D1
	75/76	34		1	P
	76/77	30		2	P
	77/78	26	1	3	P
	78/79	27	1	7	P
	79/80	1			P
Philadelphia Fury	80	23		4	NA
Montreal Manic	81	27		4	NA

LYNCH Simon George
b. Montreal 19.5.1982

Celtic	99/00	1	1	1	P

LYONS Alan
b. Falkirk 23.3.1964
Fraserburgh

Aberdeen	82/83				
St Johnstone	83/84	18	6	5	P
	84/85	34	2	8	D1
Forfar A	85/86	27	6	2	D1
Montrose	86/87	29	2	1	D1
	87/88	16	3		D2
	88/89	36		8	D2
	89/90	33	3		D2
	90/91	16	7		D2
	91/92	1	1		D1

LYONS Andrew
b. Blackpool 19.10.1966
Wigan A

Partick T	95/96	9			P
	96/97	29	6	3	D1
	97/98	26	1	5	D1
Ayr U	98/99	31	1	8	D1
	99/00	18	9		D1

LYTWYN Charles
b. Edinburgh 1.10.1964
Hibernian

Falkirk	85/86	5	7	5	D1
	86/87	2	1		P
Brechin C	86/87	17	8	4	D1
	87/88	1			D2
Berwick R	87/88	19		3	D2
Alloa A	88/89	36	1	13	D2
	89/90	14	5	1	D1
East Stirlingshire	90/91	26	1	10	D2
	91/92	19	1	11	D2
	92/93	13	4	3	D2

MAASKANT Robert
b. Scheidam 10.1.1969
Emmen

Motherwell	91/92	12			P
Go Ahead Eagles					

MACKIN Alan
b. Lennoxtown 29.7.1955

Queens Park	76/77	36		2	D2
	77/78	38		2	D2
Motherwell	78/79	7	1		P
	79/80	8	1		D1
Falkirk	80/81	33		4	D1
	81/82	31		4	D1
	82/83	38		4	D1
	83/84	39		4	D1
Morton	84/85	11			P
Partick T	84/85	14			D1
	85/86	11		1	D1
	86/87	4			D1
East Stirlingshire	86/87	4		1	D1
Alloa A	86/87	8			D2
Queen of the South	87/88	40		3	D1
	88/89	11			D1
Clyde	88/89	8			D1
East Stirlingshire	89/90	6			D2
	90/91	1			D2

MADDISON Lee Robert
b. Bristol 5.10.1972

Bristol R	91/92	8	2		FL
	92/93	12			FL
	93/94	36	1		FL
	94/95	12	2		FL
	95/96				
Northampton T	95/96	21			FL
	96/97	34			FL
Dundee	97/98	19	5	1	D1
	98/99	21			P
	99/00	19	1		P

MAGEE Darren
b. Glasgow 14.4.1977
Milngarvie W

Dundee	95/96	0	1		D1
	96/97				
	97/98	11	6		D1
	98/99	1	1		P

MAGEE Kevin
b. Bathgate 10.4.1971
Armadale Thistle

Partick T	91/92	0	6		D1
	92/93	0	5		P
Preston NE	93/94	5	2		FL
	94/95	14		1	FL
	95/96	4	1		FL
Plymouth A	95/96	0	4		FL
Scarborough	95/96	26	2	1	FL
Dundee	96/97	10	15		D1
Livingston	97/98	18	13	2	D2
	98/99	2	1		D2
Montrose	98/99	13		5	D3
Berwick R	99/00	20	9		D3

MAHE Stephane
b. Puteaux 23.9.1968

Auxerre	88/89				
	89/90				
	90/91				
	91/92				
	92/93				
	93/94				
	94/95				
Paris St Germain	95/96				
Stade Rennes	96/97				
Celtic	97/98	23			P
	98/99	24			P
	99/00	19		4	P

MAHER John
b. Glasgow 18.12.1966
Anniesland U

Clydebank	84/85	8			D1
	85/86	23	3		P
	86/87	42			P
	87/88	37			D1
	88/89	11			D1
	89/90	28			D1
	90/91	29			D1
	91/92	38	1		D1
	92/93	33	1		D1
	93/94	1			D1

MAHOOD Alan Scott
b. Kilwinning 26.3.1973

Morton	88/89	0	1		D1
	89/90				
	90/91	4	4		D1
	91/92	17		6	D1
Nottingham F L	92/93				
Morton	92/93	17		6	D1
	93/94	11	1	3	D1
	94/95	18	3	1	D2
	95/96	31	4	4	D1
	96/97	27		3	D1
	97/98	24		6	D1
Kilmarnock	98/99	16	12	2	P
	99/00	6	12	1	P

MAILER John
b. Bridge of Allan 11.6.1961
Campsie Black Watch

Dumbarton	80/81	11			D1
	81/82	0	2		D1
Stirling A	81/82	1	1		D2
Campsie Black Watch	82/83				
Kirkintilloch Rob Roy	83/84				
Maryhill	84/85				
Glasgow Perthshire	85/86				
Hamilton A	86/87	11	8	3	P
Clyde	87/88	33		11	D1
	88/89	22	8	6	D1
Cowdenbeath	89/90	14	2	3	D2
Stirling A	90/91	6	3	1	D2

MAIN Alan David
b. Elgin 5.12.1967
Lossiemouth
Elgin C

Dundee U	86/87	2			P
	87/88	8			P
Cowdenbeath	88/89	3			D1
East Stirlingshire	88/89	2			D2
Dundee U	89/90	27			P
	90/91	31			P
	91/92	17			P
	92/93	43			P
	93/94	18			P
	94/95	6			P
St Johnstone	94/95	17			D1
	95/96	34			D1
	96/97	34			D1
	97/98	34			P
	98/99	34			P
	99/00	21			P

MAIR Gordon
b. Bothwell 18.12.1958

Notts Co	75/76				
	76/77	3	2		FL
	77/78				
	78/79	4		1	FL
	79/80	42		5	FL
	80/81	2	2		FL
	81/82	32	2	9	FL
	82/83	25		3	FL
	83/84	15	2		FL
Lincoln C	84/85	31			FL
	85/86	26		3	FL
Motherwell	86/87	18	11	1	P
	87/88	16	5	1	P
	88/89	6	6		P
	89/90	7	2		P
	90/91	2			P
Clydebank	90/91	7		2	D1
	91/92	28	3	2	D1
Ayr U	92/93	20	2	7	D1
	93/94	25	1		D1

MAKEL Lee Robert
b. Sunderland 11.1.1973

Newcastle U	90/91	1	2		FL
	91/92	5	4	1	FL
Blackburn R	92/93	1			FL
	93/94	0	2		FL
	94/95				
	95/96	0	3		FL
Huddersfield T	95/96	33		2	FL
	96/97	19		3	FL
	97/98	10	3		FL
Heart of Midlothian	97/98	3	2		P
	98/99	6	8	1	P
	99/00	11	6		P
Portsmouth L	99/00				

MAKELA Janne
b. 23.7.1971

St Mirren	95/96	1			D1
Raith R	96/97	8		1	P

MALCOLM Robert
b. Glasgow 12.11.1980

Rangers	99/00	1	2		P

MALPAS Maurice Daniel Robert
b. Dunfermline 3.8.1962

Leven Royals						
Dundee U		81/82	15	4		P
		82/83	31	3	1	P
		83/84	33	1	2	P
		84/85	35		2	P
		85/86	36		2	P
		86/87	36		2	P
		87/88	44			P
		88/89	36		1	P
		89/90	30		2	P
		90/91	36		1	P
		91/92	44		3	P
		92/93	37			P
		93/94	35			P
		94/95	31			P
		95/96	30		2	D1
		96/97	26		1	P
		97/98	31		1	P
		98/99	31			P
		99/00	8	4		P

MANLEY Roderick
b. Glasgow 23.7.1965

Falkirk		84/85	8	3		D1
		85/86	31			D1
		86/87	37	2		P
		87/88	37	6	1	P
		88/89	35		1	D1
St Mirren		89/90	30			P
		90/91	18			P
		91/92	32			P
		92/93	20			D1
Instant Dict		93/94				
		94/95				
Dundee		95/96	17			D1

MARCH James
b. Glasgow 21.4.1954

St Rochs						
Airdrieonians		74/75	2	5	4	D1
		75/76	11	7	1	D1
		76/77	32		2	D1
		77/78	12		2	D1
		78/79	25	2	4	D1
		79/80	17	4		D1
		80/81	22	2	3	P
		81/82	28	2		P
		82/83	21	2	1	D1
		83/84	20	2		D1
Ayr U		84/85	12	1		D1
		85/86	27	2		D1

MARGAARD Carsten

Morton		87/88	8	1		P

MARINELLO Peter
b. Edinburgh 20.2.1950

Hibernian		67/68	11			D1
		68/69	17	2	1	D1
		69/70	14		4	D1
Arsenal		69/70	14		1	FL
		70/71	1	2		FL
		71/72	4	4	1	FL
		72/73	13		1	FL
Portsmouth		73/74	39		3	FL
		74/75	38	1	2	FL
		75/76	15	2	2	FL
Motherwell		75/76	16	2	3	P
		76/77	16	6	3	P
		77/78	31	4	5	P
		78/79	14		1	P
Fulham		78/79	8	1		FL
		79/80	17	1	1	FL
Phoenix Inferno		80/81				
Heart of Midlothian		81/82	10	8	2	D1
		82/83	2	2		D1
Partick T		83/84	1	5		D1

MARKLUND Goran Mathius
b. Stockholm 2.10.1975

Vasalund						
Dundee U		97/98	1	2		P

MARR John Gerard
b. 3.6.1956

Petershill						
Partick T		74/75	0	1		D1
		75/76	14	5		D1
		76/77	31	1		P
		77/78	33	1		P
		78/79	29			P
		79/80	10			P
		80/81	2	2		P
Morton		80/81	6	1		P
		81/82	0	1		P

MARSHALL Gordon George Banks
b. Edinburgh 19.4.1964

Rangers		79/80				
		80/81				
		81/82				
		82/83				
East Stirlingshire	L	82/83	15			D2
Broxburn		82/83				
East Fife		82/83	10			D2
		83/84	32			D2
		84/85	39			D1
		85/86	39			D1
		86/87	36			D1
Falkirk		86/87	10			P
		87/88	44			P
		88/89	39			D1
		89/90	39			D1
		90/91	39			D1
Celtic		91/92	25			P
		92/93	11			P
		93/94	1			P
Stoke C	L	93/94	10			FL
Celtic		94/95	16			P
		95/96	36			P
		96/97	11			P
		97/98	1			P
St Mirren		97/98	1			D1
Kilmarnock		97/98	12			P
		98/99	36			P
		99/00	14			P

MARSHALL Scott Roderick
b. Edinburgh 1.5.1973

Arsenal		91/92				
		92/93	2			FL
		93/94				
Rotherham U	L	93/94	10		1	FL
Oxford U	L	93/94				
Arsenal		94/95				
Sheffield U	L	94/95	17			FL
Arsenal		95/96	10	1	1	FL
		96/97	6	2		FL
		97/98	1	2		FL
Celtic		98/99	1	1		P

MARTIN Brian
b. Bellshill 24.2.1963

Albion R		80/81	9	1		D2
Stenhousemuir		80/81	2			D2
Shotts Bon Accord		81/82				
		82/83				
		83/84				
		84/85				
Falkirk		85/86	23	2	1	D1
		86/87	33	1	1	P
Hamilton A		86/87	7			P
		87/88	21	2		D1
St Mirren		87/88	12		1	P
		88/89	34		2	P
		89/90	35		2	P
		90/91	32		2	P
		91/92	17		2	P
Motherwell		91/92	25			P
		92/93	43	1	3	P
		93/94	43		2	P
		94/95	32		2	P
		95/96	33		2	P
		96/97	34			P
		97/98	26		1	P
Stirling A		98/99	33		1	D2
		99/00	11			D2
Partick T		99/00	12	4		D2

MARTIN Craig
b. Uphall 10.11.1978

Dunfermline A		98/99	2	1		P
Albion R		99/00	7			D3

MARTIN John

Dundee		75/76	10		2	P
		76/77	12	2		D1

MARTIN John Galloway King
b. Edinburgh 27.10.1958

Tranent Jnrs						
Airdrieonians		80/81	22			P
		81/82	27			P
		82/83	39		1	D1
		83/84	39			D1
		84/85	36			D1
		85/86	36			D1
		86/87	44			D1
		87/88	44			D1
		88/89	36			D1
		89/90	39			D1
		90/91	38			D1
		91/92	41			P
		92/93	43			P
		93/94	44			D1
		94/95	35			D1
		95/96	20			D1
		96/97	27			D1
		97/98	20			D1
Albion R		97/98	3			D3
Airdrieonians		98/99	28			D1
Preston A						

MARTIN Lee Andrew
b. Hyde 5.2.1968

Manchester U		87/88	0	1		FL
		88/89	20	4	1	FL
		89/90	28	4		FL
		90/91	7	7		FL
		91/92	0	1		FL
		92/93				
		93/94				
Celtic		93/94	15			P
		94/95	4			P
		95/96				
Bristol R		96/97	25			FL
Huddersfield T	L	97/98	2	1		FL

MARTIN Paul J
b. Bellshill 8.3.1965

Fir Park BC						
Kilmarnock		84/85	19			D1
		85/86	31		1	D1
		86/87	40		2	D1
		87/88	39		1	D1
		88/89	11		1	D1
Hamilton A		88/89	20	1		P
		89/90	21	2	1	D1
Stranraer		89/90	1			D2
Dumbarton		90/91	14		1	D2
		91/92	38		2	D2
		92/93	40		2	D1
		93/94	17	2		D1
		94/95	28		2	D2
		95/96	12		1	D1
Albion R		96/97	25		1	D3
		97/98	18		1	D3
Queens Park		98/99	28		6	D3
		99/00	27	1	1	D3

MASKREY Stephen William
b. Edinburgh 16.8.1962

Falkirk						
East Stirlingshire		84/85	36	1	12	D2
		85/86	21		12	D2
Queen of the South		85/86	6	6	2	D2
		86/87	23	8	2	D1
St Johnstone		87/88	28	5	5	D2
		88/89	31		12	D1
		89/90	22	7	12	D1
		90/91	33	1	7	P
		91/92	12	12	2	P
		92/93	3	16	2	P
		93/94	1	3		P
Kilmarnock		94/95	19	11	4	P
		95/96	13	9	1	P
Partick T		96/97	29	2	2	D1
Livingston		97/98	4	10	1	D2
Cowdenbeath		97/98	5			D3

MASON Paul David
b. Liverpool 3.9.1963

Groningen						
Aberdeen		88/89	21	7	4	P
		89/90	33	1	9	P
		90/91	25	1	3	P
		91/92	28	3	7	P
		92/93	31	8	4	P
Ipswich T		93/94	18	4	3	FL
		94/95	19	2	3	FL
		95/96	24	2	7	FL
		96/97	41	2	12	FL
		97/98	1			FL

MASTERTON Daniel
b. Ayr 5.9.1954

Ayr U	76/77	26	2	9	P
	77/78	25	2	7	P
	78/79	17	7	5	D1
	79/80	0	2		D1
Clyde	80/81	36		19	D2
	81/82	33	2	23	D2
	82/83	18	9	14	D1
	83/84	23	4	11	D1
Queen of the South	84/85	1			D2

MASTERTON Robert
b. 3.8.1956

Stenhousemuir *	78/79	1			D2
Heart of Midlothian	79/80	9	6		D1
	80/81	8	3		P
Meadowbank T	81/82	11	3		D2
Falkirk	82/83	3	1		D1
East Fife	83/84	3			D2

MATHERS Paul
b. Aberdeen 17.1.1970

Dundee	89/90	8			P
	90/91	6			D1
	91/92	31			D1
	92/93	36			P
	93/94	33			P
	94/95	2	1		D1
	95/96	1	1		D1
Falkirk	96/97	16			D1
	97/98	29			D1
	98/99	31			D1

MATHIE Alexander
b. Bathgate 20.12.1968

Celtic	88/89	0	1		P
	89/90	5	1		P
	90/91	2	2		P
Morton	91/92	42		18	D1
Port Vale L	92/93	0	3		FL
Newcastle U	93/94	0	16	3	FL
	94/95	3	6	1	FL
Ipswich T	94/95	13		2	FL
	95/96	39		18	FL
	96/97	11	1	4	FL
	97/98	25	12	13	FL
	98/99	2	6	1	FL
Dundee U	98/99	13	9	1	P
	99/00	10	2	3	P
Preston NE L	99/00	5	7	2	FL

MATHISEN Sven

Hibernian	78/79	2			P

MATTHAEI Rob
b. Amsterdam 20.9.1966
Haarlem
De Graafshad
Volendam

Motherwell	98/99	14	3		P
	99/00	2	1		P

MAUCHLEN Alistair Henry
b. Kilwinning 26.6.1960
Irvine Meadow

Kilmarnock	78/79	20			D1
	79/80	30		2	P
	80/81	31		3	P
	81/82	31	6	4	D1
Motherwell	82/83	25		3	P
	83/84	20			P
	84/85	29	1	1	D1
	85/86	1			P
Leicester C	85/86	35	2	2	FL
	86/87	30		1	FL
	87/88	33	3	2	FL
	88/89	38		3	FL
	89/90	38		1	FL
	90/91	40		1	FL
	91/92	14	6	1	FL
Heart of Midlothian	92/93	16	2		P

MAUCHLEN J Stewart
b. Kilwinning 22.10.1957

Morton	79/80	1	3		P
	80/81	0	1		P
	81/82				
Stranraer	82/83	2			D2
Irvine Meadow	83/84				
	84/85				
Stranraer	85/86	27	1	8	D2
Ayr U	86/87	3	2		D2

MAXWELL Alistair Elspie
b. Hamilton 16.2.1965

Motherwell	83/84	4			P
	84/85	15			D1
	85/86	4			P
	86/87	21			P
	87/88	1			P
Clydebank	87/88	1			D1
Motherwell	88/89	17			P
	89/90	36			P
	90/91	36			P
	91/92				
Rangers	92/93	10			P
	93/94	31	1		P
	94/95	10	1		P
Dundee U	95/96	34			D1
	96/97	10			P
	97/98				
Morton	98/99	30			D1
	99/00	33			D1

MAXWELL Samuel George
b. Stevenston 9.6.1950
Irvine Royal Academy
Kilmarnock Amateurs
Dreghorn Jnrs

Kilmarnock	68/69				
	69/70	1	1		D1
	70/71	17	2	1	D1
	71/72	34		8	D1
	72/73	33		4	D1
	73/74	35		9	D2
	74/75	29	2	6	D1
	75/76	15	3		D1
	76/77	25	5	2	P
	77/78	35		9	D1
	78/79	36	1	11	D1
	79/80	19	3	3	P
	80/81	9	6		P
	81/82				
Queen of the South	82/83	7	3		D2
Stranraer	82/83	14	1		D2
Whittlets V					

MAXWELL Scott Stewart
b. Edinburgh 26.8.1963

Heart of Midlothian	80/81	1		1	P
	81/82				
Stirling A	82/83	0	3		D2
	83/84	24	1		D2
	84/85	39		4	D2
	85/86	39		3	D2
	86/87	31		5	D2
	87/88	38		2	D2
	88/89	16	7	1	D2

MAY Edward Skillion
b. Edinburgh 30.8.1967
Dundee U

Hibernian	85/86	15	4	1	P
	86/87	28	2	5	P
	87/88	32	2	2	P
	88/89	13	12	2	P
	89/90				
Falkirk	90/91	13		6	P
	91/92	33	3	9	P
	92/93	40	2	6	P
	93/94	34	4	9	D1
	94/95	24		2	P
Motherwell	94/95	10		2	P
	95/96	28		1	P
	96/97	34		2	P
	97/98	20	5		P
	98/99	10	2		P
Dunfermline A	99/00	19	4	3	D1

MAYER Andreas
b. Burgau 13.9.1972
Rofingen
Augsburg

Bayern Munich	92/93				
St Pauli	93/94				
	94/95				
	95/96				
Stabaek	95				
	96				
	97				
Rosenborg Trondheim	97				
Aberdeen	98/99	13		2	P
	99/00	20	1		P

MEADE Raphael Joseph
b. Islington 22.11.1962

Arsenal	81/82	8	8	4	FL
	82/83	2	2	2	FL
	83/84	9	4	5	FL
	84/85	6	2	3	FL
Sporting Lisbon	85/86				
	86/87				
	87/88				
Dundee U	88/89	8	3	4	P
Luton T	88/89	2	2		FL
BK09 Odense					
Ipswich T	89/90	0	1		FL
BK 09 Odense					
Plymouth A	90/91	2	3		FL
Brighton	91/92	35	5	9	FL
Hong Kong	92/93				
	93/94				
Brighton	94/95	0	3		FL

MEIKLE David
b. 19.1.1960
Rancel Amateurs

Motherwell	78/79	1			P
	79/80	4	2		D1

MELDRUM Colin George
b. Kilmarnock 26.11.1975
Kilwinning R

Kilmarnock	94/95	4			P
	95/96	1			P
	96/97	6			P
	97/98	11			P
Stranraer	98/99	7			D1
Ross Co	98/99	2			D3
Kilmarnock	99/00	18			P

MELROSE James Millsopp
b. Glasgow 7.10.1958
Eastercraigs Amateurs
Sighthill Amateurs

Partick T	75/76	0	2		D1
	76/77	22	5	8	P
	77/78	21	4	4	P
	78/79	29	4	10	P
	79/80	31	4	9	P
Leicester C	80/81	28	4	9	FL
	81/82	24	11	11	FL
	82/83	5		1	FL
Coventry C	82/83	21	3	8	FL
Celtic	83/84	20	10	7	P
Wolverhampton W L	84/85	6	1	2	FL
Manchester C	84/85	23	1	7	FL
	85/86	4	6	1	FL
Charlton A	85/86	11		5	FL
	86/87	30	4	14	FL
	87/88	3			FL
Leeds U	87/88	3	1		FL
Shrewsbury T	87/88	6	3	1	FL
	88/89	16	5	2	FL
	89/90	5	14		FL

MENNIE Vincent
b. Dortmund 19.5.1964
1FC Cologne

Dundee	85/86	11		1	P
	86/87	13	7	1	P
	87/88	27	2	1	P
	88/89	0	4		P
Forfar A	89/90	1		1	D1

MICHELS Jan
b. Deventer 8.9.1970
Go Ahead Eagles

Motherwell	98/99	7	3		P

MIKHAILITCHENKO Alexei
b. Kiev 30.3.1963
Sampdoria

Rangers	91/92	24	3	10	P
	92/93	16	13	3	P
	93/94	24	10	5	P
	94/95	4	5	2	P
	95/96	6	5		P

MILLAR Blair
b. Paisley 16.10.1956
Glentyne Thistle

Clydebank	77/78	9	1	1	P
	78/79	37		28	D1
	79/80	38		17	D1
	80/81	37	2	18	D1
	81/82	37		20	D1
Airdrieonians	82/83	34	1	12	D1
	83/84	5	3		D1
	84/85	1	6	1	D1
Kilmarnock	84/85	22		12	D1
	85/86	21		7	D1
	86/87	4	3		D1
	87/88				
Stirling A *	88/89	1	5		D2

MILLAR John
b. Coatbridge 8.12.1966
Dundee BC

Chelsea		84/85				
		85/86	7			FL
		86/87	4			FL
Northampton T	L	86/87	1			FL
Hamilton A	L	86/87	10			P
Blackburn R		87/88	13	2		FL
		88/89	37	1		FL
		89/90	38	1	1	FL
		90/91	34			FL
Heart of Midlothian		91/92	40	1	7	P
		92/93	23	1	1	P
		93/94	16	4	4	P
		94/95	25	3	6	P
		95/96	16	4	4	P
Raith R		95/96	3		1	P
		96/97	25	2		P
		97/98	19	5	1	D1
Livingston		98/99	30		4	D2
		99/00	27	3	2	D1

MILLAR Marc
b. Dundee 10.4.1969
Riverside A

Brechin C		91/92	12	5	1	D2
		92/93	30	1	11	D2
		93/94	39		10	D1
		94/95	8		1	D2
Dunfermline A		94/95	22	2	2	D1
		95/96	25		5	D1
		96/97	19	4	6	P
		97/98	10	2	2	P
		98/99	13	8	1	P
Livingston		99/00	24		2	D1
St Johnstone		99/00	3	5	2	P

MILLAR Peter

Forth W

Arbroath		68/69				
		69/70				
Dunfermline A		69/70				
		70/71	5	4		D1
		71/72	15	3	3	D1
Motherwell		72/73	17	1	5	D1
		73/74	30	1	2	D1
		74/75	27	1	4	D1
		75/76	23	5	4	P
		76/77	31	1		P
		77/78	24	5	1	P
		78/79	13		1	P
Dundee		78/79	16			D1
		79/80	26	2	2	P

MILLEN Andrew Francis
b. Glasgow 10.6.1965
Eastercraigs
Pollok Jnrs

St Johnstone		84/85	3			D1
		85/86	35	1	1	D2
		86/87	30	1	1	D2
Alloa A		87/88	36		4	D2
		88/89	38		3	D2
		89/90	37		2	D1
Hamilton A		90/91	39			D1
		91/92	40		1	D1
		92/93	41		3	D1
Kilmarnock		93/94	44			P
		94/95	8			P
Ipswich T	L	94/95				
Hibernian		94/95	13			P
		95/96	25			P
		96/97	16	3		P
Raith R		96/97	13			P
		97/98	6			D1
Ayr U		97/98	26		2	D1
		98/99	34		1	D1
Morton		99/00	28			D1

MILLER Alexander
b. 7.4.1949

Rangers		68/69	0	1		D1
		69/70				
		70/71	21		1	D1
		71/72	2			D1
		72/73	2	1	2	D1
		73/74				
		74/75	15	3	2	D1
		75/76	25	2	1	P
		76/77	17	7	4	P
		77/78	16	8	2	P
		78/79	10	7		P
		79/80	13	5	3	P
		80/81	24	1	2	P
		81/82	14	2		P
South China		82/83				
Morton		83/84	8		1	D1

MILLER Charles D
b. Glasgow 18.3.1976

Rangers		93/94	2	1		P
		94/95	21		3	P
		95/96	17	6	3	P
		96/97	7	6	1	P
		97/98	5	2		P
		98/99	2	14	3	P
Leicester C	L	98/99	1	3		FL
Rangers		99/00				
Watford		99/00	9	5		FL

MILLER Colin Fyfe
b. Lanark 4.10.1964

Toronto Blizzard		82	2			NA
		83	10		2	NA
		84	11			NA
Rangers		85/86	2			P
Albion R	L	85/86	1	1		D2
Doncaster R		86/87	20		2	FL
		87/88				
Hamilton Steelers		88				
Hamilton A		88/89	20	1		P
		89/90	37		1	D1
		90/91	37			D1
		91/92	43		1	D1
		92/93	29		3	D1
		93/94	31			D1
St Johnstone		93/94	12			P
		94/95	12			D1
Heart of Midlothian		94/95	16		1	P
		95/96	2	1		P
Dunfermline A		95/96	24			D1
		96/97	19	3		P
		97/98	13	2		P
Ayr U		97/98	8			D1
		98/99	4	2		D1
Hamilton A		98/99	7	1		D1
		99/00	1			D2

MILLER Graeme
b. Glasgow 21.2.1973

Hibernian		92/93	1			P
		93/94	0	1		P
		94/95				
		95/96	0	1		P
Berwick R		96/97	2	5	1	D2
Queens Park *		97/98	10	6	1	D3

MILLER Greg Alan
b. Glasgow 1.4.1976

Hibernian		95/96	1	2		P
		96/97	3	3		P
		97/98	0	3	1	P
Livingston	L	97/98	1	4		D2
Motherwell		98/99	1	3		P
Clydebank		99/00	24	11	2	D1

MILLER James
b. Greenock 4.1.1953

Aberdeen		73/74	4	1		D1
Queen of the South		74/75	38			D2
		75/76	17	4	1	D1
		76/77	27		1	D1
Motherwell		76/77	14	1		P
		77/78	3	5	1	P
Morton		77/78	14			D1
		78/79	33			P
		79/80	20	1		P
Clyde		80/81	28	2		D2
		81/82	1			D2
Queen of the South		81/82	16	1		D1
		82/83	2			D2
Albion R		83/84	2			D2

MILLER Joseph
b. Glasgow 8.12.1967

Aberdeen		84/85	0	1		P
		85/86	17	2	3	P
		86/87	22	5	6	P
		87/88	12	2	4	P
Celtic		87/88	24	3	3	P
		88/89	16	6	8	P
		89/90	16	8	5	P
		90/91	24	6	6	P
		91/92	23	3	2	P
		92/93	10	13	2	P
Aberdeen		93/94	24	3	4	P
		94/95	21	6		P
		95/96	31		9	P
		96/97	26	4	4	P
		97/98	20	8	1	P
Dundee U		98/99	14	10	2	P

MILLER Kenneth
b. Edinburgh 23.12.1979

Hibernian		97/98	1	6		P
		98/99	5	2	1	D1
Stenhousemuir	L	98/99	11		8	D3
Hibernian		99/00	23	8	11	P

MILLER Liam William Peter
b. Cork 13.2.1981
Ballincollig

Celtic		99/00	0	1		P

MILLER William Ferguson
b. Glasgow 2.5.1955
Eastercraigs U

Aberdeen		71/72				
Peterhead	L	71/72				
Aberdeen		72/73	0	1		D1
		73/74	31		1	D1
		74/75	34		1	D1
		75/76	36			P
		76/77	36			P
		77/78	36		2	P
		78/79	34			P
		79/80	31		1	P
		80/81	33		2	P
		81/82	36			P
		82/83	36		1	P
		83/84	34		2	P
		84/85	34		3	P
		85/86	33		1	P
		86/87	36		2	P
		87/88	42		3	P
		88/89	21		1	P
		89/90	15			P

MILLER William Nesbit
b. Edinburgh 1.11.1969

Hibernian		89/90	11			P
		90/91	24	1	1	P
		91/92	29	1		P
		92/93	29	5		P
		93/94	37			P
		94/95	34			P
		95/96	13			P
		96/97	31			P
		97/98	31			P
Dundee		98/99	26			P

MILNE Callum
b. Edinburgh 27.8.1965

Hibernian		84/85	1			P
		85/86	7	1		P
		86/87	2			P
		87/88	1	1		P
		88/89	18	1		P
		89/90	3			P
		90/91	21			P
		91/92	7	1		P
		92/93	10	5		P
Partick T		93/94	29	2	1	P
		94/95	3	1		P
		95/96	19	3		P
		96/97	22	3		D1
		97/98	23	1	1	D1

MILNE Kenneth
b. Stirling 26.8.1979

Cowdenbeath		98/99	23		6	D3
Heart of Midlothian		99/00	0	1		P

MILNE Ralph
b. Dundee 13.5.1961

Dundee U		79/80	4	9	2	P
		80/81	16	5	7	P
		81/82	32	2	8	P
		82/83	30	4	16	P
		83/84	19	6	5	P
		84/85	14	5	4	P
		85/86	10	8	1	P
		86/87	7	7	1	P
Charlton A		86/87	10	2		FL
		87/88	9	1		FL
Bristol C		87/88	19		4	FL
		88/89	10	1	2	FL
Manchester U		88/89	19	3	3	FL
		89/90	0	1		FL

MIMMS Robert Andrew
b. York 12.10.1963
Halifax T

Rotherham U		81/82	2			FL
		82/83	13			FL
		83/84	22			FL
		84/85	46			FL
Everton		85/86	10			FL
Notts Co	L	85/86	2			FL
Everton		86/87	11			FL
Sunderland	L	86/87	4			FL
Blackburn R	L	86/87	6			FL
Everton		87/88	8			FL
Manchester C	L	87/88	3			FL
Tottenham H		87/88	13			FL
		88/89	20			FL
		89/90	4			FL
Aberdeen	L	89/90	6			P
Blackburn R		90/91	22			FL
		91/92	45			FL
		92/93	42			FL
		93/94	13			FL
		94/95	3	1		FL
		95/96	1	1		FL
Crystal Palace		96/97	1			FL
Preston NE		96/97	27			FL
Rotherham U		97/98	43			FL
York C		98/99	35			FL
		99/00	28			FL

MISSE-MISSE Jean-Jacque
b. Yaounde 7.8.1968
RAA La Louviere
Ethnikos
RAA La Louviere
Trabzonspor
Sporting Lisbon

Dundee U		97/98	4			P
Chesterfield		97/98	1			FL

MITCHELL Alistair Robert
b. Kirkcaldy 3.12.1968
Ballingry R

East Fife		88/89	18		4	D2
		89/90	35		12	D2
		90/91	29	5	7	D2
Kilmarnock		91/92	42		10	D1
		92/93	26	6	6	D1
		93/94	34		5	P
		94/95	33	2	4	P
		95/96	29	1	3	P
		96/97	23	7	2	P
		97/98	22	11	4	P
		98/99	27	5	4	P
		99/00	22	4	2	P

MITCHELL Charles Brian
b. Stonehaven 16.7.1963

Aberdeen		81/82	1			P
		82/83	1			P
		83/84	6	3		P
		84/85	7	7	1	P
		85/86	18	5		P
		86/87	15	2		P
Bradford C		86/87	16			FL
		87/88	42		6	FL
		88/89	44	1	1	FL
		89/90	32	3	2	FL
		90/91	16	4		FL
		91/92	20			FL
Bristol C		92/93	15	1		FL
Hull C		93/94	9			FL

MITCHELL David Stuart
b. Glasgow 13.6.1962
Hakoah

Rangers		83/84	7	5	2	P
		84/85	11	3	4	P
Feyenoord		85/86				
		86/87				
		87/88				
		88/89				
Chelsea		88/89	6			FL
		89/90				
		90/91	1			FL
Newcastle U	L	90/91	2		1	FL
Swindon T		91/92	24	3	5	FL
		92/93	37	4	11	FL
Altay Izmir		93/94				
Millwall		93/94	26	1	9	FL
		94/95	23	5	6	FL

MITCHELL Graham
b. Glasgow 2.11.1962
Auchengill BC

Hamilton A		80/81	2	2		D1
		81/82	32	5		D1
		82/83	27	3		D1
		83/84	14	7	1	D1
		84/85	27	3		D1
		85/86	32		6	D1
		86/87	23		1	P
Hibernian		86/87	17		1	P
		87/88	41		1	P
		88/89	20			P
		89/90	28	3		P
		90/91	25	3		P
		91/92	26	1		P
		92/93	41			P
		93/94	36		1	P
		94/95	18			P
		95/96	6			P
Falkirk		96/97	17	3	1	D1
Raith R		97/98	2	1		D1

MITCHELL Graham Lee
b. Shipley 16.2.1968

Huddersfield T		86/87	16	1		FL
		87/88	28	1	1	FL
		88/89	33	1		FL
		89/90	28			FL
		90/91	46			FL
		91/92	43			FL
		92/93	3	1		FL
		93/94	20	2		FL
Bournemouth	L	93/94	4			FL
Huddersfield T		94/95	11	1		FL
Bradford C		94/95	26			FL
		95/96	32	1	1	FL
		96/97	6			FL
Raith R		96/97	20			P
Cowdenbeath		97/98	11		1	D3
Raith R		97/98	2	1		D1

MJALLBY Johan
b. Sweden 9.2.1971

AIK Stockholm		89				
		90				
		91				
		92				
		93				
		94				
		95				
		96				
		97				
		98				
Celtic		98/99	17		1	P
		99/00	26	4	2	P

MOBILIO Domenic
b. Vancouver 14.1.1969
Vancouver 86ers

Dundee		93/94	0	2		P

MOLS Michael
b. Amsterdam 17.12.1970

FC Twente		92/93				
		93/94				
		94/95				
		95/96				
FC Utrecht		96/97				
		97/98				
		98/99				
Rangers		99/00	9		9	P

MOLS Tonny
b. Eeklo 8.1.1969
FC Bruges
RWD Molenbeek
Lokeren

Dundee U		98/99	11			P
Arbroath		99/00	5			D2
Clyde		99/00	1			D2
Ross Co		99/00	1			D2

MONEY Israel Campbell
b. Maybole 31.8.1960

St Mirren		81/82	1			P
		82/83	1			P
		83/84	6			P
		84/85	30			P
		85/86	33			P
		86/87	42			P
		87/88	41			P
		88/89	21			P
		89/90	28			P
		90/91	26			P
		91/92	27			P
		92/93	25		2	D1
		93/94	28			D1
		94/95	15			D1
		95/96	12			D1

MONTGOMERIE Samuel Raymond
b. Irvine 17.4.1961
Saltcoats V
Newcastle U

Dumbarton		81/82	17	3	5	D1
		82/83	25		2	D1
		83/84	39		1	D1
		84/85	6			P
		85/86	22	2		D1
		86/87	35			D1
		87/88	31			D1
Kilmarnock		88/89	31		2	D1
		89/90	32	3	3	D1
		90/91	35	2		D1
		91/92	26	4	1	D1
		92/93	42			D1
		93/94	42			P
		94/95	9	3		P
		95/96	12	2		P
		96/97	20	2	1	P
		97/98	27			P
		98/99	22			P
Partick T		99/00	31	1		D2

MOONEY Martin James
b. Alexandria 25.9.1970

Falkirk		88/89	1	5		P
		89/90	8	7	2	D1
Stirling A		89/90	2			D2
Falkirk		90/91	1	3		P
		91/92	0	4		P
Dumbarton		92/93	27	7	12	D1
		93/94	41	2	9	D1
		94/95	33	3	17	D2
		95/96	31	5	5	D1
		96/97	18	4	1	D2
		97/98	26	4	5	D3
		98/99	28	4	4	D3
Stenhousemuir		99/00	17	14	8	D2

MOORE Allan
b. Glasgow 25.12.1964

Dumbarton		83/84	2	2		D1
		84/85	1	3		P
		85/86	26	7	4	D1
		86/87	18		3	D1
Heart of Midlothian		86/87	2	8		P
		87/88	2	5	1	P
		88/89	5	7	2	P
St Johnstone		89/90	33		13	D1
		90/91	31		5	P
		91/92	18	3	1	P
		92/93	17	9	3	P
		93/94	7	6	1	P
Dunfermline A		93/94	2	6		D1
		94/95	11	1	1	D1
		95/96	28		5	D1
		96/97	13	13	3	P
		97/98	11	11		P
Livingston		97/98	6	1	1	D2
Airdrieonians		98/99	21	7	4	D1
		99/00	23	4	2	D1

MOORE Craig Andrew
b. Canterbury (Aus) 12.12.1975

Rangers		93/94	1			P
		94/95	19	2	2	P
		95/96	9	2	1	P
		96/97	23		1	P
		97/98	8	2		P
		98/99	8		1	P
		99/00	22		1	P

MOORE Vincent
b. Scunthorpe 21.8.1964
Campsie Black Watch

Clydebank		84/85	3			D1
		85/86	15	8	2	P
		86/87	6	7	1	P
Airdrieonians		86/87	21		3	D1
		87/88	36		7	D1
		88/89	6	3		D1
Stirling A		88/89	14		4	D2
		89/90	36		14	D2
		90/91	31	4	13	D2
		91/92	27	11	6	D1
		92/93	28	3	4	D1
		93/94	5			D1
Ayr U		93/94	19		2	D1
		94/95	13	4	2	D1
		95/96	11		2	D2
Albion R		95/96	8		2	D3
		96/97	27		5	D3
		97/98	17		1	D3

MORAVCIK Lubomir
b. Slovakia 22.6.1965

St Etienne	90/91				
	91/92				
	92/93				
	93/94				
	94/95				
	95/96				
Bastia	96/97				
	97/98				
MSV Duisburg	97/98				
Celtic	98/99	14		6	P
	99/00	29	1	8	P

MORE Colin David
b. Edinburgh 13.11.1960

Heart of Midlothian	78/79	4			P
	79/80	6			D1
	80/81	21	3		P
	81/82	3			D1
Raith R	82/83	32		4	D1
	83/84	34	2		D1
	84/85	30		1	D2
	85/86	33			D2

MORGAN Andrew Alan
b. Glasgow 10.12.1974

St Johnstone	93/94	0	3		P
	94/95	0	3		D1
Forfar A	94/95	20		5	D3
	95/96	34		6	D2
	96/97	36		15	D3
	97/98	3		1	D2
Partick T	97/98	18		5	D1
	98/99	12	1	6	D2

MORRIS Christopher Barry
b. Newquay 24.12.1963
Newquay

Sheffield W	82/83				
	83/84	8	5	1	FL
	84/85	11	3		FL
	85/86	29	1		FL
	86/87	13	4		FL
Celtic	87/88	44		3	P
	88/89	33		4	P
	89/90	32		1	P
	90/91	15	3		P
	91/92	29	3	1	P
	92/93	3			P
Middlesbrough	92/93	22	3	1	FL
	93/94	14	1		FL
	94/95	14	1		FL
	95/96	22	1	2	FL
	96/97	3	1		FL

MORRIS Eric
b. Stranraer 30.9.1951

Rangers	76/77	1			P
	77/78				
	78/79	1			P
Ayr U	79/80	34		11	D1
	80/81	36		10	D1
	81/82	36	2	8	D1
	82/83	26	2		D1
	83/84	18			D1
	84/85	32	2	1	D1
	85/86	1	1		D1

MORRISON Albert
b. Kilwinning 29.10.1960
Bellfield BC
Ardrossan Winton R

Kilmarnock	79/80				
	80/81	1			P
	81/82				
	82/83				
Auchinleck Talbot					

MORRISON Francis
b. Glasgow 17.4.1967

St Mirren	85/86	0	1		P
Arbroath	86/87	19	11	2	D2
	87/88	16	13	2	D2

MORRISON Stephen
b. St Andrews 15.8.1961
St Mirren BC
Aberdeen
Perth Azzuri

Dunfermline A	81/82	26	4	4	D1
	82/83	24	5	8	D1
	83/84	37	1	9	D2
	84/85	34	3	8	D2
	85/86	24	5	5	D2
	86/87	30	6	5	D1
	87/88	17	12	3	P
	88/89	6	10		D1
Hamilton A	88/89	8	1		P
	89/90	17	3	7	D1
Dumbarton	89/90	17		4	D2
	90/91	32	5	8	D2
Clyde	91/92	18	16	7	D2
	92/93	15	9	7	D2
	93/94	13	7	1	D1
Kilbirnie Ladeside	94/95				
Alloa A	94/95	5			D3
Larne	94/95				
Alloa A	95/96	21	5	2	D3
?	96/97				
	97/98				
Clydebank	98/99	2	1		D1
	99/00	1	3		D1

MORROW John James
b. Belfast 20.11.1971

Rangers	91/92	3			P
	92/93				
	93/94	2			P
	94/95				
	95/96				
Oldham A	96/97	1	1		FL
Morton	97/98	4	5	1	D1
	98/99	4	1		D1

MORTON James
b. Dundee 29.10.1956

Brechin C	74/75	31	2	3	D2
	75/76	23	2	2	D2
	76/77	33		7	D2
	77/78	33		10	D2
Berwick R	78/79	36		20	D2
	79/80	18		6	D1
St Johnstone	79/80	18	2	1	D1
	80/81	35		9	D1
	81/82	38		17	D1
	82/83	32	1	7	D1
	83/84	31	1	2	P
	84/85	17	2		D1
	85/86	28		9	D2
Brisbane Lions	86/87				
Forfar A	87/88	19	3	1	D1
	88/89	37		1	D1
	89/90	17	4	4	D1
Arbroath	90/91	18		5	D2
	91/92	15	12	4	D2

MOULE Andrew Gareth
b. Neath 16.4.1977
Dyce Jnrs

Dundee U	94/95	0	1		P

MOWAT John

St Mirren	74/75	3	1		D2
	75/76	6		1	D1
	76/77	12	1	1	D1
	77/78	5			P
	78/79	2			P

MOWBRAY Anthony Mark
b. Saltburn 22.11.1963

Middlesbrough	81/82				
	82/83	25	1		FL
	83/84	33	2	1	FL
	84/85	40		3	FL
	85/86	35		4	FL
	86/87	46		7	FL
	87/88	44		3	FL
	88/89	37		3	FL
	89/90	28		2	FL
	90/91	40		3	FL
	91/92	17			FL
Celtic	91/92	14	1	2	P
	92/93	26		2	P
	93/94	20	2	1	P
	94/95	15		1	P
Ipswich T	95/96	19		2	FL
	96/97	8			FL
	97/98	23	2		FL
	98/99	40		2	FL
	99/00	35	1	1	FL

MOYES David William
b. Glasgow 25.4.1963
Drumchapel Amateurs

Celtic	81/82	15	4		P
	82/83	4	1		P
Cambridge U	83/84	30			FL
	84/85	40		1	FL
	85/86	9			FL
Bristol C	85/86	27		2	FL
	86/87	41		3	FL
	87/88	15		1	FL
Shrewsbury T	87/88	17		2	FL
	88/89	28	5	1	FL
	89/90	46		8	FL
Dunfermline A	90/91	35		7	P
	91/92	39		5	P
	92/93	30		1	D1
	93/94	1			D1
Hamilton A	93/94	5			D1
Preston NE	93/94	29		4	FL
	94/95	38		4	FL
	95/96	41		3	FL
	96/97	26		4	FL
	97/98	8	1		FL

MUGGLETON Carl David
b. Leicester 13.9.1968

Leicester C		86/87				
		87/88				
Chesterfield	L	87/88	17			FL
Blackpool	L	87/88	2			FL
Leicester C		88/89	3			FL
Hartlepool U	L	88/89	8			FL
Leicester C		89/90				
Stockport Co	L	89/90	4			FL
Leicester C		90/91	22			FL
		91/92	3			FL
		92/93	17			FL
		93/94				
Stoke C	L	93/94	6			FL
Celtic		93/94	12			P
Stoke C		94/95	24			FL
		95/96	6			FL
Rotherham U	L	95/96	6			FL
Sheffield U	L	95/96	0	1		FL
Stoke C		96/97	33			FL
		97/98	34			FL
		98/99	40			FL
		99/00				
Mansfield T	L	99/00	9			FL
Chesterfield	L	99/00	5			FL

MUIR James
b. 27.12.1956

Motherwell	76/77	2			P
	77/78	4			P
	78/79				
Hamilton A	79/80	4			D1
	80/81	1			D1
Hurlford U					

MUIR John
b. 4.9.1947
Alloa A

St Johnstone	69/70	3	3		D1
	70/71	7		1	D1
	71/72	5	2	1	D1
	72/73	19	4	6	D1
	73/74	25	7	12	D1
	74/75	32	1	14	D1
	75/76	24	2	3	P
Alloa A	76/77	32	4	11	D2
	77/78	14	1	4	D1
	78/79	7		2	D2
	79/80	13	3	3	D2

MUIR Lindsay
b. Linlithgow 10.5.1956

Hibernian	75/76	6	4	1	P
	76/77	4	4		P
	77/78				
St Johnstone	78/79	37		3	D1
	79/80	24	2	1	D1
Berwick R	80/81	20			D1
	81/82	28			D2
	82/83	36		1	D2
	83/84	33	2		D2
	84/85	36			D2
	85/86	27			D2
	86/87	38		1	D2
Cowdenbeath	87/88	36			D2
	88/89	2			D2
Berwick R	88/89	33			D2
	89/90	11			D2

MUIR William
b. Kilmarnock 24.2.1964
Kilmarnock BC

Aberdeen		80/81				
Rangers		81/82				
Kilmarnock		82/83	4	3		P
Queen of the South		83/84	0	2		D2
Irvine Meadow		83/84				
Craigmark Bruntonians		84/85				
		85/86				
Cumnock Jnrs		86/87				
		87/88				
		88/89				
Stranraer		89/90	3	2		D2
		90/91	0	1		D2

MULLER Jochen
b. Erbach 18.4.1963
Mannheim

Dundee U		91/92	4	1		P

MULVANEY Francis
b. Chapelhall 5.4.1962

Albion R		80/81	9	9	4	D2
Stenhousemuir *		81/82	1			D2
Forth W		82/83				
		83/84				
		84/85				
Motherwell		85/86	4	1		P
East Stirlingshire		86/87	6	1		D2

MUNGALL Steven Henry
b. Bellshill 22.5.1958

Motherwell		76/77	3			P
		77/78	10	3		P
		78/79	1	3		P
Tranmere R		79/80	19	5		FL
		80/81	37	1	3	FL
		81/82	43	1	1	FL
		82/83	30	1	1	FL
		83/84	25	1		FL
		84/85	22	1		FL
		85/86	46		1	FL
		86/87	46			FL
		87/88	45			FL
		88/89	42		1	FL
		89/90	16	1	1	FL
		90/91	32	1	1	FL
		91/92	17	1		FL
		92/93	29	6	3	FL
		93/94	8	4		FL
		94/95	19	7	1	FL
		95/96				

MUNOZ Victor
b. Spain 15.3.1957

St Mirren		90/91	18		1	P

MUNRO Alexander Iain Fordyce
b. Bellshill 24.8.1951
Drumchapel Amateurs

St Mirren		68/69				
		69/70	4	1		D1
		70/71	30	2	3	D1
		71/72	36		6	D1
		72/73	31	1	7	D1
Hibernian		73/74	8	6	2	D1
		74/75	28	2	8	D1
St Mirren	L	75/76	6	2		D1
Hibernian		75/76	17		1	P
Rangers		76/77	3	2		P
		77/78				
St Mirren		77/78	24		3	P
		78/79	33			P
		79/80	32			P
		80/81				
Stoke C		80/81	32			FL
Sunderland		81/82	34			FL
		82/83	37			FL
		83/84	9			FL
Dundee U		83/84	9			P
		84/85	5			P
Hibernian		84/85	6			P
		85/86	26			P

MUNRO Francis Michael
b. Broughty Ferry 25.10.1947

Chelsea		62/63				
Dundee U		63/64				
		64/65	19		1	D1
		65/66	28		13	D1
		66/67	2	1		D1
Aberdeen		66/67	29		6	D1
		67/68	13	1	2	D1
Wolverhampton W		67/68	7		1	FL
		68/69	12	4	2	FL
		69/70	32	1	1	FL
		70/71	36			FL
		71/72	37		3	FL
		72/73	32		2	FL
		73/74	36		2	FL
		74/75	35		3	FL
		75/76	30			FL
		76/77	33		1	FL
Hereford U	L	76/77				
Celtic		77/78	14	1		P

MUNRO Stuart
b. Falkirk 15.9.1962

St Mirren		80/81	1			P
		81/82				
Alloa A		82/83	39		5	D1
		83/84	19	2		D1
Rangers		83/84	2	3		P
		84/85	13			P
		85/86	28	1		P
		86/87	43			P
		87/88	16	1		P
		88/89	21	1	2	P
		89/90	36		1	P
		90/91	14			P
Blackburn R		91/92	1			FL
Bristol C		92/93	16			FL
		93/94	43	1		FL
		94/95	29	2		FL
		95/96	3			FL
Falkirk		95/96	13			P
St Mirren		96/97	25	1	1	D1

MURDOCH Andrew Gerard
b. Greenock 20.7.1968
Johnstone Burgh

Celtic		88/89	13			P
		89/90	13			P
Hamilton A	L	89/90	4			D1
Partick T		90/91	18			D1
		91/92	32			D1
		92/93	17			P
		93/94	5	1		P
		94/95	2			P

MURDOCH William
b. Rutherglen 21.4.1949
Drumchapel Amateurs

Kilsyth R		67/68				
		68/69				
Celtic		69/70				
Bristol C		70/71				
Stenhousemuir		71/72	23	3	5	D2
		72/73	26	1	4	D2
		73/74	26		7	D2
		74/75	34		2	D2
		75/76	14	3		D2
Kilmarnock		75/76	4			D1
		76/77	34	1	1	P
		77/78	17	7	2	D1
		78/79	1	2		D1
		79/80				
Stirling A		80/81				
Stenhousemuir		80/81	5	1		D2
Cumbernauld U						

MURIE David
b. Edinburgh 2.8.1976

Heart of Midlothian		96/97	6	1		P
		97/98	0	1		P
		98/99	0	4		P
Morton		98/99	6	1		D1
		99/00	33	1	2	D1

MURPHY James
b. Hamilton 14.10.1956
Bellshill A

Dundee		78/79	10	6	2	D1
		79/80	28	3	3	P
		80/81	20	15	5	D1
		81/82	7			P
		82/83	6	4	2	P
Hamilton A		82/83	6		1	D1
Ayr U		83/84	37	2	8	D1
		84/85	35	2	6	D1
		85/86	20	7	5	D1
Clyde		86/87	24	11	11	D1
		87/88	1	12	1	D1

MURPHY John

Darvel Jnrs

Ayr U		63/64				
		64/65				
		65/66				
		66/67	34		1	D1
		67/68				
		68/69				
		69/70	32			D1
		70/71	34			D1
		71/72	34			D1
		72/73	34		1	D1
		73/74	27	1	1	D1
		74/75	34			D1
		75/76	35		1	P
		76/77	24	1		P
		77/78	5			P
East Stirlingshire *		78/79	1			D2

MURRAY Derek R
b. Dunfermline 26.11.1960
Oakley U

Dundee U		80/81	1			P
		81/82	12			P
		82/83	1			P
		83/84	2			P
Motherwell		84/85	34		5	D1
		85/86	24	1		P
		86/87	13	7		P
		87/88	22			P
Raith R		88/89	38		2	D1
		89/90	28	1		D1
		90/91	14	3		D1

MURRAY Donald James
b. Elgin 18.1.1949
Burghead Thistle

Cardiff C		62/63	1			FL
		63/64	21			FL
		64/65	31			FL
		65/66	32			FL
		66/67	40			FL
		67/68	40		1	FL
		68/69	42		1	FL
		69/70	42		1	FL
		70/71	42		1	FL
		71/72	36			FL
		72/73	36		1	FL
		73/74	35		1	FL
		74/75	9			FL
Swansea C	L	74/75	5			FL
Heart of Midlothian		74/75				
		75/76	22			P
		76/77				
Newport Co		76/77	16	2		FL
Barry Town						
Cardiff C						

MURRAY Gary S
b. Dundee 19.8.1959

Montrose		78/79	24	4	12	D1
		79/80	36	2	15	D2
		80/81	19		12	D2
Hibernian		80/81	15		5	D1
		81/82	27	1	5	P
		82/83	22	4	6	P
		83/84	4	6		P
Forfar A		84/85	5	6	2	D1
		85/86	13	1	7	D1
Montrose		86/87	11	19	1	D1
		87/88	22	2	10	D2
		88/89	34	4	21	D2
		89/90	22	10	10	D2
		90/91	19	14	11	D2

MURRAY Gavin
b. Dunfermline 4.8.1957

Clydebank		77/78	2		1	P
		78/79				
Stenhousemuir		79/80	27		4	D2
		80/81	18	2	8	D2
		81/82	38	1	7	D2
		82/83	34	2	15	D2
		83/84	38		13	D2
East Fife		84/85	39		12	D1
		85/86	35		9	D1
		86/87	0	1		D1

MURRAY Grant Robert
b. Edinburgh 29.8.1975
Bonnyrigg Rose

Heart of Midlothian		96/97	2	2		P
		97/98	8	2		P
		98/99	18	3		P
		99/00	15	6		P

MURRAY Ian William
b. Edinburgh 20.3.1981
Dundee U

Hibernian		99/00	8	1		P

MURRAY John
b. Motherwell 30.11.1959
Coltness U

Partick T		79/80	1			P
		80/81	6			P
		81/82	9			P
		82/83	37			D1
		83/84	35			D1
		84/85	22	1		D1
		85/86	18	5		D1
Clyde		86/87	5	1		D1

MURRAY Malcolm
b. Buckie 26.7.1964

Heart of Midlothian		83/84	1			P
		84/85	4			P
		85/86				
		86/87	8			P
		87/88	7			P
Stirling A	L	87/88	5			D2
Heart of Midlothian		88/89	8			P
St Johnstone	L	88/89	2			D1
Hull C		88/89	6	2		FL
		89/90	3			FL
Mansfield T		89/90	28			FL
		90/91	28	2		FL
Partick T		91/92	23			D1
Meadowbank T		91/92	1			D1
Clydebank		92/93	6			D1
Meadowbank T		92/93	32			D1
		93/94	39		4	D2
Arbroath		94/95	24		3	D3

MURRAY Neil
b. Bellshill 21.2.1973

Rangers		92/93	11	5		P
		93/94	20	2		P
		94/95	14	6	1	P
		95/96	2	3		P
Switzerland		96/97				
		97/98				
Dundee U		98/99	2	1		P
FSV05 Mainz						

MURRAY Stephen
b. Dumbarton 9.10.1944
Dumbarton St Patricks

Dundee		63/64	2			D1
		64/65	23		5	D1
		65/66	33		8	D1
		66/67	32		1	D1
		67/68	33			D1
		68/69	31		1	D1
		69/70	25		3	D1
Aberdeen		69/70	7			D1
		70/71	33		6	D1
		71/72	32		10	D1
		72/73	29		4	D1
Celtic		73/74	32		3	D1
		74/75	28		8	D1
		75/76	2	1		P
		76/77				
		77/78				
		78/79				
Dundee U		79/80	2	1		P
Clydebank	T	79/80				

MURRAY William
b. 28.8.1954

Hibernian		73/74	1	6		D1
		74/75	3	5		D1
		75/76	6	3	1	P
		76/77	11	3	1	P
		77/78	21	1	3	P
		78/79	6	1		P
		79/80	12	1	2	P
		80/81	1	1		D1
Cowdenbeath		80/81	3			D2

MUSEMIC Husref
b. Janja 4.7.1961
Red Star Belgrade

Heart of Midlothian		89/90	4	2	3	P

MYERS Christopher
b. Yeovil 1.4.1969

Torquay U		86/87	8	1		FL
Dawlish T		87/88				
		88/89				
		89/90				
Torquay U		90/91	24	5	2	FL
		91/92	36	3	4	FL
		92/93	28		1	FL
Dundee U		93/94	4	1		P
Torquay U	L	93/94	6			FL
Dundee U		94/95	0	1		P
Dunfermline A	T	95/96				
Wrexham	T	95/96				
Scarborough		95/96	8	1		FL
Exeter C		95/96	7	1		FL
		96/97	31	2	2	FL

MYHRE Thomas
b. Sarpsborg 16.10.1973
Viking Stavanger

Everton		97/98	22			FL
		98/99	38			FL
		99/00	4			FL
Rangers		99/00	3			P

McADAM Colin
b. Glasgow 28.8.1951

Dumbarton		71/72	11	1		D2
		72/73	4			D1
		73/74	19	3	5	D1
		74/75	18	1	6	D1
Motherwell		75/76	15	9		P
		76/77	24	4		P
		77/78	9	1	3	P
Partick T		77/78	10	2	3	P
		78/79	22	4	4	P
		79/80	32		17	P
Rangers		80/81	31		12	P
		81/82	15	7	2	P
		82/83	2	2		P
		83/84	8		1	P
Adelaide Juventus		84/85				
Heart of Midlothian		85/86	0	6		P
Partick T		86/87	16	3	1	D1
		87/88	20	5		D1

McADAM Thomas Ian
b. Glasgow 9.4.1954
Clydebank Colts
Weirs Recreation

Dumbarton		70/71				
		71/72				
		72/73	16	2	9	P
		73/74	16	3	5	P
		74/75	32	1	11	P
		75/76	6		4	D1
Dundee U		75/76	26		12	P
		76/77	29	4	9	P
		77/78	0	2		P
Celtic		77/78	32	1	8	P
		78/79	24	4	7	P
		79/80	34		8	P
		80/81	35		4	P
		81/82	33	1	5	P
		82/83	35		3	P
		83/84	28		1	P
		84/85	25	1		P
		85/86	5			P
Stockport Co	T	86/87	5		1	FL
Hamilton A	T	86/87	3			P
Motherwell		86/87	31		1	P
		87/88	33	1	1	P
		88/89	28		1	P
		89/90	6			P
Airdrieonians		89/90	15		1	D1
		90/91	9			D1

McALLISTER Gary
b. Motherwell 25.12.1964

Motherwell		81/82	0	1		D1
		82/83	0	1		P
		83/84	17	4		P
		84/85	34	1	6	D1
		85/86	1			P
Leicester C		85/86	31		7	FL
		86/87	39		9	FL
		87/88	40	2	9	FL
		88/89	46		11	FL
		89/90	43		10	FL
Leeds U		90/91	38		2	FL
		91/92	41	1	5	FL
		92/93	32		5	FL
		93/94	42		8	FL
		94/95	41		6	FL
		95/96	36		5	FL
Coventry C		96/97	38		6	FL
		97/98	14			FL
		98/99	29		3	FL
		99/00	38		11	FL

McALLISTER Ian
b. Irvine 8.2.1960

Ayr U		77/78	4	4	1	P
		78/79	39		1	D1
		79/80	36		3	D1
		80/81	10		1	D1
		81/82	39		3	D1
		82/83	33	1	4	D1
		83/84	36		1	D1
		84/85	23	1	4	D1
		85/86	35		2	D1
		86/87	36	1	5	D2
		87/88	25	2	2	D2
		88/89	22		1	D1
		89/90	31		2	D1
		90/91	17	3	3	D1
		91/92	4	3	2	D1

McALLISTER James Reynolds
b. Glasgow 26.4.1978

Queen of the South		95/96	2			D2
		96/97	4	2		D2
		97/98	3	12		D2
		98/99	25	2		D2
Aberdeen		99/00	29	5		P

McALLISTER Kevin
b. Falkirk 8.11.1962

Falkirk		83/84	35		11	D1
		84/85	24	5	7	D1
Chelsea		85/86	13	7		FL
		86/87	7	1		FL
		87/88	4	1		FL
Falkirk	L	87/88	6		3	P
Chelsea		88/89	28	8	6	FL
		89/90	21	3	1	FL
		90/91	5	8		FL
Falkirk		91/92	42		9	P
		92/93	40	1	3	P
Hibernian		93/94	36		6	P
		94/95	17	6	1	P
		95/96	29	2	4	P
		96/97	10	9	1	P
Falkirk		96/97	14	1	3	D1
		97/98	35		2	D1
		98/99	25	2		D1
		99/00	6	3	2	D1

McALLISTER Patrick F
b. Belfast 3.2.1972
Cliftonville

Dunfermline A		90/91	0	1		P
		91/92	2	2		P
		92/93	0	1		D1

McALPINE Hamish
b. Kilspindie 21.1.1948

Dundee U		68/69	1			D1
		69/70				
		70/71	24			D1
		71/72	29			D1
		72/73	24			D1
		73/74	19			D1
		74/75	34			D1
		75/76	36		1	P
		76/77	36		2	P
		77/78	35			P
		78/79	36			P
		79/80	29			P
		80/81	36			P
		81/82	35			P
		82/83	36			P
		83/84	34			P
		84/85	25			P
		85/86	8			P
Dunfermline A		85/86	1			D2
Raith R		86/87	37			D2
		87/88	35		1	D1
Arbroath		88/89	10			D2

McANESPIE Alexander

Craigmark Bruntonians

Ayr U		64/65				
		65/66				
		66/67	18			D1
		67/68				
		68/69				
		69/70	13	2		D1
		70/71	13	1	1	D1
		71/72	18			D1
		72/73	33		1	D1
		73/74	31			D1
		74/75	24	2		D1
		75/76	23			P
		76/77	19			P
		77/78	20			P

McANESPIE Kieran Liam
b. Gosport 11.9.1979

St Johnstone		96/97	1	8	2	D1
		97/98	1	2		P
		98/99	8	10	2	P
		99/00	14	6	1	P

McANESPIE Stephen
b. Kilmarnock 1.2.1972
Vasterhauringe

Raith R		93/94	2	1		P
		94/95	33	1		D1
		95/96	2	1		P
Bolton W		95/96	7	2		FL
		96/97	11	2		FL
		97/98	1	1		FL
Fulham		97/98	2	2		FL
Bradford C	L	97/98	7			FL
Fulham		98/99	1	2		FL
		99/00				

McARTHUR James
b. Dunfermline 27.2.1952

Cowdenbeath		68/69				
		69/70				
		70/71	11			D1
		71/72	35			D2
		72/73	10			D2
Hibernian		72/73	11			D1
		73/74	27			D1
		74/75	30			D1
		75/76	20			P
		76/77				
		77/78				
		78/79	18			P
		79/80	29			P
		80/81	37			D1
		81/82	33			P
		82/83	12			P
Meadowbank T		82/83	1			D2
Cowdenbeath		83/84	1			D2
Raith R		83/84	12			D1
Morton *		83/84	3			D1

McARTHUR Michael
b. Kilwinning 10.2.1970

Aberdeen		87/88	1	2		P
		88/89				
Kilmarnock		89/90	2	1	1	D2

McAULEY Sean
b. Sheffield 23.6.1972

Manchester U						
St Johnstone		92/93	24	2		P
		93/94	28			P
		94/95	7	1		D1
Chesterfield	L	94/95	1		1	FL
Hartlepool U		95/96	46			FL
		96/97	38		1	FL
Scunthorpe U		96/97	9			FL
		97/98	30	5	1	FL
		98/99	16	1		FL
Scarborough	L	98/99	6	1		FL

McAVEETY Phillip
b. Glasgow 27.10.1960

St Mirren		77/78	3			P
Berwick R		78/79	16			D2
St Mirren		79/80	0	1		P
		80/81	7	1		P
		81/82	1			P
		82/83	4			P
		83/84	3			P
Morton		83/84	1	3		D1

McAVENNIE Francis
b. Glasgow 22.11.1959

Johnstone Burgh						
Partick T	T					
St Mirren		80/81				
		81/82	29	2	13	P
		82/83	36		8	P
		83/84	34		12	P
		84/85	34		16	P
West Ham		85/86	41		26	FL
		86/87	36		7	FL
		87/88	8			FL
Celtic		87/88	32		15	P
		88/89	23		12	P
West Ham U		88/89	8	1		FL
		89/90	1	4		FL
		90/91	24	10	10	FL
		91/92	16	4	6	FL
Aston Villa		92/93	0	3		FL
Celtic		92/93	19		9	P
		93/94	8	3	1	P
Swindon T	L	93/94	3	4		FL
Falkirk		94/95	1	2	2	P
St Mirren		94/95	7			D1

McBAIN Roy Adam
b. Aberdeen 7.11.1974

Dundee U		93/94	0	1		P
		94/95				
Dundee		95/96	3	3		D1
Ross Co		96/97	26	1	4	D3
		97/98	27	6	4	D3
		98/99	33		5	D3
		99/00	18	10	1	D2

McBEAN Stewart

Glasgow U						
St Johnstone		74/75				
		75/76	5			P
		76/77	16	1		D1
		77/78	12	1		D1
Canada						

McBRIDE James
b. Johnstone 19.10.1959

Feguslie U						
Kilmarnock		80/81	17	5	1	P
		81/82	5	2	1	D1
Stranraer		82/83	35	2	8	D2
		83/84	37		3	D2
		84/85	30		3	D2
Australia						
Queen of the South		85/86	37		8	D2
		86/87	37		2	D1
Australia		87/88				
Queen of the South		88/89	2			D1

McBRIDE John Paul
b. Hamilton 28.11.1978

Celtic		96/97	0	2		P
		97/98				
		98/99	0	1		P
St Johnstone		98/99	2	1		P
		99/00	18	1	1	P

McBRIDE Joseph
b. Glasgow 17.8.1960

Everton		78/79				
		79/80	17	1	1	FL
		80/81	27	4	7	FL
		81/82	7	1	1	FL
Rotherham U		82/83	42		11	FL
		83/84	3		1	FL
Oldham A		83/84	19	6	4	FL
		84/85	9	2	1	FL
Hibernian		84/85	10	2	2	P
		85/86	12	2	1	P
		86/87	35	3	7	P
		87/88	5	8	1	P
		88/89	4			P
Dundee		88/89	13	4	2	P
		89/90	10	8	1	P
		90/91	4	10	2	D1
East Fife		91/92	38	1	8	D2
		92/93	33	1	9	D2
		93/94	8	7	2	D2
Albion R		93/94	8			D2
		94/95	31	4	5	D3
		95/96	12	1	5	D3
Livingston		95/96	0	2		D3
Hamilton A		96/97	2	1		D2
Maryhill Jnrs						

McBRIDE Martin
b. Glasgow 28.11.1967

Wishaw BC						
Motherwell		85/86	0	1		P
		86/87	0	2		P
		87/88	4	6		P
		88/89	10	6	1	P
		89/90	1			P
East Stirlingshire		90/91	25	2	2	D2
Albion R		91/92	1			D2
		92/93	31	6		D2
		93/94	24	8	2	D2
		94/95	22	4		D3
East Stirlingshire		95/96	28	3	8	D3
		96/97	31		5	D3
		97/98	20	16	1	D3
Albion R		98/99	0	1		D3

McBRIDE Stephen
b. Lurgan 2.5.1964

Linfield						
Motherwell		83/84	0	4		P
Glenavon						

MacCABE David
b. Port Glasgow 3.4.1962

Airdrieonians		83/84	12	9	3	D1
		84/85	37		21	D1
		85/86	25	12	9	D1
		86/87	32	4	13	D1
		87/88	44		20	D1
		88/89	5			D1
Motherwell		88/89	12	1		P
		89/90	0	1		P
Kilmarnock		89/90	4		1	D2
Morton		90/91	35		21	D1
		91/92	4	8		D1
		92/93	10	3	6	D1

McCABE Gerard
b. Hamilton 26.9.1956

Polkemmet Jnrs						
Hibernian						
Windsor Star						
Toronto Italia						
Clyde		77/78	20			D2
		78/79	33	4	3	D1
		79/80	39		8	D1
Clydebank		80/81	38		1	D1
		81/82	37		8	D1
		82/83	37		4	D1
		83/84	37		4	D1
		84/85	32	1	4	D1
		85/86	24			P
		86/87	10			P
Hamilton A		86/87	19	5	2	P
		87/88	25	8	7	D1
Dumbarton	L	87/88	5	1	1	D1
Hamilton A		88/89	7	1		P
Clyde		88/89	25	1	2	D1
		89/90	31	4	5	D1
Victoria Vistas		90/91				
Hamilton A		90/91	9	7		D1
Cork C		91/92				
		92/93				
Glentoran		93/94				
Hamilton A		94/95				
Arbroath		95/96	12	7		D3
Dumbarton		96/97	4			D2

McCAFFERTY Thomas
b. Wishaw 7.5.1960

Fauldhouse U						
Airdrieonians		80/81	0	1		P
		81/82	1	1		P
		82/83	10	1	2	D1
		83/84	12	4		D1
		84/85	10	3	1	D1
Kilmarnock		85/86	22	4	1	D1
		86/87	4	2		D1
Stenhousemuir *		86/87	1			D2
East Stirlingshire		86/87	7			D2
Falkirk		86/87	2			P
Stenhousemuir		87/88	37	1		D2
		88/89	16	2		D2
Queen of the South		89/90	27	2		D2
		90/91	20	2		D2

McCAFFREY Stuart Muir
b. Glasgow 30.5.1979

Hibernian		97/98	0	2		P

McCAHILL Stephen Joseph
b. Greenock 3.9.1966

Gleniffer Thistle						
Dumbarton		84/85	26			P
		85/86	19		1	D1
St Etenne	T	85/86				
Dumbarton		86/87	37	2	2	D1
		87/88	41	1	1	D1
		88/89	21		1	D2
Celtic		88/89	4	1		P
		89/90	2			P
		90/91				
		91/92				
Morton		92/93	23	1		D1
		93/94	8		1	D1
		94/95	27		2	D2
		95/96	24	1	1	D1
		96/97	11			D1

McCAIG David
b. Kilsyth 22.9.1956

Falkirk		75/76	10	2	4	D1
Clyde		76/77	13	1		D2
Bailieston		77/78				
East Stirlingshire		78/79	4		1	D2
		79/80	27	5	4	D2
		80/81	23	9	7	D1
		81/82	21	5	3	D1
		82/83	15	3	3	D2
Dumbarton		82/83	7	1	1	D1
		83/84	10	19	3	D1
		84/85	0	3		P
East Fife		85/86	1			D1

McCALL Ian Holland
b. Dumfries 30.9.1965

Bellevue						
Queens Park		83/84	2	1	1	D2
		84/85	24	4		D2
		85/86	33	2	8	D2
Dunfermline A		86/87	29	14	8	D1
		87/88	4			P
Rangers		87/88	8	4	1	P
		88/89	2	3	1	P
		89/90	2	2		P
Bradford C		89/90	11	1	1	FL
Dunfermline A		90/91	28	1	4	P
		91/92	9		1	P
Dundee		91/92	27	1	9	D1
Falkirk		92/93	27	8	6	P
		93/94	32	3	2	D1
		94/95	3	2	1	P
Hamilton A		94/95	5	1	1	D1
Hong Kong		95/96				
Partick T		96/97	1	6		D1
Clydebank		97/98	2	19	1	D2

McCALL Stuart Murray
b. Leeds 10.6.1964

Bradford C		82/83	25	3	4	FL
		83/84	46		5	FL
		84/85	46		8	FL
		85/86	38		4	FL
		86/87	36		7	FL
		87/88	44		9	FL
Everton		88/89	29	4		FL
		89/90	37		3	FL
		90/91	33		3	FL
Rangers		91/92	35	1	1	P
		92/93	35	1	5	P
		93/94	34		3	P
		94/95	30		2	P
		95/96	19	2	3	P
		96/97	7			P
		97/98	26	4		P

McCALL Walker
b. Irvine 29.3.1954

Aberdeen		73/74	4	3	2	D1
		74/75	10	4	6	D1
		75/76	1			P
Ayr U		76/77	32	1	16	P
		77/78	34	1	12	P
San Diego Sockers		78	19		11	NA
St Johnstone		78/79	5			D1
San Diego Sockers		79	17		6	NA
		80	11		1	NA
Atlanta Chiefs		80	14		2	NA
Aberdeen		80/81	13	4	10	P
		81/82	6	2	4	P
		82/83	0	2		P
South China						
Dundee		83/84	30	1	13	P
		84/85	14	10	1	P
		85/86	0	2		P

McCALLAN Joseph
b. 1.4.1949

Clydebank		72/73	18		6	D2
		73/74	18	5	3	D2
		74/75	33	1	10	D2
		75/76	26		12	D2
		76/77				
		77/78	21	2	2	P
Falkirk		77/78	14		2	D2
		78/79	32	5	9	D2
		79/80	14	12	3	D2

McCALLUM Mungo
b. Glasgow 28.10.1965

Morton		82/83	0	1		P
		83/84	1	4		D1
Larkhall Thistle		84/85				
		85/86				
		86/87				
		87/88				
Alloa A		88/89	15	2	7	D2
		89/90	13	2	8	D1
		90/91	5	2	1	D2
		91/92	8	2	3	D2
Stenhousemuir		91/92	7		5	D2
Stirling A		92/93	9	10	4	D1
		93/94	8	3	1	D1
East Stirlingshire		93/94	16		12	D2
		94/95	11	1	4	D3

McCANN Neil Docherty
b. Greenock 11.8.1974

Dundee		92/93	2	1		P
		93/94	20	2	1	P
		94/95	29	3	2	D1
		95/96	22		2	D1
Heart of Midlothian		96/97	25	5	5	P
		97/98	35		10	P
		98/99	8		3	P
Rangers		98/99	15	4	5	P
		99/00	16	5	3	P

McCANN Ryan
b. Bellshill 21.9.1981

Celtic		99/00	1			P

McCARRISON Dugald
b. Lanark 22.12.1969

Celtic		87/88	1			P
		88/89	0	1	1	P
		89/90				
		90/91	0	1		P
Ipswich T	L	90/91				
Celtic		91/92				
Darlington	L	91/92	5		2	FL
Celtic		92/93	0	1		P
Kilmarnock		92/93	6	2	1	D1
		93/94				
		94/95	0	1		P
Hamilton A		95/96	0	3		D1
Lesmagahow Jnrs						

McCART Christopher
b. Motherwell 17.4.1967

Motherwell		85/86	12	1		P
		86/87				
		87/88	0	1		P
		88/89	25	1		P
		89/90	33	1	1	P
		90/91	36			P
		91/92	22		2	P
		92/93	28	1	3	P
		93/94	36			P
		94/95	24			P
		95/96	20			P
		96/97	16	3		P
Falkirk		97/98	14	2	1	D1
		98/99	12	2	1	D1

McCARTHY Michael Joseph
b. Barnsley 7.2.1959

Worsbrough BC						
Barnsley		77/78	46		1	FL
		78/79	46		2	FL
		79/80	44		1	FL
		80/81	43		1	FL
		81/82	42		1	FL
		82/83	39		1	FL
		83/84	12			FL
Manchester C		83/84	24		1	FL
		84/85	39			FL
		85/86	38			FL
		86/87	39		1	FL
Celtic		87/88	22			P
		88/89	26			P
Olympique Lyon		89/90				
Millwall		89/90	6			FL
		90/91	11	1		FL
		91/92	14	3	2	FL

McCATHIE Norman
b. Edinburgh 23.3.1961

Cowdenbeath		80/81	6	5		D2
Dunfermline A		81/82	17	2	4	D1
		82/83	24		2	D1
		83/84	38		5	D2
		84/85	36	1	8	D2
		85/86	37		8	D2
		86/87	44		6	D1
		87/88	38	1	1	P
		88/89	19	1	1	D1
Ayr U		88/89	2			D1
Dunfermline A		89/90	36			P
		90/91	36		1	P
		91/92	38	2	1	P
		92/93	30	2	2	D1
		93/94	43		8	D1
		94/95	32		4	D1
		95/96	18		3	D1

McCLAIR Brian John
b. Airdrie 8.12.1963

Aston Villa		80/81				
Motherwell		81/82	7	4	4	D1
		82/83	26	3	11	P
Celtic		83/84	28	7	23	P
		84/85	25	7	19	P
		85/86	33	1	22	P
		86/87	43	1	35	P
Manchester U		87/88	40		24	FL
		88/89	38		10	FL
		89/90	37		5	FL
		90/91	34	2	13	FL
		91/92	41	1	18	FL
		92/93	41	1	9	FL
		93/94	12	14	1	FL
		94/95	35	5	5	FL
		95/96	12	10	3	FL
		96/97	4	15		FL
		97/98	2	11		FL
Motherwell		98/99	8	3		P

McCLELLAND John
b. Belfast 7.12.1955

Portadown						
Cardiff C		74/75	1	3	1	FL
Bangor C		75/76				
		76/77				
		77/78				
Mansfield T		78/79	33	3	1	FL
		79/80	43		1	FL
		80/81	46		6	FL
Rangers		81/82	14			P
		82/83	35		2	P
		83/84	36		2	P
		84/85	11			P
Watford		84/85	29		1	FL
		85/86	31		1	FL
		86/87	41		1	FL
		87/88	40			FL
		88/89	43			FL
Leeds U		89/90	3			FL
Watford	L	89/90	1			FL
Leeds U		90/91	3			FL
		91/92	16	2		FL
Notts Co	L	91/92	6			FL
St Johnstone		92/93	25	1		P
		93/94	1			P
Arbroath		93/94	2			D2
Darlington		94/95				
		95/96				
		96/97	1			FL

McCLOY Peter
b. Girvan 16.11.1946

Crosshill Thistle						
Motherwell		63/64				
		64/65	5			D1
		65/66	32			D1
		66/67	32			D1
		67/68	34			D1
		68/69	19			D2
		69/70	15			D1
Rangers		69/70	7			D1
		70/71	31			D1
		71/72	34			D1
		72/73	33			D1
		73/74	30			D1
		74/75				
		75/76	24			P
		76/77	5			P
		77/78	14			P
		78/79	36			P
		79/80	34			P
		80/81	26			P
		81/82	10			P
		82/83	17			P
		83/84	26			P
		84/85	21			P
		85/86	2			P

McCLOY Steven
b. Girvan 28.4.1975

Craigmark Burntonians						
Kilmarnock		93/94	1	5	1	P
		94/95				
Sheffield U	L	94/95				
Hamilton A		95/96	1	4		D1
Ireland						
Auchinleck Talbot						

McCLURG John
b. Greenock 1.11.1957

Port Glasgow R						
Kilmarnock		80/81	3			P
		81/82				
		82/83	10	3		P
		83/84	8	4	2	D1
Morton		84/85	7	2		P
Pollok Jnrs						
Largs Thistle						

McCLUSKEY George McKinlay Cassidy
b. Hamilton 19.9.1957

Club		Season	Apps	Sub	Gls	Div
Celtic						
Thorniewood U	L	73/74				
Celtic		74/75				
		75/76	0	1	1	P
		76/77	2	2		P
		77/78	12	3	6	P
		78/79	16	5	5	P
		79/80	22	1	10	P
		80/81	15	7	10	P
		81/82	35		21	P
		82/83	7	3	2	P
Leeds U		83/84	24	8	8	FL
		84/85	13	6	5	FL
		85/86	20	2	3	FL
Hibernian		86/87	33	2	9	P
		87/88	24	7	4	P
		88/89	4	12	3	P
Hamilton A		89/90	27	1	8	D1
		90/91	35		14	D1
		91/92	29	3	12	D1
Kilmarnock		92/93	29	2	11	D1
		93/94	16	7	2	P
		94/95	2	1		P
Clyde		94/95	18	1	5	D2
		95/96	5	11	3	D2

McCLUSKEY Patrick
b. Kilsyth 13.4.1952

Club		Season	Apps	Sub	Gls	Div
Millwall	T					
Berwick R	T					
Albion R	T					
Chelsea	T					
Glasgow U		67/68				
Maryhill Jnrs		68/69				
Celtic		69/70				
Sligo R	L	69/70				
Celtic		70/71				
		71/72	2	2		D1
		72/73	14	1	3	D1
		73/74	23	2	1	D1
		74/75	28	1	3	D1
		75/76	34		3	P
		76/77	4	4		P
Dumbarton		77/78	38		1	D1
		78/79	38		3	D1
		79/80	36		8	D1
Darmstadt	T					
Airdrieonians		80/81	27			P
		81/82	19			P
Pittsburgh Spirit		82/83				
Queen of the South		83/84	34		1	D2
		84/85	17			D2

McCLUSKEY Stuart Campbell
b. Bellshill 29.10.1977

Club	Season	Apps	Sub	Gls	Div
St Johnstone	94/95	2			D1
	95/96	2			D1
	96/97	7	3	1	D1
	97/98	12	6	1	P
	98/99	5	2		P
	99/00	5	1		P

McCLYMONT John
b. 12.2.1959

Club	Season	Apps	Sub	Gls	Div
Airdrieonians	78/79	0	2		D1
	79/80	10	4	5	D1
	80/81	0	2		P

McCOIST Alistair Murdoch
b. Glasgow 24.9.1962

Club	Season	Apps	Sub	Gls	Div
Fir Park BC					
St Johnstone	78/79	4			D1
	79/80	9	6		D1
	80/81	38		22	D1
	81/82				
Sunderland	81/82	19	9	2	FL
	82/83	19	9	6	FL
Rangers	83/84	29	1	9	P
	84/85	22	3	12	P
	85/86	33		24	P
	86/87	44		33	P
	87/88	40		31	P
	88/89	18	1	9	P
	89/90	32	2	14	P
	90/91	15	11	11	P
	91/92	37	1	34	P
	92/93	32	2	34	P
	93/94	16	5	7	P
	94/95	4	5	1	P
	95/96	18	7	16	P
	96/97	13	12	10	P
	97/98	7	8	5	P
Kilmarnock	98/99	16	10	7	P
	99/00	5	4	1	P

McCOLL William
b. Glasgow 25.12.1954

Club	Season	Apps	Sub	Gls	Div
Clydebank	72/73	22	1	2	D2
	73/74	18	6		D2
	74/75	28	1	3	D2
	75/76	4	3		D2
	76/77	37		15	D1
	77/78	33		3	P
Ayr U	78/79	34	2	6	D1
	79/80	30	2	1	D1
	80/81	19	1		D1
Clyde	81/82	36			D2
	82/83	11			D1
Albion R *	83/84	1			D2

McCOLLIGAN Brian
b. Glasgow 31.10.1980

Club	Season	Apps	Sub	Gls	Div
Celtic	99/00	1			P

McCONALOGUE Stephen
b. Glasgow 16.6.1981

Club	Season	Apps	Sub	Gls	Div
Dundee U	98/99	0	1		P
	99/00	9	7		P

McCONDICHIE Andrew Morrison
b. Glasgow 21.8.1977

Club		Season	Apps	Sub	Gls	Div
Celtic		95/96				
		96/97				
		97/98				
Hamilton A	L	97/98	5			D1
Celtic		98/99	1			P
Albion R		99/00	2			D3
Clydebank		99/00	1			D1
Raith R		99/00	1			D1

McCORMACK John D
b. Glasgow 25.4.1955

Club	Season	Apps	Sub	Gls	Div
Clydebank	76/77	3			D1
	77/78	32	2	5	P
	78/79	39		10	D1
	79/80	37	1	9	D1
St Mirren	80/81	28	1	3	P
	81/82	25			P
	82/83	19			P
	83/84	36		3	P
Dundee	84/85	34		7	P
	85/86	15	12	2	P
Airdrieonians	86/87	42			D1
	87/88	2			D1
Partick T *	87/88	18	1		D1

McCORMACK John Thomas
b. Stirling 22.7.1965

Club	Season	Apps	Sub	Gls	Div
Bonnybridge Jnrs					
Falkirk	83/84	4	1		D1
	84/85	19	1		D1
	85/86	17	2	1	D1
	86/87	15	1	1	P
	87/88	5	1		P
Meadowbank T	87/88	4	1		D1
	88/89	26		1	D1
	89/90	25			D1
	90/91	11	1		D1
Stirling A	91/92	18	2		D1
	92/93	18			D1
	93/94	10			D1
Alloa A	93/94	7			D2
	94/95	34			D3
	95/96	15	4		D3
	96/97	25	2	2	D3
	97/98	10	5		D3
	98/99				
Dumbarton	99/00	8	10		D3

McCORMICK Stephen
b. Dumbarton 14.8.1969

Club		Season	Apps	Sub	Gls	Div
Queens Park		91/92	31	1	17	D2
		92/93	30	2	5	D2
		93/94	29	7	7	D2
		94/95	18	4	8	D3
Stirling A		95/96	33		25	D2
		96/97	29	2	8	D1
		97/98	5	3		D1
Dundee		97/98	6	8	5	D1
		98/99	0	1		P
Leyton Orient	L	98/99	1	3		FL
Morton		98/99	3	2	1	D1
Airdrieonians		98/99	4	8	2	D1
		99/00	11	4	4	D1
East Fife		99/00	11		1	D3

McCRACKEN David
b. Glasgow 16.10.1981

Club	Season	Apps	Sub	Gls	Div
Dundee U	99/00	2			P

McCREADY Gordon
b. Glasgow 19.4.1959

Club	Season	Apps	Sub	Gls	Div
Port Glasgow Jnrs					
Kilmarnock	80/81	4	1	1	P
	81/82	10		1	D1
Port Glasgow Jnrs					

McCREERY David
b. Belfast 16.9.1957

Club	Season	Apps	Sub	Gls	Div
Manchester U	74/75	0	2		FL
	75/76	12	16	4	FL
	76/77	9	16	2	FL
	77/78	13	4	1	FL
	78/79	14	1		FL
QPR	79/80	42		4	FL
	80/81	14	1		FL
Tulsa Roughnecks	81	27			NA
	82	18			NA
Newcastle U	82/83	23	3		FL
	83/84	40			FL
	84/85	34	1	1	FL
	85/86	39	2		FL
	86/87	30			FL
	87/88	35		1	FL
	88/89	36			FL
Heart of Midlothian	89/90	20	2		P
	90/91	4	3		P
Hartlepool U	91/92	27	3		FL
Carlisle U	92/93	19	3		FL
	93/94	6	7		FL
Hartlepool U	94/95	7	2		FL

McCUE James
b. 29.6.1975

Club	Season	Apps	Sub	Gls	Div
Partick T	95/96	2	1		P

McCULLOCH Alan William
b. Barrhead 19.8.1953

Club		Season	Apps	Sub	Gls	Div
Kilbirnie Ladeside						
Kilmarnock		72/73				
		73/74	1			D2
		74/75	16			D1
		75/76				
		76/77	1			P
		77/78				
St Mirren	L	77/78	10			P
Kilmarnock		78/79	39			D1
		79/80	36			P
		80/81	19			P
		81/82	39			D1
		82/83	35			P
		83/84	39			D1
		84/85	38			D1
		85/86	38			D1
		86/87	40			D1
		87/88	36			D1
		88/89	39			D1
		89/90	24			D2

McCULLOCH David

Club	Season	Apps	Sub	Gls	Div
Kilsyth R					
Ayr U	67/68				
	68/69				
	69/70	33		2	D1
	70/71	9	3	1	D1
	71/72	8			D1
	72/73	30	2	4	D1
	73/74	31	1	2	D1
	74/75	29	2	5	D1
	75/76	25	4	4	P
	76/77	29	3	2	P
	77/78	17	4	2	P
Clydebank	78/79	3	4		D1
Hamilton A	78/79	14		2	D1
	79/80	20	3	1	D1

McCULLOCH Gordon

Club	Season	Apps	Sub	Gls	Div
St Johnstone	75/76	1			P

McCULLOCH Lee
b. Bellshill 14.5.1978

Club	Season	Apps	Sub	Gls	Div
Cumbernauld U					
Motherwell	95/96	0	1		P
	96/97	1	14		P
	97/98	6	19	2	P
	98/99	14	12	3	P
	99/00	28	1	9	P

McCULLOCH Scott Anderson James
b. Cumnock 29.11.1975

Club	Season	Apps	Sub	Gls	Div
Rangers	92/93				
	93/94				
Hamilton A	94/95	8		1	D1
	95/96	4	6	1	D1
	96/97	19	5	1	D2
	97/98	15		1	D1
Dunfermline A	97/98	18			P
	98/99	19		1	P
Dundee U	98/99	9			P
	99/00	10	5		P

McCULLOCH William
b. 7.1.1948

Airdrieonians		73/74	25		5	D2
		74/75	28	2	7	D1
		75/76	16	3	2	D1
		76/77	35		7	D1
		77/78	10			D1
		78/79	7	1	1	D1
		79/80	17	5	5	D1
		80/81	11	5	3	P
Berwick R		81/82	27	6	6	D2

McCULLOCH William
b. Baillieston 2.4.1973

Linlithgow Rose						
Airdrieonians		91/92	1			P
		92/93	1			P
		93/94	0	1		D1
		94/95	1	1		D1
Ayr U		95/96				
		96/97				
East Fife		97/98	17			D2
		98/99	34			D2
		99/00	36			D3

McCURDY Patrick
b. Greenock 12.11.1964

Shamrock BC						
Hibernian		82/83	0	4	1	P
		83/84	1			P
Alloa A		83/84	3			D1
Hamilton A		83/84	7		5	D1
		84/85	17	5	4	D1
Morton		84/85	2			P
		85/86	0	2		D1
Stranraer		85/86	11		4	D2
Alloa A						
Dalry Thistle						
Largs Thistle						

McCUTCHEON Derek
b. Kilmarnock 17.2.1960

Ayr U		77/78	3	1	1	P
		78/79	8		5	D1
		79/80	1	1		D1
		80/81	13	1	5	D1
Clyde		81/82	32	2	8	D2
		82/83	8	7	3	D1
Glenafton A		83/84				
		84/85				
		85/86				
		86/87				
		87/88				
Stranraer		88/89	31		9	D2
		89/90	34		5	D2
		90/91	10	6	2	D2

McCUTCHEON Gary Kyle
b. Dumfries 8.10.1978

Kilmarnock		95/96				
		96/97				
		97/98				
Stenhousemuir	L	97/98	20		7	D2
Kilmarnock		97/98	0	1		P
		98/99	2	11	2	P
		99/00	0	2		P
Clydebank		99/00	4			D1

McDERMOTT Murray
b. Edinburgh 2.2.1950

Raith R		71/72	20			D2
		72/73	32			D2
		73/74	33			D2
		74/75	38			D2
		75/76	26			D2
		76/77	39			D1
		77/78	33			D2
		78/79	39			D1
		79/80	39			D1
		80/81	39			D1
Berwick R		81/82	36			D2
		82/83	24			D2
Morton		83/84	32			D1
		84/85	31			P
		85/86	4			D1
Arbroath		86/87	12			D2
Meadowbank T		86/87	12			D2
		87/88	3			D1
Partick T *		87/88	1			D1

McDICKEN Derrick Schendal
b. Auchinleck 4.4.1955

Ayr Boswell						
Bellfield BC						
Troon Jnrs						
Darvel Jnrs						
Kilmarnock		72/73				
		73/74	5	5	1	D2
		74/75	33		4	D1
		75/76	16	1	1	D1
		76/77	29	1	4	P
		77/78	36			D1
		78/79	36		2	D1
		79/80	34		1	P
		80/81	33		1	P
		81/82	20	7	8	D1
		82/83	28	3	1	P
		83/84	30	3	7	D1
		84/85	22	2		D1
Clyde		85/86	7	4		D1
Auchinleck Talbot						

McDONAGH James
b. Bellshill 22.6.1957

Livingston U						
Albion R	T	81/82	3			D2
Airdrieonians		81/82	5	3	1	P
		82/83	6	2	3	D1

MacDONALD Alexander
b. Glasgow 17.3.1948

Luncarty Jnrs						
Glasgow U						
St Johnstone		65/66	8		3	D1
		66/67	16		3	D1
		67/68	29	1	9	D1
		68/69	11		2	D1
Rangers		68/69	8	1	1	D1
		69/70	15		2	D1
		70/71	27	6	6	D1
		71/72	31	1	11	D1
		72/73	27	2	4	D1
		73/74	29	1	3	D1
		74/75	29	1	2	D1
		75/76	34	1	4	P
		76/77	29	1	9	P
		77/78	34		3	P
		78/79	33		5	P
		79/80	23	3	1	P
Heart of Midlothian		80/81	28		3	P
		81/82	15	1	1	D1
		82/83	29	2	5	D1
		83/84	19	5	1	P
		84/85	14	8	2	P
		85/86	0	1		P

McDONALD Anthony
b. Helensburgh 22.10.1964

Arthurlie						
St Mirren		91/92	0	3		P

McDONALD Colin
b. Edinburgh 10.4.1974

Falkirk		93/94	5	12	1	D1
		94/95	26	5	9	P
		95/96	4	5	1	P
Swansea C		95/96	3	5		FL
		96/97	3	7		FL
Ayr U		97/98	2	2		D1
Clydebank		97/98	23		13	D1
		98/99	22	8	9	D1
Falkirk		99/00	26	4	6	D1

McDONALD Daniel
b. Hamilton 11.1.1954

Muirkirk Jnrs						
Ayr U		73/74	2	1		D1
		74/75	9	1		D1
		75/76	20	2	1	P
		76/77	14	6	1	P
		77/78	4	1		P
Stranraer		78/79	37		6	D2
		79/80	35		2	D2
		80/81	36			D2
		81/82	38		2	D2
		82/83	36		3	D2
		83/84	37		8	D2
		84/85	25	2	1	D2
		85/86	10			D2

McDONALD Iain
b. 26.8.1952

Rangers		69/70	1		1	D1
		70/71	3			D1
		71/72	7		1	D1
		72/73				
		73/74				
Dundee U		74/75	25	2	6	D1
		75/76	1	2		P

MacDONALD Iain Campbell Aitken
b. Rintein 30.8.1953

Elgin C						
St Johnstone		72/73	14	1		D1
		73/74	30		1	D1
		74/75	33		1	D1
		75/76	30			P
Carlisle U		76/77	42		2	FL
		77/78	34		2	FL
		78/79	41		1	FL
		79/80	40		1	FL
		80/81	29	1	1	FL
Dundee		81/82	17		2	P
		82/83	34			P
		83/84	17	2	1	P
Arbroath		84/85	20		1	D2
		85/86	6			D2

McDONALD Ian
b. Glasgow 28.12.1958

Partick T		76/77	0	2		P
		77/78				
		78/79	1	2		P
		79/80	12	4	3	P
		80/81	16	8	1	P
		81/82	19	9		P
		82/83	27	8	1	D1
		83/84	28	3	5	D1
		84/85	22			D1
Motherwell		84/85	10	3	4	D1
Partick T		85/86	23	1	5	D1
		86/87	34	3	1	D1
		87/88	33	2	9	D1
		88/89	3	1		D1
Morton		89/90	22	3	1	D1
		90/91	34	2	1	D1
		91/92	11	6		D1
		92/93	14	11	1	D1
		93/94	3	2		D1

MacDONALD John
b. Glasgow 15.4.1961

Rangers		77/78	34		3	P
		78/79	0	2		P
		79/80	21	5	5	P
		80/81	26	4	11	P
		81/82	32	3	14	P
		82/83	25	3	10	P
		83/84	2	16	1	P
		84/85	8	10	3	P
		85/86	2			P
Hong Kong		85/86				
Charlton A		86/87	2			FL
Barnsley		86/87	25		7	FL
		87/88	31	2	7	FL
		88/89	28	4	5	FL
		89/90	3	1	1	FL
Scarborough		89/90	29		5	FL
		90/91	10	1	1	FL
Airdrieonians		90/91	3	9		D1
		91/92				
		92/93				
Dumbarton		93/94	3	3	2	D1
Inverness CT		94/95	2		1	D3

MacDONALD Kenneth Stewart
b. Dundee 9.3.1961

Broughty A						
St Johnstone		81/82	4	5	2	D1
		82/83	0	1		D1
Forfar A		82/83	25		16	D2
		83/84	23	3	13	D2
		84/85	29	4	14	D1
Hong Kong		85/86				
Forfar A		86/87	41	1	17	D1
		87/88	41	2	20	D1
Airdrieonians		88/89	36		22	D1
		89/90	5	3	5	D1
Raith R		89/90	25	1	10	D1
		90/91	10	1	2	D1
St Johnstone		90/91	5	6		P
		91/92				
Arbroath		92/93	28	1	4	D2
Cowdenbeath *		93/94	10		1	D2
Stirling A		93/94	0	1		D1
East Stirlingshire		93/94	11	3	5	D2

MacDONALD Kevin Duncan
b. Inverness 7.9.1959
Inverness Caledonian

Club		Season				
Leicester C		80/81	16	4	2	FL
		81/82	24	1	1	FL
		82/83	42		4	FL
		83/84	38		1	FL
		84/85	13			FL
Liverpool		84/85	13			FL
		85/86	10	7	1	FL
		86/87	3	3		FL
		87/88	0	1		FL
Leicester C	L	87/88	3			FL
Liverpool		88/89	3			FL
Rangers	L	88/89	2	1		P
Coventry C		89/90	19	3		FL
		90/91	7	2		FL
Cardiff C	L	90/91	8			FL
Walsall		91/92	20		3	FL
		92/93	28	5	3	FL

McDONALD Michael Flynn
b. Glasgow 8.11.1950

Club		Season				
Clydebank		71/72	36			D2
Stoke C		72/73	1			FL
		73/74	4			FL
		74/75				
Hibernian		75/76	15			P
		76/77	36			P
		77/78	36			P
		78/79	18			P
		79/80	4			P
Berwick R		80/81	15			D1
Vale of Leithen		81/82				
St Johnstone		82/83	31			D1
		83/84	11			P
Arbroath		84/85	2			D2

McDONALD Paul Thomas
b. Motherwell 20.4.1968
Fir Park BC

Club		Season				
Hamilton A		86/87	3	2		P
		87/88	6	12		D1
		88/89	27	7		P
		89/90	37	1	3	D1
		90/91	36	2	7	D1
		91/92	34	4	5	D1
		92/93	44		11	D1
Southampton		93/94				
		94/95	0	2		FL
		95/96	0	1		FL
Burnley	L	95/96	8	1	1	FL
Brighton		95/96	5			FL
		96/97	40	5	4	FL
		97/98	7	4	1	FL
Dunfermline A		97/98	1	2		P
Partick T		98/99	29	2	3	D2
Morton		99/00	16	8	3	D1

McDONALD Roderick D W
b. Alness 30.8.1964
Invergordon Academy
Easter Ross
Brora R

Club		Season				
Celtic		72/73				
		73/74	2			D1
		74/75	12	3		D1
		75/76	27		3	P
		76/77	24		2	P
		77/78	36		7	P
		78/79	18		2	P
		79/80	27	2	6	P
		80/81	14		2	P
Heart of Midlothian		81/82	35		6	D1
		82/83	39		3	D1
		83/84	34		2	P
		84/85	28		1	P
		85/86	10		2	P
		86/87	27		5	P
Morton		87/88	31			P
		88/89	26		2	D1
Partick T		89/90	17			D1
Queen of the South	T	90/91	8		2	D2
Irvine Meadow						

McDONALD Rodney
b. Westminster 20.3.1967
Colne Dynamos

Club		Season				
Walsall		90/91	31	5	5	FL
		91/92	38	1	18	FL
		92/93	39		12	FL
		93/94	34	1	6	FL
Partick T		94/95	22	3	5	P
		95/96	12	4	5	P
Southport		96/97				
Chester C		96/97	22		6	FL
		97/98	21	10	5	FL

MacDONALD William James
b. Irvine 17.9.1976
WBA

Club		Season				
Partick T		95/96	11	6	1	P
		96/97	10	5	1	D1
		97/98	21	5		D1
Dunfermline A		98/99	0	1		P
Livingston		98/99	5			D2
		99/00	0	1		D1
Clydebank		99/00	3	1		D1
Stranraer		99/00	14		1	D2

McDOUGALL D Francis
b. Glasgow 21.2.1958

Club		Season				
Clydebank		78/79	36	2	25	D1
St Mirren		79/80	16		5	P
		80/81	20	3	10	P
		81/82	15	3	7	P
		82/83	23	7	9	P
		83/84	28	1	12	P
Aberdeen		84/85	27	1	22	P
		85/86	22	3	14	P
		86/87	0	1		P

McDOUGALL Gordon
b. Bellshill 17.2.1971
Musselburgh A

Club		Season				
Falkirk		91/92	4			P
		92/93	5			P
East Stirlingshire		93/94	38			D2
		94/95	30			D3
		95/96	28			D3
		96/97	22			D3
		97/98	34			D3
		98/99	13			D3

McDOUGALL Ian
b. 14.8.1954

Club		Season				
Rangers		73/74	8	1		D1
		74/75	11	3	2	D1
		75/76	3	1	1	P
		76/77	1	3		P
Dundee		77/78	36	1	1	D1
		78/79	8	8	1	D1

McDOWALL Kenneth
b. Glasgow 29.7.1963
Drumchapel Amateurs

Club		Season				
Partick T		81/82	0	1		P
		82/83	10	14	5	D1
		83/84	35	1	13	D1
		84/85	6		1	D1
St Mirren		84/85	17	6	3	P
		85/86	5	7	1	P
		86/87	15	4	1	P
		87/88	19	8	3	P
		88/89	4	5		P
		89/90	20	3	3	P
		90/91	11	12	4	P
		91/92	19	10	2	P
		92/93	12	1	3	D1

McDOWELL Donald
b. Glasgow 11.9.1952

Club		Season				
Partick T		71/72				
		72/73				
		73/74	5	3	1	D1
		74/75				
St Mirren		74/75				
		75/76	24		12	D1
		76/77	27	6	12	D1
		77/78	1			P
Kilmarnock		77/78	36		13	D1
		78/79	5	3	2	D1
Falkirk		78/79	11	1	3	D2
		79/80	12	7	6	D2
		80/81	0	1		D1
Arbroath		80/81	6	2	1	D2

McEACHRAN John
b. Greenock 22.7.1963
Port Glasgow Jnrs

Club		Season				
St Mirren		80/81	0	1		P
		81/82	10	4	1	P
		82/83	1	2	1	P
		83/84	0	6	1	P
Kilmarnock		84/85	11	4	1	D1
Largs Thistle						

McEWAN Alexander Ian
b. Glasgow 15.5.1970
Rangers

Club		Season				
St Mirren		89/90	2			P
		90/91	1		1	P
		91/92	0	1		P
Morton		92/93	1	2	2	D1
		93/94	12	6	6	D1
Albion R		94/95	10	2	2	D3
		95/96	5	2	1	D3

McEWAN Gerard T
b. Glasgow 16.1.1968
St Columbas BC

Club		Season				
Hamilton A		86/87	2			P
		87/88				
Arbroath		88/89	22			D2
Petershill						
Wishaw Jnrs						
Ashfield						

McFADDEN Paul
b. Glasgow 14.9.1965
Duntocher BC

Club		Season				
Motherwell		83/84	10	3	2	P
		84/85	2	6	2	D1
		85/86	0	1		P

MacFARLANE David
b. Irvine 16.1.1967

Club		Season				
Rangers		84/85	1	1		P
		85/86				
		86/87	2	2		P
		87/88	1			P
Kilmarnock	L	87/88	4		3	D1
Dundee	L	87/88	1	1		P
Kilmarnock		88/89	19	4	3	D1
		89/90	5	2	1	D2
Partick T		89/90	5	4	1	D1

McGACHIE John
b. Edinburgh 13.11.1965
Salvesen BC

Club		Season				
Aberdeen		82/83				
		83/84				
Hibernian		83/84	3	5	1	P
		84/85	0	3		P
Hamilton A		84/85	23	4	8	D1
		85/86	5	4	1	D1
Meadowbank T		85/86	21		12	D2
		86/87	39		21	D2
		87/88	39		14	D1
		88/89	15	3	5	D1
		89/90	5	1	1	D1
Hamilton A		89/90	21	5	5	D1
		90/91	0	1		D1
Stirling A		90/91	8	12	5	D2
Montrose		91/92	28	1	9	D1
Peterhead						
Keith						

McGARR Ernest
b. Glasgow 9.3.1944
Kilbirnie Ladeside

Club		Season				
Aberdeen		65/66				
		66/67				
		67/68	1			D1
		68/69	20			D1
		69/70	22			D1
		70/71				
Dunfermline A		70/71	14			D1
		71/72	11			D1
		72/73				
East Fife		72/73	17			D1
		73/74	26			D1
		74/75				
		75/76	26			D1
		76/77	18			D1
Cowdenbeath		77/78	39			D2
		78/79	5			D2
Airdrieonians		78/79	33			D1
		79/80	39			D1
		80/81	3			P
Berwick R		80/81	6			D1

McGARVEY Francis Peter
b. Glasgow 17.3.1956
Colston Amateurs
Kilsyth R

Club		Season				
St Mirren		74/75	0	1		D1
		75/76	16	9		D1
		76/77	37	1	17	D1
		77/78	35		17	P
		78/79	33		13	P
Liverpool		79/80				
Celtic		79/80	11	1	2	P
		80/81	34		23	P
		81/82	25	1	10	P
		82/83	32	2	17	P
		83/84	28	2	10	P
		84/85	30	3	15	P
St Mirren		85/86	35		6	P
		86/87	38	2	10	P
		87/88	18	7	2	P
		88/89	18	13	2	P
		89/90	2	1		P
Queen of the South		90/91	12	7	6	D2
Clyde		91/92	12		6	D2
		92/93	33	1	16	D2

McGEACHIE George
b. Skinflats 5.2.1959
Bo'ness U

Dundee	77/78	12	3	2	D1
	78/79	3	2		D1
	79/80	28		1	P
	80/81	27	3	2	D1
	81/82	28	1	3	P
	82/83	20	2		P
	83/84	22	1		P
	84/85	35		1	P
	85/86	1	1		P
	86/87	23	5		P
	87/88	12	2	1	P
	88/89	6			P
	89/90	2			P
Raith R	89/90	14			D1
	90/91	30	1		D1
	91/92	18			D1
	92/93	29	1		D1
	93/94	18	2		P
Stenhousemuir	94/95	21	1		D2
	95/96	21	1		D2
	96/97	20	5		D2

McGEACHY Archibald M
b. Campbeltown 26.11.1969
Ferguslie U

Morton	87/88	7	2		P
	88/89	4	6		D1

McGETTRICK James

St Mirren	76/77	2	5		D1
	77/78	4	3		P
Clyde	78/79	13	2		D1
	79/80	3	5		D1

McGHEE Alexander

Hibernian	71/72	1			D1
	72/73				
Morton	73/74	12		2	D1
	74/75	27		3	D1
Hibernian	75/76	5	1	3	P
	76/77	7	2		P
	77/78	9	1	3	P
Dundee	78/79	20		2	D1
	79/80	0	1		P
Cowdenbeath	80/81	3	1		D2

McGHEE Mark Edward
b. Glasgow 20.5.1957
Cumbernauld Borough

Bristol C	73/74				
	74/75				
Celtic T	75/76				
Morton	75/76	2	3	1	D1
	76/77	39		20	D1
	77/78	20		16	D1
Newcastle U	77/78	17	1	3	FL
	78/79	4	6	2	FL
Aberdeen	78/79	11		4	P
	79/80	15	6	6	P
	80/81	36		13	P
	81/82	29	2	8	P
	82/83	31	1	17	P
	83/84	30	3	16	P
SV Hamburg	84/85				
Celtic	85/86	13	5	4	P
	86/87	6	11	1	P
	87/88	15	9	6	P
	88/89	28	1	16	P
Newcastle U	89/90	46		19	FL
	90/91	17	4	5	FL
Reading	91/92	23	9	5	FL
	92/93	9	4	2	FL

McGHIE William
b. Glasgow 13.11.1961

Clydebank	81/82	35			D1
	82/83	39		4	D1
	83/84	39			D1
	84/85	33	2	2	D1
	85/86	10	5		P
	86/87	12	2		P
Partick T	87/88	40			D1
	88/89	9			D1
Queen of the South	89/90	35		4	D2
	90/91	35	1	1	D2
	91/92	27	1	2	D2
	92/93	31	3	4	D2
	93/94	30	1	2	D2

McGIFFEN Ian

Ayr U	77/78	4			P

McGILL Daniel
b. Paisley 7.7.1971
Gleniffer Thistle

St Mirren	89/90	1	1		P
	90/91	1	2		P
	91/92	3	10		P
	92/93	6	3	2	D1
Clyde	92/93	7	2	1	D2
	93/94	4	12	2	D1
	94/95	2	4	1	D2

McGILL Derek
b. Lanark 14.10.1975
Dunfermline A

Hamilton A	93/94	13	3	3	D1
	94/95	4	3	1	D1
Glentoran	94/95				
Falkirk	95/96				
Hamilton A	96/97	8		4	D2
Raith R	96/97	3	6		P
	97/98	11	5	4	D1
Queens Park	98/99	4			D3
	98/99	3			D3

McGINLAY Patrick David
b. Glasgow 30.5.1967

Blackpool	85/86				
	86/87	2	9	1	FL
	87/88				
Hibernian	88/89	0	2		P
	89/90	20	8	3	P
	90/91	29	3	1	P
	91/92	43		9	P
	92/93	40		10	P
Celtic	93/94	39	2	10	P
	94/95	7	1	1	P
Hibernian	94/95	24		7	P
	95/96	30	1	5	P
	96/97	29		6	P
	97/98	33		4	P
	98/99	29	1	12	D1
	99/00	22	9	3	P

McGINNIS Gary
b. Dundee 21.10.1963
Celtic

Dundee U	81/82				
	82/83				
	83/84	2	2		P
	84/85	7	3		P
	85/86	3	1		P
	86/87	16	4		P
	87/88	9	2		P
	88/89	7	4		P
	89/90	4	3		P
St Johnstone	89/90	10	1		D1
	90/91	32			P
	91/92	28	1		P
	92/93	26	1		P
	93/94	28	1		P
	94/95	10			D1
Happy Valley					

McGINTY Brian
b. East Kilbride 10.12.1976

Rangers	94/95	1			P
	95/96	2			P
	96/97				
Hull C	97/98	21		2	FL
	98/99	22	10	4	FL
Airdrieonians	99/00	4			D1

McGIVERN Samuel Walker
b. Kilwinning 9.10.1963
Glenfield BC

Kilmarnock	81/82	18	10	2	D1
	82/83	32	2	3	P
	83/84	35	2	7	D1
	84/85	28	4	5	D1
	85/86	36		11	D1
	86/87	15	4	2	D1
Falkirk	86/87	13	3	3	P
	87/88	9	1	1	P
	88/89	30	4	8	D1
	89/90	13	3	2	D1
	90/91	28	2	15	D1
	91/92	23	7	3	P
	92/93	1			P
Ayr U	92/93	9			D1
	93/94	38	2	12	D1
	94/95	9	2	1	D1
Dumbarton	95/96	9	2		D1
	96/97	1	1	1	D2

McGLASHAN Colin
b. Perth 17.3.1964

Dundee	82/83	0	2		P
	83/84	2	7	1	P
Dunfermline A	84/85	9	7	1	D2
Cowdenbeath	84/85	11		5	D2
	85/86	34		15	D2
	86/87	15		7	D2
Clyde	86/87	21		5	D1
	87/88	42	1	16	D1
	88/89	37		16	D1
	89/90	39		11	D1
Partick T	90/91	34	2	10	D1
	91/92	43	1	18	D1
	92/93	12	10	2	P
	93/94	0	1		P
Ayr U	93/94	34	2	3	D1
Montrose	94/95	34		19	D3
	95/96	33		16	D2
	96/97	30		11	D3
	97/98	36		20	D3
	98/99	8		1	D3
Arbroath	98/99	27		12	D2
	99/00	34		16	D2

McGLINCHEY Paul
b. 6.1.1961

Hibernian	79/80	2	3		P
	80/81	8	1		D1
Berwick R	81/82	14	4	2	D2

McGOVERN Paul
b. 31.10.1968

Hibernian	87/88	1	6	1	P
	88/89				
	89/90				
Partick T	90/91	10	8	4	D1
	91/92	1	4		D1
Berwick R	92/93	2		1	D2
Montrose *	92/93	2			D2

McGOWAN Jamie
b. Morecambe 5.12.1970

Dundee	92/93	21		1	P
	93/94	11	3		P
Falkirk	93/94	6	3	2	D1
	94/95	27	4	1	P
	95/96	27	2	1	P
	96/97	29		2	D1
	97/98	33		2	D1
Motherwell	98/99	32		1	P
	99/00	10	3		P

McGOWAN Martin
b. Glasgow 11.8.1962
Campsie Black Watch

Dumbarton	80/81	0	1		D1
	81/82	26	3	1	D1
	82/83	22	4	1	D1
	83/84	34		1	D1
	84/85	28			P
	85/86	19			D1
Stranraer	86/87	7			D2
East Stirlingshire	86/87	3			D2
Albion R	86/87	17			D2
	87/88	29	1	4	D2
	88/89	36		3	D2
	89/90	20			D1

McGOWAN Patrick
b. Bellshill 4.8.1959
Glenboig Jnrs

Dumbarton	80/81	21	4	1	D1
	81/82	16		4	D1
	82/83	31	3	3	D1
	83/84	14	7		D1
	84/85	13	1	1	P
	85/86	25	4	2	D1
	86/87	17	15	2	D1
	87/88	39	2	4	D1
	88/89	34		1	D2

McGOWNE Kevin
b. Kilmarnock 16.12.1969

St Mirren	89/90	1	1		P
	90/91	10			P
	91/92	31	5	1	P
St Johnstone	92/93	25	1	1	P
	93/94	37	4		P
	94/95	30		1	D1
	95/96	23		2	D1
	96/97	2			D1
Kilmarnock	96/97	30	1		P
	97/98	21	5		P
	98/99	32		4	P
	99/00	9			P

McGRAIN Daniel Fergus
b. Finnieston 1.5.1950

Celtic		67/68				
		68/69				
		69/70				
		70/71	7			D1
		71/72	2	1		D1
		72/73	30			D1
		73/74	29	1	1	D1
		74/75	30			D1
		75/76	35			P
		76/77	36			P
		77/78	7			P
		78/79	18		3	P
		79/80	34			P
		80/81	33			P
		81/82	27			P
		82/83	34		1	P
Blackpool	L	82/83				
		83/84	33			FL
		84/85	30			FL
		85/86	27	1		FL
		86/87	21	5		FL
Rochdale Rovers		87				
Hamilton A		87/88	20	1		D1

McGRAW Mark Robertson
b. Rutherglen 5.1.1971

Morton		88/89	0	1		D1
		89/90	5	6	3	D1
Hibernian		90/91	4	9		P
		91/92	14	10	1	P
		92/93	1	1		P
		93/94	0	2		P
		94/95	2	6	2	P
Falkirk		95/96	2	7		P
		96/97	20	9	8	D1
		97/98	0	2		D1
Morton		97/98	7	6		D1
Clyde		97/98	9		4	D2
		98/99	5		2	D2
		99/00	4	2	1	D2

McGREGOR James Gordon

St Johnstone		74/75	0	2		D1
		75/76	15	9	2	P
		76/77	11	6	2	D1
Australia		77/78				
Partick T		78/79	0	1		P
		79/80	3	1		P
Stirling A		80/81	6	1		D1
Clyde		80/81	0	1		D2

McGREGOR John Reid
b. Airdrie 5.1.1963

Queens Park		79/80	30		2	D2
		80/81	38		13	D2
		81/82	37		4	D1
Liverpool		82/83				
St Mirren	L	83/84	5		1	P
Liverpool		84/85				
		85/86				
Leeds U	L	85/86	5			FL
Liverpool		86/87				
Rangers		87/88	20	5		P
		88/89				
		89/90				
		90/91				
		91/92	1			P

McGRILLEN Paul Alexander
b. Glasgow 19.8.1971

Motherwell		90/91	0	2		P
		91/92	5	11		P
		92/93	12	10	6	P
		93/94	20	20	5	P
		94/95	2	5	2	P
Falkirk		94/95	6		1	P
		95/96	24	6	6	P
		96/97	24	7	7	D1
		97/98	19	11	7	D1
Airdrieonians		98/99	20	3	1	D1
East Fife		99/00	3		1	D3
Stirling A		99/00	23	6	11	D2

McGROARTY Christopher
b. Bellshill 6.2.1981

Dunfermline A		98/99	3	1		P
		99/00	13	7		D1

McGUGAN Paul Joseph
b. Glasgow 17.7.1964
Eastercraigs Amateurs

Celtic		83/84	1			P
		84/85	3			P
		85/86	19	2	2	P
		86/87	21	1		P
		87/88	1	1		P
Barnsley		87/88	28	1	1	FL
		88/89	19	1	1	FL
		89/90				
Chesterfield		90/91	22		1	FL
		91/92	37		3	FL
		92/93	13		2	FL
		93/94	2	3		FL

McGUIRE Douglas John
b. Bathgate 6.9.1967

Celtic		86/87	0	1		P
		87/88	0	1		P
Dumbarton	L	87/88	3	3		D1
Sunderland	L	87/88	1			FL
Coventry C		88/89				
		89/90	1	3		FL
		90/91				
Cumnock Jnrs		90/91				
Queen of the South		91/92	17	8		D2
		92/93	19	7	5	D2
		93/94	19	9	6	D2
		94/95	5	2	1	D2
Stranraer		94/95	1	5		D1
		95/96	5	10	2	D2
Albion R		96/97	8	8	3	D3

McGUIRE Philip
b. Glasgow 4.3.1980
Dyce Jnrs

Aberdeen		99/00	0	3		P

McGUIRE William
b. Bellshill 24.1.1957
Petershill

Airdrieonians		77/78	8	8	1	D1
		78/79	33	3	8	D1
		79/80	38	1	12	D1
		80/81	21	7	4	P
		81/82	23	7	2	P
		82/83	21	6	5	D1
		83/84	33	2	7	D1
		84/85	16	8	4	D1
Falkirk		85/86	11	7	6	D1
		86/87	8	17	1	P
Partick T		87/88	27	13	10	D1
		88/89	3	1	1	D1
		89/90	4	4		D1
Dumbarton		90/91	12	1	1	D2

McILWRAITH James
b. Glasgow 17.4.1954
Troon Jnrs
Kilwinning

Motherwell		73/74				
		74/75	18	5	5	D1
		75/76	3	2	1	P
Bury		75/76	19	4	3	FL
		76/77	29	2	11	FL
		77/78	32	3	7	FL
Portsmouth		78/79	16	3		FL
Ayr U	L	78/79	0	2		D1
Bury		79/80	28	1	3	FL
Halifax T		80/81	29		5	FL
		81/82	4	3	1	FL

McINALLY Alan Bruce
b. Ayr 10.2.1963

Ayr U		80/81	3	3		D1
		81/82	15	2	9	D1
		82/83	32	3	7	D1
		83/84	34	1	13	D1
Celtic		84/85	4	8	1	P
		85/86	5	11	1	P
		86/87	29	9	15	P
Aston Villa		87/88	18	8	4	FL
		88/89	32	1	14	FL
Bayern Munich		89/90				
		90/91				
		91/92				
		92/93				
Ayr U		93/94				
Kilmarnock		93/94	2	6		P

McINALLY James Edward
b. Glasgow 19.2.1964

Celtic		80/81				
		81/82				
		82/83	0	1		P
		83/84				
Dundee	L	83/84	11		2	P
Nottingham F		84/85	24			FL
		85/86	12			FL
Coventry C		85/86	5			FL
Dundee U		86/87	32		1	P
		87/88	35	1	2	P
		88/89	29		1	P
		89/90	35		3	P
		90/91	33		1	P
		91/92	32		4	P
		92/93	27	6	5	P
		93/94	29	2		P
		94/95	23	2		P
Raith R		95/96	23	2		P
		96/97	4			P
Dundee U		96/97	12	4	1	P
Dundee		97/98	32		1	D1
		98/99	14	1		P

McINNES Derek John
b. Paisley 5.7.1971

Morton		87/88	1	1		P
		88/89	24	5	1	D1
		89/90	15	8	1	D1
		90/91	24	7	3	D1
		91/92	38	4	7	D1
		92/93	40		2	D1
		93/94	16		1	D1
		94/95	26		3	D2
		95/96	12	1	1	D1
Rangers		95/96	5	1		P
		96/97	10	11	1	P
		97/98				
		98/99	0	7		P
Stockport Co	L	98/99	13			FL
Rangers		99/00	0	1		P

McINTOSH David

Dundee		75/76	4		1	P
		76/77	2	1		D1

McINTOSH Martin
b. East Kilbride 19.3.1971
Rangers
Tottenham H

St Mirren		88/89	1	1		P
		89/90	1	1		P
		90/91				
Clydebank		91/92	25	3	5	D1
		92/93	32	1	4	D1
		93/94	2	2	1	D1
Hamilton A		93/94	13		2	D1
		94/95	30		2	D1
		95/96	23		1	D1
		96/97	33		7	D2
		97/98	1			D1
Stockport Co		97/98	38		2	FL
		98/99	41		3	FL
		99/00	17	3		FL
Hibernian		99/00	9			P

McINTYRE Brendan
b. Glasgow 28.1.11965
Heart of Midlothian

Partick T		85/86	9	5		D1
		86/87	2	1		D1
Queen of the South		86/87	6	5		D1
Stranraer		87/88	24	1		D2
Falkirk		87/88	7			P
		88/89	3			D1
Stranraer		88/89	4		1	D2

McINTYRE James
b. Kilwinning 26.10.1962
Irvine Meadow

Rangers		81/82	0	1		P

McINTYRE James
b. Alexandria 24.5.1972
Duntocher BC

Bristol C		91/92	1			FL
Exeter C	L	92/93	12	3	3	FL
Airdrieonians		93/94	8	5		D1
		94/95	2	10	1	D1
		95/96	22	7	9	D1
Kilmarnock		95/96	7		2	P
		96/97	29	2	6	P
		97/98	6	2	1	P
Reading		97/98	6			FL
		98/99	22	10	6	FL
		99/00	15	11	4	FL

McINTYRE Paul
b. Girvan 18.1.1967
Maybole Jnrs

St Mirren		90/91	4		1	P
		91/92	20	3		D1
		92/93	14	6	1	D1
		93/94	39	3	8	D1
		94/95	19	1		D1
		95/96	19	6		D1
Stranraer		96/97	28		7	D2
		97/98	23	4	7	D2
		98/99	22	1		D1
Clydebank		99/00	4	5	1	D1
Partick T		99/00	7	6		D2

McINTYRE Thomas
b. Bellshill 26.12.1963

Aberdeen		83/84	7	3		P
		84/85				
		85/86	2	3		P
		86/87	0	4		P
Hibernian		86/87	15			P
		87/88	21	5		P
		88/89	16	1	2	P
		89/90				
		90/91	9			P
		91/92	37		6	P
		92/93	12		1	P
		93/94	11			P
Airdrieonians		94/95	15	2		D1
		95/96	12	5	2	D1
		96/97	5	2		D1

MacIVER Stuart
b. Glasgow 12.11.1966

Dumbarton		84/85	1	2		P
		85/86	13	16	10	D1
		86/87	18	13	7	D1
		87/88	12	12	4	D1
		88/89	27		13	D2
		89/90	32	2	19	D2
		90/91	19	2	6	D2
		91/92	0	3	1	D2
		91/92	6	1		D1

MacKAY Gary
b. Edinburgh 23.1.1964

Heart of Midlothian		80/81	11	1		P
		81/82	10	7	2	D1
		82/83	26	6	6	D1
		83/84	29	2	4	P
		84/85	16	1	2	P
		85/86	30	2	4	P
		86/87	31	5	7	P
		87/88	40	1	5	P
		88/89	29		2	P
		89/90	31	2	1	P
		90/91	27	3	3	P
		91/92	41	2	1	P
		92/93	36	1	2	P
		93/94	34	2	1	P
		94/95	21	13	2	P
		95/96	21	5	2	P
		96/97	20	7	1	P
Airdrieonians		96/97	8		1	D1
		97/98	23	3		D1
		98/99	4	6		D1

McKAY James

Hibernian		77/78	3	1	1	P

MacKAY John
b. Falkirk 15.12.1957
Dunipace Jnrs

St Johnstone		75/76	0	1		P
		76/77	39		1	D1
		77/78	29	2	1	D1
		78/79	11			D1
Toronto Blizzard		79	3			NA
St Johnstone		79/80	20	1		D1
		80/81	31			D1
Cleveland		81				
St Johnstone		81/82	13		1	D1
		82/83	4			D1
		83/84	1	1		P
East Stirlingshire	L	84/85	2			D2
Stirling A		84/85	3			D2
Hamilton A		84/85	4			D1
Queen of the South		84/85	11			D2
East Stirlingshire		85/86	16	1	1	D2
		86/87	17	2		D2
		87/88	7	1		D2
Alloa A *		87/88	1			D2
Stenhousemuir *		87/88	1			D2

MacKAY Malcolm George
b. Bellshill 19.2.1972

Queens Park		90/91	10			D2
		91/92	25	2	3	D2
		92/93	33		3	D2
		93/94				
Celtic		94/95	1			P
		95/96	9	2	1	P
		96/97	18	2	1	P
		97/98	3	1	1	P
		98/99	1		1	P
Norwich C		98/99	24	3	1	FL
		99/00	16	5		FL

MacKAY William
b. Glenrothes 27.10.1960

Rangers		77/78	1			P
		78/79	0	1		P
		79/80	0	2		P
		80/81	0	6		P
		81/82	1	6	1	P
		82/83	2	2		P
		83/84	1	1		P
		84/85				
Heart of Midlothian		85/86	0	3		P
		86/87	0	2		P
Dunfermline A *		86/87	0	6		D1

McKEAN Robert Munro
b. East Kilbride 15.3.1952 d. 15.3.1978
Blantyre V

St Mirren		69/70				
		70/71	20	3	2	D1
		71/72	28		8	D2
		72/73	33	2	6	D2
		73/74	34		19	D2
Rangers		74/75	25	1	5	D1
		75/76	32	1	5	P
		76/77	14	8	2	P
		77/78	6	4		P

McKECHNIE James
b. Glasgow 5.11.1964

Celtic		78/79				
		79/80				
		80/81				
Nottingham F		80/81				
		81/82				
		82/83				
		83/84				
Celtic		83/84				
		84/85	1	1		P
		85/86				
Norwich C	L	85/86				
Derry C						

McKEE Colin
b. Glasgow 22.8.1973

Manchester U		91/92				
		92/93				
Bury	L	92/93	2			FL
Manchester U		93/94	1			FL
Kilmarnock		94/95	22	3	6	P
		95/96	19	9	4	P
		96/97	14	11	2	P
Partick T		97/98	1			D1
Falkirk		98/99	2	2		D1
Queen of the South		98/99	2			D2
Ross Co		98/99	0	1		D3
Stirling A		98/99	1	1		D2
Queens Park		99/00	2	5		D3

McKEE Kevin George
b. Edinburgh 10.6.1966
Whitburn Centre
Polbeth U

Hibernian		82/83	2	2		P
		83/84	11	5		P
		84/85	16	2		P
		85/86	1	1		P
Hamilton A		86/87	25	4	4	P
		87/88	37	3		D1
		88/89	36			P
		89/90	39		1	D1
		90/91	38			D1
		91/92	34		1	D1
		92/93	19	1	1	D1
Partick T		93/94	22	1		P
		94/95	16	1		P
		95/96	10	1		P
Stenhousemuir		96/97	13			D2

McKELLAR David
b. Irvine 22.5.1956

Ipswich T		74/75				
Colchester U	L	74/75				
Peterborough U	L	74/75				
Ipswich T		75/76				
Dundee U		76/77				
Ardrossan Winton R		77/78				
Derby Co		78/79	16			FL
		79/80	25			FL
Brentford		80/81	39			FL
		81/82	45			FL
		82/83				
Carlisle U		83/84	42			FL
		84/85	40			FL
Hibernian		85/86				
Newcastle U	L	85/86	10			FL
Hamilton A		86/87	36			P
		87/88	16			D1
Dunfermline A		87/88	6			P
Hartlepool U	L	88/89	5			FL
Carlisle U		88/89	34			FL
		89/90	35			FL
Kilmarnock		89/90	5			D2
		90/91	1			D1

McKENNA Adrian Paul
b. Glasgow 31.3.1971
Hibernian

Airdrieonians		91/92	0	2		P
Stirling A		92/93	17	2	1	D1
		93/94	6	1	2	D1
		94/95				
		95/96				
Albion R		96/97	0	1		D3

McKENZIE Roderick
b. Bellshill 8.8.1975
Heart of Midlothian

Stenhousemuir		95/96	36			D2
Heart of Midlothian		96/97	3			P
		97/98	4			P
		98/99	19			P
		99/00	3	2		P

MacKENZIE Scott
b. Glasgow 7.7.1970
Musselburgh A

Falkirk		91/92	0	2		P
		92/93	2	1		P
		93/94	14	5		D1
		94/95	36		1	P
		95/96	27	3	1	P
		96/97	26	2	1	D1
		97/98	29		3	D1
		98/99	33	2	1	D1
		99/00	34		1	D1

McKEOWN Brian
b. Motherwell 31.10.1956
Fauldhouse U

Airdrieonians		78/79	6	6	1	D1
		79/80	39		6	D1
		80/81	24	5		P
		81/82	30	5	2	P
		82/83	24	2	3	D1
		83/84	28	3		D1
		84/85	33			D1
		85/86	33	1	1	D1
		86/87	40	1		D1
		87/88	33			D1
		88/89	37			D1
		89/90	21			D1
Queen of the South		90/91	25			D2
		91/92	16		2	D2
		92/93	12	1		D2
		93/94	35			D2
		94/95	30	1		D2
		95/96	30	1		D2
		96/97	26		1	D2

McKEOWN Gary Joseph
b. Oxford 19.10.1970

Arsenal		88/89				
		89/90				
		90/91				
		91/92				
Shrewsbury T	L	91/92	8		1	FL
Dundee		92/93	1			P
		93/94	2			P
		94/95	0	1		D1
		95/96	13	4	1	D1
		96/97	17	3	1	D1
Exeter C	L	96/97	3			FL

McKEOWN Kevin						
b. Glasgow 12.10.1967						
Stenhousemuir		86/87	17			D2
Motherwell		86/87	1			P
		87/88				
		88/89	2			P
Stirling A		88/89	5			D2
Stenhousemuir		89/90	11			D2
Crusaders		90/91				
		91/92				
		92/93				
		93/94				
		94/95				
		95/96				
		96/97				
Ayr U		97/98	2			D1

MacKIE Darren Graham						
b. Inverurie 5.1.1982						
Aberdeen		99/00	2	2		P

MacKIE George S						
b. Edinburgh 18.5.1954						
Dundee		75/76	14	1		P
Partick T		76/77	16	3		P
		77/78	27	4		P
		78/79	1			P
		79/80	1	1		P
Albion R		80/81	14	1	1	D2
Brechin C		81/82	38		5	D2
		82/83	21	3	4	D2
		83/84	19	11	4	D1
		84/85	25	1	2	D1
Arbroath		84/85	6			D2
		85/86	27	5	2	D2
		86/87	24	5		D2
		87/88	13	3		D2

MacKIE Peter						
b. Glasgow 17.1.1958						
Celtic						
Cumbernauld U	L					
Celtic		77/78	1			P
		78/79	0	2		P
Dundee		79/80	22		2	P
		80/81	25	9	5	D1
		81/82	22	10	4	P
		82/83	32	4	5	P
		83/84	18	8	3	P
St Mirren		84/85	10	11	2	P
		85/86	19	5	2	P
Blackpool	T	86/87				
Partick T		86/87	31	3	3	D1
Stranraer *		87/88	1			D2
		88/89				
		89/90				
		90/91				
		91/92				
East Stirlingshire *		92/93	0	1		D2
Stenhousemuir		92/93	8	5	1	D2

McKILLIGAN Neil						
b. Falkirk 2.1.1974						
Southampton						
Partick T		92/93	3	2		P
		93/94	1	2		P
Ayr U		93/94	8		1	D1
		94/95	30	4		D1
		95/96	7	3		D2
Raith R		95/96	1	2		P
Albion R		96/97	28	2	1	D3
		97/98	27	4		D3

McKIMMIE Stewart						
b. Aberdeen 27.10.1962						
Dundee		80/81	15	2		D1
		81/82	16			P
		82/83	29	3		P
		83/84	16			P
Aberdeen		83/84	17	1	1	P
		84/85	34		3	P
		85/86	34		3	P
		86/87	37			P
		87/88	42			P
		88/89	35			P
		89/90	33			P
		90/91	25		1	P
		91/92	39			P
		92/93	14			P
		93/94	40			P
		94/95	34		1	P
		95/96	29			P
		96/97	14			P
Dundee U		96/97	6			P
		97/98	3	1		P

McKINLAY Thomas Valley						
b. Glasgow 3.12.1964						
Dundee		82/83	1			P
		83/84	36		3	P
		84/85	33	1	3	P
		85/86	22			P
		86/87	32		2	P
		87/88	19			P
		88/89	18			P
Heart of Midlothian		88/89	17		1	P
		89/90	29		1	P
		90/91	31	2	2	P
		91/92	37	2	2	P
		92/93	32	2	1	P
		93/94	43			P
		94/95	11			P
Celtic		94/95	17			P
		95/96	3			P
		96/97	24	3		P
		97/98	2	3		P
Stoke C	L	97/98	3			FL
Celtic		98/99	11	7		P
Kilmarnock		99/00	14	1		P

McKINLAY William						
b. Glasgow 22.4.1969						
Hamilton Thistle						
Dundee U		86/87	3			P
		87/88	10	2	1	P
		88/89	29	1	1	P
		89/90	13			P
		90/91	29	5	2	P
		91/92	22		1	P
		92/93	35	1	1	P
		93/94	39		9	P
		94/95	25	1	4	P
		95/96	5		4	D1
Blackburn R		95/96	13	6	2	FL
		96/97	23	2	1	FL
		97/98	26	4		FL
		98/99	14	2		FL

McKINNA Lawrie						
b. Kilmarnock 8.7.1961						
Galston U						
Darvel Jnrs						
Kilmarnock		82/83	0	3		P
		83/84	18	6	8	D1
		84/85				
		85/86	11	13	1	D1
Boxhill						
Heidelberg U						
Apia-Leichhardt						

MacKINNON David D						
b. Glasgow 23.5.1956						
Dundee		75/76	4			P
		76/77	2	2		D1
		77/78	25		3	D1
Partick T		78/79	35			P
		79/80	29	1		P
		80/81	7	1		P
		81/82	24	2		P
Rangers		82/83	30	1	1	P
		83/84	12	5		P
		84/85	30			P
		85/86	18	6		P
Airdrieonians		86/87	27	3	1	D1
		87/88	40		1	D1
		88/89	28		1	D1
Kilmarnock		89/90	33		2	D2
		90/91	20	1		D1
Forfar A		91/92	27	1		D1

McKINNON Raymond						
b. Dundee 5.8.1970						
Dundee U		88/89	1			P
		89/90	7	3		P
		90/91	17		2	P
		91/92	21	4	4	P
Nottingham F		92/93	5	1	1	FL
Aberdeen		93/94	5			P
		94/95	17	3		P
		95/96	0	1		P
Dundee U		95/96	5	4		D1
		96/97	17	9	6	P
		97/98	7	2		P
		98/99				
Livingston		99/00	17	2	2	D1

McKINNON Robert						
b. Glasgow 31.7.1966						
Rutherglen Glencairn						
Newcastle U		85/86	1			FL
Hartlepool U		86/87	45			FL
		87/88	41	1	2	FL
		88/89	46		2	FL
		89/90	46		1	FL
		90/91	45		1	FL
		91/92	23		1	FL
Motherwell		91/92	16		1	P
		92/93	35			P
		93/94	42		4	P
		94/95	32		3	P
		95/96	27			P
		96/97				
		97/98				
Heart of Midlothian		98/99	14	2		P
		99/00	3			P

McKNIGHT Allen Darrell						
b. Antrim 27.1.1964						
Distillery						
Celtic		86/87				
Albion R	L	86/87	36			D2
Celtic		87/88	12			P
West Ham U		88/89	23			FL
		89/90				
		90/91				
Falkirk	T	91/92				
Airdrieonians		91/92	2			P
Stockport Co		91/92				
Rotherham U		91/92	3			FL
Walsall		91/92	8			FL
South China		92/93				
Exeter C		93/94	9	1		FL

McKNIGHT Paul						
b. Belfast 8.2.1977						
Rangers		94/95	0	1		P
		95/96				
		96/97				
		97/98				
		98/99				
St Mirren		99/00	1	3	2	D1

McLAREN Alan James						
b. Edinburgh 4.1.1971						
Cavalry Park						
Heart of Midlothian		87/88	1			P
		88/89	11	1	1	P
		89/90	26	1	1	P
		90/91	18	5	1	P
		91/92	38		1	P
		92/93	34		1	P
		93/94	37		1	P
		94/95	10		1	P
Rangers		94/95	24		2	P
		95/96	36		3	P
		96/97	17	1		P

McLAREN Andrew						
b. Glasgow 5.6.1973						
Dundee U		91/92	7	6		P
		92/93	4	1		P
		93/94	18	9	2	P
		94/95	16	4		P
		95/96	23	8	3	D1
		96/97	29	5	3	P
		97/98	15	12	4	P
		98/99	3	5		P
Reading		98/99	7		1	FL
		99/00	2			FL
Livingston	L	99/00	5	4		D1

McLAREN Stewart						
b. Larkhall 6.4.1953						
WBA		71/72				
		72/73				
		73/74				
Motherwell		74/75	22			D1
		75/76	29	2	2	P
		76/77	25	2		P
		77/78	29	2	2	P
		78/79	12		1	P
Dundee		78/79	21		4	D1
		79/80	28		3	P
		80/81	31			D1
Heart of Midlothian		81/82	34			D1
		82/83	8	6		D1
		83/84	18	1		P
		84/85	1			P

McLAREN William R
b. Glasgow 7.6.1948

Queen of the South		73/74	35		3	D2
		74/75	35	1		D2
		75/76	25		2	D1
		76/77	35		3	D1
		77/78	35		5	D1
		78/79	2	1		D1
Morton		78/79	18	1		P
		79/80	25	4	1	P
		80/81	7	1		P
Hibernian		80/81	18			D1
		81/82	18	2		P
Clyde		82/83	14	2	1	D1
Queen of the South		82/83	5			D2
		83/84	24		1	D2
Partick T		84/85	5			D1

McLAUGHLIN Brian
b. Falkirk 7.10.1954

Linlithgow Rose						
Celtic		71/72				
		72/73	0	2		D1
		73/74	2	1	1	D1
		74/75	0	1		D1
		75/76				
Finn Harps	L	75/76				
Celtic		76/77				
		77/78	1			P
Ayr U		77/78	22	2	5	P
		78/79	38	1	19	D1
		79/80	5		1	D1
Motherwell		79/80	34		11	D1
		80/81	32	4	6	D1
		81/82	36	1	19	D1
		82/83	6	3	1	P
Hamilton A		82/83	15		8	D1
		83/84				
Falkirk		83/84	5	6		D1
		84/85	0	1		D1
West Adelaide		85/86				
Ayr U		86/87	15	3	1	D2

McLAUGHLIN Brian
b. Bellshill 14.5.1974

Giffnock North						
Celtic		93/94	0	8		P
		94/95	19	2		P
		95/96	11	15	4	P
		96/97	8	12	1	P
		97/98				
Dundee U		98/99	1	2		P

McLAUGHLIN Gerard
b. Clydebank 21.6.1958

Dumbarton U						
Clydebank		76/77	20	8	2	D1
		77/78	9			P
		78/79	11	2	1	D1
		79/80	39		2	D1
		80/81	34	1	2	D1
		81/82	14	4	1	D1
Airdrieonians		82/83	35		2	D1
		83/84	24		1	D1

McLAUGHLIN Joseph
b. Greenock 2.6.1960

Morton		79/80	30		2	P
		80/81	34		1	P
		81/82	36			P
		82/83	34			P
Chelsea		83/84	41			FL
		84/85	36		1	FL
		85/86	40		1	FL
		86/87	36		2	FL
		87/88	36		1	FL
		88/89	31			FL
Charlton A		89/90	31			FL
Watford		90/91	24		1	FL
		91/92	22		1	FL
Falkirk		92/93	8		1	P
		93/94	37		2	D1
		94/95	28		2	P
		95/96	15	1	1	P
Hibernian		95/96	9			P
		96/97	9			P
Clydebank		97/98	32		2	D2
		98/99	32		3	D1
		99/00	12			D1
St Mirren		99/00	3		1	D1

McLAUGHLIN Paul Gerard
b. Johnstone 9.12.1965

Anniesland Waverley						
Clydebank		82/83	4			D1
		83/84				
Queens Park		84/85	32	1		D2
		85/86	22	1	1	D2
		86/87	30			D2
		87/88	33		2	D2
		88/89	34		1	D2
		89/90				
Celtic		90/91	2	1		P
Partick T		90/91	18			D1
		91/92	30	3		D1
		92/93	22	1		P

McLEAN Alan J

Rangers Amateurs						
Celtic						
Kilmarnock		76/77	3	5		P
		77/78	30	1		D1
East Kilbride Thistle						
Cumbernauld U						
Claremont						

McLEAN Alistair

Ardrossan Winton R						
Ayr U		70/71				
		71/72	12			D1
		72/73	4			D1
		73/74	29			D1
		74/75	10			D1
		75/76				
Aberdeen		76/77	9			P
Ayr U		77/78	3			P
St Mirren		78/79	2			P
Partick T		78/79	1			P
Aberdeen		79/80				
Motherwell		80/81	1			D1

McLEAN James

Morton		77/78	4	3		D1
		78/79	1			P

McLEAN Paul
b. Johnstone 25.7.1964

Queens Park		83/84	4	1		D2
		84/85	0	1		D2
		85/86	11	2	2	D2
		86/87	14	5		D2
		87/88	39		3	D2
		88/89	36	3	2	D2
Motherwell		89/90	0	2		P
		90/91	0	1		P
Ayr U		91/92	30	1	3	D1
		92/93	2			D1
Stranraer		92/93	22	1	5	D2
		93/94	20	5	1	D2
		94/95	14	12		D1
		95/96	1	3		D2

McLEAN Stewart Donald
b. Glasgow 13.12.1955

Kilmarnock Star						
Darvel Jnrs						
Kilmarnock		73/74				
		74/75	19	1		D1
		75/76	20	2	2	D1
		76/77	14	4		P
		77/78	30	1		D1
		78/79	38			D1
		79/80	34			P
		80/81	32	2	1	P
		81/82	28	4	1	D1
		82/83	19	2	2	P
		83/84	19	3		D1
		84/85	33	3	2	D1
		85/86	31	1	3	D1
		86/87	34	4	2	D1
		87/88	44			D1
		88/89	29	3		D1
		89/90	19	2		D2

McLEAN Thomas
b. Ashgill 2.6.1947

Birkenshaw Amateurs						
Kilmarnock		62/63				
		63/64				
		64/65	19		3	D1
		65/66	33		9	D1
		66/67	31		8	D1
		67/68	34		4	D1
		68/69	33		5	D1
		69/70	33		9	D1
		70/71	33		10	D1
Rangers		71/72	21	1	1	D1
		72/73	22	2	5	D1
		73/74	21	3	4	D1
		74/75	32	1	14	D1
		75/76	34	1	4	P
		76/77	36		1	P
		77/78	29	2	1	P
		78/79	34	1	1	P
		79/80	22	6	2	P
		80/81	23	5		P
		81/82	2	1	1	P

McLEISH Alexander
b. Glasgow 21.1.1959

Glasgow U						
Aberdeen		77/78	1			P
		78/79	18	1	1	P
		79/80	35		2	P
		80/81	32		3	P
		81/82	32		5	P
		82/83	33	1	2	P
		83/84	32		2	P
		84/85	30		1	P
		85/86	34		3	P
		86/87	40		3	P
		87/88	36		1	P
		88/89	34			P
		89/90	32		2	P
		90/91	33			P
		91/92	7			P
		92/93	27			P
		93/94	35			P
Motherwell		94/95	2			P
		95/96	1			P

McLELLAND Charles
b. Glasgow 24.3.1953

Aberdeen		73/74	15		1	D1
		74/75	33		1	D1
		75/76	29	1		P
		76/77	25		1	P
		77/78	25			P
		78/79	25			P
Motherwell		79/80	34		1	D1
		80/81	15	2		D1
Dundee		81/82	15			P
		82/83	0	1		P
Motherwell		82/83	14	1	1	P
Montrose		83/84	29			D2
		84/85	36	1		D2
		85/86	28			D1
		86/87	33	1		D1
		87/88	27			D2
		88/89	16			D2
		89/90	3	2		D2

McLELLAND Steven
b. Aberdeen 25.8.1957

Eadie Star						
Largs Thistle						
Ayr U		77/78	5	4	1	P
		78/79	20	1	1	D1
		79/80	2	2		D1
Motherwell		80/81	27		3	D1
		81/82	37		3	D1
Hamilton A		82/83	14			D1
Australia						

McLEOD Alexander Hector McMillan
b. Glasgow 1.1.1951

Renfrew Jnrs						
St Mirren		69/70				
		70/71				
		71/72	36		7	D2
		72/73	34		23	D2
Southampton		73/74	2	1		FL
		74/75				
Huddersfield T	L	74/75	3	1	1	FL
Hibernian		74/75	9	1	3	D1
		75/76	16	1	7	P
		76/77	19		7	P
		77/78	35	1	16	P
		78/79	36		8	P
		79/80	25	1	8	P
		80/81	27	3	15	D1
		81/82	33	1	7	P
		82/83				
Dundee U	T	82/83				
Hamilton A		82/83	1	2		D1

MacLEOD Alistair Fraser
b. Glasgow 20.10.1960

Club		Season				
Glasgow Amateurs						
Dumbarton		76/77				
		77/78	12	6		D1
		78/79	29	3	1	D1
		79/80	31	1		D1
		80/81	39		4	D1
		81/82	2			D1
Kilmarnock		81/82	32	1	1	D1
		82/83	34		1	P
		83/84	31	1	2	D1
		84/85	11	6		D1
		85/86	12	1		D1
		86/87	14	6	3	D1
Raith R		87/88	29	1		D1

MacLEOD Andrew Donald
b. Glasgow 14.8.1969

Club		Season				
Aberdeen		88/89	1			P
Fortuna Sittard		89/90				
		90/91				
		91/92				
		92/93				
		93/94				
Ross Co		94/95	27	3	9	D3
		95/96	15	10	3	D3
		96/97	16	8	6	D3
		97/98	1			D3

MacLEOD Duncan
b. 23.5.1949

Club		Season				
Southampton						
Dundee		72/73				
Dundee U		73/74	12	1	3	D1
		74/75	7	5		D1
St Johnstone		75/76	1	1		P
Brechin C		76/77	33	1	2	D2
		77/78	33			D2
		78/79	18			D2
		79/80	20	1		D2
		80/81	18		1	D2

McLEOD Gordon Thomas
b. Edinburgh 2.9.1967

Club		Season				
Dundee U		84/85	1	2		P
		85/86	3			P
		86/87	7	1		P
		87/88	10	2	3	P
		88/89	1			P
Airdrieonians		88/89	9		1	D1
Dundee		89/90	24	3		P
		90/91	23	1	2	D1
		91/92	11	3		D1
Meadowbank T		92/93	28		3	D1
		93/94	35		9	D2
		94/95	31		1	D2
Livingston		95/96	34		4	D3
		96/97	19		5	D2
		97/98	9	1	4	D2

MacLEOD Ian Murdo
b. East Kilbride 19.11.1959

Club		Season				
Claremont						
Motherwell		77/78	4	1		P
		78/79	21	4		P
		79/80	24			D1
		80/81	25		1	D1
		81/82	37			D1
		82/83	31		1	P
		83/84	28	1		P
		84/85	38			D1
		85/86	28	1	1	P
Falkirk		86/87	31	4		P
		87/88	33			P
		88/89				
Raith R		89/90	37			D1
		90/91	26		1	D1
		91/92	44		1	D1
		92/93	34	2	2	D1
		93/94	3			P
Meadowbank T		93/94	19	2		D2

McLEOD Joseph
b. Edinburgh 30.12.1967

Club		Season				
Dundee U		86/87	0	2		P
Dumbarton	L	86/87	4	1		D1
Dundee U		87/88	4	6	1	P
		88/89	0	3		P
		89/90	0	2		P
Motherwell		90/91	10	12	1	P
		91/92	9	5		P
		92/93	4	6		P
Portadown	L	92/93				
Stirling A		93/94	17	1		D1
		94/95	36		8	D2
		95/96	23	3	2	D2
		96/97	5	1		D1
Berwick R		97/98	4			D3
		98/99	7	1		D3

McLEOD Kenneth
b. 25.9.1960

Club		Season				
Heart of Midlothian		78/79	2	1		P

MacLEOD Murdo Davidson
b. Glasgow 24.9.1958

Club		Season				
Glasgow Amateurs						
Dumbarton		74/75				
		75/76	1	6		D1
		76/77	25	2	7	D1
		77/78	38	1	1	D1
		78/79	14		1	D1
Celtic		78/79	23		3	P
		79/80	36		7	P
		80/81	14	4	8	P
		81/82	36		10	P
		82/83	35		11	P
		83/84	34		7	P
		84/85	30	1	3	P
		85/86	29	1	3	P
		86/87	37	1	4	P
Borussia Dortmund		87/88				
		88/89				
		89/90				
Hibernian		90/91	25		2	P
		91/92	22			P
		92/93	26	5		P
Dumbarton		93/94	42		1	D1
		94/95	24			D2
Partick T		95/96	1			P

MacLEOD William
b. 17.7.1961

Club		Season				
Ipswich T						
Partick T		80/81	2			P
Queen of the South		81/82	19		3	D1

McLURE Brian
b. 29.8.1959

Club		Season				
St Mirren		77/78	0	1		P
Johnstone Burgh		78/79				
Queen of the South		79/80	5	1		D2
		80/81	1			D2

McMAHON Gerard Joseph
b. Belfast 29.12.1973

Club		Season				
Glenavon						
Tottenham H		94/95	2			FL
Barnet	L	94/95	10		2	FL
Tottenham H		95/96	7	7		FL
Stoke C		96/97	31	4	3	FL
		97/98	7	10		FL
St Johnstone		97/98	9	1		P
		98/99	13	6	1	P
		99/00	9	10		P

McMAHON Steven
b. Glasgow 22.4.1970

Club		Season				
Ferguslie U						
Swansea C		92/93	2			FL
Carlisle U		93/94	2			FL
Cowdenbeath		93/94	2			D2
Foshan		94/95				
Darlington		95/96	6	4	1	FL
Partick T		95/96	0	1		P
Clydebank		96/97	12	9	3	D1

McMANUS Allan William
b. Paisley 17.11.1974

Club		Season				
Links U						
Heart of Midlothian		95/96	16	1	2	P
		96/97	10	5		P
		97/98	8	4		P
Livingston		98/99	31		1	D2
		99/00	28			D1

McMANUS Michael
b. Glasgow 27.3.1954

Club		Season				
Possil YM						
Ashfield Jnrs						
Motherwell		75/76	1	2		P
		76/77				
Hamilton A		77/78	37		7	D1
		78/79	19	6	2	D1
		79/80	17	8	6	D1
		80/81	25	6	4	D1
Montrose		81/82	24	3	3	D2
		82/83	27	1	6	D2
		83/84	33	1		D2
		84/85	7	6	1	D2
		85/86	27	5	4	D1
		86/87	6	15		D1
Newburgh Jnrs						

McMANUS Michael
b. Bathgate 24.10.1967

Club		Season				
Edina Hibs						
Hibernian		84/85	0	1		P

McMANUS Thomas Kelly
b. Glasgow 28.2.1981

Club		Season				
Hibernian		98/99	0	1		D1
East Fife		99/00	11		3	D3
Hibernian		99/00	1	1		P

McMARTIN Grant Thomas
b. Linlithgow 31.12.1970

Club		Season				
Dunipace Jnrs						
Dundee		89/90	3	1		P
		90/91	15	4	1	D1
		91/92	17	7	1	D1
		92/93	2	1		P
		93/94	1	2		P
St Johnstone		93/94	0	6		P
		94/95	12	10	3	D1
Livingston		95/96	36		3	D3
		96/97	33	1	3	D2
		97/98	35	1		D2
		98/99	0	4		D2
Stranraer		98/99	13			D1
		99/00	14	3	2	D2

McMASTER John
b. Greenock 23.2.1955

Club		Season				
Port Glasgow Jnrs						
Aberdeen		72/73				
		73/74				
		74/75	1	1		D1
		75/76	18	3	3	P
		76/77	1	1		P
		77/78	30	2	4	P
		78/79	24	2	3	P
		79/80	32	1	4	P
		80/81	10		2	P
		81/82	21	10	1	P
		82/83	19	6	2	P
		83/84	11	1		P
		84/85	0	1		P
		85/86	5	2	1	P
		86/87	2			P
Morton		86/87	5	4		D1
		87/88	19	1	2	P

McMILLAN Ian
b. Broxburn 9.6.1976

Club		Season				
Armadale Thistle						
Raith R		94/95	0	1		D1
		95/96	4	4		P

McMILLAN Stephen
b. Edinburgh 19.1.1976

Club		Season				
Motherwell		93/94	0	1		P
		94/95	2	1		P
		95/96	10	2		P
		96/97	13	3		P
		97/98	33	1	1	P
		98/99	30		2	P
		99/00	31		3	P

McMINN Kevin Clifford
b. Castle Douglas 28.9.1962

Club		Season				
Glenafton A						
Queen of the South		82/83	21	1	1	D2
		83/84	27	5	3	D2
		84/85	8			D2
Rangers		84/85	13	7	1	P
		85/86	15	13	2	P
		86/87	9	6	1	P
Seville		86/87				
		87/88				
Derby Co		87/88	7		1	FL
		88/89	32		4	FL
		89/90	15			FL
		90/91	13			FL
		91/92	35	2	2	FL
		92/93	6	13	2	FL
Birmingham C		93/94	10	3		FL
Burnley		93/94	14		3	FL
		94/95	17	5		FL
		95/96	7	3		FL

McNAB Douglas
b. Edinburgh 3.7.1956

Club		Season				
Penicuik A						
Alloa A		77/78	12			D1
		78/79	39			D2
		79/80	24			D2
Partick T		79/80	2			P
		80/81	3			P
		81/82				
		82/83	24			D1
		83/84	17			D1
Hamilton A		83/84	12			D1
Dumbarton		84/85	1			P
Meadowbank T		84/85	8			D1

McNAB Edward
b. Luton 15.8.1962

Shamrock BC						
Morton		80/81	1	4		P
		81/82	4	3		P
		82/83	29		5	P
		83/84	6	13	2	D1
		84/85	6	6		P
Kilmarnock		85/86	11	12	3	D1
		86/87	3			D1
Stranraer		86/87	14	4	1	D2
		87/88	5	5	2	D2
Port Glasgow Jnrs						

McNAIR Colin J
b. Glasgow 20.3.1969

Falkirk		87/88	6	6		P
		88/89	29	4	4	D1
		89/90	6	1		D1
Motherwell		89/90	1	1		P
Dumbarton		90/91	24	1	2	D2
		91/92	0	1		D2

McNALLY Mark
b. Motherwell 10.3.1971

Celtic		90/91	17	2		P
		91/92	21	3	1	P
		92/93	25	2		P
		93/94	30	2	2	P
		94/95	19	1		P
Southend U		95/96	20		2	FL
		96/97	32	2		FL
Stoke C		96/97				
		97/98	3	1		FL
Dundee U		98/99	4	1		P
Ayr U		99/00	5	3		D1

McNAMARA Jackie
b. Glasgow 24.10.1973

Gairdoch U						
Dunfermline A		92/93	1	2		D1
		93/94	38	1		D1
		94/95	30		2	D1
		95/96	7		1	D1
Celtic		95/96	26		1	P
		96/97	30		1	P
		97/98	28	3	2	P
		98/99	15	1		P
		99/00	22			P

McNAMARA John
b. Glasgow 19.9.1952

Eastercraigs Amateurs						
Cumbernauld U						
Celtic		70/71				
		71/72				
		72/73				
		73/74	1	1		D1
		74/75	1			D1
		75/76	16	2	2	P
Hibernian		76/77	10	1		P
		77/78	33	1		P
		78/79	35			P
		79/80	30			P
		80/81	36		1	D1
		81/82	27	2		P
		82/83	27	1	1	P
		83/84	10			P
		84/85	23			P
Morton		85/86	23			D1
		86/87	26	1	2	D1
		87/88	7			P

McNAUGHT John
b. Glasgow 19.6.1964 d. 1997

Auchengill YC						
Hamilton A		82/83	24	3	1	D1
		83/84	24	4	3	D1
		84/85	19	8	4	D1
		85/86	20	4	11	D1
Chelsea		85/86	0	1		FL
		86/87	8		2	FL
		87/88	36			FL
Partick T		87/88	10		3	D1
Hamilton A		87/88	4		1	D1
		88/89	3		1	P
Blantyre V						

McNAUGHTON Alexander
b. Motherwell 1.12.1953

Queens Park		72/73	6			D2
		73/74	17	5	4	D2
		74/75	9	11		D2
		75/76	22		8	D2
		76/77	24	2	10	D2
Clydebank		77/78	11	5		P
Clyde		78/79	0	6		D1
Stenhousemuir		78/79	25		16	D2
Dunfermline A		79/80	39		17	D1
		80/81	39		20	D1
		81/82	30	1	13	D1
Ayr U		82/83	21	5	3	D1
		83/84	14	6	5	D1
East Stirlingshire		84/85	5		2	D2
Stenhousemuir		84/85	20	1	6	D2
		85/86	19	6	6	D2

McNAUGHTON Brian
b. Edinburgh 22.1.1963

Broxburn A						
Heart of Midlothian		84/85	3	5	2	P
		85/86	2	2		P
East Fife		86/87	36	3	15	D1
		87/88	14		7	D1
		88/89	17	3	7	D2
Forfar A		88/89	8	2	4	D1
		89/90	0	4		D1
Meadowbank T		89/90	24	4	8	D1
		90/91	3	4		D1
		91/92	0	5	1	D1
Arbroath		91/92	24	1	7	D2
		92/93	12	6	3	D2

McNEIL Donald
b. Glasgow 20.2.1958

Eastercraigs						
Dumbarton		75/76	11	3		D1
		76/77	14	8		D1
		77/78	31	1	2	D1
		78/79	22		3	D1
		79/80	24	1	4	D1
		80/81	2			D1
		81/82	18	1	1	D1
		82/83	27	1		D1
		83/84	31	1	3	D1
		84/85	24	3	1	P
		85/86	16		1	D1
		86/87	12		1	D1
		87/88	24		1	D1

McNEIL John
b. Greenock 12.2.1959

Morton		75/76	3	2		D1
		76/77	9	8	1	D1
		77/78	4	11	1	D1
		78/79	21	6	4	P
		79/80	16	3	2	P
		80/81	20	6	4	P
		81/82	22	5	5	P
Dundee U	L	82/83	0	1		P
Morton		82/83	18	4	3	P
		83/84	34	3	17	D1
		84/85	13	8	3	P
		85/86	29	1	14	D1
		86/87	31	7	10	D1
		87/88	12	4	1	P
		88/89	10	5	1	D1
		89/90	7	1	1	D1
		90/91	3			D1

McNICOLL David
b. 23.9.1951

Butterburn YC						
Dunfermline A		69/70	20			D1
		70/71	24	1	2	D1
		71/72	34		1	D1
		72/73	36		2	D2
		73/74	8			D1
		74/75	9		1	D1
Montrose		75/76	26		3	D1
		76/77	31		3	D1
		77/78	12			D1
Heart of Midlothian		77/78	27		1	D1
		78/79	16	1		P
St Johnstone		79/80	16	1	1	D1
East Fife		80/81	1			D2

McPARLAND John Ian
b. Edinburgh 4.10.1961

Ormiston Primrose						
Notts Co		80/81	0	2		FL
		81/82	7	5		FL
		82/83	4	7	1	FL
		83/84	15	6	2	FL
		84/85	16	4		FL
		85/86	43	1	15	FL
		86/87	45		24	FL
		87/88	41	2	21	FL
		88/89	19	4	6	FL
Hull C		88/89	11		1	FL
		89/90	13	7	5	FL
		90/91	7	9	1	FL
Walsall	L	90/91	11		6	FL
Dunfermline A		91/92	11	5	2	P
Lincoln C		92/93	3	1		FL
Northampton T		92/93	11		3	FL
Hong Kong		93/94				
		94/95				
Hamilton A		95/96	0	1		D1
Berwick R		96/97	8	1		D2

McPHAIL John
b. Dundee 7.12.1955

Dundee		75/76	5	1		P
		76/77	23	2		D1
		77/78	34			D1
		78/79	2	1		D1
Sheffield U		78/79	15		1	FL
		79/80	44		5	FL
		80/81	39			FL
		81/82	26		1	FL
		82/83	11			FL
York C		82/83	11	1	2	FL
		83/84	46		10	FL
		84/85	42		5	FL
		85/86	42		7	FL
Bristol C		86/87	26			FL
Sunderland		87/88	46		16	FL
		88/89	45		4	FL
		89/90	38		2	FL
		90/91	1			FL
Hartlepool U		90/91	42		1	FL
		91/92	40	1	1	FL
		92/93	42		1	FL
		93/94	29	3	1	FL
		94/95	6			FL

McPHEE Ian
b. Perth 31.1.1961

Forfar A		78/79	11	1	1	D2
		79/80	38	1	6	D2
		80/81	35		1	D2
		81/82	30	1	4	D2
		82/83	39		6	D2
		83/84	39		5	D2
		84/85	39		3	D1
		85/86	37		2	D1
		86/87	41		4	D1
		87/88	1			D1
Dundee U		87/88	9	1	1	P
		88/89	1	1	1	P
Airdrieonians		88/89	27		3	D1
		89/90	19		1	D1
		90/91	36		1	D1
		91/92	0	1		P
Forfar A		91/92	16			D1
		92/93	36		3	D2
		93/94	35		2	D2
		94/95	32	1	4	D3
		95/96	19			D2
		96/97	6	3	1	D3
		97/98	4		1	D2

MacPHERSON Angus Ian
b. Glasgow 11.10.1968

Rangers		89/90				
Exeter C	L	89/90	11		1	FL
Kilmarnock		90/91	11			D1
		91/92	42	1	3	D1
		92/93	39	1	5	D1
		93/94	43		2	P
		94/95	33		1	P
		95/96	35		1	P
		96/97	33			P
		97/98	25			P
		98/99	31		1	P
		99/00	30		1	P

McPHERSON David
b. Paisley 28.1.1964

Gartcosh U					
Rangers	82/83	15	5	1	P
	83/84	32	4	2	P
	84/85	27	4		P
	85/86	34		5	P
	86/87	42		8	P
Heart of Midlothian	87/88	44		4	P
	88/89	32		4	P
	89/90	35		4	P
	90/91	34		2	P
	91/92	44		2	P
Rangers	92/93	34		2	P
	93/94	27	1	1	P
	94/95	9			P
Heart of Midlothian	94/95	23		2	P
	95/96	22	4	1	P
	96/97	26		1	P
	97/98	10	3	3	P
	98/99	17	1		P

McQUADE Denis
b. 6.1.1951

St Rochs					
Partick T	69/70	0	1		D1
	70/71				
	71/72	26	6	12	D1
	72/73	23	7	5	D1
	73/74	3	6		D1
	74/75	33		7	D1
	75/76	16	6	7	D1
	76/77	16	4	4	P
	77/78	10	4	1	P
	78/79	13	9	4	P
Heart of Midlothian	78/79	13	9	4	P
Hamilton A	79/80	7	6	2	D1

McQUEEN Eric
b. Johnstone 31.12.1963

Beith					
St Mirren	84/85				
	85/86	1	2		P
	86/87				
Stranraer	87/88	31		1	D2
	88/89	8		1	D2
Kilmarnock	88/89	4			D1

McQUEEN Thomas Feeney
b. Bellshill 1.4.1963

Clyde	81/82	39			D2
	82/83	36			D1
	83/84	38		1	D1
Aberdeen	84/85	33	2	3	P
	85/86	15	2	1	P
	86/87	1			P
West Ham U	86/87	9			FL
	87/88	10	2		FL
	88/89	0	2		FL
	89/90	5	2		FL
Falkirk	90/91	32		2	P
	91/92	26		1	P
	92/93	30		4	P
	93/94	26			D1
	94/95	3	1		P
Dundee	95/96	21			D1
	96/97	15	1		D1

McQUILKEN James Charles
b. Glasgow 3.10.1974

Celtic	92/93	1			P
	93/94				
	94/95				
	95/96	3	1		P
Dundee U	95/96	6	3		D1
	96/97	6	3		P
Hibernian	96/97	9			P
	97/98	1			P
Falkirk	98/99	21	1		D1
	99/00	28	3	1	D1

McQUILLAN John
b. Stranraer 20.7.1970

Stranraer	85/86	0	1		D2
	86/87				
Dundee	87/88				
	88/89				
	89/90	1	1		P
	90/91	8	6	1	D1
	91/92	39	1	3	D1
	92/93	27	2		P
	93/94	27	7	1	P
	94/95	30	2		D1
St Johnstone	95/96	25		2	D1
	96/97	32			D1
	97/98	34		1	P
	98/99	27	1	1	P
	99/00	11			P
Dundee U	99/00	18		1	P

McSHANE Patrick
b. 21.10.1960

Heart of Midlothian	79/80	0	2		D1
	80/81	3	1	1	P
	81/82				
East Stirlingshire	82/83	0	5		D2
Albion R	82/83	1	1		D2

McSHERRY James
b. Larkhall 12.2.1952

Fairholm Amateurs					
Lesmagahow					
Kilmarnock	70/71	7	2		D1
	71/72	33		1	D1
	72/73	27		4	D1
	73/74	32	1	3	D2
	74/75	12	1		D1
Ayr U	75/76	28	5		P
	76/77	29	3	2	P
	77/78	21	5		P
	78/79	27	5	5	D1
	79/80	31	4	3	D1
	80/81	9	7		D1
	81/82	12	4		D1
Berwick R	82/83	24		1	D2
Stirling A	82/83	7			D2
Pezoporikos	83/84				
Stirling A	84/85	7	4		D2

McSKIMMING Shaun Peter
b. Stranraer 29.5.1970

Stranraer					
Dundee	87/88	1			P
	88/89				
	89/90	6	1		P
	90/91	15	1	3	D1
Kilmarnock	91/92	23	7	1	D1
	92/93	35		5	D1
	93/94	40		3	P
	94/95	8			P
Motherwell	94/95	10	4	2	P
	95/96	13	2	1	P
	96/97	23		4	P
	97/98	11	1		P
Dundee	98/99	25	4	2	P
	99/00	7	5		P

McSTAY John
b. Larkhall 24.12.1965

Gartcosh U					
Motherwell	83/84	0	1		P
	84/85	4	2	1	D1
	85/86	5	5		P
	86/87	2	2		P
Raith R	87/88	37	2	6	D1
	88/89	37		5	D1
	89/90	38		3	D1
	90/91	36		1	D1
	91/92	34		2	D1
	92/93	41		5	D1
	93/94	35	2	2	P
Falkirk	94/95	0	1		P
Hamilton A	94/95	2			D1
Clydebank	94/95	19	1		D1
East Fife	95/96	34		1	D2
	96/97	9			D1
Ayr U	96/97	6	4		D2
Clyde	97/98	35		5	D2
Albion R	98/99	32		3	D3
	99/00	26	1	6	D3

McSTAY Paul Michael Lyons
b. Hamilton 22.10.1964

Hamilton Thistle					
Celtic	81/82	7	3	1	P
	82/83	36		6	P
	83/84	34		3	P
	84/85	32		4	P
	85/86	34		8	P
	86/87	43		3	P
	87/88	44		5	P
	88/89	33		5	P
	89/90	35		3	P
	90/91	30		2	P
	91/92	32		7	P
	92/93	43		4	P
	93/94	35		2	P
	94/95	28	1	1	P
	95/96	29	1	2	P
	96/97	14	1	1	P

McSTAY William James
b. Hamilton 26.11.1961

Celtic		82/83	0	1		P
		83/84	15	4	1	P
		84/85	11	3	1	P
		85/86	14	4		P
		86/87	15	1		P
Huddersfield T		86/87	0	1		FL
		87/88	4	4		FL
Notts Co		87/88	6	3		FL
		88/89	27	6	1	FL
		89/90	0	3		FL
Hartlepool U	L	89/90	3			FL
Partick T	L	89/90	4	1		D1
Kilmarnock		90/91	18	2		D1
		91/92	5	4		P
		92/93	0	1		P
Sligo R						

McSWEGAN Gary
b. Glasgow 24.9.1970

Rangers	87/88	0	1		P
	88/89	0	1		P
	89/90				
	90/91	1	2		P
	91/92	0	4		P
	92/93	8	1	4	P
Notts Co	93/94	28	9	15	FL
	94/95	19	3	6	FL
	95/96	0	3		FL
Dundee U	95/96	19	6	17	D1
	96/97	15	16	7	P
	97/98	17	14	5	P
	98/99	5		3	P
Heart of Midlothian	98/99	17	4	7	P
	99/00	23	7	13	P

McVEIGH John
b. Coatbridge 25.1.1957

Coatbridge St Patricks					
Airdrieonians	75/76	3	3		D1
	76/77	19	2	4	D1
	77/78	25	5	3	D1
	78/79	11		4	D1
	79/80	11	3	2	D1
	80/81	4	1		P
Brisbane C	81/82				
Clyde	82/83	29		2	D1
	83/84	35			D1
	84/85	37		2	D1
	85/86	34		2	D1
Hamilton A	86/87	18	2		P
Kilmarnock	86/87	18		4	D1
	87/88	11	1		D1
Falkirk	87/88	20	1		P
	88/89	2	1		D1

McVICAR Donald Fredrick
b. Perth 6.11.1962

Blairgowrie					
St Johnstone	81/82	8	5		D1
	82/83	25	1		D1
	83/84	20	1		P
	84/85	26		1	D1
Tranmere R	85/86	7			FL
Montrose	85/86	8	4		D1
	86/87	4	2		D1
St Johnstone	86/87	23		2	D2
	87/88	38		1	D2
	88/89	28		3	D1
	89/90	35		3	D1
	90/91	18	5	1	P
	91/92	3	1		P
Partick T	91/92	10			D1
	92/93	38			P
Airdrieonians	93/94	20	1		D1
Ayr U	93/94	10			D1
	94/95	5			D1
Forfar A	94/95	15	1	1	D3
	95/96	23			D2
Arbroath	95/96	8			D3
	96/97	20	1	2	D3

McVIE William
b. 7.8.1948

Lesmagahow Jnrs					
Clyde	68/69	4			D1
	69/70	7	1		D1
	70/71	5	1		D1
	71/72	16	1	2	D1
	72/73	12	3	5	D2
	73/74	24	2	2	D1
	74/75	34		1	D1
Motherwell	75/76	32		1	P
	76/77	12	1	1	P
	77/78	25	1		P
	78/79	16			P
Toronto Blizzard	79	25			NA
	80	3			NA
Heart of Midlothian	80/81	12			P
Blantyre V					

McWALTER Mark Nicoll
b. Arbroath 20.6.1968

Club		Season	Apps	Sub	Gls	Lge
Arbroath		84/85	9	5	2	D2
		85/86	35	2	14	D2
		86/87	17	2	4	D2
St Mirren		87/88	3	1		P
		88/89	22	10	5	P
		89/90	13	9		P
		90/91	16	6	3	P
Partick T		91/92	5	2		D1
		92/93	7	5		P
Ballymena U		93/94				
		94/95				
		95/96				
Arbroath		96/97	23	1	3	D3
		97/98	28	2	6	D3
		98/99	3	2		D2

McWHIRTER Norman
b. Johnstone 4.9.1969
Linwood

Club		Season	Apps	Sub	Gls	Lge
St Mirren		86/87	1	4		P
		87/88	22	2	1	P
		88/89	1	3		P
		89/90	20	1		P
		90/91	25			P
		91/92	9	2		P
		92/93	34		1	D1
		93/94	27		7	D1
		94/95	23		1	D1
		95/96	17			D1
		96/97	26	1		D1
		97/98	32		1	D1
		98/99	24	1		D1

McWILLIAM Ian
b. Malta 19.3.1953
Duntocher Hibs

Club		Season	Apps	Sub	Gls	Lge
Queens Park		74/75	10	1	1	D2
		75/76	15			D2
		76/77	19	1	3	D2
Celtic		77/78	1			P
Seiko		78/79				
		79/80				
Blackpool	T	80/81				
Rutherglen Glencairn						

McWILLIAMS Derek
b. Broxburn 16.1.1966
Broxburn A

Club		Season	Apps	Sub	Gls	Lge
Dundee		84/85	7	8	2	P
		85/86	6	5	1	P
		86/87	4	2		P
Stirling A	L	86/87	3	1		D2
Falkirk		87/88	31		4	P
		88/89	28		11	D1
		89/90	32		16	D1
		90/91	29		10	D1
Dunfermline A		91/92	21	3	3	P
		92/93	22	3	3	D1
		93/94	12	8	3	D1
Partick T		94/95	27	2	3	P
		95/96	25	2	3	P
		96/97	19	4	2	D1
Clydebank		97/98	26		7	D2
		98/99	5	4	1	D1
		99/00	14	6		D1
Partick T		99/00	7		3	D2

NAPIER Craig Cameron
b. East Kilbride 14.11.1965
Kirkton U

Club		Season	Apps	Sub	Gls	Lge
Clyde		84/85	1	15		D1
		85/86	3	5		D1
		86/87	42			D1
		87/88	42		1	D1
		88/89	14			D1
Hamilton A		88/89	19	1		P
		89/90	39		6	D1
		90/91	39		6	D1
		91/92	18	4	2	D1
		92/93	27	2	1	D1
		93/94	27		2	D1
Kilmarnock		93/94	10	5		P
		94/95	2	1		P
Falkirk		95/96	3	1		P
Ayr U		95/96	10			D2

NAREY David
b. Dundee 21.6.1956
St Columba BC
Dundee
Chelsea

Club		Season	Apps	Sub	Gls	Lge
Dundee U		73/74	10	2		D1
		74/75	31		6	D1
		75/76	33			P
		76/77	32		2	P
		77/78	35			P
		78/79	36		5	P
		79/80	35		1	P
		80/81	32			P
		81/82	34		1	P
		82/83	36		5	P
		83/84	34		1	P
		84/85	29		1	P
		85/86	35			P
		86/87	33			P
		87/88	39			P
		88/89	33			P
		89/90	31			P
		90/91	4			P
		91/92	24			P
		92/93	27	1		P
		93/94	6			P
Raith R		94/95	21		1	D1

NAYSMITH Gary Andrew
b. Edinburgh 16.11.1978
Whitehill Welfare

Club		Season	Apps	Sub	Gls	Lge
Heart of Midlothian		95/96	0	1		P
		96/97	10			P
		97/98	16		2	P
		98/99	23	3		P
		99/00	34	1	1	P

NEGRI Marco
b. Milan 27.10.1970

Club		Season	Apps	Sub	Gls	Lge
Udinese		88/89				
Novara		89/90				
Udinese		90/91				
		91/92				
Ternana		91/92				
		92/93				
Cosenza		92/93				
		93/94				
Bologna		93/94				
Cosenza		94/95				
Perugia		95/96				
		96/97				
Rangers		97/98	28	1	32	P
		98/99				
		99/00				

NELSON Craig Robert
b. Coatbridge 28.5.1971
Cork C

Club		Season	Apps	Sub	Gls	Lge
Partick T		90/91	1			D1
		91/92	11			D1
		92/93	27			P
		93/94	39			P
		94/95	13			P
Heart of Midlothian		94/95	20			P
		95/96	4			P
Falkirk		96/97	20			D1
		97/98	7			D1
Ayr U		98/99	15			D1
		99/00	18			D1

NELSON Martin
b. Glasgow 9.5.1967
Rutherglen Glencairn
Dumbarton

Club		Season	Apps	Sub	Gls	Lge
Alloa A		86/87	34		3	D2
		87/88	27		6	D2
Hamilton A		87/88	2			D1
		88/89	2	5		P
Raith R		88/89	8	1	2	D1
		89/90	27	5	4	D1
		90/91	33		4	D1
		91/92	32	2	3	D1
Montrose		92/93	5		1	D2
Clydebank		93/94	0	3		D1
Dumbarton		93/94	0	3		D1
Alloa A *		94/95	17	8	1	D3

NEVIN Patrick Kevin Francis Michael
b. Glasgow 6.9.1963
Gartcosh U

Club		Season	Apps	Sub	Gls	Lge
Clyde		81/82	25	9	12	D2
		82/83	35	4	5	D1
Chelsea		83/84	38		14	FL
		84/85	41		4	FL
		85/86	39	1	7	FL
		86/87	36	1	5	FL
		87/88	36	1	6	FL
Everton		88/89	20	5	2	FL
		89/90	23	7	4	FL
		90/91	31	6	8	FL
		91/92	7	10	2	FL
Tranmere R		91/92	8			FL
		92/93	43		13	FL
		93/94	45		8	FL
		94/95	44		4	FL
		95/96	39	1	3	FL
		96/97	10	11	2	FL
Kilmarnock		97/98	26	5	5	P
		98/99	2	1	1	P
Motherwell		98/99	14	16		P
		99/00	6	22	2	P

NEWELL Michael Colin
b. Liverpool 27.1.1965
Liverpool

Club		Season	Apps	Sub	Gls	Lge
Crewe A		83/84	3			FL
Wigan A		83/84	5	4		FL
		84/85	35	4	9	FL
		85/86	24		16	FL
Luton T		85/86	16		6	FL
		86/87	42		12	FL
		87/88	4	1		FL
Leicester C		87/88	36		8	FL
		88/89	45		13	FL
Everton		89/90	20	6	7	FL
		90/91	20	9	7	FL
		91/92	8	5	1	FL
Blackburn R		91/92	18	2	6	FL
		92/93	40		13	FL
		93/94	27	1	6	FL
		94/95	2	10		FL
		95/96	26	4	3	FL
Birmingham C		96/97	11	4	1	FL
West Ham U	L	96/97	6	1		FL
Bradford C	L	96/97	7			FL
Aberdeen		97/98	18	3	4	P
		98/99	14	9	2	P

NEWMAN Robert Nigel
b. Bradford on Avon 13.12.1963

Club		Season	Apps	Sub	Gls	Lge
Bristol C		81/82	15	6	3	FL
		82/83	42	1	3	FL
		83/84	29	1	1	FL
		84/85	34		3	FL
		85/86	37	2	3	FL
		86/87	43	2	6	FL
		87/88	44		11	FL
		88/89	46		6	FL
		89/90	46		8	FL
		90/91	46		8	FL
Norwich C		91/92	41		7	FL
		92/93	16	2	2	FL
		93/94	32		2	FL
		94/95	23	9	1	FL
		95/96	15	8	1	FL
		96/97	44		1	FL
		97/98	10	5		FL
Wigan A	L	97/98	8			FL
Motherwell		97/98	11			P

NICHOLAS Charles
b. Glasgow 30.12.1961
St Columba of Iona

Club		Season	Apps	Sub	Gls	Lge
Celtic		80/81	26	3	16	P
		81/82	7	3	3	P
		82/83	35		29	P
Arsenal		83/84	41		11	FL
		84/85	35	3	9	FL
		85/86	41		10	FL
		86/87	25	3	4	FL
		87/88	3			FL
Aberdeen		87/88	16		3	P
		88/89	28	1	16	P
		89/90	32	1	11	P
Celtic		90/91	12	2	6	P
		91/92	32	5	21	P
		92/93	12	4	2	P
		93/94	30	5	8	P
		94/95	5	7		P
Clyde		95/96	31		5	D2

NICHOLAS Peter
b. Newport 10.11.1959

Crystal Palace		77/78	23		1	FL
		78/79	37		3	FL
		79/80	39		2	FL
		80/81	28		1	FL
Arsenal		80/81	8		1	FL
		81/82	28	3		FL
		82/83	21			FL
Crystal Palace		83/84	25		3	FL
		84/85	22		4	FL
Luton T		84/85	19			FL
		85/86	41			FL
		86/87	42		1	FL
Aberdeen		87/88	39		3	P
Chelsea		88/89	39		1	FL
		89/90	29			FL
		90/91	11	1	1	FL
Watford		90/91	15			FL
		91/92	25		1	FL

NICHOLAS Steven
b. Stirling 8.7.1981

Stirling A		97/98	0	7		D1
		98/99	27		5	D2
Motherwell		98/99	1	6	1	P
		99/00	2	19	1	P

NICHOLL James Michael
b. Canada 28.12.1956

Manchester U		74/75	0	1		FL
		75/76	15	5		FL
		76/77	39			FL
		77/78	37		2	FL
		78/79	19	2		FL
		79/80	42			FL
		80/81	36		1	FL
		81/82	0	1		FL
Sunderland	L	81/82	3			FL
Toronto Blizzard		82				
Sunderland		82/83	29			FL
Rangers		83/84	17			P
Toronto Blizzard		84				
WBA		84/85	27			FL
		85/86	29			FL
Rangers		86/87	33	1		P
		87/88	21	1		P
		88/89	1			P
Dunfermline A		89/90	17			P
		90/91	7			P
Raith R		90/91	10			D1
		91/92	32		1	D1
		92/93	38		4	D1
		93/94	33	1	1	P
		94/95	13			D1
		95/96	0	1		P

NICHOLLS David Clarkson
b. Bellshill 5.4.1972

Ferguslie U						
Hibernian		90/91	1			P
		91/92	5			P
Coleraine		92/93				
Hamilton A		93/94	4			D1
		94/95	3			D1
Cork C		94/95				
Clydebank		95/96	35		3	D1
		96/97	32	1	2	D1
		97/98	32		1	D2
		98/99	34		1	D1
Falkirk		99/00	32	1	12	D1

NICHOLSON Barry
b. Dumfries 24.8.1978

Rangers		98/99	3	3		P
		99/00	0	1		P

NICOL Andrew
b. Falkirk 3.12.1960

Falkirk		78/79	2			D2
		79/80				
		80/81	15			D1
		81/82	39			D1
		82/83	39			D1
		83/84	39			D1
		84/85	34		2	D1
		85/86	35			D1
		86/87	22	2		P
		87/88	31			P
		88/89	38			D1
		89/90				
		90/91	10	1		D1
Meadowbank T		91/92	33	1	1	D1
		92/93	11			D1

NICOLL David

St Johnstone		74/75	2			D1
		75/76	4			P
		76/77	6			P
Forfar A		77/78	32			D2

NICOLSON Keith Derek
b. Perth 16.7.1968

East Craigie Jnrs						
St Johnstone		87/88	1			D2
		88/89	3			D1
		89/90	1			D1
		90/91	5			P
Brechin C		91/92	16		2	D2
		92/93				
		93/94	24	3	1	D1
		94/95	9			D2

NIEMI Antti
b. Oulu 31.5.1972

HJK Helsinki		91				
		92				
		93				
		94				
		95				
FC Copenhagen		95/96				
		96/97				
Rangers		97/98	5			P
		98/99	7			P
		99/00	1			P
Charlton A	L	99/00				
Heart of Midlothian		99/00	17			P

NIJHOLT Luc
b. Zaandam 29.7.1961

Haarlem						
AZ67 Alkmaar						
FC Utrect						
FC Basel						
Motherwell		90/91	21	2		P
		91/92	39		5	P
		92/93	31	3		P
Swindon T		93/94	31	1	1	FL
		94/95	35			FL

NISBET Scott
b. Edinburgh 30.1.1968

Rangers		85/86	4	1		P
		86/87	0	1		P
East Fife		86/87	6			D1
Rangers		87/88	22	3		P
		88/89	5	2	1	P
		89/90	4	3		P
		90/91	15			P
		91/92	20		5	P
		92/93	10			P

NISH Colin
b. Edinburgh 7.3.1981

Dunfermline A		98/99	0	2		P
		99/00	0	2		D1
Alloa A		99/00	9	4	5	D2

NIXON Jerren Kendall
b. Trinidad 25.6.1973

EMC Motown						
Dundee U		93/94	7	8	1	P
		94/95	8	20	6	P
FC Zurich		95/96				
		96/97				
Watford	L	96/97				

NOTMAN Alexander
b. Edinburgh 10.12.1979

Manchester U		96/97				
		97/98				
		98/99				
Aberdeen	L	98/99	0	2		P
Manchester U		99/00				
Sheffield U	L	99/00	7	3		FL

NUMAN Arthur
b. Heemskerk 14.12.1969

SV Eindhoven						
Rangers		98/99	8	2		P
		99/00	29	1	1	P

NYYSSONEN Kai Juhani
b. Kuopio 10.6.1972

Finland						
Belgium						
CD Cordoba						
Motherwell		98/99	3		1	P

O'BOYLE George
b. Belfast 14.12.1967

Linfield						
Dunfermline A		89/90	28		3	P
		90/91	15	1	6	P
		91/92	12	4	1	P
		92/93	3		2	D1
		93/94	28	4	17	D1
St Johnstone		94/95	32		19	D1
		95/96	35		21	D1
		96/97	23	2	12	D1
		97/98	29	4	10	P
		98/99	12	1	2	P
		99/00	4	4		P

O'BRIEN Gerard
b. Glasgow 10.11.1949

Clydebank		68/69				
Southampton		69/70	5			FL
		70/71	2			FL
		71/72	21	2	1	FL
		72/73	10	1		FL
		73/74	2	6		FL
Bristol R	L	73/74	3			FL
Southampton		74/75	19	1	1	FL
Swindon T		75/76	12			FL
		76/77	12	3		FL
Clydebank		77/78	24		1	P
Hibernian		78/79	2	5		P

O'BRIEN Paul
b. Edinburgh 27.4.1962

Dundee U						
Heart of Midlothian		80/81	13	2	2	P
		81/82	0	1		D1
St Johnstone		81/82	4	7		D1
		82/83	1	4		D1
Liberton Cropley		83/84				
		84/85				
		85/86				
		86/87				
East Stirlingshire		87/88	34		5	D2
		88/89	15	6	1	D2
		89/90	16	1	3	D2
		90/91	7			D2

O'BRIEN Paul Patrick
b. Glasgow 3.12.1965

Queens Park		86/87	36	1	11	D2
		87/88	37	1	17	D2
		88/89	22	9	4	D2
		89/90	39		9	D2
Dunfermline A		90/91	0	2		P
		91/92				
Brechin C		92/93	20	3	2	D2
		93/94	10	4		D1
?		94/95				
		95/96				
		96/97				
Queens Park		97/98	26	4	4	D3

O'CONNOR Derek A
b. Edinburgh 8.1.1955

East Fife		73/74	9	4	2	D1
		74/75	18	1	7	D2
		75/76	17	1	4	D1
		76/77	14	1	4	D1
St Johnstone		76/77	12	1	3	D1
		77/78	37	1	19	D1
		78/79	11		1	D1
Heart of Midlothian		78/79	18		8	P
		79/80	25	2	12	D1
		80/81	13	3	4	P
		81/82	12	2	4	D1
Berwick R	L	81/82	10		6	D2
Heart of Midlothian		82/83	37	1	17	D1
		83/84	5	6	1	P
		84/85	0	3	1	P
Meadowbank T		84/85	6		1	D1
Dunfermline A		84/85	9		1	D2
Brechin C		84/85	5	2	1	D1
Berwick R		85/86	12	2	6	D2
		86/87	24	7	6	D2

O'CONNOR Gary
b. Newtongrange 7.4.1974

Berwick R		92/93	13			D2
		93/94	26			D2
		94/95				
Heart of Midlothian		95/96	3			P
Doncaster R		95/96	8			FL
		96/97	18			FL
Partick T		97/98	3			D1
Berwick R		97/98	27			D3
		98/99	35			D3
		99/00	29			D3

O'CONNOR Sean
b. Wolverhampton 7.8.1981

Hednesford T						
Dundee U		99/00	1			P

O'DONNELL Philip
b. Bellshill 25.3.1972

Motherwell		90/91	11	1		P
		91/92	42		4	P
		92/93	32		4	P
		93/94	35		7	P
		94/95	3			P
Celtic		94/95	25	2	6	P
		95/96	14	1	3	P
		96/97	19		2	P
		97/98	6	8	2	P
		98/99	13	2	2	P

O'DRISCOLL Jerry
b. Aberdeen 4.4.1978

Crombie Jnrs						
Dundee		95/96	1	4	1	D1
		96/97	18	3	10	D1
		97/98	1	12	1	D1
		98/99	0	1		P
Arbroath		98/99	3	1		D2
Montrose		98/99	9			D3
		99/00	20	4	5	D3

O'HALLORAN Keith James
b. Dublin 27.3.1977

Cherry Orchard BC						
Middlesbrough		94/95	1			FL
		95/96	2	1		FL
Scunthorpe U	L	95/96	6	1		FL
Cardiff C	L	96/97	8			FL
St Johnstone		96/97	4	1		D1
		97/98	11	11	1	P
		98/99	10	6	1	P
		99/00	31	1	1	P

OHANLON Kelham Gerard
b. Saltburn 16.5.1962

Middlesbrough		82/83	19			FL
		83/84	30			FL
		84/85	38			FL
Rotherham U		85/86	46			FL
		86/87	40			FL
		87/88	40			FL
		88/89	46			FL
		89/90	43			FL
		90/91	33			FL
Carlisle U		91/92	42			FL
		92/93	41			FL
Preston NE		93/94	23			FL
Dundee U		94/95	29			P
		95/96	2			D1
Preston NE		96/97	13			FL

O'HARA Alexander C
b. Glasgow 21.10.1956

Rangers		73/74	18	1	4	D1
		74/75	2	2	1	D1
		75/76	1	3		P
		76/77	5		2	P
Partick T		77/78	25	3	10	P
		78/79	26	8	8	P
		79/80	33	1	5	P
		80/81	32		7	P
		81/82	17	6	3	P
		82/83	32		3	D1
		83/84	21	3	8	D1
Morton		84/85	24	3	1	P
		85/86	32	1	4	D1
		86/87	40		2	D1
		87/88	35	5	1	P
		88/89	21	2		D1
		89/90	19	10	3	D1
Hamilton A		90/91	19	5	1	D1
Glenafton A						

O'HARA Thomas
b. Bellshill 17.8.1953

St Columbas BG						
Celtic						
Kirkintilloch Rob Roy	L					
Queen of the South		74/75	37	1	5	D2
		75/76	22			D1
		76/77	39		2	D1
		77/78	22			D1
Washington Diplomats		78	28			NA
Queen of the South		78/79	13			D1
Washington Diplomats		79	29		2	NA
		80	32			NA
Jacksonville Teamen		81	31			NA
Motherwell		81/82	17	3		D1
		82/83	30	3		P
Falkirk		83/84	33	3	3	D1
Partick T		84/85	15	2		D1

O'LEARY Pierce
b. Dublin 5.11.1959

Shamrock R		77/78				
Philadelphia Fury		78	14			NA
Shamrock R		78/79				
		79/80				
		80/81				
Vancouver Whitecaps		81	22		1	NA
		82	15			NA
		83	16			NA
		84	8			NA
Celtic		84/85	11			P
		85/86	12	1		P
		86/87	15	1	1	P
		87/88				

OLIVER Neil
b. Berwick 11.4.1967

Berwick R		85/86	3	2		D2
		86/87	36	1		D2
		87/88	10	2		D2
		88/89	39			D2
Blackburn R		89/90	3			FL
		90/91	2	1		FL
Falkirk		91/92	34	1		P
		92/93	24	1		P
		93/94	31	2	2	D1
		94/95	26	1		P
		95/96	3			P
		96/97	14	1	1	D1
		97/98	23	1		D1
		98/99	7	1		D1
Hamilton A		98/99	6			D1
Clydebank		99/00	18			D1
Berwick R		99/00	9			D3

OLOFSSON Kjell
b. Gothenburg 23.7.1965

Moss						
Dundee U		96/97	22	3	12	P
		97/98	31	1	18	P
		98/99	32	2	7	P

OMOYINMI Emmanuel
b. Nigeria 28.12.1977

West Ham U		96/97	0	1		FL
Bournemouth	L	96/97	5	2		FL
West Ham U		97/98	1	4	2	FL
Dundee U	L	97/98	1	3		P
West Ham U		98/99	0	3		FL
Leyton Orient	L	98/99	3	1	1	FL
West Ham U		99/00				
Gillingham	L	99/00	7	2	3	FL
Scunthorpe U	L	99/00	6		1	FL
Barnet	L	99/00	1	5		FL

O'NEIL Brian
b. Paisley 6.9.1972

Old Kilpatrick						
Celtic						
Porirua Viard U	L	91				
Celtic		91/92	25	3	1	P
		92/93	11	6	3	P
		93/94	14	13	2	P
		94/95	24	2		P
		95/96	3	2		P
		96/97	15	1	2	P
Nottingham F	L	96/97	4	1		FL
Aberdeen		97/98	24	4	1	P

O'NEIL John
b. Bellshill 6.7.1971

Dundee U		88/89	0	1		P
		89/90	6	4		P
		90/91	11	4		P
		91/92	11	1		P
		92/93	21	7	3	P
		93/94	8	4	1	P
St Johnstone		94/95	26	1	3	D1
		95/96	34		6	D1
		96/97	25	4	3	D1
		97/98	26	4	5	P
		98/99	33		2	P
		99/00	31	2	3	P

O'NEIL Kris
b. Edinburgh 29.9.1980

Musselburgh Jnrs						
Heart of Midlothian		98/99	0	3		P
Clydebank		99/00	9	3	1	D1

O'NEILL Colin
b. Belfast 14.6.1963

Ards						
Larne						
Ballymena U						
Portadown						
Motherwell		88/89	19		2	P
		89/90	24		1	P
		90/91	21		1	P

O'NEILL John Joseph
b. Glasgow 3.1.1974

Queens Park		91/92	12	13	6	D2
		92/93	19	8	6	D2
		93/94	39		18	D2
Celtic		94/95	0	1		P
		95/96				
Bournemouth		95/96	2	4		FL
		96/97	7	11	1	FL
		97/98	34	9	3	FL
		98/99	18	6	3	FL
		99/00	18	12	3	FL

O'NEILL Martin
b. Glasgow 17.6.1975

Clyde		93/94	8	1	1	D1
		94/95	20	1	2	D2
		95/96	19	4	2	D2
		96/97	21	8	4	D2
Kilmarnock		97/98	0	2		P
Stranraer		98/99	1			D1
Clydebank		99/00	9	8		D1

O'NEILL Michael Andrew Martin
b. Portadown 5.7.1969

Coleraine						
Newcastle U		87/88	19	2	12	FL
		88/89	17	10	3	FL
Dundee U		89/90	15	3	5	P
		90/91	7	6		P
		91/92	5	3	4	P
		92/93	22	3	2	P
Hibernian		93/94	36		3	P
		94/95	33		10	P
		95/96	27	2	6	P
Coventry C		96/97	1			FL
		97/98	2	2		FL
Reading	L	97/98	9		1	FL
Aberdeen		97/98	4	2		P

O'NEILL Thomas
b. Bellshill 24.12.1955

Shotts Bon Accord						
Motherwell		76/77	2	2		P
		77/78	3	5	1	P
Clyde		77/78	14		6	D2
		78/79	34			D1
		79/80	22	3	5	D1
		80/81	37		7	D2
		81/82	38		11	D2
		82/83	34	2	10	D1
		83/84	19	3	2	D1
		84/85	2	7		D1
Hamilton A		84/85	8	1	1	D1
		85/86	38		4	D1
		86/87	9	1		P
Airdrieonians		86/87	21	1	1	D1
New Stevenston Thistle		87/88				
		88/89				
		89/90				
		90/91				
Stirling A		91/92	5			D1

O'ROURKE James

Holycross Academy						
Hibernian		62/63	17		2	D1
		63/64	10		3	D1
		64/65	1			D1
		65/66	21		10	D1
		66/67	23		6	D1
		67/68	13	5	4	D1
		68/69	27	2	6	D1
		69/70	8	3	1	D1
		70/71	18		6	D1
		71/72	25	2	11	D1
		72/73	25	3	17	D1
		73/74	16	3	14	D1
St Johnstone		74/75	34		15	D1
		75/76	34		8	P
Motherwell		76/77	19	4	9	P
		77/78	15	8	5	P

ORR Neil Ian
b. Greenock 13.5.1959

Morton		75/76	4			D1
		76/77	20	4		D1
		77/78	39			D1
		78/79	35			P
		79/80	35		1	P
		80/81	33			P
		81/82	16			P
West Ham U		81/82	24		1	FL
		82/83	9	5		FL
		83/84	28	1		FL
		84/85	17	3		FL
		85/86	33	3	2	FL
		86/87	21	1	1	FL
		87/88	1			FL
Hibernian		87/88	38		1	P
		88/89	33			P
		89/90	24	5	1	P
		90/91	15	2	1	P
		91/92	21	7		P
		92/93	20	1		P
St Mirren		93/94	24		1	D1
		94/95	4	1		D1
Queen of the South		94/95	7		1	D2

O'SULLIVAN Desmond P
b. 12.2.1961

Heart of Midlothian		78/79	2			P
		79/80	2	6	1	D1
Stirling A		80/81	4	1		D1
Stenhousemuir *		81/82	1			D2

PAATELAINEN Mika Matti
b. Helsinki 3.2.1967
Valkeakosken Haka

Dundee U		87/88	17	2	9	P
		88/89	33		10	P
		89/90	27	4	7	P
		90/91	9	11	1	P
		91/92	15	15	6	P
Aberdeen		91/92	6		1	P
		92/93	33		16	P
		93/94	14	22	6	P
Bolton W		94/95	43	1	12	FL
		95/96	12	3	1	FL
		96/97	3	7	2	FL
Wolverhampton W		97/98	10	13		FL
Hibernian		98/99	25	1	12	D1
		99/00	25	6	9	P

PAGE James
b. Dundee 29.10.1964

Dundee U		83/84	1			P
		84/85				
		85/86	0	4		P
		86/87	6	2	1	P

PAGEAUD Michel
b. Paris 30.8.1966
Valenciennes

Dundee U		93/94				
Dundee		93/94	11			P
		94/95	34			D1
		95/96	35			D1
Valenciennes						

PAILLE Stephane
b. 27.6.1965

Heart of Midlothian		96/97	12	7	2	P

PALIN Leigh Granville
b. Worcester 12.9.1965

Aston Villa		83/84				
Shrewsbury T	L	84/85	2			FL
Nottingham F		85/86				
Bradford C		86/87	19	2	3	FL
		87/88	18	2	3	FL
		88/89	28	2	4	FL
Stoke C		89/90	17	2	3	FL
Hull C		89/90	9		1	FL
		90/91	35		5	FL
		91/92	13		1	FL
Rochdale	L	91/92	3			FL
Burnley		92/93	1			FL
Partick T		92/93	5			P

PARK Donald J
b. Inverness 19.7.1953
Inverness Caledonian

Heart of Midlothian		72/73	16	2	6	D1
		73/74	13	2	4	D1
		74/75	7	4	1	D1
		75/76	18	9	3	P
		76/77	26	6	3	P
		77/78	32	1	6	D1
		78/79	2	1	1	P
Partick T		78/79	30	1	2	P
		79/80	29	2	3	P
		80/81	31	2	3	P
		81/82	34	2	5	P
		82/83	33		12	D1
Heart of Midlothian		83/84	26	4	4	P
		84/85	16	6	3	P
Brechin C		85/86	21	12	1	D1
		86/87	4	1		D1
Meadowbank T		86/87	12	2	2	D2
		87/88	27	4	3	D1
		88/89	5	12	2	D1
		89/90	9	11	4	D1
		90/91	2			D1

PARKER Keigan
b. Livingston 8.6.1982

St Johnstone		98/99	0	2		P
		99/00	6	4	2	P

PARKS Anthony
b. Hackney 28.1.1963

Tottenham H		81/82	2			FL
		82/83	1			FL
		83/84	16			FL
		84/85				
		85/86				
		86/87	2			FL
Oxford U	L	86/87	5			FL
Tottenham H		87/88	16			FL
Gillingham	L	87/88	2			FL
Brentford		88/89	33			FL
		89/90	37			FL
		90/91	1			FL
Fulham		90/91	2			FL
West Ham U		91/92	6			FL
Stoke C		92/93	2			FL
Falkirk		92/93	15			P
		93/94	41			D1
		94/95	28			P
		95/96	28			P
Blackpool		96/97				
Burnley		97/98				
Doncaster R	L	97/98	6			FL

PARLANE Derek James
b. Helensburgh 5.5.1953
Queens Park

Rangers		70/71	2	2		D1
		71/72	2			D1
		72/73	29	1	19	D1
		73/74	28	1	14	D1
		74/75	30	1	17	D1
		75/76	17	7	5	P
		76/77	31	2	16	P
		77/78	6	16	5	P
		78/79	21	3	4	P
		79/80	2	1		P
Leeds U		79/80	11		3	FL
		80/81	22	4	5	FL
		81/82	12		2	FL
		82/83	0	1		FL
Hong Kong	L	82/83				
Manchester C		83/84	40	1	16	FL
		84/85	7		4	FL
Swansea C		84/85	21		3	FL
Racing Jet		85/86				
Rochdale		86/87	23		7	FL
		87/88	19		3	FL
Airdrieonians		87/88	9		4	D1

PARTRIDGE David
b. London 26.11.1978
West Ham U

Dundee U		98/99	0	1		P
		99/00	29			P

PASCUAL Bernard
b. Aubervilliers 10.4.1967

Le Havre		93/94				
		94/95				
		95/96				
		96/97				
		97/98				
Dundee U		98/99	16			P
		99/00	30	2		P

PATERSON Craig
b. South Queensferry 2.10.1959
Bonnyrigg Rose

Hibernian		77/78	0	3	1	P
		78/79				
		79/80	30			P
		80/81	38		3	D1
		81/82	36		1	P
Rangers		82/83	20			P
		83/84	21		1	P
		84/85	22		2	P
		85/86	18		1	P
		86/87	2			P
Motherwell		86/87	16		1	P
		87/88	44		2	P
		88/89	33		1	P
		89/90	33		2	P
		90/91	28	4	2	P
Kilmarnock		91/92	28			D1
		92/93	21		1	D1
		93/94	4	2		P
		94/95				
Hamilton A		95/96	9			D1
Glenafton A						
Forth W						

PATERSON Derek
b. Dundee 1.3.1964

Dundee		83/84	2			P
Arbroath		84/85	26	3	3	D2
		85/86	11	7		D2

PATERSON Garry
b. Dunfermline 10.11.1969
Lochore Welfare

Dundee		92/93	11	9	2	P
		93/94	17	3	2	P
Ayr U		94/95	10	1		D1
Dunfermline A		94/95	5			D1
Stirling A		94/95	11		1	D2
		95/96	26		4	D2
		96/97	33		4	D1
		97/98	30			D1
Cowdenbeath *		98/99	1			D3
Montrose		98/99	14		4	D3
		99/00	24		2	D3

PATERSON Ian
b. Cardenden 22.8.1956

Heart of Midlothian		77/78	0	2		D1
		78/79	0	2		P
Brechin C		78/79	1			D2
		79/80	35	3	14	D2
		80/81	21	2	6	D2
		81/82	23	7	8	D2
		82/83	36	3	12	D2
		83/84	7	3	3	D1
Cowdenbeath		83/84	23	3	7	D2
		84/85	30	7	12	D2
		85/86	7	3	3	D2
Falkirk		85/86	2	4	2	D1
Montrose		85/86	5	2		D1
		86/87	37	7	10	D1
		87/88	7	1	1	D2
Brechin C		87/88	30		6	D2
		88/89	32	6	10	D2
		89/90	23	6	5	D2
		90/91	8	10	1	D1
Forfar A		91/92	16	8	2	D1
Brechin C *		92/93	0	2		D2

PATERSON James
b. Bellshill 25.9.1979

Dundee U		98/99	8	7		P
		99/00	8		1	P

PATERSON Jamie Ryan
b. Dumfries 26.4.1973

Halifax T		90/91	3	3	1	FL
		91/92	13	2	2	FL
		92/93	18	5	2	FL
		93/94				
Falkirk		94/95	1	3		P
Scunthorpe U		95/96	23	3	2	FL
		96/97	11	18		FL

PATERSON William

Albion R		74/75	19		2	D2
		75/76	9	1	2	D2
Hibernian		75/76	1	2		P
		76/77	1	4	1	P
		77/78				
Falkirk		78/79	9		3	D2
		79/80	0	2		D2

PATON William

Ayr U		74/75	1			D1
		75/76	11			P
		76/77	2			P

PATTERSON Darren James
b. Belfast 15.10.1969

Club	L	Season	Apps	Sub	Gls	Div
WBA		88/89				
Wigan A		89/90	12	17	1	FL
		90/91	18	10	4	FL
		91/92	39	1	1	FL
Crystal Palace		92/93				
		93/94				
		94/95	22		1	FL
Luton T		95/96	21	2		FL
		96/97	8	2		FL
Preston NE	L	96/97	2			FL
Luton T		97/98	23			FL
Dundee U		98/99	17	2		P
		99/00	6			P

PAYNE Graeme
b. Dundee 13.2.1956

Club	L	Season	Apps	Sub	Gls	Div
Dundee U		73/74	18	5	1	D1
		74/75	8	3		D1
		75/76	15	4	2	P
		76/77	34	2	1	P
		77/78	31	2	1	P
		78/79	19	7	3	P
		79/80	18	1		P
		80/81	19	3	3	P
		81/82	3	3	1	P
		82/83	2	1		P
Morton	L	82/83	16	2	2	P
Dundee U		83/84	0	1		P
Arbroath		83/84	12		1	D2
		84/85	32		3	D2
Brechin C		84/85	5	2	2	D1
		85/86	23	6	1	D1
		86/87	2	2		D1
St Johnstone		86/87	18	8	6	D2

PAYTON Andrew Paul
b. Clitheroe 23.10.1967

Club	L	Season	Apps	Sub	Gls	Div
Hull C		86/87	0	2		FL
		87/88	11	10	2	FL
		88/89	18	10	4	FL
		89/90	34	5	17	FL
		90/91	43		25	FL
		91/92	10		7	FL
Middlesbrough		91/92	8	11	3	FL
Celtic		92/93	19	10	13	P
		93/94	1	6	2	P
Barnsley		93/94	25		12	FL
		94/95	38	5	12	FL
		95/96	37	3	17	FL
Huddersfield T		96/97	38		17	FL
		97/98	4	1		FL
Burnley		97/98	19		9	FL
		98/99	39	1	19	FL
		99/00	39	2	27	FL

PEDERSON Erik
b. Porsgrunn 11.10.1967

Club	L	Season	Apps	Sub	Gls	Div
Viking Stavanger						
Dundee U		96/97	25			P
		97/98	32			P
		98/99	6			P

PEEBLES Gary James
b. Johnstone 6.2.1967

Club	L	Season	Apps	Sub	Gls	Div
St Mirren		86/87	6	1		P
		87/88	1			P
Partick T		88/89	12		1	D1
		89/90	22	2	1	D1
		90/91	26	7	3	D1
		91/92	1	1		D1
		92/93	8	1		P

PELOSI John
b. Glasgow 29.2.1956

Club	L	Season	Apps	Sub	Gls	Div
Possil YM						
Aston Villa						
Motherwell						
Glasgow Perthshire						
St Johnstone		76/77	1	1		D1
		77/78	15	4	4	D1
		78/79	31	1	5	D1
		79/80	29	3	5	D1
		80/81	21	1	5	D1
		81/82	9		2	D1
		82/83	23	5	5	D1
		83/84	0	1		P
Hamilton A		83/84	14		1	D1
		84/85	16	3	2	D1
Kilmarnock	L	84/85	8		1	D1
Hamilton A		85/86	27	4	5	D1
		86/87	12	1		P
Queen of the South		87/88	17	12	1	D1
Stenhousemuir		88/89	2			D2

PENNEY Steven Alexander
b. Ballymena 6.1.1974

Club	L	Season	Apps	Sub	Gls	Div
Ballymena U						
Brighton		83/84	22	3	1	FL
		84/85	24	2	4	FL
		85/86	30	7	3	FL
		86/87	27		3	FL
		87/88	13		3	FL
		88/89	9	1	1	FL
		89/90				
		90/91				
		91/92				
Heart of Midlothian		91/92	3	6		P
Burnley		92/93	10	1	3	FL

PENTILLA Tero
b. Finland 9.3.1975

Club	L	Season	Apps	Sub	Gls	Div
FC Haka						
Rangers		99/00	3			P

PEPPER Colin Nigel
b. Rotherham 2.4.1968

Club	L	Season	Apps	Sub	Gls	Div
Rotherham U		85/86	4	3		FL
		86/87	1	1		FL
		87/88	14	1		FL
		88/89	1	1		FL
		89/90	15	4	1	FL
York C		90/91	38	1	3	FL
		91/92	33	2	4	FL
		92/93	34		8	FL
		93/94	18	5		FL
		94/95	35		4	FL
		95/96	39	1	8	FL
		96/97	26	3	12	FL
Bradford C		96/97	11		5	FL
		97/98	31	1	5	FL
Aberdeen		98/99	7	3		P
		99/00	10	8		P
Southend U	L	99/00	9	3	2	FL

PERRY Mark George
b. Aberdeen 7.2.1971

Club	L	Season	Apps	Sub	Gls	Div
Dundee U		92/93	17	1	1	P
		93/94	8	1		P
		94/95	9			P
		95/96	18	2	2	D1
		96/97	33	2		P
		97/98	32		1	P
Aberdeen		98/99	32		4	P
		99/00	10	8		P

PETRIC Gordan
b. Belgrade 30.7.1969

Club	L	Season	Apps	Sub	Gls	Div
Partizan Belgrade						
Dundee U		93/94	27		1	P
		94/95	33		2	P
Rangers		95/96	32	1	1	P
		96/97	23	3	2	P
		97/98	6			P
		98/99				
Crystal Palace		98/99	18		1	FL
Heart of Midlothian		99/00	17	1		P

PETRIE Stewart James John
b. Dundee 27.2.1970

Club	L	Season	Apps	Sub	Gls	Div
East Craigie						
Forfar A		90/91	32	4	6	D1
		91/92	36	5	7	D1
		92/93	37		21	D2
		93/94	3		3	D2
Dunfermline A		93/94	30	7	6	D1
		94/95	31	2	14	D1
		95/96	31	3	13	D1
		96/97	24	4	3	P
		97/98	19	8	2	P
		98/99	19	11	2	P
		99/00	32		3	D1

PETROV Stilian
b. Bulgaria 5.7.1979

Club	L	Season	Apps	Sub	Gls	Div
CSKA Sofia						
Celtic		99/00	21	6	1	P

PETTA Bobby Alfred Manuel
b. Rotterdam 6.8.1974

Club	L	Season	Apps	Sub	Gls	Div
Feyenoord						
Ipswich T		96/97	1	5		FL
		97/98	28	4	7	FL
		98/99	26	6	2	FL
Celtic		99/00	2	10		P

PETTIGREW William
b. Motherwell 29.9.1953

Club	L	Season	Apps	Sub	Gls	Div
Bonkle Amateurs						
Hibernian						
East Kilbride Thistle						
Motherwell		72/73				
		73/74	10	1	4	D1
		74/75	21	7	20	D1
		75/76	35		22	P
		76/77	35	1	21	P
		77/78	26		7	P
		78/79	30		6	P
Dundee U		79/80	34	1	14	P
		80/81	14	6	6	P
		81/82	2	1	1	P
Heart of Midlothian		81/82	35		16	D1
		82/83	26	7	9	D1
Morton		83/84	17		9	D1
		84/85	10	5	1	P
Hamilton A		84/85	3			D1

PHILLIBEN John
b. Stirling 14.3.1964

Club	L	Season	Apps	Sub	Gls	Div
Gairdoch U						
Stirling A		80/81	15			D1
		81/82	37		1	D2
		82/83	34		1	D2
		83/84	23			D2
Doncaster R		83/84	12			FL
		84/85	33	3	1	FL
		85/86	20	2		FL
Cambridge U	L	85/86	6			FL
Doncaster R		86/87	1			FL
Motherwell		86/87	35	2		P
		87/88	33	2	2	P
		88/89	17	2		P
		89/90	19	5		P
		90/91	11		1	P
		91/92	30	2	1	P
		92/93	31			P
		93/94	18	10	2	P
		94/95	30	1		P
		95/96	19	5		P
		96/97	11	6	1	P
		97/98	10	3		P
Stirling A		98/99	20	2		D2
		99/00	10	7		D2

PHILLIP Iain Frederick
b. Broughty Ferry 12.2.1951

Club	L	Season	Apps	Sub	Gls	Div
Broughty U						
Broughty A						
Dundee		69/70				
		70/71	29	1		D1
		71/72	32			D1
		72/73	4			D1
Crystal Palace		72/73	30		1	FL
		73/74	5			FL
Dundee		73/74	26			D1
		74/75	17			D1
		75/76	23	4		P
		76/77	36		1	D1
		77/78	14	1		D1
		78/79	8		1	D1
Dundee U		78/79	9	1		P
		79/80	26		1	P
		80/81	28	2		P
		81/82	14	1		P
		82/83	5			P
Raith R		83/84	3	6		D1
		84/85	39			D2
		85/86	22			D2
Arbroath		86/87	36			D2
		87/88	24	1		D2

PHILLIPS Gerard
b. Cheltenham 23.6.1956

Club	L	Season	Apps	Sub	Gls	Div
Cumnock Jnrs						
Ayr U		74/75	13	2	4	D1
		75/76	12	3	4	P
		76/77	4	8		P
		77/78	7	3	2	P
		78/79	21	6	14	D1
Queen of the South		79/80	21		11	D2
		80/81	17	2	6	D2
		81/82	24	2	12	D1
Hamilton A		82/83	21		4	D1
		83/84	33	3	8	D1
		84/85	27	7	6	D1
		85/86	6	12	1	D1
		86/87	14	6	2	P
Cumnock Jnrs						

PHILLIPS James Neil
b. Bolton 8.2.1966

Bolton W		83/84	0	1		FL
		84/85	37	3	1	FL
		85/86	33		1	FL
		86/87	33	1		FL
Rangers		86/87	0	6		P
		87/88	19			P
Oxford U		88/89	45		4	FL
		89/90	34		3	FL
Middlesbrough		89/90	12			FL
		90/91	44		2	FL
		91/92	43		2	FL
		92/93	40		2	FL
Bolton W		93/94	41	1		FL
		94/95	46		1	FL
		95/96	37			FL
		96/97	36			FL
		97/98	21	1	1	FL
		98/99	14	1		FL

PIRIE William

Arbroath		71/72	10		7	D2
		72/73	34		14	D2
		73/74	24		12	D2
Aberdeen		73/74	9			D1
		74/75	7	4	4	D1
		75/76	8	10	7	P
Dundee		76/77	33		36	D1
		77/78	39		35	D1
		78/79	30	1	16	D1
		79/80	9		4	P

PITTMAN Stephen Lee
b. Livingston 18.7.1967

East Fife		86/87	5	6		D1
		87/88	29	2	2	D1
		88/89	25		8	D2
Shrewsbury T		88/89	11	1		FL
		89/90	20		2	FL
Dunfermline A	L	89/90				
USA		90/91				
		91/92				
Dundee		92/93	20		1	P
		93/94	35	1	1	P
		94/95	3		1	D1
Partick T		94/95	27		4	P
		95/96	14			P

POCHETTINO Jose Luis
b. 29.7.1965
Cobras

Dundee U		91/92	0	2		P

POINTON Neil Geoffrey
b. Church Warsop 28.11.1964

Scunthorpe U		81/82	5			FL
		82/83	46		1	FL
		83/84	45		1	FL
		84/85	46			FL
		85/86	17			FL
Everton		85/86	14	1		FL
		86/87	10	2	1	FL
		87/88	32		3	FL
		88/89	20	3		FL
		89/90	19		1	FL
Manchester C		90/91	35		1	FL
		91/92	39		1	FL
Oldham A		92/93	34		3	FL
		93/94	23	2		FL
		94/95	32			FL
		95/96	3	1		FL
Heart of Midlothian		95/96	21	1	1	P
		96/97	24	1		P
		07/98	19	1		P

PORRINI Sergio
b. Milan 8.11.1968

AC Milan		88/89				
Atalanta		89/90				
		90/91				
		91/92				
		92/93				
Juventus		93/94				
		94/95				
		95/96				
		96/97				
Rangers		97/98	26		4	P
		98/99	35		2	P
		99/00	11	1		P

PORTEOUS Ian
b. Glasgow 21.11.1964

Aberdeen		82/83	1			P
		83/84	5	9	3	P
		84/85	7	6	1	P
		85/86	0	6		P
		86/87	3	6	2	P
		87/88	1	2	1	P
		88/89				
Kilmarnock		89/90	5	2	1	D2
		90/91				
		91/92	16	8	1	D1
		92/93	17	3	6	D1
		93/94	7	6	1	P
Arbroath		94/95	14		4	D3
		95/96	10	6	4	D3

POTTER Brian
b. Dunfermline 26.1.1977
Rosyth Recreation

Raith R		93/94	1			P

POUNEWATCHY Stephane Zeusnagapa
b. Paris 10.2.1968
Martigues
Gueugnon

Carlisle U		96/97	42		1	FL
		97/98	39		2	FL
Dundee		98/99	2	1		P

POWER Lee Michael
b. Lewisham 30.6.1972

Norwich C		89/90	0	1		FL
		90/91	13	3	3	FL
		91/92	2	2	1	FL
		92/93	11	7	6	FL
Charlton A	L	92/93	5			FL
Norwich C		93/94	2	3		FL
Sunderland	L	93/94	1	2		FL
Portsmouth	L	93/94	1	1		FL
Bradford C		93/94	2	1		FL
		94/95	12	15	3	FL
Peterborough U		95/96	25	13	5	FL
Dundee		96/97	9	1	4	D1
Hibernian		96/97	6		1	P
		97/98	3	2	1	P
Ayr U		97/98	0	4		D1

PREECE David Douglas
b. Sunderland 26.8.1976
Sunderland

Darlington		97/98	45			FL
		98/99	46			FL
Aberdeen		99/00	9	1		P

PREGET Antoine
b. 5.10.1972

Dundee U		99/00	3	1		P
Raith R		99/00	2			D1

PRENTICE Alan
b. Edinburgh 30.10.1964

Meadowbank T		87/88	32	2	7	D1
		88/89	21	1	2	D1
Hamilton A		88/89	9			P
		89/90	4	1		D1
Meadowbank T		89/90	20			D1
		90/91	21	6	2	D1

PRENTICE Robert
b. 27.9.1953

Heart of Midlothian		73/74	26	2	3	D1
		74/75	5	9	2	D1
		75/76	30	3	3	P
		76/77	25	8	2	P
		77/78	17	7	2	D1
		70/79	6	6		P
Toronto Blizzard		79	5			NA
		80	24			NA

PRESSLEY Steven
b. Elgin 11.10.1973
Inverkeithing BC

Rangers		91/92	0	1		P
		92/93	8			P
		93/94	17	6	1	P
		94/95	2			P
Coventry C		94/95	18	1	1	FL
Dundee U		95/96	35		2	D1
		96/97	36		2	P
		97/98	29		2	P
Heart of Midlothian		98/99	29	1	1	P
		99/00	36			P

PRESTON Allan
b. Edinburgh 16.8.1969

Dundee U		87/88	1	1		P
		88/89	8	1	1	P
		89/90	8			P
		90/91	1	2		P
		91/92	2			P
Heart of Midlothian		92/93	19	2	2	P
Dunfermline A		93/94	20	6	5	D1
St Johnstone		93/94	3	6		P
		94/95	24	2	2	D1
		95/96	25	2	2	D1
		96/97	23	9	1	D1
		97/98	32	3	1	P
		98/99	8	7	1	P
Queen of the South		99/00	6	2	1	D2

PROVAN David Alexander
b. Gourock 8.5.1956
Port Glasgow R

Kilmarnock		74/75	20	2	1	D1
		75/76	23	1	3	D1
		76/77	34		1	P
		77/78	36		3	D1
		78/79	4			D1
Celtic		78/79	30		4	P
		79/80	35		1	P
		80/81	31	2	7	P
		81/82	19	1	4	P
		82/83	33		5	P
		83/84	14	4	2	P
		84/85	19	6	2	P
Sydney Olympic	L	85				
Celtic		85/86	11	1	2	P

PRYTZ Robert
b. Malmo 12.1.1960
Malmo FF

Rangers		82/83	24	6	5	P
		83/84	22	4	4	P
		84/85	17	4	3	P
Gothenburg						
Young Boys Bern						
Bayer Uerdingen						
Atalanta						
Verona						
Young Boys Bern						
Kilmarnock		96/97	1	2		P
East Fife		97/98	18		3	D2
Cowdenbeath		97/98	1			D3
Dumbarton		97/98	3			D3

PURAS Roberto Matute
b. San Asencio 26.8.1972
Belenenses

Dundee		99/00	1	4		P

PURDIE Bryan
b. Bo'ness 1.1.1959

Berwick R		76/77	1			D2
Cowdenbeath		77/78	25	5	5	D2
		78/79	25	7	4	D2
		79/80	20	7	2	D2
Alloa A		80/81	31		1	D2
		81/82	36		7	D2
		82/83	23		4	D1
		83/84	24	5	2	D1
Falkirk		84/85	22	2		D1
		85/86	37		1	D1
		86/87	25	2	1	P
Raith R		86/87	8	2		D2
		87/88	9	1		D1
Partick T		87/88	15			D1
		88/89	8		1	D1
East Stirlingshire		88/89	19			D2
		89/90	14			D2

PURDIE Ian
b. Bellshill 7.3.1953

Aberdeen		71/72	0	1		D1
		72/73	3		2	D1
		73/74	6	2	1	D1
		74/75	27		7	D1
Dundee		75/76	22	3		P
		76/77	33	1	7	D1
Motherwell		77/78	11	5	3	P
Wigan A		78/79	46		11	FL
		79/80	8	1	1	FL
Portsmouth		79/80	4	1	1	FL

QUITONGO Jose Manuel
b. Angola 18.11.1974

Benfica						
St Johnstone	T					
Malmo						
Waterford U	T					
Darlington		95/96	1			FL
Hamilton A		95/96	18	4	4	D2
		96/97	31	3	3	D1
		97/98	6		2	D1
Heart of Midlothian		97/98	3	14	3	P
		98/99	5	7		P
		99/00	0	1		P
Hamilton A		99/00	15		1	D2

RAE Alexander Scott
b. Glasgow 30.9.1969

Bishopbriggs					
Falkirk	87/88	3	9		P
	88/89	34	3	12	D1
	89/90	34		8	D1
Millwall	90/91	37	2	10	FL
	91/92	36	2	11	FL
	92/93	23	7	6	FL
	93/94	34	2	13	FL
	94/95	38		10	FL
	95/96	37		13	FL
Sunderland	96/97	13	10	2	FL
	97/98	24	5	3	FL
	98/99	12	3	2	FL
	99/00	22	4	3	FL

RAE David G
b. Glasgow 12.2.1959

Dundee U					
Morton	77/78	2	1		D1
	78/79	1	3		P
	79/80				
Alloa A	80/81	22	4	1	D2
Clyde	81/82	9	4	1	D2
	82/83	19	1		D1
	83/84	0	2		D1
Stenhousemuir	83/84	33		2	D2
	84/85	3	1		D2
East Stirlingshire	84/85	8			D2

RAE Gavin
b. Aberdeen 28.11.1977

Dundee	95/96	4	2		D1
	96/97	11	6	2	D1
	97/98	1	5		D1
	98/99	23	7	1	P
	99/00	35		4	P

RAE Gordon
b. Edinburgh 3.5.1958

Whitehill Welfare					
Musselburgh Windsor					
Hibernian	77/78	2		1	P
	78/79	24	3	7	P
	79/80	31	2	4	P
	80/81	34		13	D1
	81/82	27	2	11	P
	82/83	31		6	P
	83/84	14	2		P
	84/85	34			P
	85/86	27	5	2	P
	86/87	34	1	2	P
	87/88	40			P
	88/89	32		1	P
	89/90	2			P
Partick T	89/90	9			D1
	90/91	29	1		D1
	91/92	36	2	3	D1
Hamilton A	92/93	9			D1
Meadowbank T	92/93	21		2	D1

RAE Robin
b. Musselburgh 18.1.1964

Musselburgh Windsor					
Hibernian	81/82	3			P
	82/83				
	83/84	9			P
	84/85	1			P
Morton	85/86	11			D1
Hamilton A	85/86	2			D1
Ormiston Primrose					
Bonnyrigg Rose					

RAESIDE Robert
b. South Africa 7.7.1972

St Andrews U					
Raith R	90/91	12	2		D1
	91/92	12	1		D1
	92/93	10			D1
	93/94				
	94/95	9	1		D1
	95/96	6	2	1	P
Dundee	96/97	34		4	D1
	97/98	9	2		D1
	98/99	19	2		P
	99/00	1			P

RAFFERTY Stuart
b. Port Glasgow 6.3.1961

Port Glasgow Jnrs					
Motherwell	78/79	4	1		P
	79/80	2	5	2	D1
	80/81	2	3	2	D1
	81/82	8	5	5	D1
	82/83	30	3	4	P
	83/84	25	1	4	P
Dundee	84/85	35	1	4	P
	85/86	23	6	3	P
	86/87	28	8	4	P
	87/88	27	3		P
	88/89	31	1	1	P
Dunfermline A	89/90	31	1	1	P
	90/91	12	2		P
	91/92	37	6	3	D1
	92/93	31	7	2	D1
	93/94	19	7		D1

RAMSAY Douglas
b. Irvine 26.4.1979

Motherwell	98/99	0	4	1	P
	99/00	0	2		P

RAMSEY Paul Christopher
b. Londonderry 3.9.1962

Leicester C		80/81	1	2		FL
		81/82	10			FL
		82/83	40		1	FL
		83/84	33		1	FL
		84/85	38	1		FL
		85/86	13		1	FL
		86/87	29		6	FL
		87/88	41	1	1	FL
		88/89	22			FL
		89/90	31	4	3	FL
		90/91	20	4		FL
Cardiff C		91/92	39		3	FL
		92/93	30		4	FL
St Johnstone		93/94	22			P
		94/95	9	2		D1
Cardiff C	L	94/95	11			FL
Telford U		95/96				
Torquay U		95/96	18			FL

RATCLIFFE Kevin
b. Deeside 12.11.1960

Everton		79/80	2			FL
		80/81	20	1		FL
		81/82	25			FL
		82/83	29		1	FL
		83/84	38			FL
		84/85	40			FL
		85/86	39		1	FL
		86/87	42			FL
		87/88	24			FL
		88/89	30			FL
		89/90	24			FL
		90/91	35	1		FL
		91/92	8	1		FL
Dundee	L	92/93	4			P
Everton		92/93				
Cardiff C		92/93	19		1	FL
		93/94	6			FL
Nottingham F		93/94				
Derby Co		93/94	6			FL
Chester C		94/95	23			FL

RAYNES Steven
b. Edinburgh 4.9.1971

Hibernian	91/92	0	1		P
	92/93	2			P
Dundalk	93/94				
	94/95				
	95/96				
	96/97				
Livingston	97/98	31	1	2	D2
Forfar A	98/99	27	5		D2
Brechin C	99/00	24			D3

REDFORD Ian Petrie
b. Perth 5.4.1960

Errol R					
Dundee	76/77	0	1		D1
	77/78	25	9	10	D1
	78/79	33	4	15	D1
	79/80	13		9	P
Rangers	79/80	13			P
	80/81	35		9	P
	81/82	20	12	2	P
	82/83	29	4	3	P
	83/84	28	4	4	P
	84/85	24	2	5	P
Dundee U	85/86	25	5	5	P
	86/87	31	6	8	P
	87/88	22	3	6	P
	88/89	9		2	P
Ipswich T	88/89	22	2	2	FL
	89/90	14	4	2	FL
	90/91	23	3	4	FL
St Johnstone	91/92	28		3	P
	92/93	12	4	2	P
Brechin C	93/94	40	3	3	D1
	94/95	1			D2
Raith R	94/95	11	1		D1

REFVIK Isaak

Hibernian	78/79	5			P

REID Alan
b. Paisley 21.10.1980

Renfrew V					
Hibernian	98/99	0	1		D1
	99/00	0	1		P

REID Brian Robertson
b. Paisley 15.6.1970

Morton	88/89	2			D1
	89/90	36		1	D1
	90/91	19			D1
Rangers	90/91	3			P
	91/92				
	92/93	2			P
	93/94				
	94/95				
Morton	95/96	9			D1
	96/97	26		1	D1
	97/98	33		2	D1
Burnley	98/99	30	1	3	FL
Dunfermline A	99/00	21	2	3	D1

REID Christopher Thomas
b. Edinburgh 4.11.1971

Hibernian	89/90	2			P
	90/91	1			P
	91/92	9			P
	92/93	14			P
	93/94				
	94/95				
	95/96				
	96/97	1			P
	97/98	8			P
Hamilton A	98/99	6			D1
	99/00	24			D1

REID David

Hibernian	79/80	0	1		P

REID Dennis Alexander
b. Glasgow 2.3.1947

Glasgow Perthshire					
Rangers	64/65				
	65/66				
	66/67	2		2	D1
Dundee U	68/69	31	3	3	D1
	69/70	20		1	D1
	70/71	29	1	6	D1
	71/72	6	1	1	D1
Newcastle U	71/72	12	6		FL
	72/73	3	2		FL
Morton	72/73	7		1	D1
	73/74	25	1	5	D1
	74/75	22		4	D1
	75/76	17		1	D1
Dundee U	75/76	8	2	3	P
	76/77	0	1		P
Ayr U	76/77	2			P

REID Joseph
b. Cumbernauld 27.9.1963
Kilsyth St Patricks

St Johnstone		81/82	0	1		D1
		82/83	0	2		D1
		83/84	6	3	3	P
		84/85	24	14	7	D1
		85/86	8			D2
Hamilton A		85/86	21	1	9	D1
		86/87	6			P
Kilmarnock		86/87	11	6	9	D1
		87/88	11	3	6	D1
Cowdenbeath		87/88	9	1	3	D2
		88/89	15	6	5	D2
Stirling A		89/90	28	7	16	D2
		90/91	27	6	11	D2
		91/92	7	13		D1
Stenhousemuir *		92/93	1			D2
Armadale Thistle						
Shettleston						
Kilbirnie Ladeside						

REID Mark
b. Kilwinning 15.9.1961

Celtic		80/81	22			P
		81/82	36		2	P
		82/83	24	2	1	P
		83/84	23	1	2	P
		84/85	15	1		P
Charlton A		85/86	42		8	FL
		86/87	42			FL
		87/88	36		4	FL
		88/89	36		1	FL
		89/90	30	1		FL
		90/91	23	1	2	FL
St Mirren		91/92	11	4		P
		92/93	5			D1

REID Robert

St Mirren		73/74	17		1	D2
		74/75	31		5	D2
		75/76	25		1	D1
		76/77	39		10	D1
		77/78	32		5	P
		78/79				
		79/80	1			P

REID Wesley Andrew
b. Lewisham 10.9.1968

Arsenal						FL
Millwall		88/89	1			FL
		89/90	4	1		FL
Bradford C		90/91	14	2		FL
		91/92	17	2	3	FL
Airdrieonians		91/92	5	2		P
		92/93	18	7		P
		93/94	14	4	2	D1

REILLY John

Aberdeen		76/77	1			P
		77/78				
Hamilton A		78/79	1	1		D1
Albion R *		78/79	1			D2

REILLY John
b. Dundee 21.3.1962

Dundee U		80/81	0	1		P
		81/82	3	5	1	P
		82/83	8	8	7	P
		83/84	15	4	7	P
		84/85	3	7	4	P
Motherwell		85/86	24	6	9	P
		86/87	18	8	3	P
		87/88				
		88/89				
		89/90				
		90/91				
Dunfermline A		91/92	1	4		P
		92/93	0	1		D1
East Fife		93/94	7	2	5	D2
Cowdenbeath		93/94	10	3		D2
Arbroath		94/95	3		2	D3
Forfar A		94/95	0	1		D3
Albion R		95/96	7	3	1	D3

REILLY Mark Francis
b. Bellshill 30.3.1969
Wishaw Jnrs

Motherwell		89/90	3	1		P
		90/91				
Kilmarnock		91/92	15	4		D1
		92/93	18	1	3	D1
		93/94	37	1		P
		94/95	31	1		P
		95/96	22	6		P
		96/97	31	2	2	P
		97/98	36		3	P
Reading		98/99				
Kilmarnock		98/99	17	1		P
		99/00	28	1	3	P

REILLY Robert Piper
b. Kilmarnock 23.9.1959

Ayr U		78/79	1	4	1	D1
		79/80				
		80/81	8	2	4	D1
Clyde		81/82	22	7	11	D2
		82/83	28	6	8	D1
		83/84	21	4	1	D1
		84/85	23	10	3	D1
		85/86	25	5	4	D1
		86/87	6	3		D1
Hamilton A		86/87	3	4	1	P
Airdrieonians		86/87	5	2	1	D1
		87/88	18	4		D1
Meadowbank T		87/88	8	4	2	D1
		88/89	8	4	1	D1
Kilmarnock		88/89	17		2	D1
		89/90	30	1	4	D2
		90/91	13	13	2	D1
Stirling A		91/92	30		4	D1
		92/93	24	9	4	D1
		93/94	17	5	1	D1
Stranraer		94/95	16	9	1	D1
		95/96	14	9	1	D2
Albion R		95/96	3		1	D3
		96/97	4	10		D3
Dumbarton		96/97	2	6	1	D2
Queens Park		96/97	0	1		D3
Dumbarton		97/98	4	2	1	D3

RENNIE Alexander

United Crossroads						
Rangers		64/65				
		65/66				
		66/67				
Stirling A		67/68				
St Johnstone		67/68	5			D1
		68/69	16	8	3	D1
		69/70	9	4	1	D1
		70/71	32		1	D1
		71/72	33		2	D1
		72/73	32			D1
		73/74	30			D1
		74/75	28			D1
Dundee U		75/76	25	2		P
		76/77	18			P
		77/78	17	1		P
		78/79				

RENNIE Allan
b. Glasgow 26.10.1960

Queens Park		78/79	5			D2
		79/80	17			D2
		80/81	33			D2
		81/82	27	1		D1
		82/83	27	1		D1
		83/84	12	1		D2
		84/85	5			D2
Clydebank		85/86	2	1		P
		86/87	0	2		P

RENNIE Stewart
b. Edinburgh 24.4.1947
Royston BC

Falkirk		67/68				
		68/69	25			D1
		69/70	31			D2
		70/71	29			D1
		71/72	18			D1
		72/73	29			D1
		73/74				
Motherwell		73/74	27			D1
		74/75	25			D1
		75/76	36			P
		76/77	26			P
		77/78	32			P
		78/79	28			P
Ayr U		79/80	39			D1
		80/81	39			D1
		81/82	29			D1
		82/83	18			D1

RENWICK Michael
b. Edinburgh 29.2.1976

Hibernian		94/95	0	1		P
		95/96	1	1		P
		96/97	6	3		P
		97/98	3	3		P
		98/99	15	1		D1
		99/00	11	2		P

RESCH Franz
b. Vienna 4.5.1969
Rapid Vienna

Motherwell		97/98	3			P
Darlington		97/98	15	2	1	FL

REYNA Claudio
b. Livingston, NJ 20.7.1973

Bayer Leverkusen		95/96				
		96/97				
Wolfsburg		97/98				
		98/99				
Rangers		98/99	6			P
		99/00	25	4	5	P

RHODES Andrew Charles
b. Askern 23.8.1964

Barnsley		83/84	31			FL
		84/85	5			FL
Doncaster R		85/86	30			FL
		86/87	41			FL
		87/88	35			FL
Oldham A		87/88	11			FL
		88/89	27			FL
		89/90	31			FL
Dunfermline A		90/91	35			P
		91/92	44			P
St Johnstone		92/93	44			P
		93/94	44			P
		94/95	19			D1
Airdrieonians		95/96	16			D1
		96/97	9			D1
		97/98	4			D1
Scarborough	L	97/98	11			FL

RICCIO Luigi
b. Naples 28.12.1977
Perugia

Rangers		98/99	0	1		P

RICE Brian
b. Bellshill 11.10.1963

Hibernian		80/81	0	1		D1
		81/82	0	1		P
		82/83	22		2	P
		83/84	19	7	5	P
		84/85	34	1	4	P
Nottingham F		85/86	19		3	FL
		86/87	3		1	FL
Grimsby T	L	86/87	4			FL
Nottingham F		87/88	30		2	FL
		88/89	19	1	1	FL
WBA	L	88/89	2	1		FL
Nottingham F		89/90	15	3	2	FL
		90/91	0	1		FL
Stoke C	L	90/91	18			FL
Falkirk		91/92	14	2	1	P
		92/93	15	2	2	P
		93/94	36	1	3	D1
		94/95	19	7	2	P
		95/96	1	4		P
Dunfermline A		95/96	5	1		D1
		96/97	4	4		P
Clyde		97/98	31		2	D2
		98/99	8	10		D2
Morton		99/00	1			D1

RICHARDSON Alexander
b. Glasgow 15.11.1954
Arthurlie

St Mirren		76/77	37	1	3	D1
		77/78	26	4	1	P
		78/79	28	4	1	P
		79/80	30		2	P
		80/81	33		6	P
		81/82	17	2	4	P
		82/83	31	1	1	P
		83/84	4			P
Dundee		83/84	28	1		P
		84/85	7	15	1	P
Morton		85/86	36		6	D1
		86/87	32	1	5	D1
Arbroath		87/88	26	2	4	D2
		88/89	28	1	4	D2
		89/90	28		4	D2
Albion R		90/91	29	1	3	D2

RICHARDSON Lee James
b. Halifax 12.3.1969

Halifax T		86/87	1			FL
		87/88	20	10	1	FL
		88/89	22	3	1	FL
Watford		88/89	9			FL
		89/90	31	1	1	FL
Blackburn R		90/91	32	6	2	FL
		91/92	18	6	1	FL
Aberdeen		92/93	28	1	2	P
		93/94	31	4	4	P
Oldham A		94/95	28	2	6	FL
		95/96	27		11	FL
		96/97	27	4	4	FL
Stockport C	L	97/98	4	2		FL
Huddersfield T		97/98	16	5	3	FL
		98/99	13	2		FL
		99/00				
Bury	L	99/00	5		1	FL
Livingston		99/00	6			D1

RIDDELL Gary E
b. Ellon 9.8.1966

Aberdeen						
Dunfermline A		87/88	22			P
		88/89	21	1		D1

RIDEOUT Paul David
b. Bournemouth 14.8.1964

Swindon T		80/81	12	4	4	FL
		81/82	34	1	14	FL
		82/83	44		20	FL
Aston Villa		83/84	22	3	5	FL
		84/85	28	1	14	FL
Bari		85/86				
		86/87				
		87/88				
Southampton		88/89	20	4	6	FL
		89/90	30	1	7	FL
		90/91	14	2	6	FL
Swindon T	L	90/91	9		1	FL
Southampton		91/92	4			FL
Notts Co		91/92	9	2	3	FL
Rangers		91/92	7	4	1	P
		92/93	0	1		P
Everton		92/93	17	7	3	FL
		93/94	21	3	6	FL
		94/95	25	4	14	FL
		95/96	19	6	6	FL
		96/97	4	6		FL

RIEPER Marc Jensen
b. Copenhagen 5.6.1968

AGF Aarhus						
Brondby						
West Ham U		94/95	17	4	1	FL
		95/96	35	1	2	FL
		96/97	26	2	1	FL
		97/98	5		1	FL
Celtic		97/98	30		2	P
		98/99	7			P

RIIPA Juha
b. 12.9.1968

Hibernian		96/97	1			P

RILEY Paul John
b. Edinburgh 7.8.1975

Hibernian		96/97	0	1		P
		97/98				
Brechin C		98/99	12			D3
		99/00	28			D3

RING Michael Paul
b. Brighton 13.2.1961

Brighton		81/82	1			FL
Morton	L	81/82	4			P
Brighton		82/83	0	1		FL
		83/84	0	3		FL
Ballymena U		83/84				
Hull C		84/85	13	2	1	FL
		85/86	4	5	1	FL
Bolton W	L	85/86	1	2		FL
Aldershot		86/87	24	9	8	FL
		87/88	21	11	6	FL
		88/89	8	6	2	FL

RISETH Vidar
b. Levanger 21.4.1972

Rosenborg		93/94				
Kongsvingur		94/95				
Luton T		95/96	6	5		FL
Linzer ASK		96/97				
		97/98				
Celtic		98/99	26	1	3	P
		99/00	28			P

RISTIC Dragutin
b. Pula 5.8.1964

Benevento Sporting						
Dundee		93/94	16	2	6	P
Falkirk		93/94	12		4	D1
Dundee U		94/95	8	2	2	P

RITCHIE Andrew
b. Bellshill 23.2.1956

Bellshill Academy						
Bellshill YMCA						
Celtic		71/72				
Kirkintilloch Rob Roy	L	71/72				
		72/73				
Celtic		73/74	0	1		D1
		74/75				
		75/76	5	3	1	P
		76/77				
Morton		76/77	26	1	22	D1
		77/78	37		20	D1
		78/79	35		22	P
		79/80	34		19	P
		80/81	29	3	8	P
		81/82	23	2	6	P
		82/83	16	7	3	P
Motherwell		83/84	6	2	1	P
Clydebank	T	83/84	1			D1
East Stirlingshire	T	83/84	1			D2
Hannover 96	T	83/84				
Albion R		83/84	2	1	1	D2
		84/85	2	1	1	D2

RITCHIE Innes
b. Edinburgh 24.8.1973

Bathgate Thistle						
Motherwell		94/95	1			P
		95/96	5	5		P
East Fife		96/97	13			D1
		97/98	30		2	D2
Clydebank		98/99	11	2		D1
Berwick R		98/99	9			D3
		99/00	29	2	5	D3

RITCHIE Paul Michael
b. St Andrews 25.1.1969

Kirkcaldy YMCA						
Dundee		86/87				
		87/88				
Brechin C		87/88	7	1	3	D2
		88/89	18		7	D2
		89/90	25	13	9	D2
		90/91	34	4	14	D1
		91/92	24		12	D2
Dundee		91/92	4	3	1	D1
		92/93	17	2	3	P
Gillingham	L	92/93	6		3	FL
Dundee		93/94	10	7	2	P
		94/95	6	9	2	D1
Gillingham	L	94/95	5		1	FL
Dundee		95/96				
Hamilton A		96/97	36		31	D2
		97/98	23	6	7	D1

RITCHIE Paul Simon
b. Glasgow 21.8.1975

Heart of Midlothian		95/96	28		1	P
		96/97	27	1	3	P
		97/98	34			P
		98/99	29		1	P
		99/00	14		1	P
Bolton W		99/00	13	1		FL

RITCHIE Stephen Kilcar
b. Edinburgh 17.2.1954

Bristol C		71/72				
		72/73	1			FL
Morton		72/73	11		1	D1
		73/74	26		1	D1
		74/75	28		1	D1
Hereford U		75/76	46		1	FL
		76/77	32		1	FL
		77/78	24		1	FL
Aberdeen		77/78	9			P
		78/79	1			P
Torquay U		78/79	17			FL
		79/80	41		2	FL

RITCHIE William

Largs Thistle						
St Johnstone		72/73	2			D1
		73/74	28	2		D1
		74/75	12	1		D1
		75/76	21	1		P
Clyde *		76/77	6	2		D2

RIX Graham
b. Askern 23.10.1957

Arsenal		76/77	4	3	1	FL
		77/78	37	2	2	FL
		78/79	39		3	FL
		79/80	38		4	FL
		80/81	35		5	FL
		81/82	39		9	FL
		82/83	36		6	FL
		83/84	34		4	FL
		84/85	18		2	FL
		85/86	38		3	FL
		86/87	13	5	2	FL
		87/88	7	3		FL
Brentford	L	87/88	6			FL
SM Caen		88/89				
		89/90				
		90/91				
		91/92				
Dundee		92/93	12	2	2	P
		93/94				
Chelsea		94/95	0	1		FL

ROBB David Thomson
b. Broughty Ferry 15.12.1947

Chelsea						
Newburgh Jnrs						
Aberdeen		65/66				
		66/67	2	1	1	D1
		67/68	16	2	4	D1
		68/69	24	2	9	D1
		69/70	34		16	D1
		70/71	32		9	D1
		71/72	34		10	D1
		72/73	19		4	D1
		73/74	21		11	D1
		74/75	6		4	D1
		75/76	30	2	4	P
		76/77	6	6	1	P
Tampa Bay Rowdies		77	15		8	NA
Aberdeen		77/78	13		5	P
Tampa Bay Rowdies		78	27		13	NA
Norwich C		78/79	4	1	1	FL
Philadelphia Fury		79	30		16	NA
Vancouver Whitecaps		80	15			NA
Tulsa Roughnecks		80	12		4	NA
Dunfermline A		80/81	3			D1

ROBERTS Graham Paul
b. Southampton 3.7.1959

Sholing Sports						
Portsmouth		76/77				
Weymouth						
Tottenham H		80/81	21	3		FL
		81/82	35	2	6	FL
		82/83	20	4	2	FL
		83/84	35		6	FL
		84/85	40		7	FL
		85/86	32		1	FL
		86/87	17		1	FL
Rangers		86/87	18		2	P
		87/88	37		1	P
Chelsea		88/89	46		15	FL
		89/90	24		3	FL
WBA		90/91	27		4	FL
		91/92	12		2	FL

ROBERTS Mark Kinsley
b. Irvine 29.10.1975

Kilmarnock		91/92	0	1		D1
		92/93	4	1		D1
		93/94	7	6	2	P
		94/95	0	4	1	P
		95/96	2	9		P
		96/97	2	9	2	P
		97/98	17	15	7	P
		98/99	9	13	3	P
		99/00	2			P
Raith R		99/00	3		1	D1

ROBERTS Philip

Arsenal						FL
Grimsby T						
St Johnstone		74/75	2			D1
		75/76	20	1		P
		76/77	32	1	1	D1

ROBERTSON Allan David
b. Irvine 22.9.1952

Eastercraigs BC					
Troon Jnrs					
Kilmarnock	72/73	27			D1
	73/74	34		1	D2
	74/75	33			D1
	75/76	26			D1
	76/77	36		2	P
	77/78	28		1	D1
	78/79	36	1		D1
	79/80	24			P
	80/81	18	1		P
	81/82	37	2	2	D1
	82/83	13			P
	83/84	38			D1
	84/85	30		1	D1
	85/86	32			D1
	86/87	26			D1
	87/88	27			D1
	88/89	12			D1

ROBERTSON Alexander
b. Edinburgh 26.4.1971

Rangers	88/89	1	1		P
	89/90	0	1		P
	90/91	7	8	1	P
	91/92	3	3		P
	92/93	0	2		P
Coventry C	93/94	0	3		FL
	94/95	0	1		FL
	95/96				
Dundee U	96/97	1	3		P
Airdrieonians	97/98	3			D1
Inverness CT	97/98	16		1	D2
Livingson	97/98	6			D2
Clydebank	98/99	7	4	1	D1

ROBERTSON Christopher J G
b. Edinburgh 25.12.1957

Rangers	76/77	7	4	1	P
	77/78	2	1		P
	78/79	0	2	1	P
	79/80				
Heart of Midlothian	80/81	14	1		P
	81/82	24	4	7	D1
Meadowbank T	82/83	8		4	D2
Cowdenbeath	82/83	3	4	1	D2
Raith R	83/84	1			D1
Meadowbank T	83/84	25	6	10	D1
	84/85	17	14	8	D1
	85/86	5	12	1	D2
	86/87	0	1		D2
Berwick R *	86/87	9	2	1	D2

ROBERTSON Craig Peter
b. Dunfermline 22.4.1963

Raith R	81/82	11			D1
	82/83	21			D1
	83/84	37	1	3	D1
	84/85	39		11	D2
	85/86	24	1	2	D2
	86/87	35		3	D2
Dunfermline A	87/88	42		11	P
	88/89	13		5	D1
Aberdeen	88/89	2	2	1	P
	89/90	10	12	2	P
	90/91	2	6	1	P
Dunfermline A	91/92	31	2	1	P
	92/93	34		3	D1
	93/94	40		3	D1
	94/95	35		6	D1
	95/96	27	1	5	D1
	96/97	31			P
	97/98	21			P

ROBERTSON David
b. Aberdeen 17.10.1968

Aberdeen	86/87	32	2		P
	87/88	23			P
	88/89	23			P
	89/90	20		1	P
	90/91	35		1	P
Rangers	91/92	42		1	P
	92/93	39		3	P
	93/94	32		1	P
	94/95	23		3	P
	95/96	25		3	P
	96/97	21	1	4	P
Leeds U	97/98	24	2		FL
	98/99				
	99/00				

ROBERTSON Derek

Petershill					
St Johnstone	66/67	1			D1
	67/68	14			D1
	68/69	28			D1
	69/70	6			D1
	70/71				
	71/72	18			D1
	72/73				
	73/74	16			D1
	74/75	32			D1
	75/76	32			P
	76/77	33			D1
	77/78	23			D1
	78/79	19			D1

ROBERTSON Douglas
b. Torpichen 15.3.1963

Rangers	81/82	1	1		P
	82/83	2	2		P
Morton	83/84	38		16	D1
	84/85	22	4	1	P
	85/86	34	1	8	D1
	86/87	40		18	D1
	87/88	8	5	2	P
	88/89	11	9	2	D1
Falkirk	89/90	4	1	1	P
Morton	89/90	7	1	1	D1

ROBERTSON Graeme William T
b. Dumfries 4.6.1962

Lochar Amateurs					
Queen of the South	78/79	1			D1
	79/80	27	1	5	D2
	80/81	8	6	2	D2
	81/82	19	7	1	D1
	82/83	15	1	1	D2
	83/84	34		8	D2
	84/85				
	85/86	39		1	D2
	86/87	42	1		D1
Dunfermline A	87/88	17			P
	88/89	27	2	1	D1
	89/90	15	2	2	P
Partick T	90/91	34	1		D1
	91/92	33	3		D1
Ayr U	92/93	43	1	1	D1
	93/94	20	1		D1

ROBERTSON Hugh Scott
b. Aberdeen 19.3.1975

Lewis U					
Aberdeen	93/94	6	2		P
	94/95	2	1	2	P
	95/96	5	6		P
Dundee	96/97	15		1	D1
Brechin C	97/98	5	2		D2
Dundee	98/99	9	1		P
Inverness CT	98/99	12		1	D2
Dundee	99/00	15	9	2	P

ROBERTSON Ian William
b. Inverness 14.10.1966

Aberdeen	83/84	1			P
	84/85				
	85/86	2	2		P
	86/87	4			P
	87/88				
	88/89	7			P
	89/90	5			P
	90/91	0	1		P
Montrose	91/92	23	1	2	D1
	92/93	36		1	D2
	93/94	35			D2
	94/95	32		1	D3
	95/96	11			D2

ROBERTSON James T
b. Glasgow 3.12.1955

Motherwell	77/78	5			P
Stranraer	78/79	37		2	D2
	79/80	14		2	D2
Queen of the South	79/80	25		5	D2
	80/81	39		19	D2
	81/82	21		1	D2
	82/83	37		11	D2
	83/84	32		9	D2
	84/85	16		1	D2
	85/86	35		5	D2
	86/87	43		11	D1
Morton	87/88	22	5	2	P
	88/89	10	6	3	D1
Queen of the South	89/90	17	1	5	D2
	90/91	17	5	4	D2
	91/92	27	2	2	D2
	92/93	15	8	4	D2

ROBERTSON John Grant
b. Edinburgh 2.10.1964

Heart of Midlothian	81/82	0	1		D1
	82/83	19	4	21	D1
	83/84	34	1	15	P
	84/85	33		8	P
	85/86	34	1	20	P
	86/87	31	6	16	P
	87/88	39		26	P
	88/89	8	7	4	P
Newcastle U	88/89	7	5		FL
Heart of Midlothian	89/90	25	7	17	P
	90/91	31		12	P
	91/92	42		14	P
	92/93	41	1	11	P
	93/94	32	4	8	P
	94/95	27	4	10	P
	95/96	28	5	11	P
	96/97	25	2	14	P
	97/98	10	11	6	P
Livingston	98/99	30	6	12	D2
	99/00	1	4	1	D1

ROBERTSON Lee
b. Edinburgh 25.8.1973

Rangers	91/92	1			P
	92/93	1			P
	93/94				
	94/95	0	1		P

ROBERTSON Malcolm
b. 7.7.1951

Raith R	71/72	29	2	9	D2
	72/73	35		6	D2
	73/74	29	4	21	D2
	74/75	25		8	D2
	75/76	14		9	D2
Ayr U	75/76	22		6	P
	76/77	14	4	1	P
Heart of Midlothian	76/77	7		1	P
	77/78	26	1	6	D1
	78/79	27	2	4	P
	79/80	28	2	3	D1
	80/81	4	1		P
Toronto Blizzard	81	19		2	NA
Dundee U	81/82	1	1		P
Hibernian	82/83	2	3		P

ROBERTSON Robert
b. Leslie 14.2.1959

Kirkcaldy YMCA					
Dunfermline A	77/78	28	3		D2
	78/79	37		1	D2
	79/80	39		2	D1
	80/81	39			D1
	81/82	38			D1
	82/83	33			D1
	83/84	22	1	1	D2
	84/85	39			D2
	85/86	27	1		D2
	86/87	31			D1
	87/88	20	2		P
Alloa A	87/88	7		1	D2
	88/89	22	1		D2
	89/90	13	4		D1

ROBERTSON Stephen
b. Glasgow 16.3.1977

Stenhousemuir *	93/94	3			D2
	94/95				
Albion R *	95/96	1			D3
St Johnstone	95/96	2			D1
Clydebank	96/97	2			D1
St Johnstone	96/97	2			D1
	97/98	2			P
Hamilton A	98/99	6			D1
St Johnstone	99/00	12	1		P

ROBERTSON Stuart
b. Glasgow 29.9.1959

Doncaster R					
Dumbarton	83/84	23	3	4	D1
	84/85	21	2	1	P
Falkirk	85/86	16	6		D1
Brechin C *	86/87	4			D1
Queen of the South	87/88	19	3	1	D1
	88/89	4	1	1	D1
Dumbarton *	88/89	24	3	2	D2
Pollok Jnrs	89/90				
	90/91				
	91/92				
	92/93				
	93/94				
	94/95				
	95/96				
Albion R	96/97	1			D3

ROBIN Keith
b. 26.8.1960

Ferguslie U						
Irvine Meadow						
Kilmarnock		79/80				
		80/81	8	1		P
		81/82	3			D1

ROBINSON Brian
b. Glasgow 20.11.1965

Glenboig Jnrs						
Morton		87/88	2	1		P
Stenhousemuir		88/89	21	4	7	D2

ROBINSON Robert Sharp
b. Edinburgh 10.11.1950 d. Forfar 24.12.1996

Newtongrange						
Falkirk		71/72	2			D1
Dundee		72/73	31		2	D1
		73/74	30	2	4	D1
		74/75	33		6	D1
		75/76	17	3	2	P
		76/77	20	11	2	D1
		77/78	0	1		D1
Dundee U		77/78	14	5		P
		78/79	8	3		P
Heart of Midlothian		79/80	31	4	1	D1
		80/81	13	6		P
Raith R		81/82	25	3	2	D1
		82/83	21		1	D1
Forfar Albion						
Coupar Angus						

RODDIE Andrew Robert
b. Glasgow 4.11.1971

Aberdeen		91/92	1	9	2	P
		92/93	1	10	2	P
		93/94	3	3	1	P
Motherwell		94/95	4	15		P
		95/96	12	12		P
		96/97	8	4		P
St Mirren		97/98	19		1	D1
		98/99				
Clydebank		99/00	4			D1
Stranraer		99/00	9		3	D2
Ross Co		99/00	1			D2

RODGER James
b. Dumbarton 30.3.1958

East Kilbride Thistle						
Albion R	T	77/78	1			D2
Airdrieonians		78/79	1			D1
		79/80	9	1	1	D1
		80/81	35		2	P
		81/82	35		2	P
		82/83	37	1	5	D1
		83/84	35	2	4	D1
		84/85	25		2	D1
		85/86	39		1	D1
		86/87	6	1		D1
Clydebank		86/87	26		2	P
		87/88	37	1	1	D1
		88/89	16	1	3	D1
		89/90	28			D1
		90/91	26		2	D1

RODGER Paul
b. Edinburgh 2.9.1958

Heart of Midlothian		76/77	3			P
		77/78	5			D1
		78/79	2			P
Alloa A *		79/80	20	3		D2
Happy Valley		80/81				
		81/82				
		82/83				
		83/84				
Dunfermline A		84/85	4	2		D2
Bonnyrigg Rose						
Arbroath		85/86	7		1	D2
		86/87	4			D2

RODGERS James

Ayr U		77/78	0	2		P
Aberdeen		78/79				
Clyde		79/80	1	2		D1
Stranraer		80/81	19	11	1	D2

RODIER Derick
b. Edinburgh 4.2.1959

Hibernian		79/80	3			P
		80/81	1	6		D1
		81/82	9	10		P
		82/83	0	2		P
Dunfermline A		82/83	20	1	1	D1
		83/84	8	3		D2
Berwick R		83/84	17	1	2	D2
		84/85	23	3	1	D2

RODMAN Brian William
b. Kilmarnock 3.5.1949

Bellfield BC						
Dreghorn Jnrs						
Kilmarnock		66/67	1			D1
		67/68	8	1		D1
		68/69	0	1		D1
		69/70	8			D1
		70/71	11	1		D1
		71/72	33			D1
		72/73	29		1	D1
		73/74	36			D2
		74/75	34			D1
		75/76	20	2	2	D1
Ayr U		76/77	8			P
		77/78	18			P
Partick T		78/79	0	1		P

ROGAN Anton Gerard Patrick
b. Belfast 25.3.1966

Distillery						
Celtic		86/87	10		1	P
		87/88	25	8	1	P
		88/89	34		1	P
		89/90	17	2		P
		90/91	25	2	1	P
		91/92	5			P
Sunderland		91/92	33		1	FL
		92/93	12	1		FL
Oxford U		93/94	29		2	FL
		94/95	27	2	1	FL
Millwall		95/96	4	4		FL
		96/97	26	2	8	FL
Blackpool		97/98	1			FL
		98/99	9	5		FL

ROGERS David Raymond
b. Liverpool 25.8.1975

Tranmere R						
Chester C		95/96	14	6	1	FL
		96/97	4	1		FL
Dundee		97/98	31	1	1	D1
		98/99	7	4		P
Ayr U		99/00	13	3	1	D1
Partick T	L	99/00	6			D2

ROGERS James
b. Glasgow 19.1.1964

Albion R *		86/87	2			D2
Stenhousemuir *		86/87	1			D2
Morton		87/88	6	1		P
Stranraer		88/89	5			D2

ROLLAND Andrew
b. 12.11.1942

Cowdenbeath		61/62				
		62/63				
		63/64				
		64/65				
		65/66				
		66/67				
Dundee U		67/68	29		3	D1
		68/69	34		4	D1
		69/70	32		2	D1
		70/71	33		1	D1
		71/72	30		5	D1
		72/73	24	1	3	D1
		73/74	24	2	4	D1
		74/75	30	2	3	D1
		75/76	32	1	1	P
		76/77	29		2	P
		77/78	22	1	1	P
Fort Lauderdale Strikers		78	15		1	NA
Los Angeles Aztecs		78	12			NA
Dunfermline A		78/79	31		1	D2
		79/80	11		2	D1
Cowdenbeath		79/80	24		3	D2
		80/81	33			D2
		81/82	19	2		D2

ROMAINES Stuart
b. Seahouses 6.2.1960

Seahouses						
Berwick R		78/79	16	3		D2
		79/80	27		1	D1
		80/81	34	3		D1
		81/82	26	6		D2
		82/83	31		8	D2
		83/84	27	1	3	D2
		84/85	29		3	D2
		85/86	33		2	D2
		86/87	32		4	D2
Falkirk		87/88	27	2	2	P
		88/89	2	2		D1
Raith R		88/89	14	11		D1
		89/90	26	3	1	D1
		90/91	8	5	1	D1
Alloa A		91/92	35		1	D2
		92/93	4	1		D2
Berwick R		93/94	4			D2

RONALD Gerald
b. Glasgow 31.12.1959

Glasgow U						
Clydebank		76/77	5	6		D1
		77/78	10	4		P
		78/79				
		79/80	33	1	9	D1
		80/81	28	2	1	D1
		81/82	35		5	D1
		82/83	33	1	6	D1
		83/84	36		6	D1
		84/85	16	8	2	D1
		85/86	16	3		P
		86/87				
Dundee U		87/88				
Morton		87/88	0	2		P
		88/89	25	2	1	D1
		89/90	13	2	1	D1

ROONEY James
b. Glasgow 1.1.1956

Queens Park		74/75	12	6	4	D2
		75/76	24		1	D2
		76/77	35	2	4	D2
		77/78	39		3	D2
Morton		78/79	26	2	1	P
		79/80	17		1	P
		80/81	36		5	P
		81/82	33		4	P
		82/83	36		6	P
		83/84	36		8	D1
St Mirren		84/85	25	2	2	P
		85/86	28	4	6	P
		86/87	0	1		P
Dumbarton		86/87	23	1	2	D1
		87/88	42		4	D1
Clyde		88/89	17	1	1	D1
		89/90	24	3	1	D1
East Stirlingshire		90/91	30	1		D2
		91/92	19	3	1	D2

ROSEBURGH David
b. Loanhead 30.6.1959

Bonnyrigg Rose						
Meadowbank T		86/87	39		11	D2
		87/88	35	1	12	D1
Hamilton A		88/89	26	1		P
Meadowbank T		88/89	10		6	D1
		89/90	35		7	D1
		90/91	39		15	D1
		91/92	30		8	D1
		92/93	35	2	8	D1
Stenhousemuir		93/94	28		7	D2
		94/95	8	5		D2
		95/96	6	4		D2
		96/97	8	14	2	D2
		97/98	12	13	3	D2
		98/99				
		99/00	0	2		D2

ROSS Ian
b. Broxburn 27.8.1974

Motherwell		95/96	1			P
		96/97	21	9	2	P
		97/98	16	6	1	P
		98/99	8	4		P
St Mirren		99/00	30	1	3	D1

ROSS Maurice
b. Dundee 3.2.1981

Rangers		99/00	0	1		P

ROUGH Alan Roderick
b. Gorbals 25.11.1951

Lincoln Amateurs						
Partick T						
Sighthill Amateurs	L					
Partick T		69/70	2			D1
		70/71				
		71/72	34			D1
		72/73	34			D1
		73/74	34			D1
		74/75	19			D1
		75/76	26			D1
		76/77	36			P
		77/78	36			P
		78/79	35			P
		79/80	34			P
		80/81	33			P
		81/82	36			P
		82/83	15			D1
Hibernian		82/83	24			P
		83/84	27			P
		84/85	35			P
		85/86	36			P
		86/87	42			P
		87/88	11			P
Orlando Lions						
Celtic		88/89	5			P
Hamilton A		88/89	5			P
Ayr U		89/90	1			D1
Glenafton A						

ROUGIER Antony Leo
b. Trinidad 17.7.1971

Trinity Pros						
Raith R		94/95	14	6		D1
		95/96	17	6	1	P
		96/97	27	3	1	P
Hibernian		97/98	24	6	3	P
		98/99	26			D1
Port Vale		98/99	8	5		FL
		99/00	33	5	8	FL

ROUGVIE Douglas
b. Lochore 24.5.1956

Dunfermline U						
Aberdeen		74/75				
		75/76	1	1		P
		76/77	2	4	1	P
		77/78	1			P
		78/79	16	4		P
		79/80	22	3	2	P
		80/81	25	3	3	P
		81/82	28		6	P
		82/83	32	3	3	P
		83/84	35		4	P
Chelsea		84/85	27		1	FL
		85/86	34		2	FL
		86/87	13			FL
Brighton		87/88	35		2	FL
Shrewsbury T		88/89	20	1	3	FL
Fulham		88/89	18		1	FL
Dunfermline A		89/90	28			P
Montrose		90/91	29		2	D2
		91/92	16			D1

ROUSSET Gilles
b. Hyeres 22.8.1963

Stade Rennes						
Heart of Midlothian		95/96	25			P
		96/97	33			P
		97/98	32			P
		98/99	26			P
		99/00	16			P

ROWBOTHAM Jason
b. Cardiff 3.1.1969

Plymouth A						
Raith R		93/94	33	3	1	P
		94/95	14	6		D1

ROWELL Gary
b. Seaham 6.6.1957

Sunderland		75/76	3	1	1	FL
		76/77	27	5	5	FL
		77/78	38	1	18	FL
		78/79	32	3	21	FL
		79/80	8	9		FL
		80/81	26	5	10	FL
		81/82	30		9	FL
		82/83	34	1	16	FL
		83/84	31	3	8	FL
Norwich C		84/85	2	4	1	FL
Middlesbrough		85/86	27		10	FL
Brighton		86/87	8	2		FL
		87/88	1	1		FL
Dundee	L	87/88	0	1		P
Carlisle U		87/88	7			FL
Burnley		88/89	8	10	1	FL
		89/90	0	1		FL

ROWSON David Andrew
b. Aberdeen 14.9.1976

Stoneywood						
Aberdeen		95/96	7	2		P
		96/97	30	4	2	P
		97/98	24	6	5	P
		98/99	18	4		P
		99/00	2	3	1	P
Livingston	L	99/00	6		1	D1

ROZENTHAL Sebastian Igault
b. Santiago 1.9.1976

Universidad Catolica						
Rangers		96/97	0	1		P
		97/98	1	1		P
		98/99	0	3		P
		99/00	6	5	3	P

RUSSELL Craig Stewart
b. South Shields 4.2.1974

Sunderland		91/92	1	3		FL
		92/93				
		93/94	29	6	9	FL
		94/95	28	10	5	FL
		95/96	35	6	13	FL
		96/97	10	19	4	FL
Manchester C		97/98	17	7	1	FL
		98/99	5	2	1	FL
Tranmere R	L	98/99	3	1		FL
Port Vale		98/99	8		1	FL
Manchester C		99/00				
Oxford U	L	99/00	5	1		FL
St Johnstone	L	99/00	1		1	P

RUSSELL Robert
b. Glasgow 11.2.1957

Sunderland						
Shettleston						
Rangers		77/78	33		3	P
		78/79	36		4	P
		79/80	22	1	7	P
		80/81	23	5	6	P
		81/82	32		6	P
		82/83	18	3	1	P
		83/84	27	4	4	P
		84/85	9	9		P
		85/86	17	10		P
		86/87	1			P
Motherwell		87/88	28	4	3	P
		88/89	28	3	5	P
		89/90	32	1	3	P
		90/91	15	4	2	P
		91/92	7	9	2	P
Ayr U		92/93	4		1	D1
Arbroath		93/94	1			D2
Cowdenbeath		93/94	2	4		D2
		94/95				
Albion R		95/96	5	7		D3
		96/97	0	1		D3

RUSSELL Robert S
b. Falkirk 22.5.1955

Alloa A		73/74	5		3	D2
		74/75	26	5	9	D2
		75/76	22		4	D2
		76/77	20		11	D2
		77/78	21	1	5	D1
Morton		78/79	23	4	5	P
		79/80	7			P
Airdrieonians		79/80	10		4	D1
		80/81	18	1		P
Raith R		80/81	9		2	D1
		81/82	17	8		D1
		82/83	31	1	13	D1
East Stirlingshire		83/84	6		2	D2
Queen of the South		83/84	5		1	D2
East Fife		83/84	5		4	D1
Falkirk		84/85	5	6		D1

RUTHERFORD Andrew
b. Edinburgh 4.10.1953

East Fife		73/74	13	4		D1
		74/75	23	4	4	D2
		75/76	19	2	8	D1
		76/77	18	3	3	D1
St Johnstone		76/77	14			D1
		77/78	39			D1
		78/79	39		7	D1
		79/80	38		3	D1
		80/81	35			D1
		81/82	37		6	D1
		82/83	39		2	D1
		83/84	34			P
		84/85	21	2		D1
Cowdenbeath		85/86	30	2		D2
		86/87	0	2		D2

RUTHERFORD Johnathan Paul
b. Sunderland 23.2.1967

Newcastle U		86/87				
Alloa A		87/88	31		14	D2
		88/89	7		1	D2
Falkirk		88/89	24	4	9	P
		89/90	18	10	7	D1
		90/91	3	3	3	D1
		91/92	2	3		P
Meadowbank T		92/93	27		9	D1
		93/94	32		8	D2
		94/95	4			D2
Scarborough		94/95	6	2	1	FL
Berwick R		94/95	1			D2
		95/96	6	3	2	D2

RUTKIEWICZ Kevin
b. Glasgow 10.5.1980

Larkhall Thistle						
Aberdeen		99/00	1	9		P

SALENKO Oleg
b. St Petersburg 25.10.1969

Valencia						
Rangers		95/96	14	2	7	P

SALVATORI Stefano
b. Rome 29.12.1967

AC Milan		86/87				
Virescit		87/88				
Parma		88/89				
Fiorentina		88/89				
AC Milan		89/90				
		90/91				
Fiorentina		90/91				
		91/92				
		92/93				
Spal		93/94				
		94/95				
Atalanta		94/95				
		95/96				
Heart of Midlothian		96/97	12	2		P
		97/98	29	3	1	P
		98/99	11	1		P

SANDISON James William
b. Edinburgh 22.6.1965

Edinburgh Emmet						
Heart of Midlothian		84/85	2	1		P
		85/86	2	1		P
		86/87	12	1		P
		87/88	2			P
		88/89	11	3		P
		89/90	8	4	2	P
		90/91	24	1	1	P
Airdrieonians		91/92	40			P
		92/93	37	1		P
		93/94	33			D1
		94/95	32	1		D1
		95/96	30		1	D1
		96/97	36		1	D1
		97/98	31			D1
		98/99	33	1		D1
		99/00	24	1	5	D1

SAUNDERS Wesley
b. Sunderland 23.2.1963

Newcastle U		81/82	29			FL
		82/83	13			FL
		83/84	16			FL
		84/85	21			FL
Bradford C	L	84/85	1	3		FL
Carlisle U		85/86	35		3	FL
		86/87	37		3	FL
		87/88	25		5	FL
Dundee		87/88	11			P
		88/89	30		1	P
		89/90	7	2	1	P
Torquay U		90/91	37		3	FL
		91/92	17	1	3	FL
		92/93	6			FL

SAUZEE Franck Gaston Henri
b. Aubenas 28.10.1965

Sochaux		83/84				
		84/85				
		85/86				
		86/87				
		87/88				
Marseille		88/89				
		89/90				
Monaco		90/91				
Marseille		91/92				
		92/93				
Atalanta		93/94				
Strasbourg		94/95				
		95/96				
Montpellier		96/97				
		97/98				
Hibernian		98/99	9		2	D1
		99/00	33		2	P

SCANLON John
b. Birkenshaw 13.7.1952

East Stirlingshire		71/72	25	2	15	D2
Notts Co		72/73	2	2		FL
		73/74	1	1		FL
		74/75	31	1	14	FL
		75/76	37	1	12	FL
		76/77	25	6	5	FL
		77/78	3	1		FL
Aberdeen		77/78	0	1	1	P
		78/79	22	6	2	P
		79/80	25	4	4	P
		80/81	32	2	6	P
St Mirren		81/82	25		5	P
		82/83	19	2	7	P
		83/84	30		12	P
		84/85	13	8	4	P
		85/86	0	1		P

SCHAEDLER Erich Peter
b. Biggar 6.8.1949 d. 24.12.1985

Melbourne Thistle						
Stirling A		68/69				
		69/70				
Hibernian		69/70	5			D1
		70/71	15			D1
		71/72	29			D1
		72/73	32		1	D1
		73/74	31			D1
		74/75	30	1		D1
		75/76	32	1	1	P
		76/77	24			P
		77/78	10			P
Dundee		77/78	15			D1
		78/79	27	1	1	D1
		79/80	27			P
		80/81	31	1		D1
		81/82	1			P
Hibernian		81/82	23	5		P
		82/83	6	1		P
		83/84	29			P
		84/85	23			P
Dumbarton		85/86	14			D1

SCHEIDT Raphael
b. 10.2.1976

Celtic		99/00	1	2		P

SCHMUGGE Thorsten

Hibernian		96/97	1			P

SCOTT Alistair
b. 26.8.1950

Rangers		73/74	21	3	8	D1
		74/75	7	2	1	D1
		75/76	1	1		P
Hibernian		76/77	23	8	3	P
		77/78	5	2	1	P
Morton		78/79	24	6	3	P
		79/80	13	13	3	P
		80/81	1	1		P
Partick T		80/81	0	2		P
Quen of the South		80/81	6		1	D2
East Stirlingshire *		81/82	3			D1

SCOTT Colin George
b. Glasgow 19.5.1970

Dalry Thistle						
Rangers		87/88				
		88/89				
		89/90				
Brentford	L	89/90	6			FL
Rangers		90/91				
Airdrieonians	L	90/91	1			D1
Rangers		91/92				
		92/93				
		93/94	5	1		P
		94/95	3	1		P
		95/96	3			P
Hamilton A		95/96	5			D1
Raith R		96/97	6			P
		97/98				
Clydebank		98/99	28			D1
		99/00	21			D1

SCOTT David
b. Edinburgh 18.4.1963

Heart of Midlothian		78/79	3	2		P
		79/80	0	2		D1
Alloa A	L	80/81	1	4		D2
Heart of Midlothian		81/82				
Meadowbank T		82/83	0	1		D2

SCOTT Gordon
b. Bathgate 19.7.1960

Broxburn A						
East Fife		79/80	22	5	3	D2
		80/81	35		7	D2
		81/82	34		16	D2
		82/83	35		11	D2
		83/84	16	1	1	D2
St Johnstone		83/84	12	4	3	P
		84/85	32	1	7	D1
Forfar A		85/86	26	2	7	D1
		86/87	25		10	D1
		87/88	19		11	D1
Hamilton A		87/88	16	1	4	D1
		88/89	4	5		P
Meadowbank T		88/89	16	3	4	D1
		89/90	12	1	1	D1
Australia						
Edinburgh U						
Arniston R						

SCOTT John
b. Aberdeen 14.1.1948

Chelsea						
Dundee		64/65	6		6	D1
		65/66	7			D1
		66/67	20		12	D1
		67/68	19	3	6	D1
		68/69	32	1	10	D1
		69/70	32		9	D1
		70/71	33		16	D1
		71/72	34		12	D1
		72/73	31	1	12	D1
		73/74	30		22	D1
		74/75	32		8	D1
		75/76				
Aberdeen		75/76	28	4	14	P
		76/77	13	6	3	P
Seattle Sounders		77	17		6	NA
Aberdeen		77/78	0	1		P
Dundee		77/78	19	1	4	D1
Seattle Sounders		78	22		3	NA
Dundee		78/79	1	4		D1
		79/80				
		80/81	2			D1

SCOTT Philip Campbell
b. Perth 14.11.1974

St Johnstone		92/93	2	1		P
		93/94	19	5	3	P
		94/95	9	3	1	D1
		95/96	28		8	D1
		96/97	24	5	12	D1
		97/98	19	3	1	P
		98/99	14	2	2	P
Sheffield W		98/99	0	4	1	FL
		99/00	2	3		FL

SCRIMGEOUR Brian
b. Dundee 11.8.1959

Dundee		78/79	3			D1
		79/80				
		80/81	17	4	5	D1
		81/82	6	6		P
		82/83	18	4	2	P
Chesterfield		83/84	41		3	FL
		84/85	12	3		FL
		85/86	45		9	FL
		86/87	19	1	4	FL
Falkirk		86/87	6	1	1	P
		87/88	2			P
Partick T		87/88	21		1	D1

SEATON Andrew Murray
b. Edinburgh 16.9.1977

Stoneyburn Jnrs						
Falkirk		95/96	0	1		P
		96/97	26	3		D1
		97/98	24	6		D1
		98/99	16	8		D1
		99/00	9	10		D1

SEGERS Johannes
b. Eindhoven 30.10.1961

PSV Eindhoven						
Nottingham F		84/85	28			FL
		85/86	11			FL
		86/87	14			FL
Stoke C	L	86/87	1			FL
Nottingham F		87/88	5			FL
Sheffield U	L	87/88	10			FL
Dunfermline A	L	87/88	4			P
Wimbledon		88/89	33			FL
		89/90	38			FL
		90/91	37			FL
		91/92	41			FL
		92/93	41			FL
		93/94	41			FL
		94/95	31	1		FL
		95/96	3	1		FL
Wolverhampton W		96/97				
		97/98	11			FL

SEKERLIOGLU Attila
b. Linz 27.1.1965

FC Tirol						
St Johnstone		95/96	22	2	6	D1
		96/97	17		2	D1
		97/98	16	1	1	P

SELLARS Neil Andrew
b. Kirkcaldy 9.5.1977

Raith R		95/96	0	1		P

SEVERIN Scott Derek
b. Stirling 15.2.1979

Musselburgh A						
Heart of Midlothian		98/99	5	2		P
		99/00	18	6	2	P

SHANKS David Thow
b. Bellshill 18.4.1962

Broxburn A						
Cowdenbeath		82/83	2			D2
		83/84	28	1	2	D2
Clydebank		83/84	3		1	D1
		84/85	34		2	D1
		85/86	30		3	P
		86/87	40	1	1	P
		87/88	25	1		D1
Motherwell		87/88	6	1		P
		88/89	2	2		P
Alloa A		89/90	3			D1
Clyde		89/90	8	3	1	D1
Stirling A		90/91	35		2	D2
		91/92	32	2	1	D1
		92/93	21	3	1	D1
Queen of the South		93/94	13	1		D2
Arbroath		94/95	22	1	1	D3

SHANKS Mark
b. Airdrie 19.5.1959

Blackburn R						FL
Motherwell		78/79	10	1		P
Ayr U		79/80	9	1		D1
		80/81	34		1	D1
		81/82	33	1	2	D1
		82/83	29	3		D1
		83/84	30			D1
		84/85	31			D1
Cyprus		85/86				
Dumbarton		85/86	3	2		D1
Queen of the South		86/87	12			D1
		87/88	16	5		D1
		88/89	26	3		D1
		89/90	18	3		D2

SHANNON Robert
b. Bellshill 20.4.1966

Dundee		83/84	5	1		P
		84/85	2	1		P
		85/86	33			P
		86/87	39		5	P
		87/88	41			P
		88/89	29		1	P
		89/90	36		1	P
		90/91	37		2	D1
		91/92	3			D1
Middlesbrough	L	91/92	0	1		FL
Dunfermline A		91/92	27			P
		92/93	42			D1
Motherwell		93/94	41	2		P
		94/95	23	2	3	P
Dundee U		95/96	26		1	D1
		96/97	7	2		P
Hibernian		96/97	5			P
		97/98				
		98/99	1			D1
East Fife		99/00	4			D3

SHARP Lee
b. Glasgow 22.5.1975

Ashfield					
Dumbarton	95/96	14	1	1	D1
	96/97	35		5	D2
	97/98	34		7	D3
	98/99	17		2	D3
Dundee	98/99	4	2	1	P
	99/00	11	3	1	P

SHARP Raymond
b. Stirling 16.11.1969

Stenhousemuir	88/89	5			D2
Dunfermline A	88/89	8	1		D1
	89/90	22	5		P
	90/91	30	1		P
	91/92	25			P
	92/93	27			D1
	93/94	30		1	D1
	94/95	2			D1
Preston NE	94/95	21			FL
	95/96	1			FL
	96/97	14	1		FL
	97/98	1	2		FL
Forfar A	98/99	9			D2
Alloa A	98/99	15	2		D2
	99/00	5	3		D2
East Fife	99/00	14		1	D3
Cowdenbeath	99/00	5		1	D3

SHARP Richard Cameron
b. Springburn 21.1.1956

Rangers					
Morton	75/76	19	1	5	D1
Kilmarnock	75/76	4	1		D1
	76/77	4	4		P
St Mirren	77/78	0	4		P
	78/79	2	2		P
Dunfermline A	78/79	9		4	D2
	79/80				
East Stirlingshire	80/81	19	7	2	D1
	81/82	11	4	2	D1
Strathclyde Police					

SHAW George
b. Glasgow 10.2.1969

St Mirren	87/88	0	2		P
	88/89	8	2	1	P
	89/90	18	5	2	P
	90/91	21	12	1	P
Partick T	91/92	40	3	9	D1
	92/93	28	3	10	P
	93/94	13	4	2	P
Dundee	93/94	17		6	P
	94/95	6			D1
	95/96	17	11	11	D1
	96/97	18	3	5	D1
Dunfermline A	96/97	0	3		P
	97/98	12	11	2	P
	98/99	10	8	2	P
Ross Co	99/00	32	1	13	D2

SHAW Graham
b. Edinburgh 8.10.1951

Musselburgh A					
Dunfermline A	71/72	1			D1
	72/73	36		26	D2
	73/74	28	1	8	D1
	74/75	33		12	D1
	75/76	18		6	D1
Heart of Midlothian	75/76	13		2	P
	76/77	30	5	7	P
	77/78	23	3	3	D1
	78/79	8		1	P
	79/80	15	5	2	D1
Arbroath	80/81	31	2	3	D2
	81/82	25	5	6	D2
	82/83	37	1	12	D2
	83/84	8		4	D2
	84/85	15	1	1	D2

SHAW Gregory
b. Dumfries 15.2.1970

Dalbeattie Star					
Ayr U	88/89	1	1		D1
	89/90	2	1		D1
	90/91	5	4		D1
	91/92	16	23	10	D1
	92/93	0	5		D1
Falkirk	92/93	4	2	2	P
	93/94	18	10	10	D1
	94/95	0	3		P
Dunfermline A	94/95	6			D1
	95/96	17	11	11	D1
	96/97				
Airdrieonians	97/98	0	2		D1
Clydebank	97/98	3	3		D2
Berwick R	98/99	14	7	4	D3

SHAW Robert
b. Bellshill 1.1.1965

Leicester C					
Motherwell	83/84	0	2		P

SHEARER Duncan Nichol
b. Fort William 28.8.1962

Inverness Clachnacuddin					
Chelsea	83/84				
	84/85				
	85/86	2		1	FL
Huddersfield T	85/86	7	1	7	FL
	86/87	42		21	FL
	87/88	36		8	FL
Swindon T	88/89	33	3	14	FL
	89/90	42		20	FL
	90/91	44		22	FL
	91/92	37		22	FL
Blackburn R	91/92	5	1	1	FL
Aberdeen	92/93	32	2	22	P
	93/94	39	4	17	P
	94/95	19	4	7	P
	95/96	15	15	3	P
	96/97	2	19	4	P
Inverness CT	97/98	17	7	5	D2
	98/99	21	9	12	D2
	99/00	0	1		D1

SHEED Ronald McLean
b. Provan ?.?.1947

East Kilbride Thistle					
Kilmarnock	69/70				
	70/71				
	71/72				
	72/73				
	73/74				
	74/75				
	75/76	16	1	1	D1
	76/77	18	3	1	P
Partick T	77/78	1			P
	78/79	1	1	1	P
	79/80	0	1		P
Duncanrigg Amateurs					

SHEPHERD Anthony
b. Glasgow 16.11.1966

Celtic	85/86	0	1		P
	86/87	16	5	2	P
	87/88	0	6	1	P
Bristol C L	88/89	2	1		FL
Carlisle U	89/90	30	1	2	FL
	90/91	43	1	6	FL
Motherwell	91/92	1	4		P
	92/93	2	3		P
Portadown	93/94				
	94/95				
Ayr U	95/96	10	1		D2
Stranraer	95/96	2			D2
Partick T	95/96	0	1		P
Albion R	96/97	5		1	D3
	97/98	7	5	2	D3

SHEPSTONE Paul Thomas Adam
b. Coventry 8.11.1970

Coventry C					
Birmingham C					FL
Atherstone U					
Blackburn R	90/91	15	10	1	FL
	91/92	1			FL
York C L	91/92	2			FL
Motherwell	92/93	1			P

SHIELDS Greg
b. Falkirk 21.8.1976

Rangers	95/96	1			P
	96/97	6			P
Dunfermline A	97/98	36			P
	98/99	36			P
Charlton A	99/00	21		2	FL

SHIELDS Paul Martin
b. Dunfermline 15.8.1981

Milton Green					
Raith R	98/99	6	8		D1
	99/00	1	8	1	D1
Celtic	99/00	0	1		P

SHIELDS Peter
b. Baillieston 14.8.1960

Ipswich T					
Heart of Midlothian	80/81	30			P
	81/82	37		1	D1
	82/83	22			D1
	83/84	2	1		P
Partick T	84/85	13	6		D1
Cowdenbeath	84/85	10			D2
	85/86	26			D2

SHIRRA James W
b. 10.6.1950

Gairdoch Juveniles					
Falkirk	67/68				
	68/69	0	1		D1
	69/70	8	1		D2
	70/71	32		2	D1
	71/72	31		3	D1
	72/73	32			D1
	73/74	30	3	1	D1
	74/75	23	4	14	D2
	75/76	23	3	5	D1
	76/77	11		2	D1
Aberdeen	76/77	20	6		P
	77/78	8			P
Dundee	77/78	22	1	2	D1
	78/79	30	2	5	D1
	79/80	27	4	3	P
	80/81	15	5	4	D1
South Melbourne Hellas	81/82				
	82/83				
Stirling A	83/84	27	2		D2

SHIVUTE Eliphas
b. Olujonda 27.9.1974

Eleven Arrows					
Motherwell	97/98	12	11	3	P
	98/99	0	1		P
China					

SIM Iain
b. 5.10.1958

Ayr U	77/78	3			P
	78/79				
Stranraer	79/80	24	2	3	D2
	80/81	8	1	1	D2

SIMAO Miguel Angel De La Cruz
b. Oporto 26.2.1973

CD Alaves					
St Johnstone	98/99	20	6	4	P
	99/00	6	11	1	P

SIMPSON Fitzroy
b. Bradford on Avon 26.2.1970

Swindon T	88/89	3	4		FL
	89/90	19	11	2	FL
	90/91	27	11	3	FL
	91/92	29	1	4	FL
Manchester C	91/92	9	2	1	FL
	92/93	27	2	1	FL
	93/94	12	3		FL
	94/95	10	6	2	FL
Bristol C L	94/95	4			FL
Portsmouth	95/96	27	3	5	FL
	96/97	40	1	4	FL
	97/98	17	2		FL
	98/99	38	3	1	FL
	99/00	17			FL
Heart of Midlothian	99/00	7	4		P

SIMPSON James Bowman
b. Motherwell 24.4.1959

Muirkirk Jnrs					
Kilmarnock	82/83	17	1	1	P
	83/84	23	2		D1
Dumbarton	84/85	15	10	3	P
	85/86	3	4		D1
Morton	85/86	25		1	D1
	86/87	3			D1

SIMPSON Mark D
b. Edinburgh 19.9.1972

Falkirk	91/92	0	1		P

SIMPSON Neil
b. Hackney 15.11.1961

Middlefield Wasps					
Aberdeen	78/79				
	79/80				
	80/81	15	1	2	P
	81/82	24	5	4	P
	82/83	29	4	4	P
	83/84	21	3	2	P
	84/85	33		4	P
	85/86	22		1	P
	86/87	8			P
	87/88	14	1	1	P
	88/89	16			P
	89/90	5	4		P
Newcastle U	90/91	1	3		FL
Motherwell	91/92	20	1		P
	92/93	12		1	P

SINCLAIR Christopher
b. Sheffield 11.11.1970
Sauchie A

Dunfermline A	89/90	1			P
	90/91	0	3		P
	91/92	10	7	1	P
	92/93	1	5		D1
	93/94	1	5	1	D1
	94/95	0	1		D1
Meadowbank T	94/95	13	4	1	D2
Livingston	95/96	17	4	3	D3
	96/97	4	7		D2
Albion R	97/98	24	6	2	D3
	98/99	2	2		D3

SINCLAIR David
b. Dunfermline 6.10.1969

Stenhousemuir *	88/89	1			D2
	89/90				
Raith R	90/91	15	8	1	D1
	91/92	19	3	1	D1
	92/93	25	7		D1
	93/94	29	7	2	P
	94/95	31	1	3	D1
	95/96	31	1	3	P
Millwall	96/97	6	2		FL
Dundee U	96/97	3	3		P
	97/98	0	4		P
Livingston	97/98	5			D2
Falkirk	98/99	23			D1
	99/00	19	3	1	D1

SINCLAIR Duncan Eric
b. Haggs 13.1.1954
Kilsyth R

Dundee	75/76	9	3	2	P
	76/77	30	2	11	D1
	77/78	27	7	13	D1
	78/79	27	4	10	D1
	79/80	35		8	P
	80/81	36		19	D1
	81/82	24	1	7	P
	82/83	25	6	6	P
	83/84	0	1		D1
St Mirren	83/84	2	1		P
Airdrieonians	83/84	14	2	1	D1

SINCLAIR Graeme James
b. Paisley 1.7.1957
Eastercraigs Amateurs

Dumbarton	76/77	38			D1
	77/78	36			D1
	78/79	27	1	2	D1
	79/80	39			D1
	80/81	36			D1
	81/82	24	2		D1
Celtic	82/83	25			P
	83/84	15	5	1	P
	84/85	5	1		P
Manchester C L	84/85	1			FL
Dumbarton	84/85	5			P

SINCLAIR James A
b. East Kilbride 31.7.1957
Kirkbryde KV
Sighthill Amateurs

Queens Park	75/76	1	2		D2
	76/77	6	3	1	D2
	77/78				
	78/79	22		2	D2
	79/80	37		1	D2
	80/81	36	1		D2
Clyde	81/82	37	1	1	D2
	82/83	29	5	2	D1
	83/84	4	2		D1
Stirling A	83/84	21	1		D2
	84/85	31			D2
Hamilton A	85/86	38			D1
	86/87	3			P
Queen of the South	87/88	41			D1
	88/89	16	1		D1
Stirling A *	88/89	2			D2
Stenhousemuir *	88/89	1			D2

SINNET James W
b. Blackridge 5.12.1959

Cowdenbeath	81/82	1			D2
Albion R	81/82	1		1	D2
Bo'ness U	82/83				
	83/84				
	84/85				
Stenhousemuir	85/86	35		11	D2
	86/87	3			D2
Clydebank	86/87	2	1	1	P
Cowdenbeath	87/88	9		5	D2

SKILLING Mark James
b. Irvine 6.10.1972

Kilmarnock	92/93	40		4	D1
	93/94	23		3	P
	94/95	13	4	3	P
	95/96	13	2	1	P
	96/97				
	97/98				
Stranraer	98/99	25	3	1	D1

SKINNER Justin
b. Hounslow 30.1.1969

Fulham	86/87	2	1		FL
	87/88	27	5	6	FL
	88/89	34	4	8	FL
	89/90	24	6	4	FL
	90/91	24	8	5	FL
Bristol R	91/92	41	1	3	FL
	92/93	12			FL
	93/94	27	2	5	FL
	94/95	38		2	FL
	95/96	23	5		FL
	96/97	29	5		FL
	97/98	4			FL
Walsall L	97/98	10			FL
Hibernian	97/98	5	1		P
	98/99	24		2	D1
	99/00	1	1		P
Dunfermline A	99/00	26	2		D1

SKOLDMARK Magnus
b. Langsele 22.9.1968
Orebro
Dalian Wanda

Dundee U	97/98	15	4		P
	98/99	22	3		P
	99/00	7	3	1	P

SKONHOFT Odd Harild
b. 26.9.1973

Raith R	96/97	1			P

SLATER Mark Andrew
b. Buckie 2.4.1979
Buckie Thistle

Dundee	99/00	0	1		P

SLATER Stuart Ian
b. Sudbury 27.3.1969

West Ham U	87/88	0	2		FL
	88/89	16	2	1	FL
	89/90	40		7	FL
	90/91	37	3	3	FL
	91/92	41			FL
Celtic	92/93	37	2	2	P
	93/94	3	2	1	P
Ipswich T	93/94	28		1	FL
	94/95	22	5	1	FL
	95/96	11	6	2	FL
	96/97				
Leicester C	96/97				
Watford	96/97	13	3	1	FL
	97/98	9	5		FL
	98/99				

SLAVEN Bernard Joseph
b. Paisley 13.11.1960

Morton	81/82	8	5	1	P
	82/83	3	5		P
Airdrieonians	83/84	2			D1
Queen of the South	83/84	2			D2
Albion R	83/84	3			D2
	84/85	39		27	D2
Middlesbrough	85/86	32		8	FL
	86/87	46		17	FL
	87/88	44		21	FL
	88/89	36	1	15	FL
	89/90	46		21	FL
	90/91	41	5	16	FL
	91/92	28	10	16	FL
	92/93	13	5	4	FL
Port Vale	92/93	9	1	2	FL
	93/94	20	3	7	FL
Darlington	93/94	11		2	FL
	94/95	24	2	5	FL

SLAVIN James
b. Lanark 18.1.1975

Celtic	94/95	3			P
Partick T	95/96	8			P
	96/97	17	1		D1

SLOAN Mark Scott
b. Wallsend 14.12.1967

Berwick R	88/89	26		4	D2
	89/90	32	2	16	D2
Newcastle U	90/91	11	5	1	FL
Falkirk	91/92	20	3	4	P
	92/93	21	8	6	P
	93/94	8	4	1	D1
Cambridge U L	93/94	4		1	FL
Hartlepool U	94/95	26	3	2	FL
	95/96	1	5		FL
?	96/97				
Berwick R	97/98	1			D3

SLUDDEN John
b. Falkirk 29.12.1964
Celtic

St Johnstone	83/84	1	4		P
	84/85	22	6	6	D1
Airdrieonians	85/86	8	1		D1
Ayr U	85/86	16		5	D1
	86/87	37		26	D2
	87/88	39		31	D2
	88/89	39		15	D1
	89/90	6	3	1	D1
Kilmarnock	89/90	22		7	D2
	90/91	23	3	8	D1
East Fife	91/92	39		21	D2
	92/93	31	1	13	D2
Clydebank	92/93	1			D1
Clyde	93/94	16	1	4	D1
Stenhousemuir	93/94	18		13	D2
	94/95	4	1	1	D2

SMITH Alexander

Luncarty

St Johnstone	74/75	11			D1
	75/76	23	1		P
	76/77	27			D1

SMITH Andrew Mark
b. Aberdeen 27.11.1968
Peterhead

Airdrieonians	90/91	17	11	3	D1
	91/92	22	7	4	P
	92/93	20	14	4	P
	93/94	25	13	7	D1
	94/95	24	12	12	D1
Dunfermline A	95/96	17	2	9	D1
	96/97	30	5	10	P
	97/98	33		16	P
	98/99	29	6	8	P
	99/00	11	1	3	D1
Kilmarnock	99/00	11	4	1	P

SMITH Barry Martin
b. Paisley 19.2.1974
Giffnock North

Celtic	91/92	1	2		P
	92/93	4	2		P
	93/94	6	1		P
	94/95	3			P
Dundee	95/96	20			D1
	96/97	36			D1
	97/98	34		1	D1
	98/99	29	4		P
	99/00	32			P

SMITH Charles

Falkirk	66/67	21			D1
	67/68	11	1	2	D1
	68/69	34		3	D1
Partick T	69/70	33		2	D1
	70/71				
	71/72	11	1		D1
	72/73	3			D1
Falkirk	73/74	8	1		D1
	74/75	23	4	6	D2
St Johnstone	75/76	8	1	3	P

SMITH David
b. Glasgow 28.10.1965
Leven Valley

Clydebank	84/85	5	4	1	D1
	85/86	0	1		P
Stranraer	86/87	5	3		D2

SMITH Douglas
b. Aberdeen

Dundee U		59/60	1			D2
		60/61	6			D1
		61/62	33			D1
		62/63	34		1	D1
		63/64	33			D1
		64/65	34			D1
		65/66	34			D1
		66/67	34			D1
		67/68	34			D1
		68/69	34			D1
		69/70	34		1	D1
		70/71	34		5	D1
		71/72	25		2	D1
		72/73	31		5	D1
		73/74	26		3	D1
		74/75	20	2	1	D1
		75/76	7			P

SMITH Gary
b. Glasgow 25.3.1971

Falkirk		88/89	2	1		P
		89/90	36			D1
		90/91	27	4		D1
Aberdeen		91/92	15	1	1	P
		92/93	40			P
		93/94	19	2		P
		94/95	31			P
		95/96	33			P
France		96/97				
Aberdeen		97/98	31		1	P
		98/99	30			P
		99/00	6			P

SMITH Gordon
b. Haddington 12.6.1959

Heart of Midlothian		76/77	3	1	2	P
		77/78	2	3		D1
Berwick R		78/79	23	1	8	D2
		79/80	34	1	9	D1
		80/81	8	2	2	D1
Falkirk		81/82	33		7	D1
		82/83	8	2	2	D1
Meadowbank T		82/83	18	3	6	D2
		83/84	27	6	7	D1
		84/85	31	3	11	D1
		85/86	2	1		D2
Partick T		85/86	22		11	D1
		86/87	7	2		D1
East Fife		86/87	16	1	4	D1
		87/88	23	10	5	D1
Berwick R *		88/89	4			D2

SMITH Gordon Duffield
b. Kilwinning 29.12.1954
Kilmarnock Star

Kilmarnock		71/72				
		72/73	34		4	D1
		73/74	34		11	D2
		74/75	31	2	5	D1
		75/76	25		9	D1
		76/77	32	3	7	P
Rangers		77/78	34	1	20	P
		78/79	31	2	11	P
		79/80	20	10	4	P
Brighton		80/81	36	2	10	FL
		81/82	24	3	2	FL
		82/83	26	3		FL
Rangers	L	82/83	1	1		P
Brighton		83/84	11	4	4	FL
Manchester C		83/84	9		1	FL
		84/85	31	1	12	FL
		85/86	0	1		FL
Oldham A		85/86	14	1		FL
Admira Wacker		86/87				
FC Basel		87/88				
Stirling A		88/89	3			D2
Oldham A						

SMITH Gordon Melville
b. Glasgow 3.7.1954
Rangers BC

St Johnstone		72/73	12	1		D1
		73/74	33	1	5	D1
		74/75	32	1	1	D1
		75/76	32		2	P
Aston Villa		76/77	32	2		FL
		77/78	38			FL
		78/79	6	1		FL
Tottenham H		78/79	1	1		FL
		79/80	14			FL
		80/81	18	2	1	FL
		81/82	1	1		FL
Wolverhampton W		82/83	24	3	2	FL
		83/84	23	1	3	FL
South Africa						
Pittsburgh Spirit						

SMITH Henry George
b. Lanark 10.3.1956
Leeds U

Heart of Midlothian		81/82	33			D1
		82/83	39			D1
		83/84	36			P
		84/85	36			P
		85/86	36			P
		86/87	43			P
		87/88	44			P
		88/89	36			P
		89/90	36			P
		90/91	23			P
		91/92	44			P
		92/93	25			P
		93/94	27			P
		94/95	14	1		P
		95/96	3			P
Ayr U		95/96	9			D2
		96/97	35			D2
		97/98	2	1		D1

SMITH Ian
b. 2.4.1952

Heart of Midlothian		77/78	3	5	2	D1
		78/79	0	1		P

SMITH James
b. Elderslie 14.5.1961

Dundee		81/82	17		1	P
		82/83	36		1	P
		83/84	32	3		P
		84/85	19	4	1	P
		85/86	32			P
		86/87	39			P
		87/88	39	1	2	P
		88/89	7			P
		89/90	4			P
Airdrieonians		90/91	28		1	D1
		91/92	1			P
Montrose		91/92	11		1	D1
		92/93	28			D2
		93/94	31			D2

SMITH Joseph
b. Glasgow 11.11.1953
Aberdeen

Banks o'Dee	L					
Aberdeen		72/73	13	1		D1
		73/74	23	2	1	D1
		74/75	23	3	1	D1
		75/76	33		2	P
		76/77	39			P
		77/78	7			P
		78/79	0	2		P
Motherwell		78/79	14			P
		79/80	22	2		D1
		80/81	19			D1
		81/82				
		82/83				
Dunfermline A		83/84	1			D2

SMITH Kenneth
b. Dumbarton 9.10.1959

Stenhousemuir *		81/82	1			D2
Partick T		81/82	1			P
		82/83	2			D1
East Stirlingshire		83/84	4			D2

SMITH Mark Alexander
b. Bellshill 16.12.1964
St Mirren BC

Queens Park		83/84	11	4	2	D2
		84/85	32	4	2	D2
		85/86	28	3	3	D2
Celtic		86/87	3	3		P
Dunfermline A		87/88	30		5	P
		88/89	18	4	1	D1
Hamilton A	L	89/90	5		1	D1
Stoke C	L	89/90	2			FL
Nottingham F		90/91				
Reading	L	90/91	3			FL
Mansfield T	L	90/91	6	1		FL
Shrewsbury T		91/92	19	3	1	FL
		92/93	31			FL
		93/94	4	4		FL
		94/95	10	7	2	FL
Ayr U		95/96	8	2	1	D2
Queens Park		95/96	1			D3
		96/97	12	6		D3
		97/98	4	1		D3

SMITH Paul McKinnon
b. Currie 2.11.1962
Tynecastle BC

Dundee		80/81				
		81/82				
Dundee U		82/83				
Raith R		83/84	38		8	D1
		84/85	38		19	D2
		85/86	35		21	D2
Motherwell		86/87	42	2	9	P
		87/88	25	5	4	P
		88/89	3	1		P
Dunfermline A		88/89	35		5	D1
		89/90	32	1	4	P
		90/91	25	6	2	P
Falkirk		91/92	31	1	2	P
		92/93	19		1	P
Dunfermline A		92/93	16		1	D1
		93/94	43	1	9	D1
		94/95	34		6	D1
		95/96	10	1		D1
Heart of Midlothian		95/96	4	5		P
Ayr U		96/97	27	6	9	D2
Berwick R		97/98	2	1		D3

SMITH Robert Nisbet
b. Dalkeith 21.12.1953

Hibernian		72/73	5	4		D1
		73/74	5	6	2	D1
		74/75	16	5	3	D1
		75/76	20	3	6	P
		76/77	36		8	P
		77/78	32	3		P
		78/79	17			P
Leicester C		78/79	17		6	FL
		79/80	35		12	FL
		80/81	17	2	1	FL
		81/82	2	2		FL
Peterborough U	L	81/82	5			FL
Leicester C		82/83	26		1	FL
Hibernian	L	82/83	4	1		P
Leicester C		83/84	35	1		FL
		84/85	30			FL
		85/86	13	1	1	FL
Hibernian		86/87	9	1		P
Dunfermline A		87/88	33	2		P
		88/89	32	1	1	D1
Partick T		89/90	29	1	1	D1
Berwick R		90/91	24	2		D2

SMITH Thomas William
b. Glasgow 12.10.1973

Partick T		90/91	0	1		D1
		91/92				
		92/93	2			P
		93/94	3	5	1	P
		94/95	8	6	1	P
		95/96	24	1	2	P
		96/97	0	1		D1
Ayr U		96/97	19	2	4	D2
		97/98	13	5	1	D1
Clydebank		98/99	20	1	3	D1
Hibernian		98/99	3	2		D1
		99/00	21			P

SMITH Trevor A
b. Whitburn 6.5.1965
Sauchie Juveniles

Dunfermline A		82/83	15	3		D1
		83/84	9	7	1	D2
		84/85	11	6	5	D2
		85/86	10	14	3	D2
		86/87	7	7		D1
		87/88	5	8		P
		88/89	18	5	5	D1
Hamilton A	L	89/90	3		2	D1
Kilmarnock		90/91	9	4	1	D1
Hamilton A		91/92	25	4	13	D1
		92/93	22	6	8	D1
Portadown						

SMITH Walter
b. 24.2.1948
Glasgow Ashfield

Dundee U		66/67	1			D1
		67/68	2			D1
		68/69				
		69/70	4	1		D1
		70/71	17			D1
		71/72	14	4		D1
		72/73	14		1	D1
		73/74	30	2	1	D1
		74/75	16	2		D1
		75/76	2			P
Dumbarton		75/76	21			D1
		76/77	23			D1
Dundee U		76/77	17	1		P
		77/78	0	1		P
		78/79	5			P
		79/80	1			P
		80/81	1			P

SNEDDON Alan
b. Baillieston 12.3.1958
Larkhall Thistle

Celtic		77/78	15			P
		78/79	4			P
		79/80	32		1	P
		80/81	15			P
Hibernian		80/81	14			D1
		81/82	34	2		P
		82/83	36			P
		83/84	35		1	P
		84/85	36		2	P
		85/86	30	1	2	P
		86/87	24	2		P
		87/88	32			P
		88/89	26			P
		89/90	28	1	2	P
		90/91	5	1		P
		91/92	3	2		P
Motherwell		92/93	16			P
East Fife		93/94	33	1	2	D2
		94/95	34		2	D2
		95/96	0	3		D2

SNELDERS Theodorus G A
b. Westervoort 7.12.1963
FC Twente

Aberdeen		88/89	36			P
		89/90	23			P
		90/91	21			P
		91/92	42			P
		92/93	41			P
		93/94	33			P
		94/95	24			P
		95/96	6	1		P
Rangers		95/96	2			P
		96/97	4			P
		97/98	7			P

SNODIN Glynn
b. Rotherham 14.2.1960

Doncaster R		76/77	1	3		FL
		77/78	13	9	2	FL
		78/79	28	6	3	FL
		79/80	40	1	1	FL
		80/81	44		3	FL
		81/82	40		7	FL
		82/83	38		14	FL
		83/84	41	2	13	FL
		84/85	43		20	FL
Sheffield W		85/86	27	1	1	FL
		86/87	24	7		FL
Leeds U		87/88	33	2	7	FL
		88/89	33	2	3	FL
		89/90	3	1		FL
		90/91	14	6		FL
		91/92				
Oldham A	L	91/92	8		1	FL
Rotherham U	L	91/92	3			FL
Heart of Midlothian		91/92	4	3		P
		92/93	16	11		P
Barnsley		93/94	7	4		FL
		94/95	11	3		FL

SOLBERG Thomas
b. Oslo 25.1.1970
Moss FK
Viking Stavanger

Aberdeen		99/00	26		4	P

SOMMERVILLE James

Motherwell		77/78	0	1		P
		78/79	3	4		P

SOMNER Douglas
b. East Kilbride 4.7.1951
East Kilbride R
East Kilbride Thistle

Falkirk		71/72	23	2	6	D1
		72/73	10	2	6	D1
		73/74	6	2	1	D1
Ayr U		74/75	3	2	1	D1
Partick T		74/75	21		8	D1
		75/76	26		16	D1
		76/77	33		11	P
		77/78	31		15	P
		78/79	31	2	11	P
St Mirren		79/80	32		25	P
		80/81	29		13	P
		81/82	14	2	2	P
		82/83	15	7	5	P
Hamilton A		83/84	33	3	9	D1
Montrose		84/85	31	3	12	D2
		85/86	30	2	3	D1

SOUNESS Graeme James
b. Edinburgh 6.5.1963

Tottenham H		70/71				
		71/72				
Middlesbrough		72/73				
		73/74				
		74/75				
		75/76	34	1	3	FL
		76/77	38		2	FL
		77/78	19		3	FL
Liverpool		77/78	15		2	FL
		78/79	41		8	FL
		79/80	41		1	FL
		80/81	37		6	FL
		81/82	34	1	5	FL
		82/83	41		9	FL
		83/84	37		7	FL
Sampdoria		84/85				
		85/86				
Rangers		86/87	24	1	1	P
		87/88	14	4	2	P
		88/89	0	6		P
		89/90	0	1		P

SPACKMAN Nigel James
b. Romsey 2.12.1960
Andover

Bournemouth		80/81	44		3	FL
		81/82	34	1	3	FL
		82/83	40		4	FL
Chelsea		83/84	40		3	FL
		84/85	42		1	FL
		85/86	37	2	7	FL
		86/87	20		1	FL
Liverpool		86/87	12			FL
		87/88	19	8		FL
		88/89	8	4		FL
QPR		88/89	16		1	FL
		89/90	11	2		FL
Rangers		89/90	21		1	P
		90/91	35			P
		91/92	42			P
		92/93	2			P
Chelsea		92/93	6			FL
		93/94	5	4		FL
		94/95	36			FL
		95/96	13	3		FL
Sheffield U		96/97	19	4		FL

SPALDING Derek
b. 20.12.1954

Hibernian		72/73	2			D1
		73/74	13			D1
		74/75	21	1	1	D1
		75/76	16	1		P
		76/77	18	2		P
		77/78				
Chicago Sting		78	29		2	NA
		79	23		7	NA
		80	30		4	NA
		81	28		2	NA
		82	9			NA
Toronto Blizzard		83	24			NA
		84	10			NA

SPEIRS Charles
b. Paisley 22.3.1966
Glasgow Amateurs

Hamilton A		82/83	1	1		D1
		83/84	27	1	1	D1
		84/85	33		1	D1
		85/86	24			D1
		86/87	13	1	1	P
		87/88	15	3	1	D1
Queen of the South	L	87/88	3			D1
Hamilton A		88/89	3	3		P
Clyde		88/89	17		1	D1
		89/90	38		3	D1
		90/91	33		2	D1
		91/92	23	3	1	D2
		92/93	1	2		D2
Shotts Bon Accord		93/94				
		94/95				
Albion R		95/96	9		1	D3
Shotts Bon Accord						

SPEIRS W Gardner
b. Airdrie 14.4.1963

St Mirren		80/81	1	1		P
		81/82	1	2	1	P
		82/83	0	1		P
		83/84	9	1		P
		84/85	16	1	6	P
		85/86	25	6	7	P
		86/87	19	7	2	P
		87/88				
Kilmarnock	L	88/89	4	1		D1
Dunfermline A	L	88/89	2	2		D1
Hartlepool U		89/90	0	1		FL
Airdrieonians		89/90	6	3	1	D1
		90/91				
East Stirlingshire		91/92	19		2	D2

SPENCER John
b. Glasgow 11.9.1970

Rangers		88/89				
Morton	L	88/89	4		1	D1
Rangers		89/90				
Lai Sun	L	89/90				
Rangers		90/91	3	2	1	P
		91/92	4	4	1	P
Chelsea		92/93	13	10	7	FL
		93/94	13	6	5	FL
		94/95	26	3	11	FL
		95/96	23	5	13	FL
		96/97	0	4		FL
QPR		96/97	25		17	FL
		97/98	22	1	5	FL
Everton	L	97/98	3	3		FL
Motherwell		98/99	21		7	P
		99/00	25	3	11	P

SPROAT Hugh
b. Ayr 16.11.1952
Auchinleck Talbot

Ayr U		74/75	11			D1
		75/76	36			P
		76/77	15			P
		77/78	28			P
		78/79	38			D1
Motherwell		79/80	39			D1
		80/81	34			D1
		81/82	35			D1
		82/83	21			P
		83/84	17			P
Ayr U		84/85	37			D1
		85/86	24			D1

SPROTT Adrian
b. Edinburgh 23.3.1962
North Merchiston BC

Meadowbank T		79/80	1		1	D2
		80/81	27	4	8	D2
		81/82	35	4	9	D2
		82/83	38		11	D2
		83/84	33	4	6	D1
		84/85	38	1	14	D1
		85/86	11	2	3	D2
Hamilton A		85/86	17	1	3	D1
		86/87	26		2	P
		87/88	40	1	6	D1
Meadowbank T		88/89	38		5	D1
		89/90	37	2	1	D1
		90/91	20		2	D1
		91/92	24	3	1	D1
		92/93				
Stenhousemuir		93/94	32	3	6	D2
		94/95	28	1	7	D2
		95/96	30	1	8	D2
		96/97	23	8	1	D2
		97/98	29	1	2	D2
		98/99	17	13	3	D3

SQUIRES James Alexander
b. Preston 15.11.1975

Preston NE		93/94	4			FL
		94/95	11			FL
		95/96	3	4		FL
		96/97	6	3		FL
Mansfield T	L	97/98	1			FL
Dunfermline A		97/98	2	3		P
		98/99	19	2	2	P

STAINROD Simon Allan
b. Sheffield 1.2.1959

Sheffield U		75/76	7		2	FL
		76/77	19	2	3	FL
		77/78	24	1	6	FL
		78/79	9	5	3	FL
Oldham A		78/79	14		5	FL
		79/80	37		11	FL
		80/81	18		5	FL
QPR		80/81	15		4	FL
		81/82	39		17	FL
		82/83	29	2	9	FL
		83/84	41		13	FL
		84/85	19		4	FL
Sheffield W		84/85	5	4	1	FL
		85/86	3	3	1	FL
Aston Villa		85/86	29	1	10	FL
		86/87	25	4	6	FL
		87/88	4			FL
Stoke C		87/88	11	1	2	FL
		88/89	16		4	FL
		89/90				
Strasbourg	L	89/90				
Falkirk		90/91	37		16	P
		91/92	22	1	5	P
Dundee		91/92	10	2	2	D1
		92/93	10	10	7	P
		93/94	1			P
Ayr U		93/94	7	3	2	D1
		94/95	15	4	2	D1
		95/96	2			D2

STANTON Patrick Gordon
b. Edinburgh 13.9.1944

United Crossroads						
Salvesen BC						
Dunfermline A	T					
Edina Hearts						
Bonnyrigg Rose						
Hibernian		63/64	15		1	D1
		64/65	33			D1
		65/66	34		2	D1
		66/67	33		1	D1
		67/68	26			D1
		68/69	33		1	D1
		69/70	31		6	D1
		70/71	30		3	D1
		71/72	32		9	D1
		72/73	33		8	D1
		73/74	32		9	D1
		74/75	34		6	D1
		75/76	31	2	5	P
Celtic		76/77	36			P
		77/78	1			P

STARK Derek
b. Dunfermline 19.11.1958

Glenrothes Jnrs						
Dundee U		77/78	1			P
		78/79	30	1	1	P
		79/80	32	1	1	P
		80/81	21	1		P
		81/82	18	2		P
		82/83	31	1	2	P
		83/84	23	2	3	P

STARK William
b. Glasgow 1.12.1956

Anniesland Waverley						
St Mirren		75/76	14	7		D1
		76/77	33	2	11	D1
		77/78	31	2	7	P
		78/79	32		9	P
		79/80	35	1	8	P
		80/81	33	1	5	P
		81/82	32	1	10	P
		82/83	29	2	4	P
Aberdeen		83/84	11	3	6	P
		84/85	30	2	15	P
		85/86	28	2	8	P
		86/87	31	5	12	P
Celtic		87/88	34	3	8	P
		88/89	22	3	9	P
		89/90	2			P
Kilmarnock		90/91	21		6	D1
		91/92	1			D1
Hamilton A		91/92	6	8		D1
Kilmarnock		92/93	28		3	D1
		93/94	6	2		P

STAVRUM Arild
b. Kristiansand 16.4.1972

Viking Stavanger						
Aberdeen		99/00	22		9	P

STEELE James
b. Edinburgh 11.3.1950

Dundee		67/68	1			D1
		68/69	3	1	1	D1
		69/70	23		2	D1
		70/71	28		1	D1
		71/72	19		1	D1
Southampton		71/72	16			FL
		72/73	38		1	FL
		73/74	34	1		FL
		74/75	27			FL
		75/76	32		1	FL
		76/77	13			FL
Rangers	L	76/77	5			P
Washington Diplomats						
Memphis Rogues						
Chicago						
Pittsburgh						

STEELE William
b. Dunfermline 19.5.1956

Oakley						
Rangers		71/72				
		72/73				
		73/74				
		74/75				
Dundee U		75/76	4	6		P
Dumbarton		76/77	16	4	2	D1
Cowdenbeath		77/78	34	5	20	D2
		78/79	35	2	20	D2
		79/80	35	3	13	D2
		80/81	32		10	D2
		81/82	26		7	D2
Arbroath		81/82	5	4	3	D2
		82/83	31	2	15	D2
		83/84	19	5	4	D2

STEELE William Burnie
b. Kilmarnock 12.10.1953

Hamilton A		70/71				
Stirling A		70/71				
		71/72	22	1	9	D2
		72/73	36		14	D2
		73/74	36		18	D2
		74/75	37	1	19	D2
		75/76	20	1	4	D2
		76/77	1	18	12	D2
		77/78	32	4	13	D1
		78/79	15	6	7	D1
		79/80	3			D1
		80/81	23	5	4	D1
		81/82	18		3	D2
Airdrieonians	L	81/82	0	1		P
Stirling A		82/83	18	7	5	D2

STEIN Colin Anderson
b. Linlithgow 10.5.1947

Broxburn Strollers						
Armadale Thistle						
Hibernian		65/66	13		8	D1
		66/67	18		9	D1
		67/68	32		21	D1
		68/69	7		3	D1
Rangers		68/69	18		13	D1
		69/70	33		24	D1
		70/71	30		12	D1
		71/72	28		11	D1
		72/73	2	1		D1
Coventry C		72/73	31		10	FL
		73/74	28		6	FL
		74/75	24		6	FL
Rangers		74/75	8		3	P
		75/76	3	3	1	P
		76/77	1	1		P
		77/78				
Kilmarnock	L	77/78	23	1	8	D1

STEIN Jay
b. Dunfermline 13.1.1979

Inverkeithing U						
Raith R		96/97	0	2		P
		97/98	7	12		D1
		98/99	6	14	1	D1
		99/00	32	3	5	D1

STEINMANN Gijbertus P
b. Netherlands 2.4.1961

FC Utrecht						
Dundee U		90/91	13	1	1	P

STENSAAS Stale
b. Trondheim 7.7.1971

Rosenborg Trondheim		92				
		93				
		94				
		95				
		96				
		97				
Rangers		97/98	17	3	1	P
		98/99	1			P
Nottingham F		98/99	6	1		FL

STEPHEN Raymond
b. Aberdeen 9.12.1962

Dundee		80/81	19	4	8	D1
		81/82	9	15	4	P
		82/83	27	2	5	P
		83/84	18	2	3	P
		84/85	34	1	8	P
		85/86	32	1	14	P
		86/87	17		5	P
Nancy		87/88				
		88/89				
		89/90				
		90/91				
Kilmarnock		91/92	1			D1
Cove R						

STERLAND Melvyn
b. Sheffield 9.12.1962

Sheffield W		78/79	1	1	1	FL
		79/80	2			FL
		80/81	21	1	2	FL
		81/82	27			FL
		82/83	35			FL
		83/84	39		8	FL
		84/85	21	3	2	FL
		85/86	37	1	8	FL
		86/87	30		2	FL
		87/88	38		8	FL
		88/89	22		6	FL
Rangers		88/89	7	2	3	P
Leeds U		89/90	41	1	5	FL
		90/91	38		5	FL
		91/92	29	2	6	FL
		92/93	3			FL

STEVEN Trevor McGregor
b. Berwick 21.9.1963

Burnley		80/81	0	1		FL
		81/82	36		3	FL
		82/83	38	1	8	FL
Everton		83/84	23	4	1	FL
		84/85	40		12	FL
		85/86	41		9	FL
		86/87	41		14	FL
		87/88	36		6	FL
		88/89	29		6	FL
Rangers		89/90	34		3	P
		90/91	19		2	P
		91/92	2		1	P
		92/93	24		5	P
		93/94	32		4	P
		94/95	10	1		P
		95/96	5	1		P
		96/97	5	3	1	P

STEVENS Gregor MacKenzie
b. Glasgow 13.1.1955

Motherwell		74/75	4		1	D1
		75/76	30	3	4	P
		76/77	36		2	P
		77/78	35		6	P
		78/79	31		6	P
Leicester C		79/80	4			FL
Rangers		79/80	31		1	P
		80/81	7	2		P
		81/82	13			P
		82/83	10			P
		83/84	1			P
Heart of Midlothian	L	83/84	3			P
Motherwell		84/85	8			D1
Partick T		84/85	1			D1
		85/86	2			D1
Brechin C		86/87	32			D1
		87/88	35			D2
		88/89	21			D2
		89/90	7			D2
Dumbarton		89/90	8			D2

STEVENS Michael Gary
b. Barrow 27.3.1963

Everton		81/82	19		1	FL
		82/83	28			FL
		83/84	26	1	1	FL
		84/85	37		3	FL
		85/86	41		1	FL
		86/87	25		2	FL
		87/88	31			FL
Rangers		88/89	35		1	P
		89/90	35		1	P
		90/91	36		4	P
		91/92	43		2	P
		92/93	9			P
		93/94	28	1		P
Tranmere R		94/95	37		1	FL
		95/96	33	1		FL
		96/97	31			FL
		97/98	25		1	FL

STEVENSON James

Heart of Midlothian						
St Johnstone		75/76	1	2		P

STEWART Alexander
b. Bellshill 14.10.1965
Pollok Jnrs

Heart of Midlothian		84/85				
		85/86				
		86/87				
		87/88				
		88/89				
Kilmarnock		88/89	7		1	D1
Airdrieonians		89/90	0	8	3	D1
		90/91	18	7		D1
		91/92	41		1	P
		92/93	43		1	P
		93/94	36		2	D1
		94/95	32		1	D1
		95/96	30			D1
		96/97	31		3	D1
		97/98	27	1	1	D1
		98/99	31	1		D1
		99/00	28	1		D1

STEWART George
b. 29.8.1947

Dundee		66/67	9			D1
		67/68	23			D1
		68/69	24		1	D1
		69/70	21	1		D1
		70/71	9			D1
		71/72	16		1	D1
		72/73	33		2	D1
		73/74	11			D1
		74/75	28		2	D1
		75/76	25			P
Hibernian		76/77	29			P
		77/78	36		1	P
		78/79	27	2	1	P
		79/80	13			P
		80/81	2			D1

STEWART J

Falkirk		87/88	0	1		P

STEWART James Garvin
b. Kilwinning 9.3.1954
Troon Jnrs

Kilmarnock		71/72				
Rangers	L	71/72				
Kilmarnock		72/73	22			D1
		73/74	35			D2
		74/75	18			P
		75/76	26			D1
		76/77	35			P
Middlesbrough		77/78				
		78/79	27			FL
		79/80	5			FL
		80/81	2			FL
Rangers		80/81	10			P
		81/82	26			P
		82/83	18			P
		83/84	2			P
Dumbarton	L	83/84	2			D1
St Mirren		84/85	6			P
		85/86	3			P
Partick T		86/87	8			D1

STEWART Raymond Strean McDonald
b. Perth 7.9.1959
Errol R

Dundee U		75/76				
		76/77	1			P
		77/78	6		1	P
		78/79	34		4	P
		79/80	3			P
West Ham U		79/80	38		10	FL
		80/81	41		5	FL
		81/82	42		10	FL
		82/83	39		8	FL
		83/84	42		7	FL
		84/85	37		6	FL
		85/86	39		6	FL
		86/87	23		4	FL
		87/88	33		4	FL
		88/89	5	1	2	FL
		89/90				
		90/91	5			FL
St Johnstone		91/92	17		3	P
		92/93				
		93/94				
Stirling A		94/95	1	1		D2

STEWART Robert

Heart of Midlothian		78/79	4	1		P
		79/80	3	2	1	D1

STEWART Robert
b. Airdrie 3.1.1962
Whitburn Bluebells

Dunfermline A		81/82	21	5	7	D1
		82/83	21	3	6	D1
		83/84	21	8	4	D2
Motherwell		84/85	22	4	9	D1
		85/86	3	4	1	P
Falkirk		85/86	3	4		D1
		86/87	11	3		P
		87/88	25	11	7	P
		88/89	0	2		D1
Queen of the South		88/89	8	1		D1
		89/90	1	6		D2

STICKROTH Thomas
b. Stuttgart 13.4.1965
Bayer Uerdingen

St Mirren		89/90	6	1		P
		90/91	26	5	1	P
		91/92	13	4	1	P

STILL Nelson S
b. Glasgow 6.4.1963

Partick T		85/86	15			D1
Falkirk		86/87	1			P

STILLIE Derek
b. Irvine 3.12.1973
Notts Co

Aberdeen		93/94	4	1		P
		94/95				
		95/96				
		96/97	8			P
		97/98	2			P
		98/99	8			P

STIRLING Jered
b. Stirling 13.10.1976
Shettleston
St Rochs

Partick T		95/96	2			P
		96/97	34		7	D1
		97/98	22		6	D1
Motherwell		98/99	4	1	1	P

STRACHAN Gavin David
b. Aberdeen 23.12.1978

Coventry C		97/98	2	7		FL
		98/99				
Dundee	L	98/99	4	2		P
Coventry C		99/00	1	2		FL

STRACHAN Gordon
b. Edinburgh 9.2.1957

Dundee		71/72				
		72/73				
		73/74				
		74/75	1			D1
		75/76	17	6	6	P
		76/77	33	3	7	D1
		77/78	5	4		D1
Aberdeen		77/78	10	2	2	P
		78/79	26	5	5	P
		79/80	33		10	P
		80/81	20		6	P
		81/82	30		7	P
		82/83	32		12	P
		83/84	24	1	13	P
Manchester U		84/85	41		15	FL
		85/86	27	1	5	FL
		86/87	33	1	4	FL
		87/88	33	3	8	FL
		88/89	21		1	FL
Leeds U		88/89	11		3	FL
		89/90	46		16	FL
		90/91	34		7	FL
		91/92	35	1	4	FL
		92/93	25	6	4	FL
		93/94	32	1	3	FL
		94/95	5	1		FL
Coventry C		94/95	5			FL
		95/96	5	7		FL
		96/97	3	6		FL

STRANG Shaun A
b. Dunfermline 31.3.1970

Dunfermline A		87/88	1			P
		88/89				
		89/90				
Raith R		90/91	0	4		D1
		91/92	6	7	3	D1

STREET Robert John Wainwright
b. Gourock 29.10.1953
Port Glasgow Jnrs

Aberdeen		72/73	1	1		D1
		73/74	1	1		D1
		74/75	3			D1
		75/76	0	1		P
Montrose		76/77	26	4	12	D1
		77/78	9	8	3	D1
Kilmarnock		78/79	12	6	5	D1
		79/80	26	5	9	P
		80/81	13		2	P
Keith		81/82				
Peterhead		81/82				
		82/83				
Montrose		83/84	23	11	2	D2
		84/85	0	2		D2
Brechin C		84/85	4	6		D1
Huntly						

STRICKLAND Derek
b. Stoneyburn 7.11.1959

Rangers		78/79	1			P
Leicester C		79/80	4	3	2	FL
		80/81				
Heart of Midlothian		81/82	0	1		D1
East Stirlingshire		82/83	13	2		D2

STRONG Gregory
b. Bolton 5.9.1975

Wigan A		93/94	16	2	1	FL
		94/95	12	5	2	FL
Bolton W		95/96	0	1		FL
		96/97				
		97/98				
Blackpool	L	97/98	11		1	FL
Bolton W		98/99	4	1		FL
Stoke C	L	98/99	5		1	FL
Bolton W		99/00	6			FL
Motherwell		99/00	10			P

STUBBS Alan
b. Liverpool 6.10.1971

Bolton W		90/91	16	7		FL
		91/92	26	6	1	FL
		92/93	37	5	2	FL
		93/94	41		1	FL
		94/95	37	2	1	FL
		95/96	24	1	4	FL
Celtic		96/97	20			P
		97/98	29		1	P
		98/99	22	1	1	P
		99/00	23			P

STURROCK Paul Whitehead
b. Ellon 10.10.1956
Grandtully Vale
Vale of Atholl
Bankfoot Jnrs

Dundee U		74/75	9	3	6	D1
		75/76	10	7	3	P
		76/77	36		15	P
		77/78	32	1	3	P
		78/79	31	2	6	P
		79/80	31	2	4	P
		80/81	35		13	P
		81/82	28		8	P
		82/83	28		8	P
		83/84	15	2	4	P
		84/85	28	2	14	P
		85/86	31	1	8	P
		86/87	30		6	P
		87/88	8	1	3	P
		88/89	5	5	1	P

SULLEY Christopher Stephen
b. Camberwell 3.12.1959

Chelsea		78/79				
		79/80				
		80/81				
Bournemouth		80/81	7	1		FL
		81/82	46			FL
		82/83	46		1	FL
		83/84	46		2	FL
		84/85	23			FL
		85/86	37			FL
Dundee U		86/87	7			P
Blackburn R		86/87	13			FL
		87/88	34			FL
		88/89	19			FL
		89/90	36			FL
		90/91	25			FL
		91/92	7			FL
Port Vale		92/93	40		1	FL
Preston NE		93/94	21		1	FL

SULLIVAN Dominick
b. Glasgow 1.4.1951
Provanmill Gasworks
St Roch

Clyde		69/70				
		70/71	28			D1
		71/72	27	2	3	D1
		72/73	30	3	7	D2
		73/74	33	1	1	D1
		74/75	34		4	D1
		75/76	12	4	1	D1
Aberdeen		76/77	28	4	3	P
		77/78	25	4	3	P
		78/79	32		4	P
		79/80	2	3		P
Celtic		79/80	15		4	P
		80/81	30		3	P
		81/82	31		3	P
		82/83	7	1	1	P
Dundee U	T	83/84				
Manchester C	T	83/84				
Morton		83/84	24	1	3	D1
		84/85	23	4	3	P
Alloa A		85/86	20	2	1	D1
		86/87	21	2	3	D2
		87/88	14			D2

SWEENEY Joseph
b. 19.2.1957
Pollok Jnrs

Clydebank		79/80	26	2	11	D1
		80/81	10	6	4	D1
Partick T		80/81	4	1		P
		81/82	2	6		P

SWEENEY Paul Martin
b. Glasgow 10.1.1965

Raith R		82/83	1			D1
		83/84	24	5	1	D1
		84/85	31	1		D2
		85/86	37		3	D2
		86/87	38			D2
		87/88	39		2	D1
		88/89	28		2	D1
Newcastle U		88/89	6	2		FL
		89/90	14	5		FL
		90/91	8	1		FL
St Johnstone		90/91	8			P
		91/92				
		92/93	2			P
Gateshead		93/94				
Hartlepool U		94/95	1			FL

SWEENEY Sean Brian
b. Glasgow 17.8.1969

Clydebank		86/87	2			P
		87/88	12	2		D1
		88/89	14	5		D1
		89/90	33	1	1	D1
		90/91	33			D1
		91/92	18			D1
		92/93	36		2	D1
		93/94	31			D1
		94/95	27		2	D1
Airdrieonians		95/96	24			D1
		96/97	26		1	D1
		97/98	29			D1
Livingston		98/99	10			D2
		99/00	15	3	1	D1

TAGGART Craig
b. Glasgow 17.1.1973
West Park U

Falkirk		91/92	0	8		P
		92/93	3	2		P
		93/94	4	9	1	D1
Stirling A		94/95	32	2	5	D2
		95/96	33	2	8	D2
		96/97	22	3	2	D1
		97/98	4	2	2	D1
Clydebank		98/99	25	10	2	D1
Stirling A		99/00	27	1	3	D2
Ross Co		99/00	9		1	D2

TAIT Robert
b. 16.2.1962
Crosshouse Waverley

Ayr U		72/73	0	1		D1
		73/74	7	2	1	D1
		74/75	3	1		D1
		75/76	7			P
		76/77	6	1		P
		77/78	6			P
Stranraer		78/79	28	1	2	D2
		79/80	24	2		D2

TALLON Gerrit Thomas
b. Drogheda 5.9.1973
Drogheda

Blackburn R		91/92				
		92/93				
		93/94				
		94/95				
		95/96				
Kilmarnock		96/97	4			P
Chester C	L	96/97	1			FL
Mansfield T		97/98	26		1	FL
		98/99	31	5	1	FL
		99/00	11	2		FL

TAYLOR Alexander
b. Glasgow 13.6.1962
Blantyre St Josephs

Dundee U		78/79				
		79/80				
		80/81				
		81/82				
		82/83	1	2		P
		83/84	5	4	1	P
		84/85	17	4	5	P
		85/86				
Hamilton A		86/87	25	1	1	P
		87/88	41		4	D1
Walsall		88/89	13		3	FL
		89/90	30	2	3	FL
Falkirk		90/91	29		2	P
		91/92	21	1	1	P
		92/93	3	5	1	P
Partick T		92/93	8		1	P
		93/94	27	5	4	P
		94/95	17	6	2	P
Raith R		95/96	1	8		P
		96/97	13	4	2	P
Ross Co		97/98	19	8	4	D3
		98/99	24	8	4	D3
Forfar A		99/00	30	1	4	D3

TAYLOR Ian

Aberdeen		66/67	12	1	3	D1
		67/68	14	1	5	D1
		68/69	13	1	1	D1
		69/70	1			D1
		70/71	14	2	4	D1
		71/72	10	5	2	D1
		72/73	18		4	D1
		73/74	14	3	3	D1
Motherwell		73/74	2			D1
		74/75	20	3	1	D1
		75/76	17	7	4	P
St Johnstone		76/77	23	1	2	D1
		77/78	12	2	1	D1

TEALE Shaun
b. Southport 10.3.1964
Southport
Northwich V
Weymouth

Bournemouth		88/89	19	1		FL
		89/90	34			FL
		90/91	46		4	FL
Aston Villa		91/92	42			FL
		92/93	39		1	FL
		93/94	37	1	1	FL
		94/95	28			FL
Tranmere R		95/96	29			FL
		96/97	25			FL
Preston NE	L	96/97	5			FL
Tranmere R		97/98				
Motherwell		98/99	29		1	P
		99/00	16		2	P

TEASDALE Michael Joseph
b. Elgin 28.7.1969
Elgin C

Dundee		93/94	2	3		P
		94/95	13	4	1	D1
		95/96	1			D1
Inverness CT		95/96	19		2	D3
		96/97	36		2	D3
		97/98	18	4	3	D2
		98/99	36		4	D2
		99/00	23	4	2	D1

TEBILY Olivier
b. Abidjan 19.12.1975
Chateauroux

Sheffield U		98/99	7	1		FL
Celtic		99/00	19	3		P

TEMPERLEY Wiliam

Hibernian		78/79	3	5	1	P
Alloa A *		79/80	1			D2
Meadowbank T *		79/80	1			D2

TEMPLEMAN Christopher
b. Kirkcaldy 12.1.1980

Dunfermline A		98/99	5	7		P
		99/00	0	1		D1
Dumbarton		99/00	3			D3

TEN CAAT Pieter Theodour
b. Scheveld 8.12.1964
Groningen

Aberdeen		91/92	28	2	5	P
		92/93	11	4		P
		93/94	1	2		P

TERKELSEN Henrik
b. 21.4.1965

Morton		87/88	1			P

THERN Jonas
b. Falkoping 20.3.1967

Malmo FF		85				
		86				
		87				
FC Zurich		87/88				
Malmo FF		88				
		89				
Benfica		89/90				
		90/91				
		91/92				
Napoli		92/93				
		93/94				
AS Roma		94/95				
		95/96				
		96/97				
Rangers		97/98	22		5	P
		98/99	1			P

THIELE G

St Mirren		90/91	0	1		P

THOM Andreas
b. Rudersdorf 7.9.1965
Dynamo Berlin

Bayer Leverkusen		89/90				
		90/91				
		91/92				
		92/93				
		93/94				
		94/95				
Celtic		95/96	31	1	5	P
		96/97	18	5	7	P
		97/98	8	7	3	P
Hertha Berlin						

THOMAS Anthony
b. Liverpool 12.7.1971

Tranmere R		89/90	42		2	FL
		90/91	33		3	FL
		91/92	30		3	FL
		92/93	16			FL
		93/94	40		2	FL
		94/95	26			FL
		95/96	31			FL
		96/97	28	2		FL
Everton		97/98	6	1		FL
Motherwell		98/99	10			P
		99/00	6			P

THOMAS Kevin Roderick
b. Edinburgh 7.9.1965
Links U

Heart of Midlothian		92/93	2	2	2	P
		93/94	7	5		P
		94/95	11	7	5	P
		95/96	0	3		P
		96/97	4	9		P
		97/98	0	1		P
Stirling A		97/98	6			D1
Morton		98/99	22		9	D1
		99/00	2		2	D1
St Johnstone		99/00	5	7	2	P

THOMPSON David Reid
b. Blantyre 28.5.1962

Airdrieonians		80/81	8	15	3	P
		81/82	5	11	1	P
Stenhousemuir		82/83	39		8	D2
		83/84	39		7	D2
		84/85	6		2	D2
Stirling A		84/85	27	3	9	D2
		85/86	31	6	5	D2
		86/87	22	2	5	D2
		87/88	39		8	D2
		88/89	20	2	4	D2
Kilmarnock		89/90	8	7	2	D2
Clyde		89/90	12		4	D1
		90/91	14		3	D1
		91/92	31		16	D2
		92/93	19	4	8	D2
Albion R		93/94	3	2		D2
		94/95	18	2	1	D3
		95/96	7			D3

THOMPSON Gary
b. Glasgow 11.6.1956

Morton		76/77	0	1		D1
		77/78				
Falkirk		78/79	10	7	6	D2
		79/80	17	3	7	D2
		80/81	14	5	2	D1
		81/82	9	13	3	D1
		82/83	18	4	1	D1
Alloa A		83/84	26	5	1	D1
		84/85	33		4	D2
		85/86	21		2	D1
Dunfermline A		85/86	8		2	D2
		86/87	38	3		D1
		87/88	3	2		P
St Johnstone		87/88	26	3	1	D2
		88/89	30			D1
		89/90	1	6		D1
Forfar A *		89/90	11	3		D1
Arbroath *		90/91	1			D2

THOMPSON Steven
b. Paisley 14.10.1978

Dundee U		96/97	0	1		P
		97/98	3	5		P
		98/99	5	10	1	P
		99/00	16	10	1	P

THOMSON Edward
b. 25.2.1947

Heart of Midlothian		66/67	9			D1
		67/68	9		1	D1
		68/69	34			D1
		69/70	23			D1
		70/71	34			D1
		71/72	29		2	D1
		72/73	23	1	1	D1
Aberdeen		72/73	7			D1
		73/74	31	1	1	D1
		74/75	16	1		D1
		75/76	26	2		P
San Antonio Thunder		76	19		3	NA
Aberdeen		76/77	3	4		P

THOMSON Robert
b. Glasgow 21.3.1955
Glasgow U

St Johnstone		73/74	5	1		D1
		74/75	8	6		D1
		75/76	23	3	3	P
		76/77	35	1	7	D1
		77/78	35	1	7	D1
Morton		78/79	30		11	P
		79/80	27		11	P
		80/81	29		2	P
		81/82	4		1	P
Middlesbrough		81/82	18	2	2	FL
Hibernian		82/83	29	1	5	P
		83/84	16		4	P
		84/85	10	6	3	P
Morton		84/85	11		2	P
Blackpool		85/86	14	2	2	FL
		86/87	36		4	FL
Hartlepool U		87/88	2	1		FL
Hamilton A		87/88	22		4	D1
Queen of the South						

THOMSON Scott Munro
b. Aberdeen 29.1.1972
Shrewsbury T

Brechin C		90/91	26	4	3	D1
		91/92	11		3	D2
Aberdeen		92/93	0	2		P
		93/94	0	3		P
		94/95	6	4	1	P
		95/96	0	4		P
Raith R		95/96	9		1	P
		96/97	18	4	2	P
		97/98	30	1	1	D1
Dunfermline A		98/99	20	1	2	P
		99/00	28	1	2	D1

THOMSON Scott Yuill
b. Edinburgh 8.11.1966
Hutchison Vale

Dundee U		84/85				
		85/86				
Raith R	L	85/86	1			D2
Dundee U		86/87	3			P
		87/88				
		88/89	1			P
		89/90	2			P
		90/91				
Forfar A		91/92	44			D1
		92/93	39			D2
		93/94	5			D2
Raith R		93/94	34			P
		94/95	35			D1
		95/96	26			P
		96/97	27			P
St Johnstone		97/98				
Hull C		97/98	9			FL
Motherwell		97/98	1			P
Airdrieonians		98/99	8			D1
		99/00	22			D1

THOMSON William Marshall
b. Linwood 10.2.1958
Glasgow U

Partick T		75/76				
		76/77				
		77/78				
St Mirren		78/79	34			P
		79/80	36			P
		80/81	36			P
		81/82	35			P
		82/83	35			P
		83/84	30			P
Dundee U		84/85	11			P
		85/86	28			P
		86/87	39			P
		87/88	36			P
		88/89	35			P
		89/90	7			P
Clydebank	L	89/90	2			D1
Dundee U		90/91	5			P
Motherwell		91/92	43			P
		92/93	9			P
		93/94				
Rangers		94/95	5			P
		95/96	1			P
Dundee		96/97	25			D1

THORN Andrew Charles
b. Carlshalton 12.11.1966

Wimbledon		84/85	10			FL
		85/86	27	1		FL
		86/87	34		2	FL
		87/88	35			FL
Newcastle U		88/89	26		1	FL
		89/90	10		1	FL
Crystal Palace		89/90	17		1	FL
		90/91	34		1	FL
		91/92	33			FL
		92/93	34		1	FL
		93/94	10			FL
Wimbledon		94/95	22	1	1	FL
		95/96	11	3		FL
Heart of Midlothian		96/97	1			P
Tranmere R		96/97	19		1	FL
		97/98	17			FL

TIERNEY Lawrence
b. Leith 4.4.1959

Heart of Midlothian		77/78	23	5	2	D1
		78/79	8	6		P
		79/80	6	1		D1
Hibernian		79/80	7	1		P
Wigan A		80/81	4	3		FL

TIERNEY Peter Grant
b. Falkirk 11.10.1961
Heart of Midlothian

Cowdenbeath		80/81	31	1	1	D2
		81/82	32		2	D2
		82/83	33		2	D2
		83/84	30	5	1	D2
		84/85	25		3	D2
Meadowbank T		84/85	7			D1
		85/86	35		4	D2
		86/87	36		4	D2
		87/88	36		2	D1
		88/89	18			D1
Dunfermline A		88/89	18		1	D1
		89/90	33		2	P
Partick T		90/91	28		1	D1
		91/92	9	4	1	D1
		92/93	16		2	P
		93/94	18	4	1	P
		94/95	4	1		P
		95/96	1			P
Livingston		95/96	.16		2	D3
		96/97	22		1	D2
Stenhousemuir		97/98	1			D2

TOD Andrew
b. Dunfermline 4.11.1971
Kelty Hearts

Dunfermline A		93/94	19	3	11	D1
		94/95	30	5	6	D1
		95/96	36		5	D1
		96/97	35		4	P
		97/98	35		6	P
		98/99	24	1	1	P
		99/00	27	3	1	D1

TOLMIE James
b. Glasgow 20.11.1960

Morton		78/79	7	3	3	P
		79/80	15	13	2	P
		80/81	28	6	5	P
SC Lokeren		81/82				
		82/83				
Manchester C		83/84	38	3	13	FL
		84/85	7	10	2	FL
		85/86	1	2		FL
Carlisle U	L	85/86	7	1	1	FL
Sweden		86/87				
		87/88				
		88/89				
		89/90				
		90/91				
Morton		91/92	15		3	D1
		92/93	14	7	2	D1
		93/94	35	1	2	D1

TOMASCHEK Robert
b. Nitra 25.8.1972
Slovan Bratislava

Heart of Midlothian		99/00	13	1		P

TORFASON Gudmundur
b. Westmann Islands 13.12.1961
RSC Gent

St Mirren		89/90	29		12	P
		90/91	18		4	P
		91/92	27	2	8	P
		92/93	1			D1
St Johnstone		92/93	9	1	4	P
		93/94	21	8	5	P
Doncaster R		94/95	1	3		FL

TORRANCE Robert Ferguson
b. Glasgow 12.8.1958

St Mirren		76/77	9	10	12	D1
		77/78	8	2	1	P
		78/79	14	6	6	P
		79/80	6	4	3	P
Hibernian		79/80	8	3	1	P
		80/81	2			D1
Partick T		80/81	5	4		P
Stirling A		81/82	23	9	7	D2
		82/83	32		14	D2
		83/84	14	3	4	D2
Brechin C		84/85	11	12	2	D1
		85/86	3		1	D1
Arbroath		85/86	30		13	D2
		86/87	14	4	5	D2
Alloa A *		87/88	6	5	2	D2

TORTOLANO Joseph
b. Stirling 6.4.1966
WBA

Hibernian	85/86	11	9	3	P
	86/87	23	10		P
	87/88	11	10	4	P
	88/89	15	10		P
	89/90	6	1		P
	90/91	13	5	1	P
	91/92	22	3	1	P
	92/93	16	5	3	P
	93/94	12	6	1	P
	94/95	11	7		P
	95/96	14	1		P
Falkirk	96/97	11	1		D1
Clyde	97/98	16	5		D2
	98/99				
Stirling A	99/00	26	1		D2

TOSH Paul James
b. Arbroath 18.10.1973

Arbroath	91/92	3	5	1	D2
	92/93	26	8	12	D2
Dundee	93/94	14	12	1	P
	94/95	13	14	5	D1
	95/96	29	1	9	D1
	96/97	19	4	4	D1
Hibernian	96/97	6		1	P
	97/98	4	11	1	P
	98/99	1			D1
Exeter C L	98/99	8	2	2	FL
Partick T	98/99	10		1	D2
Raith R	99/00	10	8	4	D1
Arbroath	99/00	3			D2

TOSH Steven William
b. Kirkcaldy 27.4.1973

Arbroath	93/94	6	1	1	D2
	94/95	29	2	11	D3
St Johnstone	95/96	8	1	1	D1
	96/97	22	5	3	D1
	97/98	4	4	1	P
Raith R	97/98	6			D1
	98/99	23	2	3	D1
	99/00	25	6	5	D1

TOWNSLEY Derek
b. Carlisle 21.3.1973
Gretna

Queen of the South	96/97	29	2	2	D2
	97/98	27	2	7	D2
	98/99	21	6	10	D2
Motherwell	99/00	16	9	1	P

TRACEY Paul
b. Bellshill 11.8.1967

Motherwell	83/84	0	3		P
Bellshill A	84/85				
	85/86				
	86/87				
	87/88				
Clyde	88/89	0	1		D1
	89/90	1			D1

TRAYNOR John Francis
b. Glasgow 10.12.1966

Celtic	88/89	3	1		P
Clydebank	89/90	1			D1
	90/91	9	12		D1
	91/92	12	2	1	D1
Ayr U	91/92	27		4	D1
	92/93	36		7	D1
	93/94	34	8	3	D1
	94/95	9	2	2	D1
	95/96	20	4		D2
	96/97	30	4	2	D2
	97/98	29	4	2	D1
	98/99	22	7		D1
	99/00	1			D1

TRAYNOR Thomas
b. Bonnybridge c1943 d. Melbourne 22.12.1992
Dunipace Jnrs

Heart of Midlothian	62/63	1			D1
	63/64	29		1	D1
	64/65	17		3	D1
	65/66	30		9	D1
	66/67	24	1	1	D1
	67/68	24	2	6	D1
	68/69	28	1	6	D1
	69/70	16		4	D1
Dundee U	70/71	19	2	1	D1
	71/72	26		5	D1
	72/73	22	1	2	D1
	73/74	26	2	3	D1
	74/75	17	3	5	D1
	75/76	1	2		P
Morton *	75/76	4			D1
Falkirk	76/77	5	8		D1

TREANOR Mark
b. Glasgow 1.4.1962
Eastercraigs

Clydebank	79/80	1			D1
	80/81	15	1		D1
	81/82	35			D1
	82/83	36		3	D1
	83/84	11	8	1	D1
	84/85	38		1	D1
	85/86	32			P
	86/87	31	2		P
	87/88	36	1	3	D1
	88/89	27		5	D1
St Johnstone	88/89	3			D1
	89/90	30		4	D1
	90/91	30		4	P
	91/92	31	2	2	P
	92/93	7	2	1	P
Falkirk	92/93	3			P
Clydebank	93/94	14		2	D1
Stranraer	94/95	4			D1

TULLY Craig
b. Stirling 7.1.1976

Dundee	93/94	1			P
	94/95				
	95/96	2			D1
	96/97	16	5		D1
	97/98	5	10		D1
Forfar A	98/99	6		1	D2
Ross Co	98/99	8			D3
	99/00	12	1		D2

TURNBULL J Stewart
b. South Africa 22.8.1961
Polbeth U

Dundee	77/78	2			D1
	78/79				
	79/80	8			P
	80/81				
Hibernian	81/82	4	2	1	P
	82/83	28	2		P
	83/84	22	4		P
Hamilton A	84/85	15			D1
Bush Bucks					

TURNER Thomas Gibson
b. Johnstone 11.10.1963
Glentyan Thistle

Morton	84/85	7	6	1	P
	85/86	30	4	7	D1
	86/87	32	6	4	D1
	87/88	29		1	P
	88/89	29	2	10	D1
	89/90	30		6	D1
St Johnstone	90/91	26	1	3	P
	91/92	31	2	3	P
	92/93	25	3	1	P
	93/94	37	3		P
	94/95	10	1		D1
Partick T	94/95	15		2	P
	95/96	20	2	3	P
	96/97	7	4		D1
St Mirren	96/97	17		2	D1
	97/98	24	1	5	D1
	98/99	13	1		D1
Queen of the South L	98/99	5			D2
St Mirren	99/00	31		1	D1

TWADDLE Kevin
b. Edinburgh 31.10.1971
Dunbar U

St Johnstone	94/95	21	4	6	D1
	95/96	17	9	4	D1
Raith R	96/97	23	5	4	P
	97/98	4	6		D1
Morton	97/98	14		2	D1
	98/99	31		5	D1
Motherwell	99/00	18	7	5	P

TWEED Steven
b. Edinburgh 8.8.1972
MSV Duisburg
St Gallen

Hibernian	91/92	1			P
	92/93	13	1		P
	93/94	27	2	3	P
	94/95	33			P
	95/96	31			P
Ionikos	96/97				
Stoke C	97/98	35	3		FL
	98/99	0	1		FL
Dundee	98/99	10		1	P
	99/00	34		2	P

TZETANOV Tzanko
b. Svichtov 6.1.1970
Energie Cottbus
SV Waldorf-Mannheim

Aberdeen	96/97	27			P
	97/98	10	1		P

URQUHART William Murray
b. Inverness 22.11.1956

Rangers	78/79	6	4	4	P
	79/80	4		2	P
Wigan A	80/81	5	5	2	FL

VALAKARI Simo Johannes
b. Helsinki 28.4.1973

Finn PA	95				
	96				
Motherwell	96/97	11			P
	97/98	24	4		P
	98/99	35			P
	99/00	28	2		P

VALERIANI Juan

Dundee U	98/99	0	1		P

VALLE Oscar Garcia
b. Spain 11.2.1973
Atletico Madrid
Osasuna
Villareal

Dundee U	97/98	1			P

VAN BRONCKHORST Giovanni
b. Rotterdam 5.2.1975

Feyenoord	93/94				
	94/95				
	95/96				
	96/97				
	97/98				
Rangers	98/99	35		7	P
	99/00	27		4	P

VAN DE KAMP Guido
b. Den Bosch 8.2.1964
BVV Den Bosch

Dundee U	91/92	27			P
	92/93	1			P
	93/94	25			P
Dunfermline A	94/95	13			D1
	95/96	26			D1
	96/97				
Raith R	97/98	36			D1
	98/99	33			D1
	99/00	32			D1

VAN DE VEN Peter
b. Hunsel 8.1.1961
Willem II Tilburg

Aberdeen	90/91	23	9		P
	91/92	20	3	2	P
Heart of Midlothian	92/93	37			P
	93/94	2			P

VAN DER ARK Willem
b. Groningen 13.11.1963
Willem II Tilburg

Aberdeen	88/89	4	4	2	P
	89/90	16	11	7	P
	90/91	6	5	4	P
	91/92	7	11		P

VAN DER GAAG Mitchell
b. Zutphen 27.10.1971
PSV Eindhoven

Motherwell	94/95	2			P
	95/96	12		1	P
	96/97	26		6	P

VAN DER HOORN Freddy
b. Den Bosch 12.10.1963
BVV Den Bosch

Dundee U	89/90	31		2	P
	90/91	32		1	P
	91/92	41		1	P
	92/93	31	1		P
	93/94	28			P

VAN EIJS Frank
b. Geleen 6.11.1971
Winterslag

Dundee	99/00	14	2		P

VAN HOOIJDONK Pierre
b. Steenbergen 29.11.1969
RBC
NAC Breda

Celtic	94/95	13	1	4	P
	95/96	34		26	P
	96/97	19	2	14	P
Nottingham F	96/97	8		1	FL
	97/98	41	1	29	FL
	98/99	19	2	6	FL
Vitesse Arnhem					
Feyenoord					

VAN VOSSEN Peter Jacobus
b. Zierikzee 21.4.1968

Anderlecht		92/93				
Ajax Amsterdam		93/94				
		94/95				
Istanbulspor		95/96				
Rangers		95/96	3	4		P
		96/97	6	8	5	P
		97/98	0	1		P
Feyenoord		98/99				
De Grafschaap						

VAREILLE Jerome
b. Vernoux 1.6.1974

Mulhouse						
Kilmarnock		97/98	24	10	4	P
		98/99	20	3	5	P
		99/00	13	10	3	P

VATA Rudi
b. Shkoder 13.2.1969

Vllaznia Shkoder						
Dinamo Tirana						
Tours	L					
Celtic		92/93	15	7	2	P
		93/94	6	4	1	P
		94/95	7		1	P
		95/96	5	1		P
Energie Cottbus						

VENETIS Anastasios
b. Larissa 24.3.1980

Larissa						
Dundee U		99/00	12	5		P

VERHEUL Bart
b. Arnhem 23.11.1971

Go Ahead Eagles						
Motherwell		91/92	1	2		P
		92/93	0	1		P

VERLAQUE David
b. Johnstone 29.10.1966

Ferguslie U						
Morton		87/88	1	4		P
Albion R		88/89	1	3		D2

VIDMAR Antony
b. Adelaide 4.7.1970

Ekeren		92/93				
Adelaide City		93				
		94				
		95				
NAC Breda		95/96				
		96/97				
Rangers		97/98	8	4		P
		98/99	26	2	1	P
		99/00	21	6	6	P

VIDUKA Marko
b. Australia 9.10.1975

NK Dinamo		96/97				
		97/98				
Celtic		98/99	8	1	5	P
		99/00	28		25	P

VINCENT Robert
b. Glasgow 13.11.1977

Kilmarnock		97/98	0	2		P
Albion R		97/98	2	2		D3

VINNICOMBE Christopher
b. Exeter 20.10.1970

Exeter C		88/89	21	4		FL
		89/90	14		1	FL
Rangers		89/90	1	6		P
		90/91	10		1	P
		91/92	1	1		P
		92/93				
		93/94	2	2		P
Burnley		94/95	29		1	FL
		95/96	35		2	FL
		96/97	6	2		FL
		97/98	20	3		FL

VRTO Dusan
b. Banska Stiavnica 29.10.1955

Banik Ostrava						
Dundee		92/93	32		1	P
		93/94	38			P
		94/95	22			D1
		95/96	25	2		D1

WADDELL John
b. Watford 26.3.1966

Norwich C						
Dundee		84/85	1	4		P
		85/86	0	2		P
Dunfermline A		86/87	1	1		D1
Stenhousemuir		86/87	15	2	5	D2
		87/88	4		1	D2

WALES Gary
b. East Calder 4.1.1979

Hamilton A		97/98	0	3		D1
		98/99	28	2	11	D1
Heart of Midlothian		99/00	17	7	6	P

WALKER Andrew Francis
b. Glasgow 6.4.1965

Partick T						
Toronto Blizzard						
Baillieston Jnrs						
Motherwell		84/85	4	7	3	D1
		85/86	19	3	4	P
		86/87	42	1	10	P
Celtic		87/88	42		26	P
		88/89	19	3	8	P
		89/90	19	13	6	P
		90/91	6	5		P
		91/92	0	1		P
Newcastle U	L	91/92	2			FL
Bolton W		91/92	23	1	15	FL
		92/93	31	1	26	FL
		93/94	7	4	3	FL
Celtic		94/95	22	4	6	P
		95/96	4	12	6	P
Sheffield U		95/96	12	2	8	FL
		96/97	20	17	12	FL
		97/98	0	1		FL
Hibernian		97/98	7	1	3	P
Raith R		97/98	5	2	2	D1
Ayr U		98/99	31	2	15	D1
Partick T		99/00	4			D2
Alloa A		99/00	4	4	3	D2

WALKER Colin
b. Bellshill 16.3.1960

Albion R *		80/81	1			D2
Bellshill A		80/81				
Airdrieonians		81/82	12	1		P
		82/83	11	3	2	D1
		83/84	17	3		D1
		84/85	20	2	2	D1
		85/86	2	2		D1
		86/87	7	7		D1
Stenhousemuir		87/88	21		5	D2
		88/89	29	1	9	D2
		89/90	24	1	7	D2
		90/91	38		4	D2
		91/92	3	1		D2

WALKER David
b. Glasgow 9.5.1961

Johnstone Burgh						
St Mirren		81/82	9			P
		82/83	5	1		P
		83/84	4	1		P
Partick T		84/85	28			D1
		85/86	26			D1
		86/87	30	2		D1
Cowdenbeath *		87/88	3		1	D2
Stenhousemuir *		88/89	1			D2

WALKER Derek John
b. Bellshill 3.7.1966

Aberdeen BC						
Queens Park		82/83	8	5		D1
		83/84	15	1	1	D2
		84/85	34	2	4	D2
		85/86	26			D2
Hamilton A		86/87	8	3		P
Clyde		87/88	38	1	16	D1
Meadowbank T		88/89	6	5		D1
Kilmarnock		88/89	9	7	1	D1
Stenhousemuir *		88/89	1			D2
Stirling A		89/90	8	10	4	D2
East Stirlingshire		90/91	35	3	10	D2
		91/92	1	5		D2
		92/93	25	1	6	D2
Albion R		93/94	11		2	D2
Stranraer		93/94	0	2		D2

WALKER John
b. 7.10.1959

Ayr U		77/78	4	1		P
Kilwinning R		78/79				
		79/80				
		80/81				
		81/82				
		82/83				
St Mirren		83/84	0	2		P
Kilmarnock	L	83/84	4	2		D1
Cumnock Jnrs						
Irvine Meadow						
Cumnock Jnrs						

WALKER Joseph Nicol
b. Aberdeen 29.9.1962

Motherwell		82/83	15			P
		83/84	15			P
Rangers		83/84	8			P
		84/85	14			P
		85/86	34			P
		86/87	2			P
Falkirk		86/87	8			P
Rangers		87/88	5			P
Dunfermline A	L	87/88	1			P
Rangers		88/89	12			P
		89/90				
Heart of Midlothian		90/91	13			P
		91/92				
		92/93	18			P
		93/94	17			P
		94/95	2			P
Partick T		94/95	20			P
		95/96	33			P
Aberdeen		96/97	19			P
Ross Co		97/98	26			D3
		98/99	31			D3
		99/00	25			D2

WALKER Keith
b. Edinburgh 17.4.1966

ICI Juveniles						
Stirling A		84/85	31	7	6	D2
		85/86	31	1	5	D2
		86/87	20	1	6	D2
St Mirren		87/88	18	1	3	P
		88/89	13	1	1	P
		89/90	10		2	P
Swansea C		89/90	11	2		FL
		90/91	21	3		FL
		91/92	30	2	1	FL
		92/93	42		2	FL
		93/94	27		2	FL
		94/95	28			FL
		95/96	32	1		FL
		96/97	31		1	FL
		97/98	39		3	FL
		98/99	1			FL
		99/00				

WALKER Paul
b. Kilwinning 20.8.1977

Dundee U		95/96	0	2		D1
		96/97	2	1		P
		97/98	1			P
St Mirren		98/99	0	1		D1
Stranraer		98/99	8	1	1	D1
		99/00	4	4	3	D2
Queens Park		99/00	6	2	2	D3

WALKER Thomas
b. Arbroath 15.3.1952

Airdrieonians		71/72	25	2	5	D1
		72/73	24	5	5	D1
Arbroath		73/74	14	8		D1
Airdrieonians		74/75	23	2	4	D1
		75/76	10	2	1	D1
		76/77	26	2	1	D1
		77/78	37	1	2	D1
		78/79	31	2	1	D1
		79/80	36	2		D1
		80/81	34	1	2	P
		81/82	22	3	2	P
Stirling A		82/83	26		1	D2
		83/84	30			D2

WALLACE Gordon
b. 30.5.1953

Raith R		71/72	30	1	20	D2
		72/73	26	3	7	D2
		73/74	26	1	6	D2
		74/75	32		9	D2
		75/76	25	1	9	D2
Seattle Sounders		76	21		12	NA
Raith R		76/77	33		8	D1
		77/78	8	1	3	D2
Dundee U		77/78	8	6	3	P
Seattle Sounders		78	24		4	NA
Dundee U		78/79				
Berwick R		79/80	11	2	2	D1
		80/81	3	2	1	D1
Cowdenbeath *		80/81	8	3	1	D2
?		81/82				
		82/83				
Montrose *		83/84	1			D2

WALLACE Gordon G
b. Dundee 6.1.1955

Montrose						
Raith R		67/68	34		27	D1
		68/69	34		13	D1
		69/70	4		1	D1
Dundee		69/70	30		21	D1
		70/71	33		11	D1
		71/72	30	2	16	D1
		72/73	31	1	9	D1
		73/74	23	1	14	D1
Toronto Metros		74	3		1	NA
Dundee		74/75	13	1	6	D1
		75/76	29	2	12	P
Dundee U		76/77	24	1	13	P
		77/78	14	1	3	P
Raith R		77/78	14		6	D2
		78/79	34	3	14	D1
		79/80	13	1	5	D1

WALLACE Rodney Seymour
b. Greenwich 2.10.1969

Southampton		87/88	3	12	1	FL
		88/89	38		12	FL
		89/90	35	3	18	FL
		90/91	35	2	14	FL
Leeds U		91/92	34		11	FL
		92/93	31	1	7	FL
		93/94	34	3	17	FL
		94/95	30	2	4	FL
		95/96	12	12	1	FL
		96/97	17	5	3	FL
		97/98	29	2	10	FL
Rangers		98/99	34		18	P
		99/00	25	3	16	P

WALTERS Mark Everton
b. Birmingham 2.6.1964

Aston Villa		81/82	0	1		FL
		82/83	18	4	1	FL
		83/84	33	4	8	FL
		84/85	35	1	10	FL
		85/86	40		10	FL
		86/87	18	3	3	FL
		87/88	24		7	FL
Rangers		87/88	18		7	P
		88/89	30	1	8	P
		89/90	27		5	P
		90/91	26	4	12	P
Liverpool		91/92	18	7	3	FL
		92/93	26	8	11	FL
		93/94	7	10		FL
Stoke C	L	93/94	9		2	FL
Liverpool		94/95	7	11		FL
Wolverhampton W	L	94/95	11		3	FL
Southampton		95/96	4	1		FL
Swindon T		96/97	24	3	7	FL
		97/98	25	9	6	FL
		98/99	31	7	10	FL
		99/00	11	2	2	FL
Bristol R		99/00	28	2	9	FL

WARD Alan A
b. Glasgow 13.1.1946

Drumchapel Amateurs						
Kilmarnock		76/77	1			P
		77/78				
		78/79				
Queen of the South		79/80	4			D2
Blantyre V						

WARD Joseph
b. Glasgow 25.11.1954

Clyde		74/75	27	4	3	D1
		75/76	13	11	3	D1
		76/77	19	4	8	D2
		77/78	30	5	15	D2
		78/79	14	1	10	D1
Aston Villa		78/79	1			FL
		79/80	1	1		FL
Hibernian		79/80	9			P
Dundee U		80/81	4	2		P
Ayr U		81/82	12	4	2	D1
		82/83	16	6	1	D1
		83/84	0	1		D1
Stirling A		83/84	5	3	1	D2
Berwick R *		84/85	1	2		D2
St Johnstone		85/86	18	9	7	D2
		86/87	5	7	1	D2

WARD Kenneth
b. High Valley 16.6.1963

Oakley U						
Cowdenbeath		83/84	25	6	5	D2
		84/85	33	3	16	D2
		85/86	15	1	8	D2
Forfar A		85/86	8	6	1	D1
		86/87	28	5	4	D1
		87/88	23	14	7	D1
		88/89	30	5	12	D1
		89/90	1	1		D1
St Johnstone		89/90	6	12	4	D1
		90/91	1	9	1	P
		91/92	2	10	1	P
Hamilton A		91/92	12		5	D1
		92/93	25	9	10	D1
		93/94	24	6	8	D1
Dunfermline A		94/95	19	4	4	D1
		95/96				
Falkirk		96/97	9	1	1	D1
		97/98	0	2		D1
Clydebank		97/98	16	8	3	D2

WARD Noel Gerard
b. Strabane 8.12.1952

Portadown						
Aberdeen		74/75	2			D1
		75/76	4	1		P
		76/77				
		77/78				
Wigan A		78/79	44		4	FL
		79/80	3	1		FL

WARDELL Stuart C
b. Edinburgh 9.6.1965

Dunfermline A		87/88	0	2		P
Brechin C		88/89	21	6	4	D2
		89/90				
		90/91	10	2	2	D1
		91/92	5	4		D2
?		92/93				
		93/94				
Cowdenbeath		94/95	20	3	5	D3
		95/96	1			D3

WARDROBE Thomas Barrie
b. Newcastle 3.7.1963

Sunderland		81/82				
		82/83				
St Mirren	L	82/83	4	1	1	P
Sunderland		83/84				
Hartlepool U		84/85	23	4	2	FL

WARK Joseph
b. Glasgow 9.10.1947

Irvine V						
Motherwell		68/69	36		8	D2
		69/70	34		1	D1
		70/71	34		1	D1
		71/72	25			D1
		72/73	33		1	D1
		73/74	34			D1
		74/75	32			D1
		75/76	36			P
		76/77	35		2	P
		77/78	34			P
		78/79	33			P
		79/80	27	1	1	D1
		80/81	29			D1
		81/82	25	3		D1
		82/83	5	1		P
		83/84	7			P

WARNER Anthony Randolph
b. Liverpool 11.5.1974

Liverpool		93/94				
		94/95				
		95/96				
		96/97				
		97/98				
Swindon T	L	97/98	2			FL
Celtic		98/99	3			P
Aberdeen		98/99	6			P

WATSON Andrew
b. Aberdeen 3.9.1959

Aberdeen		77/78	0	1		P
		78/79	2			P
		79/80	12	5	5	P
		80/81	26	3		P
		81/82	18	12	5	P
		82/83	8	10	2	P
Leeds U		83/84	30	1	7	FL
		84/85	7			FL
Heart of Midlothian		84/85	14	2	3	P
		85/86	8	4		P
		86/87	12	16	3	P
Hibernian		87/88	23	7	3	P
		88/89	0	1		P

WATSON George
b. Bellshill 1.5.1956

Falkirk		75/76	6			D1
		76/77	39			D1
		77/78	38			D2
		78/79				
		79/80	27			D2
		80/81	27			D1
		81/82	36			D1
		82/83	39			D1
		83/84	39			D1
		84/85	39			D1
		85/86	39			D1
		86/87	25			P
St Johnstone		86/87	5			D2
Ayr U		87/88	39			D2
		88/89	39			D1
		89/90	16			D1
East Stirlingshire		89/90	17			D2
		90/91	32			D2
		91/92	35			D2
		92/93	23			D2

WATSON Graham
b. St Andrews 10.9.1970

Aberdeen		89/90	3	1	1	P
		90/91				
		91/92	5	6		P
		92/93				
		93/94				
Clyde		94/95	28	3		D2
		95/96	25			D2
Livingston		96/97	20	2		D2
		97/98	28	6		D2
Forfar A		98/99	19			D2

WATSON Gregg
b. Glasgow 21.9.1970

Aberdeen		88/89	0	4		P
		89/90	3	1		P
		90/91	2	5		P
		91/92	3	5		P
		92/93				
Partick T		93/94	37			P
		94/95	29			P
		95/96	32		1	P
		96/97	35			D1
		97/98	31	2	1	D1
Livingston		98/99	26	1	1	D2
		99/00	1			D1
Stenhousemuir		99/00	27		1	D2

WATSON John Martin
b. Edinburgh 13.2.1959

Meadowbank T		79/80	1	1		D2
		80/81	2			D2
?		81/82				
		82/83				
Dunfermline A		83/84	17	4	3	D2
		84/85	36	1	15	D2
		85/86	37		24	D2
		86/87	40		13	D1
		87/88	16	9	3	P
		88/89	31	4	14	D1
Fulham		89/90	12	2		FL
Airdrieonians		89/90	10	1	1	D1
		90/91	29	1	4	D1
		91/92	10	12	4	P
		92/93	4	4		P

WATSON Kenneth
b. Aberdeen 15.12.1951

Rangers		76/77	30		3	P
		77/78	2	2		P
		78/79	11	2	2	P
		79/80	12	3		P
Partick T		80/81	32	1	5	P
		81/82	31		5	P
		82/83	38		8	D1
		83/84	35		7	D1
		84/85	32		6	D1
		85/86	25		7	D1
		86/87	42		9	D1
		87/88	17		1	D1
		88/89	0	1		D1

WATSON Robert
b. Airdrie 1.5.1946

Club		Season				
Airdrie Academy						
Rangers		63/64				
		64/65				
		65/66	21		2	D1
		66/67	4			D1
		67/68	7	2	1	D1
		68/69	10		1	D1
		69/70	5	3		D1
Motherwell		69/70	7			D1
		70/71	29			D1
		71/72	20		1	D1
		72/73	27		1	D1
		73/74	33			D1
		74/75	33			D1
		75/76	30	3	1	P

WATSON Stephen
b. Liverpool 4.4.1973

Club		Season				
Rangers		92/93	3			P
		93/94				
St Mirren		94/95	25	4	3	D1
		95/96	18	12	1	D1
		96/97	26		4	D1
		97/98	23	4	5	D1

WATSON William
b. New Stevenston 4.12.1949

Club		Season				
Manchester U		65/66				
		66/67				
		67/68				
		68/69				
		69/70				
Huddersfield T	L	69/70				
Manchester U		70/71	8			FL
		71/72				
		72/73	3			FL
Miami Toros		73	18			NA
Burnley	T	73/74				
Motherwell		73/74	22		1	D1
		74/75	32		1	D1
		75/76	17	2		P
		76/77	18	1		P
		77/78	33	2		P
Dundee		78/79	34			D1
		79/80	4	1		P

WATT Michael
b. Aberdeen 27.11.1970

Club		Season				
Aberdeen		89/90	7			P
		90/91	10			P
		91/92	2			P
		92/93	3			P
		93/94	4			P
		94/95	12			P
		95/96	30			P
		96/97	9			P
Norwich C		97/98				
		98/99				
Kilmarnock		99/00	4			P

WDOWCZYK Dariusz
b. Warsaw 21.9.1962

Club		Season				
Gwardia Warsaw		83/84				
		84/85				
		85/86				
		86/87				
		87/88				
		88/89				
Celtic		89/90	23		1	P
		90/91	23	1		P
		91/92	18	1		P
		92/93	24	1	3	P
		93/94	24	1		P
Falkirk	T	93/94				
Reading		94/95	37	1		FL
		95/96	29	1		FL
		96/97	8			FL
		97/98	3	3		FL

WEIGHORST Morten
b. Glostrup 25.2.1971

Club		Season				
Lyngby						
Dundee		92/93	22	1	2	P
		93/94	21	3	2	P
		94/95	29		3	D1
		95/96	14		4	D1
Celtic		95/96	2	9	1	P
		96/97	11	6	2	P
		97/98	26	5	4	P
		98/99	5	2		P
		99/00	14	3	3	P

WEIR David Gillespie
b. Falkirk 10.5.1970

Club		Season				
Falkirk		92/93	30		1	P
		93/94	37		3	D1
		94/95	32		1	P
		95/96	34		3	P
Heart of Midlothian		96/97	34		6	P
		97/98	35		1	P
		98/99	23		1	P

WEIR James

Club		Season				
Fairholm						
WBA						
Partick T						
Hamilton A		78/79	5			D1
Germany		79/80				
		80/81				
		81/82				
		82/83				
		83/84				
KSV Hessen Kasselin		84/85				
Motherwell		85/86	2	1		P
Cumnock Jnrs						

WEIR James McIntosh
b. Motherwell 15.6.1969

Club		Season				
Orbiston BC						
Hamilton A		86/87	3			P
		87/88	1	5		D1
		88/89	27	2		P
		89/90	21	9	1	D1
		90/91	39		2	D1
		91/92	40		1	D1
		92/93	37		1	D1
		93/94	2			D1
Heart of Midlothian		93/94	25	1		P
		94/95	2			P
St Johnstone		94/95	17			D1
		95/96	29			D1
		96/97	32		3	D1
		97/98	25			P
		98/99	6	1	1	P
		99/00	31		1	P

WEIR John
b. Coatbridge 18.2.1960

Club		Season				
Gartcosh U						
Celtic						
Petershill	L	77/78				
Celtic		78/79				
		79/80				
		80/81	11		1	P
		81/82				
Winterslag	T	82/83				
Airdrieonians		82/83	4		1	D1
Alloa A		83/84	10	10	1	D1
Cumbernauld U						

WEIR Michael Graham
b. Edinburgh 16.1.1966

Club		Season				
Hibernian		84/85	8	4		P
		85/86	7			P
		86/87	21	3	4	P
Luton T		87/88	7	1		FL
Hibernian		87/88	18		3	P
		88/89	4	3		P
		89/90	12	6	3	P
		90/91	17	3	1	P
		91/92	30	1	11	P
		92/93	30	3	5	P
		93/94				
		94/95	8	11	1	P
		95/96	4	5	1	P
Millwall	L	95/96	8			FL
Hibernian		96/97	1	7	1	P
Motherwell		96/97	5		2	P
		97/98	13	5	4	P

WEIR Peter Russell
b. Johnstone 18.1.1958

Club		Season				
Neilston Jnrs						
St Mirren		78/79	4	2		P
		79/80	24	2	2	P
		80/81	28		2	P
Aberdeen		81/82	25		2	P
		82/83	29	2	6	P
		83/84	26	1	5	P
		84/85	15	1	3	P
		85/86	17	4	5	P
		86/87	31	3	2	P
		87/88	5			P
Leicester C		87/88	18		2	FL
		88/89	8	2		FL
St Mirren		88/89	15	1	6	P
		89/90	9	3		P
Ayr U		90/91	28	1	1	D1
		91/92	8	3		D1

WELDON Derek
b. Motherwell 27.3.1961

Club		Season				
Shotts Bon Accord						
Motherwell		83/84	1	1		P

WELLS David

Club		Season				
Ayr U		70/71	1	1		D1
		71/72	1			D1
		72/73	22	1	1	D1
		73/74	19			D1
		74/75	19	1		D1
		75/76	17	1	2	P
		76/77	25			P
		77/78	12			P
		78/79	33	1	2	D1
		79/80	3	1		D1

WELSH Brian
b. Edinburgh 23.2.1969

Club		Season				
Dundee U		86/87	1			P
		87/88	1		1	P
		88/89	1			P
		89/90	5			P
		90/91	16	1		P
		91/92	10	1	1	P
		92/93	15		1	P
		93/94	37		1	P
		94/95	26	1	4	P
		95/96	21	2	1	D1
Hibernian		96/97	17			P
		97/98	15	2	1	P

WELSH Francis
b. Glasgow 14.5.1954

Club		Season				
Avoca Amateurs						
Celtic		71/72				
Shettleston	L	71/72				
Celtic		72/73				
		73/74	3			P
		74/75	1	1		P
Coventry C	T	75/76				
Hamilton A	T	75/76	1			D1
Kilmarnock		75/76				
		76/77	24			P
		77/78	20	1		D1
		78/79	9	4		D1
		79/80	17	1		P
Partick T		80/81	26	1		P
		81/82				
		82/83	5	1		D1
Morton		83/84	38		1	D1
Hamilton A		84/85				
Morton		84/85	7	1		P
Hamilton A	T	85/86	1			D1
Morton		85/86	3			D1

WELSH Peter Martin
b. Coatbridge 19.7.1959

Club		Season				
Leicester C		76/77	1			FL
		77/78				
Houston Hurricane		78	15		4	NA
Leicester C		78/79	4	2		FL
		79/80	9	2		FL
		80/81	3	4		FL
		81/82	7	9	4	FL
Hibernian		82/83	10	2		P
Falkirk		83/84	9			D1
Alloa A *		83/84	2			D1

WELSH Steven George
b. Glasgow 19.4.1968

Club		Season				
Wimborne T						
Cambridge U		90/91	0	1		FL
Peterborough U		91/92	42			FL
		92/93	45		1	FL
		93/94	45		1	FL
		94/95	14			FL
Partick T		94/95	20			P
		95/96	35			P
Peterborough U		96/97	6			FL
Dunfermline A		96/97	20			P
		97/98	4	2		P
Ayr U		98/99	24	1		D1

WEST Colin
b. Wallsend 13.11.1962

Sunderland		81/82	13	5	6	FL
		82/83	19	4	3	FL
		83/84	36	2	9	FL
		84/85	20	3	3	FL
Watford		84/85	12		7	FL
		85/86	33		13	FL
Rangers		86/87	4	5	2	P
		87/88	0	1		P
Sheffield W		87/88	23	2	7	FL
		88/89	17	3	1	FL
WBA		88/89	17		8	FL
		89/90	18	3	4	FL
		90/91	24	4	8	FL
		91/92	5	2	2	FL
Port Vale	L	91/92	5		1	FL
Swansea C		92/93	29	4	12	FL
Leyton Orient		93/94	42	1	14	FL
		94/95	27	3	9	FL
		95/96	39		16	FL
		96/97	22	1	3	FL
		97/98	2	5		FL
Northampton T	L	97/98	1	1		FL

WEST Colin William
b. Middlesbrough 19.9.1967

Chelsea		86/87	5	2	1	FL
Partick T	L	86/87	24		10	D1
Chelsea		87/88	3	6	3	FL
		88/89				
Swansea C	L	88/89	14		3	FL
Chelsea		89/90				
Dundee		90/91	16	3	3	D1
		91/92	7	2	3	D1
		92/93	2	5		P
Hartlepool U		93/94	1	1		FL

WESTWATER Ian
b. Loughborough 8.11.1963

Heart of Midlothian		80/81	2			P
		81/82				
		82/83				
		83/84				
Dunfermline A		84/85	8			D2
		85/86	38			D2
		86/87	42			D1
		87/88	28			P
		88/89	39			D1
		89/90	36			P
		90/91	1			P
Falkirk		91/92	40			P
		92/93	24			P
		93/94	3			D1
Dunfermline A		93/94	9			D1
		94/95	17			D1
		95/96	10	1		D1
		96/97	28	1		P
		97/98	36			P
		98/99	1			P
		99/00	22			D1

WHITE Archibald
b. Dumbarton 16.1.1959

Oxford U		76/77	2			FL
		77/78	2	7		FL
		78/79	3	5	1	FL
		79/80	3	2		FL
Heart of Midlothian		79/80	9			D1
		80/81	0	2		P

WHITEFORD Andrew
b. Bellshill 22.8.1977

St Johnstone		95/96	3	1		D1
		96/97	8	3		D1
		97/98	1			P
		98/99	0	1		P
Stirling A		99/00	20		1	D2

WHITESIDE Garry Andrew
b. Glasgow 6.9.1973

St Rochs						
Falkirk		95/96	0	2		P
		96/97	0	1		D1

WHITTAKER Brian
b. Glasgow 23.9.1956 d. Edinburgh 7.9.1997

Sighthill Amateurs						
Crystal Palace	T					
Partick T		74/75	0	1		D1
		75/76	1			D1
		76/77	36		1	P
		77/78	34	1		P
		78/79	36			P
		79/80	35		1	P
Borussia Dortmund	T	80/81				
Hertha Berlin	T	80/81				
Partick T		80/81	34		1	P
		81/82	28			P
		82/83	36		1	D1
Celtic		83/84	10		2	P
Heart of Midlothian		84/85	25	3	1	P
		85/86	24	1		P
		86/87	37			P
		87/88	42			P
		88/89	24			P
		89/90	6			P
Falkirk		90/91	25		1	P
		91/92	6			P

WHITWORTH Neil Anthony
b. Wigan 12.4.1972

Wigan A		89/90	1	1		FL
Manchester U		90/91	1			FL
		91/92				
Preston NE	L	91/92	6			FL
Barnsley	L	91/92	11			FL
Manchester U		92/93				
		93/94				
Rotherham U	L	93/94	8		1	FL
Blackpool	L	93/94	3			FL
Kilmarnock		94/95	30		3	P
		95/96	28			P
		96/97	6			P
		97/98	10	1		P
Wigan A		97/98	1	3		FL

WHYTE Derek
b. Glasgow 31.8.1968

Hamilton Thistle						
Celtic		85/86	11			P
		86/87	42			P
		87/88	41		3	P
		88/89	20	2		P
		89/90	35		1	P
		90/91	24		2	P
		91/92	38	2	1	P
		92/93	0	1		P
Middlesbrough		92/93	34	1		FL
		93/94	42		1	FL
		94/95	36		1	FL
		95/96	24	1		FL
		96/97	20	1		FL
		97/98	4	4		FL
Aberdeen		97/98	19			P
		98/99	35			P
		99/00	19	1		P

WHYTE Hugh
b. Kilmarnock 24.7.1955

Hibernian		74/75	4			D1
		75/76	1			P
Dunfermline A		76/77	39			D2
		77/78	39			D2
		78/79	38			D2
		79/80	39			D1
		80/81	39			D1
		81/82	19			D1
		82/83	27			D1
		83/84	39			D2
		84/85	30			D2
		85/86				
		86/87	2			D1

WILKIE James
b. Greenock 7.10.1958

Morton		80/81	6			P
		81/82				
Queen of the South		82/83	34		1	D2
		83/84	27	2		D2

WILKIE Lee
b. Dundee 20.4.1980

Dundee		99/00	21	3		P

WILKINS Raymond Colin
b. Hillingdon 1.9.1956

Chelsea		73/74	4	2		FL
		74/75	20	1	2	FL
		75/76	42		11	FL
		76/77	42		8	FL
		77/78	33		6	FL
		78/79	35		3	FL
Manchester U		79/80	37		2	FL
		80/81	11	2		FL
		81/82	42		1	FL
		82/83	26		1	FL
		83/84	42		3	FL
AC Milan		84/85				
		85/86				
Paris St Germain		86/87				
Rangers		87/88	24		1	P
		88/89	30	1	1	P
		89/90	15			P
QPR		89/90	23		1	FL
		90/91	38		2	FL
		91/92	26	1	1	FL
		92/93	27		2	FL
		93/94	39		1	FL
Crystal Palace		94/95	1			FL
		95/96				
		96/97				
Wycombe W		96/97	1			FL
Hibernian		96/97	15	1		P
Millwall		96/97	3			FL
Leyton Orient		96/97	3			FL

WILLIAMSON Andrew
b. Kirkcaldy 4.9.1969

Glenrothes Strollers						
Dunfermline A		87/88	2			P
		88/89	5	1		D1
		89/90	1			P
		90/91	4	1		P
		91/92	6	1		P
		92/93	4	1	1	D1
East Fife		93/94	34		4	D2
		94/95	1			D2

WILLIAMSON Robert
b. Glasgow 13.8.1961

Clydebank		80/81	0	2		D1
		81/82	10	2	1	D1
		82/83	39		21	D1
		83/84	17		4	D1
Rangers		83/84	16	1	6	P
		84/85	0	1		P
		85/86	20	3	6	P
WBA		86/87	30	1	8	FL
		87/88	10	12	3	FL
Rotherham U		88/89	41	1	27	FL
		89/90	41	1	19	FL
		90/91	9		3	FL
Kilmarnock		90/91	23		14	D1
		91/92	33	3	9	D1
		92/93	26	7	6	D1
		93/94	36	2	7	P
		94/95	7	8	2	P

WILLIAMSON William
b. 29.9.1952

Aberdeen		70/71	1			D1
		71/72				
		72/73	12			D1
		73/74	2	2		D1
		74/75	27	4	9	D1
		75/76	35	1	8	P
		76/77	9		1	P
Dundee U		76/77	7	4	1	P
Dundee		77/78	37		17	D1
		78/79	20	2	4	D1
		79/80	3	5		P
		80/81	15	5	1	D1
Brisbane Lions						

WILSON Alistair
b. Kilmarnock 14.10.1961

Irvine Meadow						
Kilmarnock		80/81	8			P
		81/82				
		82/83	1			P
Auchinleck Talbot						

WILSON Barry John
b. Kirkcaldy 16.2.1972

Ross Co		94/95	3		1	D3
Raith R		94/95	14	12	5	D1
		95/96	8	5		P
Inverness CT		96/97	27	2	5	D3
		97/98	24	9	6	D2
		98/99	35	1	14	D2
		99/00	30	2	13	D1

WILSON Brian						
Arbroath		73/74	2			D1
		74/75	13			D1
		75/76	10			D1
Heart of Midlothian		76/77	9			P
Stenhousemuir		77/78	34			D2
		78/79	34			D2
		79/80	20			D2

WILSON Gordon						
b. Birmingham 3.9.1957						
Campsie Black Watch						
Kilmarnock		80/81	4	1		P
		81/82	0	1		D1
Falkirk		82/83	3	3		D1
		83/84				
		84/85	4	8		D1
Meadowbank T *		84/85	6			D1
Dunfermline A *		85/86	2			D2

WILSON James McB						
b. Greenock 26.3.1964						
Port Glasgow R						
Morton		83/84	1			D1
		84/85	23	4		P
		85/86	11	4		D1
		86/87	0	3		D1

WILSON Marvyn						
b. Bellshill 1.12.1973						
Heart of Midlothian						
Airdrieonians		92/93	2	2		P
		93/94	11		1	D1
		94/95	12	3		D1
		95/96	8	5		D1
		96/97	21	8	1	D1
		97/98	32	2	1	D1
		98/99	31		2	D1
Ayr U		99/00	23	1	2	D1

WILSON Michael						
Hibernian		75/76	2	1		P
		76/77	1			P

WILSON Paul						
b. Milngavie 23.11.1950						
Celtic		67/68				
Maryhill Jnrs	L	67/68				
Celtic		68/69				
		69/70				
		70/71	1			D1
		71/72	2	2	1	D1
		72/73	2	2	1	D1
		73/74	10	9	5	D1
		74/75	31	2	13	D1
		75/76	18	8	4	P
		76/77	19	5	5	P
		77/78	14	6	1	P
		78/79	0	1		P
Motherwell		78/79	18	3	1	P
Partick T		79/80	1	9		P
Balntyre Celtic						

WILSON Robert						
Cowdenbeath		61/62				
		62/63				
		63/64				
		64/65				
Dundee		65/66	11			D1
		66/67	15			D1
		67/68	34		1	D1
		68/69	34		1	D1
		69/70	22		1	D1
		70/71	32		3	D1
		71/72	32			D1
		72/73	32	1		D1
		73/74	31	2	1	D1
		74/75	33		1	D1
		75/76	17			P

WILSON Scott						
b. Edinburgh 19.3.1977						
Rangers		96/97	1			P
		97/98				
		98/99	7	5	1	P
		99/00	9			P

WILSON Thomas S						
b. Paisley 24.8.1961						
Queens Park		79/80	1			D2
		80/81	1			D2
		81/82	30			D1
St Mirren		82/83	36			P
		83/84	1			P
		84/85	34	1		P
		85/86	25	2		P
		86/87	18	7	1	P
		87/88	31	4		P
		88/89	30	1		P
		89/90	9			P
Dunfermline A		89/90	13	2		P
		90/91	28			P
		91/92	16			P
Kilmarnock		92/93	18	1		D1
Dumbarton *		93/94	19			D1

WINDASS Dean						
b. Hull 1.4.1969						
North Ferriby U						
Hull C		91/92	31	1	6	FL
		92/93	40	1	7	FL
		93/94	43		23	FL
		94/95	43	1	17	FL
		95/96	16		4	FL
Aberdeen		95/96	19	1	6	P
		96/97	29		10	P
		97/98	12	12	5	P
Oxford U		98/99	33		15	FL
Bradford C		98/99	6	6	3	FL
		99/00	36	2	10	FL

WINNIE David						
b. Glasgow 26.10.1966						
St Mirren		83/84	8			P
		84/85	27	3	3	P
		85/86	17	3	1	P
		86/87	12	2		P
		87/88	26		2	P
		88/89	30			P
		89/90	16	1		P
		90/91	1			P
Aberdeen		91/92	27	1	1	P
		92/93	18	3		P
		93/94	2	4		P
Middlesbrough	L	93/94	1			FL
Aberdeen		94/95	6	2		P
Heart of Midlothian		95/96	6			P
Dundee		96/97	26		1	D1
St Mirren		97/98	21	1		D1
Ayr U		98/99	13			D1

WINTERS Robert						
b. East Kilbride 4.11.1974						
Muirend Amateurs						
Dundee U		94/95	6	7	2	P
		95/96	34	1	7	D1
		96/97	27	9	8	P
		97/98	23	7	8	P
		98/99	1	2	1	P
Aberdeen		98/99	28		12	P
		99/00	23	10	7	P

WIRMOLA Jonas						
b. Sweden 17.7.1969						
Sparvagens						
Sheffield U		93/94	8			FL
Malmo FF		94/95				
		95/96				
Dundee U		96/97	1	2		P

WISHART Fraser						
b. Johnstone 1.3.1965						
Pollok Jnrs						
Motherwell		83/84	5	1		P
		84/85				
		85/86	26			P
		86/87	44		3	P
		87/88	43		1	P
		88/89	35		1	P
St Mirren		89/90	19	1		P
		90/91	19	3		P
		91/92	9			P
Dumbarton *		92/93	2			D1
Falkirk		92/93	23	1	2	P
Rangers		93/94	5			P
		94/95	3	1		P
Heart of Midlothian		94/95	8			P
		95/96	1			P
Motherwell		96/97	15	3		P
Clydebank		97/98	30		1	D2
		98/99	32			D1
		99/00	35			D1

WOODS Christopher Charles Eric						
b. Boston 14.11.1959						
Nottingham F		76/77				
		77/78				
		78/79				
QPR		79/80	41			FL
		80/81	22			FL
Norwich C		80/81	10			FL
		81/82	42			FL
		82/83	42			FL
		83/84	42			FL
		84/85	38			FL
		85/86	42			FL
Rangers		86/87	42			P
		87/88	39			P
		88/89	24			P
		89/90	32			P
		90/91	36			P
Sheffield W		91/92	41			FL
		92/93	39			FL
		93/94	10			FL
		94/95	8	1		FL
		95/96	8			FL
Reading	L	95/96	5			FL
Colorado Rapids		96				
Southampton		96/97	4			FL
Sunderland		96/97				
Burnley		97/98	12			FL

WOODS Joseph						
b. Govan 11.9.1961						
Queens Park		81/82	1	2		D1
		82/83	32	1		D1
		83/84	13			D2
St Johnstone		83/84	3	1		P
		84/85	12	2		D1
Pollok Jnrs		85/86				
		86/87				
East Stirlingshire		87/88	37		1	D2
		88/89	16		1	D2
Stirling A		89/90	18			D2

WOODS Neil Stephen						
b. York 30.7.1966						
Doncaster R		82/83	3	1		FL
		83/84	3	4	1	FL
		84/85	3	3	2	FL
		85/86	28	2	7	FL
		86/87	18	1	6	FL
Rangers		86/87	0	3		P
Ipswich T		87/88	12	7	4	FL
		88/89	0	1		FL
		89/90	3	4	1	FL
Bradford C		89/90	13	1	2	FL
Grimsby T		90/91	42	2	12	FL
		91/92	30	7	8	FL
		92/93	21	9	4	FL
		93/94	3	8		FL
		94/95	33	4	14	FL
		95/96	24	9		FL
		96/97	21	3	1	FL
		97/98	1	9		FL
Wigan A	L	97/98	1			FL
Scunthorpe U	L	97/98	2			FL
Mansfield T	L	97/98	5	1		FL

WOODS Stephen Gerard						
b. Glasgow 23.2.1970						
Clydebank		91/92	5			D1
		92/93	42			D1
		93/94	10			D1
Preston NE		93/94	19	1		FL
Motherwell		94/95	33			P
		95/96				
		96/97	6			P
		97/98	35			P
		98/99	7			P
		99/00	14	1		P

WOODTHORPE Colin John						
b. Ellesmere Port 13.1.1969						
Chester C		86/87	30		2	FL
		87/88	34	1		FL
		88/89	44		3	FL
		89/90	46		1	FL
Norwich C		90/91	1			FL
		91/92	12	3	1	FL
		92/93	5	2		FL
		93/94	18	2		FL
Aberdeen		94/95	14			P
		95/96	15		1	P
		96/97	14	5		P
Stockport Co		97/98	29	3	1	FL
		98/99	37		2	FL
		99/00	12	14		FL

WORRELL David						
b. Dublin 12.1.1978						
Blackburn R						FL
Dundee U		98/99	3	1		P
		99/00	10	3		P

WRIGHT Alexander
b. Aberdeen 22.7.1960

Montrose	78/79	3		1	D1
	79/80	14	9	1	D2
	80/81	27	3	6	D2
	81/82	19	9		D2
St Johnstone	82/83				
	83/84	1	3		P
Montrose	84/85	28	6	3	D2
	85/86	28	8	3	D1
	86/87	22	2	1	D1
	87/88	25	2	1	D2
	88/89				
	89/90	0	1		D2

WRIGHT Brian Vincent
b. Glasgow 5.10.1958
Phoenix BC

Hamilton A	76/77	8	3		D1
	77/78	24	3	1	D1
	78/79	18	2	3	D1
	79/80	33	3	3	D1
	80/81	33	2	6	D1
	81/82	36	1	5	D1
	82/83	37		6	D1
	83/84	37			D1
	84/85	35		3	D1
	85/86	3		1	D1
Motherwell	85/86	28		6	P
	86/87	39	2		P
	87/88	0	5		P
Clydebank	87/88	29		4	D1
	88/89	34	1	2	D1
Partick T	89/90	36		5	D1
	90/91	9			D1
Clydebank	90/91	21		1	D1
	91/92	36	1	4	D1
Queen of the South	92/93	25			D2

WRIGHT George
b. South Africa 22.12.1969

Heart of Midlothian	89/90	0	1		P
	90/91	14	3	2	P
	91/92	15	9	1	P
	92/93	8	4		P
	93/94	10	2		P
	94/95	0	2		P
	95/96	2			P
Falkirk	95/96	1	1		P
Livingston	95/96	7	3		D3
	96/97				
	97/98	1			D2
Cowdenbeath	97/98	2			D3

WRIGHT Ian Edward
b. Woolwich 3.11.1963
Greenwich B

Crystal Palace	85/86	16	16	9	FL
	86/87	37	1	8	FL
	87/88	41		20	FL
	88/89	41	1	24	FL
	89/90	25	1	8	FL
	90/91	38		15	FL
	91/92	8		5	FL
Arsenal	91/92	30		24	FL
	92/93	30	1	15	FL
	93/94	39		23	FL
	94/95	30	1	18	FL
	95/96	31		15	FL
	96/97	30	5	23	FL
	97/98	22	2	10	FL
West Ham U	98/99	20	2	9	FL
Celtic	99/00	4	4	3	P

WRIGHT Keith Arthur
b. Edinburgh 17.5.1965

Raith R	83/84	34	3	5	D1
	84/85	37	1	22	D2
	85/86	39		21	D2
	86/87	17		13	D2
Dundee	86/87	15	4	10	P
	87/88	40	2	15	P
	88/89	35		8	P
	89/90	34		11	P
	90/91	36		18	D1
Hibernian	91/92	40		9	P
	92/93	42		11	P
	93/94	41	1	16	P
	94/95	19		10	P
	95/96	25	3	9	P
	96/97	17	9	4	P
Raith R	97/98	17	7	10	D1
	98/99	8	4	2	D1
Morton	98/99	10	6	6	D1
	99/00	17	6	4	D1
Stenhousemuir	99/00	4	1	1	D2

WRIGHT Paul Hamilton
b. East Kilbride 17.8.1967

Aberdeen	83/84	0	1		P
	84/85				
	85/86	3	7	2	P
	86/87	13	12	4	P
	87/88	9		4	P
	88/89	15	9	6	P
QPR	89/90	9	6	5	FL
Hibernian	89/90	2	1	1	P
	90/91	31	2	6	P
St Johnstone	91/92	39	2	18	P
	92/93	42		14	P
	93/94	16	1	7	P
	94/95	5	7	1	D1
Kilmarnock	94/95	7		1	P
	95/96	35	1	13	P
	96/97	29	2	15	P
	97/98	26	2	10	P
	98/99	25	8	6	P
	99/00	12	4	5	P

WRIGHT Stephen
b. Bellshill 27.8.1971

Aberdeen	89/90	0	1		P
	90/91	17	1	1	P
	91/92	23			P
	92/93	34	2		P
	93/94	34	2		P
	94/95	33	1	1	P
Rangers	95/96	6			P
	96/97	1			P
	97/98				
Wolverhampton W L	97/98	3			FL

WRIGHT Thomas Elliott
b. Dunfermline 10.1.1966

Leeds U	82/83	3	1	1	FL
	83/84	23	2	8	FL
	84/85	41	1	14	FL
	85/86	6	4	1	FL
Oldham A	86/87	28		7	FL
	87/88	40	1	9	FL
	88/89	42	1	7	FL
Leicester C	89/90	40	1	3	FL
	90/91	40	4	7	FL
	91/92	42	2	12	FL
Middlesbrough	92/93	34	2	5	FL
	93/94	9	7		FL
	94/95	1			FL
Bradford C	95/96	28	6	4	FL
	96/97	2	9	1	FL
Oldham A	97/98	10	2	2	FL
St Johnstone	97/98	3	2		P
Livingston	97/98	8	1	1	D2

WYLIE David
b. Johnstone 4.4.1966
Ferguslie U

Morton	85/86	23			D1
	86/87	35			D1
	87/88	44			P
	88/89	39			D1
	89/90	39			D1
	90/91	38			D1
	91/92	42			D1
	92/93	44			D1
	93/94	44			D1
	94/95	36			D2
	95/96	33			D1
	96/97	32			D1
	97/98	27			D1
	98/99	6			D1
Clyde	98/99	29	1		D2
	99/00	31			D2

WYNESS Dennis Middleton
b. Aberdeen 22.3.1977

Aberdeen	96/97	1	6		P
	97/98				
	98/99	6	8	1	P
	99/00	1	2		P
Inverness CT	99/00	21	5	6	D1

XAUSA Davide Antonio
b. Vancouver 10.3.1976
Vancouver

Port Vale	97/98				
Stoke C	97/98	1			FL
St Johnstone	97/98	1			P
Netherlands	98/99				
Inverness CT	99/00	19		10	D1

YATES Michael
b. Ormskirk 7.11.1979
Burscough

Dundee	99/00	2	3	1	P

YOUNG Darren
b. Glasgow 13.10.1978
Crombie Sports

Aberdeen	96/97	22	4	1	P
	97/98	2	3		P
	98/99	11			P
	99/00	1	2		P

YOUNG David
b. Edinburgh 1.2.1962
Celtic

Arbroath	80/81	30		2	D2
	81/82	34		2	D2
	82/83	29			D2
	83/84	28		1	D2
Dunfermline A	84/85	39		2	D2
	85/86	38		3	D2
	86/87	31		1	D1
	87/88	7		2	P
Airdrieonians	87/88	14		1	D1
Cowdenbeath	87/88	10	1		D2
	88/89	26	1	1	D2

YOUNG Derek
b. Glasgow 27.5.1980
Lewis U

Aberdeen	98/99	0	4		P
	99/00	9	5		P

YOUNG George Wingate
b. 8.11.1949
Melbourne Thistle

Stirling A	69/70				
	70/71				
	71/72	36			D2
	72/73	36			D2
	73/74	36			D2
	74/75	38			D2
	75/76	25			D2
	76/77	39			D2
	77/78	38			D1
	78/79	37			D1
Rangers	79/80	2			P
	80/81				
Dunfermline A	81/82	20			D1

YOUNG John
b. Edinburgh 22.10.1951

Falkirk	72/73	15	2	3	D1
	73/74	6	9	3	D1
St Mirren	74/75	38		1	D2
	75/76	24	2	1	D1
	76/77	31	7		D1
	77/78	17	8		P
	78/79	25	2	1	P
	79/80	25	2		P
	80/81	28			P
	81/82	5			P
Queen of the South	82/83	3			D2
Brechin C	83/84	38			D1
	84/85	27			D1
Arbroath	85/86	27			D2
	86/87	10			D2
?	87/88				
	88/89				
Montrose *	89/90	1			D2

YOUNG Kenneth William
b. Edinburgh 6.5.1974
Links U

Falkirk	92/93	0	1		P
	93/94	0	1		D1
Berwick R *	93/94	9	7	3	D2

YOUNG Quintin
b. Irvine 19.9.1947
Kello R

Ayr U	69/70	33		5	D1
	70/71	34		4	D1
Coventry C	71/72	21		2	FL
	72/73	4	1		FL
Rangers	72/73	26		13	D1
	73/74	19	1	7	D1
	74/75	22	6	6	D1
	75/76	7	1	2	P
East Fife	76/77	12		3	D1
	77/78	22	1	5	D1
	78/79	10			D2
	79/80	3		1	D2
Whitletts Victoria					

YOUNG Scott Robertson
b. Glasgow 5.4.1977
West Park U

St Johnstone	94/95	1	1		D1
	95/96	1	3		D1
Dunfermline A	96/97	2		1	P

YOUNG William David
b. Edinburgh 25.11.1951

Aberdeen		75/76	3			P
Tottenham H		75/76	35		2	FL
		76/77	19		1	FL
Arsenal		76/77	14		1	FL
		77/78	35		3	FL
		78/79	33			FL
		79/80	38		3	FL
		80/81	40		4	FL
		81/82	10			FL
Nottingham F		81/82	25		1	FL
		82/83	34		4	FL
Norwich C		83/84	5	1		FL
Brighton	L	83/84	4			FL
Darlington		84/85	4			FL

ZEROULAI Hicham
b. Morocco 17.1.1977

FUS Rabat						
Aberdeen		99/00	6	8	3	P

ZETTERLUND Lars
b. Harnosant 11.2.1964

IFK Gothenburg						
AIK Stockholm						
Orebro						
Dundee U		96/97	25		1	P
		97/98	32	1	2	P
		98/99	20	1	1	P